Books by Richard Olney

SIMPLE FRENCH FOOD   1974

THE FRENCH MENU COOKBOOK   1970

Simple French Food

Earthenware poëlons *and copper* plats à sauter

Simple French Food

RICHARD OLNEY

Foreword by James Beard

Drawings by Richard Olney

NEW YORK *Atheneum* 1974

For my sister, Frances Miller

Foreword by James Beard

RICHARD OLNEY is a many-faceted artist—a painter of no mean ability, a writer of rather stylish prose, a cook of incredible facility gifted with one of the most sensitive palates I know. Almost greater than his sensual delight in fine food is his lusty enjoyment of wines. He is acutely critical of what he eats and drinks and sometimes intolerant, but he can defend his point of view knowledgeably and articulately.

Richard's first book, *The French Menu Cookbook,* published four years ago, expressed his feelings about menus and French food in a highly personal manner. Those who love experimenting with good food achieved remarkable results with it. It is filled with offbeat and, to some, quite surprising dishes, and it combines balanced, imaginative menus with very individual commentary. *Simple French Food* is again a markedly personal exploration of food—certainly French, but it may at first glance appear to be anything but simple.

Richard is a renowned teacher of cooking, and he has written very detailed recipes. If you'll read them through carefully, however, you will find that very few of them are really difficult to execute, even the intricate boned oxtail, done with a delicious stuffing and braised. There are innumerable recipes for rabbit, an animal that has been greatly neglected on American tables and that makes some of the most delectable *ragoûts* and sautés imaginable. There is also a wealth of lamb in the book, using practically everything from the head to the tail.

Throughout there are suggestions about what to eat and drink with certain dishes, and brilliant introductions precede each cookery method and each chapter.

Simple French Food is a greatly varied book that covers what is known as *cuisine bourgeoise* or *cuisine simple*. The dishes are not those found in posh restaurants but those one enjoys in comfortable little country restaurants, less prevalent since the Second World War, and in well-run homes where the traditions of good eating have been maintained. These are hearty, mouth-watering, beautifully seasoned dishes that inspire one to rush to the kitchen—braised dishes, smothered dishes, roasts, and grilled dishes. The meat, fish and vegetable recipes are legion and are offered in lovely combinations. The dessert chapter is almost nil, however, which attests to Richard's honesty. He doesn't like desserts. Why pretend?

Here, then, is a wonderful cross-section of French cookery, much of which has not appeared in published form in this country, and it thus makes a valuable supplement to the fine books produced on French cuisine in the last few years.

Contents

Simple French Food

PREFACE

T HE FOOD in this book has been culled from all the corners of France, but I have done little to prevent the spirit from veering sharply toward the south, not only because the flavors of Provençal food tend to be direct and uncomplicated, reflecting the sharp clarity of the light and the landscape, but also, in particular, because for the last ten years my shopping has been done in Mediterranean markets, my day-to-day cooking inclines to respect the local formulas, the tables I share are Provençal, and perhaps most of all because a certain intimacy has bred an uneasy sense of the gentle dissipation of regional culinary traditions and the need to succor them. The internationalizing influence is not unique to Provence—or to France. My alarm is merely greater.

The alarm is generally shared—indeed it is as familiar a topic of casual conversation as the weather—but the active countermovement is limited largely to gastronomic journalists, professional cooks, and restaurant owners, passionate defenders of *la cuisine de bonne femme*. These sympathetic warriors have done tremendous good, but theirs is a worldly and sophisticated public and they are powerless to reach the heart of the cancer lodged in the country kitchens. The result is that regional cooking is slowly being transplanted from the home to the restaurant with, except in the hands of a few cooks of unusual talent, an accompanying loss of personality.

It has seemed to me, at least among the working-class men—masons, carpenters, truck drivers, plumbers, blacksmiths with whom I have been in contact over the years as I consolidate one corner of the house or another—that they are much more attached to the time-honored eating habits of the region than the women; admittedly the men are not in the kitchen and the time-saving devices, so attractive to their wives, seem of little interest by comparison to the succulence of a *daube* remembered from a grandmother's kitchen. When the men gather around the *casse-croûte matinale,* an early morning work break, with charcuterie, cheese, and red wine, the conversation unfailingly turns to food. The descriptions of the *bons gueuletons,* past or to come, are marvelous (*gueuleton* cannot be translated in a word; it means a meal among friends comporting many dishes washed down by great quantities of better-than-ordinary wine, lasting for hours and accompanied by much gaiety and laughter. Any non-working day is an occasion for a *gueuleton.* The dimensions of such a Bacchanal may vary from *un bon petit gueuleton* to *un gueuleton à tout casser*). The regularity with which they ask me to write out recipes for their wives is astonishing (flattering and amusing as well—although the wives are sometimes not amused). It is never a question of a preparation unknown or unusual—adventurers they are not; they always ask for a traditional regional dish, something remembered sentimentally and mouth-wateringly from childhood that mothers and grandmothers prepared to perfection—dishes that belonged to every Provençal housewife's repertoire until World War II threw everything out of joint: rabbit civets and terrines, snails *à la suçarelle,* stuffed braised cabbage, sautéed chicken *à la Provençale, daube à la Provençale, pieds et paquets à la Marseillaise.* The *pieds* and *paquets* are braised mutton tripes; bourgeois families, while remaining loyal to local traditions of cooking, sift them carefully to eliminate "vulgar" elements. A neighbor now in her mid-eighties, *la grande dame du pays* and a charming and cultivated remnant of *la vieille France,* to whom I recently served *pieds et paquets,* admitted, while broad-mindedly accepting a third serving, that, although knowing well its reputation, it was her first confrontation with the dish and she added, with regret, that she would never be able to serve a preparation of that sort at her own

4

table. When she receives, the preparations are simple but the products must be noble: the fish are local rock lobsters, Mediterranean sea bass, or the little coastal red rock mullets; the roasts leg of lamb, guinea fowl, or, during the game season, pheasant, thrush, or partridge.

Inhabitants of neighboring towns consider the village near which I live to be backward—some say inbred—"because it is off the main road." It is, in fact, but a few meters off the main road, which means that "foreigners" (Parisians) are not driving in a constant stream through the heart of the village. The streets are regularly blocked by the insouciant passage of the shepherd and his troop; the women still beat their laundry along the streams; stuffed eggplant and zucchini are carried through the streets at eleven o'clock in the morning to be installed in the ovens of the local bakery and picked up an hour or so later; the men devote half the year to playing pétanque and drinking pastis and the other half to playing cards and drinking pastis, and if, upon entering the general store, a couple of housewives happen to be discussing with the shopkeeper the various merits of their respective *ratatouilles* or *soupes au pistou,* one may as well expect to wait half an hour before being served. These are picturesque details, perhaps of minor importance, but they are comforting—one is tempted to hope that the reins of stubborn habit are strong enough to frustrate the famous industrial revolution for some time to come.

Comforting also are the fantastic, crowded out-of-door morning markets, of which that in Toulon is exemplary, bearing ample witness to the fact that people still want fresh garden produce and seafood and to the certainty that, on the whole, the French willingly spend a great deal more on food than a similar budget in any other part of the world would permit. The banks of fruits and vegetables, freshly picked (depending on the season, baby violet artichokes, tender young broad beans, tiny green beans, peas, tomatoes, fennel, squash, and zucchini squash with its flower still clinging; creamy white cauliflower the size of one's fist, giant sweet peppers, and asparagus—white, violet, and green; figs, cherries, peaches, strawberries, raspberries, and medlar; the endless tresses of garlic and wild mushrooms of all kinds (including the divine amanita of the Caesars); and crates full of live snails and crabs, both of which constantly escape and wander in a wide circle around the vendor's stand. There are the odors of basil and *pissaladière;* the mongers' cants, melodic and raucous; and the Renoiresque play of light through the plane trees' foliage, an all-over sense of gaiety and well-being. The concert is a vibrant experience, the beauty of which is breathtaking. The peasants from the near countryside have stands with small quantities of varied produce—a few eggs, a couple of live chickens or rabbits, a dozen or so fresh cheeses from goat or sheep milk, squash flowers (to be dipped in batter and fried in olive oil for lunch—they will be wilted by evening), and a few handfuls of varied vegetables plus whatever they may have picked wild on the hillsides—shoots of wild asparagus, dandelions and other wild salads, bundles of thyme, rosemary, fennel, savory, and oregano. Hand-scribbled notices inform the customer that the vegetables are "untreated" and that the chickens, whose eggs were laid that morning, are grain fed.

SIMPLE FOOD

A dreary old cliché has it that "one should eat to live and not live to eat." It is typical that this imbecile concept, a deliberately fruitless paradox born of the puritan mind, should deny sensuous reaction at either pole, and it is fortunate that neither pole really exists, for man is incapable of being either altogether dumbly bestial or altogether dumbly "mental."

I have sometimes been accused of thinking of nothing but food and wine—of being bound irreparably to the bestial pole. I do, in fact, think a great deal about food and wine and I would like my readers to share with me the belief that food and wine—that the formalization of gastro-sensory pleasure—must be an essential aspect of the whole life, in which the sensuous-sensual-spiritual elements are so intimately interwoven that the incomplete exploitation of any one can only result in the imperfect opening of the great flower, symbol of the ultimate perfection which is understanding, when all things fall into place (such was the concept, thanks no doubt to its pretty if somewhat pretentious subtitle, "Méditations de Gastronomie Transcendante," that I had hoped and expected would unfold in the pages

6

of *La Physiologie du Goût*. Those pages revealed little more than the glutton that Carême had early divined in Brillat-Savarin—joined to a pompous and puzzling self-esteem; my resentment and disappointment rankle to this day).

Simple is the password in cooking today: If food is not simple, it is not good. But, unless the supremely social acts of eating and drinking, of human communion at table, of analyzing and sharing voluptuous experience evolved and refined within the nonetheless flexible boundaries of tradition, find their place as primordial and essential threads in the larger fabric of simplicity, Simple Food as a concept can have no meaning beyond that of elementary nourishment for the anti-sensualist or ease of preparation for the lazy cook.

Those definitions are often present to confuse the issue, the chameleon word assuming nearly as many meanings as there are tongues from which it so glibly slips. Simple may also imply, depending on the user or the context, "shorn of extraneous décor," the presentation being dictated by the nature of the dish rather than by the artistic conceits of its interpreter; "possibly involved preparations, the end results of which, because they are harmonious, are simple in effect" (such as the endlessly repeated preparation-type of classical cooking: a meat or fish prepared in a way least apt to modify its native qualities—poached, grilled, or roasted, accompanied by a sauce that though compounded of separately prepared essences strikes a single suave note, quietly enhancing the integrity of the basic product. Typical also, but in the agrestic tradition, are the *cassoulet* described later and the various meat stews whose souls are dissected in the meat chapter). Simple may also mean "pure," in the sense that a single flavor is sought out and accented (a terrine of foie gras nourished only by goose fat or a roast pheasant unaltered by hanging, forcemeats, alcoholic deglazings, or overcooking); "rustic" (peasant cooking whose flavors are sturdy, vigorous, and direct—sometimes rough but not necessarily "pure" in the sense of the preceding instances; inexpensive materials—salt pork, cabbage, potatoes, and dried vegetables—play important roles). Before even attempting to formulate a satisfactory definition, I think that one must, inverting the key phrase, say, "If food is not good, it is not simple."

A grain-fed farm hen's freshly laid egg, soft-boiled, has been chosen by some, defenders of an integral, naturally determined logic of the single element, as the symbol of ultimate perfection. Others of the same school lean toward the freshly plucked, vine-ripened, sun-hot August tomato, while, for those of the rustic school, the *aligot,* a gummy but tasty enough mess of potato purée and fresh Cantal cheese, has assumed the heroic dimensions of a symbol.

One well-known journalist amuses himself by pretending that the gourmet world is broken into two camps: the eaters of the rustic *aligot*—true lovers of the good and the pure—and the eaters of the elegant woodcock in its foie gras–tainted sauce—pretentious fools deceived by appearances and false gastronomic tradition. French writers on various regional cookings, while claiming respect for the traditions of other provinces, rarely fail to express a certain critical snobbism toward Parisian cooking, and if, in passing, the Parisian *concièrge*'s potato and leek soup may suffer a dig, the malice is mainly aimed at the sophistication of "rootless" professional traditions. It cannot be doubted that roots in Carême, Taillevent, and the Sun King's kitchens have nourished a somewhat exotic growth—an uneasy companion to the vigorous and essential structure rooted in lives led close to the soil and the seasons. *La vraie cuisine de bonne femme,* a near synonym of rustic cooking in the minds of those who fancy the phrase, is usually associated with *les plats mijotés:* stews that cook at a bare murmur for hours on end. When one of these little stews is thus denoted, one understands that it flirts with divinity—that it has reached heights of simple purity unattainable by a man's cooking. Shorn, through translation, of its mystical sheath, the phrase means "real home cooking."

A celebrated chef, recently interviewed, said, "Anyone can produce *la grande cuisine*—all that is necessary is a lot of foie gras and truffles and a few bottles of fine wine to throw into the sauces." But half-hidden behind the flipness is the conviction that expensive products too often replace imagination in the kitchen—that same imagination without which rustic culinary traditions could not exist (and with a bit more of which one might find fewer quails stuffed with foie gras on the menus of France's star-heavy restaurants).

But, were one to accept unaltered natural flavors or simplicity of execution as fundamental to the concept of simple food, rustic cooking (which necessarily embodies complicated aspects, one of its roles being essentially alchemical—the magical transformation of poor or vulgar elements into something transcendental) could not be admitted.

Consider the *cassoulet,* a voluptuous monument to rustic tradition: The beans are cooked apart, their flavor enhanced by prolonged contact with aromatic vegetables, herbs, and spices; the mutton is cooked apart, slowly, the wine and other aromatic elements refining, enriching, or underlining its character; apart, the goose has long since been macerated in herbs and salt and subsequently preserved in its own fat; a good sausage is famously allied to witchcraft. All of these separate products are then combined; a bit of catalytic goose fat—with the aid of gelatinous pork rind—binds them together in a velvet texture, and a further slow cooking process intermingles all the flavors while a gratin, repeatedly basted, forms, is broken, re-forms, is rebroken, a single new savor moving into dominance, cloaking, without destroying, the autonomy of the primitive members.

Escoffier wrote, *"Faites simple"* and he is often quoted. Yet, while not one to sneeze at the sun-hot tomato on the one hand nor, on the other, at the sticky *aligot* (the one representing an obvious necessity, the other a homely pleasure unrelated to his métier), he surely was aiming, rather, at safeguarding all that was valuable in the elaborate tradition of nineteenth-century professional cuisine, precisely by eliminating the encumbering decorative paring that, when not merely superfluous or distracting, was often detrimental to the basic quality of a preparation.

Curnonsky, whose entire life was devoted to eating and to thinking, talking, and writing about eating, took great pride in having been instrumental in popularizing regional cooking traditions in France and, in particular, in convincing restaurant owners and professional cooks of the virtue of presenting regional specialties. On his banner were inscribed Escoffier's two famous words, but he has bequeathed us, as well, a number of maxims of his own fabrication and a throng of disciples who regularly recite them. Coupled with the knowledge that Curnonsky's passion for the garden-fresh vegetable and the farm-kitchen stew failed to temper his admiration for the apparently involved refinements of the classical French tradition, these aphoristic pronouncements may shed a bit of light on what "simple food" means to a relatively complicated (gastronomic) intelligence:

> *En cuisine, comme dans tous les arts, la simplicité est le signe de la perfection.* ("In cooking, as in all the arts, simplicity is the sign of perfection.")

9

Presumably the analogy to the other arts applies, as well, to the means of achieving the simplicity. The painter, tortured before his canvas, effaces here, redraws there—alas, a few tiny details, overworked, constipate increasingly the effect of the whole as, discontent, he smears a clean edge, sharpens a vague contour, until, finally, in a rash of frustration, everything is scrubbed out, rebegun, and hours, days or, perhaps, months later, the unadorned statement emerges vibrant—a casual breath of life.

Happily a stew is rarely subject to quite such a complicated and uncertain conceptual process, but decidedly the simplicity that Curnonsky (more symbol than a man in this context) admired in cooking was, above all, the simplicity of art, the purity and the spontaneity of the effect justifying any means.

And:

La cuisine! C'est quand les choses ont le goût de ce qu'elles sont. ("La cuisine! That's when things taste like themselves.")

This is none other than the artist's precept, "Respect your medium," transposed into the world of food. No more, it says, should a leg of lamb be altered to imitate venison than clay should be made to imitate marble, the quality of the basic material being, in each instance, destroyed while the noble material, insolently imitated, remains aloof.

Defined as "pure in effect," not only rustic cooking but also classical French cooking, with its refined methods and subtle harmonies, must, insofar as its integrity remains unmarred by sophistication, be admitted as well to the fold of simple food.

A menu, too, must be pure in effect. Its successful composition depends, no less than the conception of a recipe, upon the cultivated art of simplicity; one of the commonest faults among France's most talented chefs is a compulsion, fired by the touching and too human desire to flatter a Sybaritic guest, to compose a menu, each of the parts of which may be of an exquisite purity but which, in its plethoric whole, adds up to something in the way of barbaric orgy, leaving the would-be Sybarite exhausted, uneasy in spirit as in body —far indeed from the beatific plane. (La Mère Fillioux, a Lyonnaise legend, is said, on the other hand, to have attained near perfection in both the confection of her individual preparations and her menu composition by limiting her talents to the execution of some six dishes—the two most celebrated were artichoke bottoms garnished with foie gras and truffled poached chicken. She claimed to have mastered only those and pretended, furthermore, that the intelligence, progressively refining over the years, that she brought to their elaboration would have been impossible in the demanding presence of a larger repertory. A goal of perfection set within such rigid and limited boundaries might easily train boredom in its wake, and it is fortunate that we, as amateurs, can afford to live more dangerously.)

I attempted in my first book to analyze a menu as I understand it and doubt that I could offer a more satisfactory dissection here. The essence of the thing is this: For a menu to emerge as a single statement, a coherent entity, it must be made up of single statements, each of which relates to the others creating larger single (or simple—or harmonious) effects within the whole. Courses relate to each other as well as each to its accompanying wine, and each wine is chosen not only in terms of its perfect fusion with a course, forming one statement, but as a harmonious prelude to the wine that follows it, forming another . . .

Simplicity—no doubt—is a complex thing. And the complexity of conceiving the larger symphony, a simple menu, must receive a bow of respect; my main objective in this book, however, is to deal with that fragment of a menu which is the single preparation: You, the cook, must also be the artist, bringing understanding to mechanical formulas, transforming each into an uncomplicated statement that will surprise or soothe a gifted palate, or from your knowledge drawing elements from many to formulate a new harmony—for such is creativity, be it in the kitchen or in the studio: the application of personal expression to an intimate understanding of the rules. The Renaissance master was lent visionary wings precisely by virtue of being bound by rules of religious and social convention, tyrannical iconography, despot-patrons' whims, and technical traditions. (His modern counterpart, exalting in the new freedom, sometimes fancies that were he so bound he would surely suffocate, the bright flame of genius snuffed. But as total freedom—never totally achieved—can exist only in a vacuum, there he flails, helpless in thin air, in desperate self-expression.)

The painter–cook analogy does not seem too far flung to me.

There are many who believe a healthy dose of imagination is all that one need bring to the kitchen. The cacophonous results are in quite the same spirit as the poignant failures of the liberated artist. When, on the other hand, to the beginner respectful of the rules, cooking appears involved and difficult, the reason is certainly that the internal logic of the thing has not been grasped: He who blindly opens a cookbook and follows to the letter a series of minutely described steps with no comprehension of their raisons d'être—of why, if at all, each was necessary—may or may not produce a masterpiece, but he is likely to heave a sigh of relief at being released from that precarious teeter-totter—nor, once executed, will any of the steps—motifs in an unperceived pattern—be remembered. They, like the child's desperate problem of pegs and holes, round and square, were too complicated—chaos is always complicated: When the logic of each step is understood in its relation to a total formula, everything falls into place; it is accepted and retained without effort. There are no secrets, no sleights of hand, no special talents unique to a culinary elite; and no technique integral to a preparation is complicated or difficult (the processes aimed at transforming a cooked preparation into a decorative object do often seem complicated—probably because, to many of us, they appear meaningless. Of course, food should be presented as attractively as possible and cold dishes in particular may support a certain amount of fantasy without their deeper qualities suffering. But, to be appetizing as well as attractive, food should always look like food, and we may be grateful that the chilly bits of baroque architecture with sumptuously inlaid façades of jewel-cut truffle, egg-white, and pimento mosaic belong largely to the past. The casual grace of a field bouquet touches us more deeply today than the formal splendor of a funeral wreath . . .).

Rules in cooking are not iron-cast (and, as in any medium of expression, they are often bent or broken by practitioners of talent—but to break rules, one must *have* rules). They are merely the expression of a well of experience formed and enriched over the centuries, re-examined, modified, or altered in terms of changing needs, habits, and tastes. They are welded out of knowledge—an understanding of what happens to a material when treated in a special way, how an ingredient may act differently if added at one point during a cooking process rather than at another, which aromatic elements fuse happily together and which, when combined, create a discordant effect, which and in what combinations will enhance the primitive qualities of a raw material, why some things should be subjected to high heat and others to the tiniest of flames or why a number of different qualities of heat must apply to a single preparation at different points in a cooking process . . .

One's own set of rules will form itself and become increasingly elaborate as one comes to understand the logic behind each detail, each step, to recognize the repetitions or variations of basic steps from one recipe to another; and the more elaborate the set of rules—that is to say, *the better one understands and is able to define an intricate framework of limitations*—the greater is the freedom lent one's creative imagination. Only a cookbook is needed to prepare a *boeuf Bourguignon* but, without rules, improvisation is impossible—and that is what cooking is all about.

THOUGHTS ABOUT IMPROVISATION

A number of friends have felt—and I agreed—that this book should contain a chapter on improvisational cooking. But the more I have worried about it, the more impossible it seems, in the context of writing, to lend life to the spirit of the thing—to make it felt that, by knowing and accepting rules, one frees oneself of rules. It is easy enough to say, "You must bring freedom, relaxation, knowledge and imagination to the thing and, above all, do not be afraid; a failure is no disgrace and may very often be more instructive than a success . . ." (The sense of failure is, in any case, always sharper in the mind of the practitioner than in those of the guests—I know that I have often diminished my table companions' pleasure in a meal that would otherwise have ravished them by a helpless compulsion to critically analyze each preparation.)

And it is the more difficult inasmuch as a recipe once set down —its pound of flesh, its ½ teaspoon of salt, its level tablespoon of flour, and ¼ cup olive oil trapped in black and white—no longer belongs to the realm of improvisation. The act of recording it robs it of the license responsible for its creation. It is self-evident: All that is recorded is born in improvisation—sometimes it has been deliberate, searching, analytical; the creation, so to speak, achieved in a single stroke, its elements drawn from the knowledge and experience of a great chef. Such are the endless appellations of classical cuisine, each conceived by a specific person to honor a personality or to commemorate an occasion. More often, in the instance of regional dishes, the improvisation is more or less unconscious, its nature dictated by "socio-economic-geographical" conditions, accident, or intuition. It is a study in depth, a continuing, slow, dumb, perfecting process stretching through generations of a family—and in horizontal penetration, the contributions of one family or another melting into a general concept. In detachment, one may think of these growing, changing, impersonal but living formulas as symbolic of a sort of culinary *anima mundi*. Their continuing evolution has often been frustrated by the intellectualizing interference of codification (and, more recently, by the leveling influence of internationalization).

It is true that nothing is more amusing than to be caught empty-handed—faced only with dibs and dabs of leftovers and (hopefully) a few staples and, on the spur of a moment, to be obliged to transform these disparate fragments into an acceptable meal. And the gratification of having been able, thanks to mere imagination, to formulate a few drab odds and ends into a bright, coherent, and often exciting statement is great. But this very excitement seems to be at odds with the solidly planted intentions of a cookbook and the expectations of its readers. I finally abandoned the notion of consecrating an entire chapter to this aspect of cooking, preferring, throughout the book, to present recipes as illustrations to theoretical discussion in the hope that they may serve as points of departure no less often than as satisfactory entities in themselves.

Note-taking is, moreover, an ill-assorted and dull companion to extemporaneous cooking, and when a good, honest, comforting dish throws itself together, I most often let myself off by commending its beauty and assuring myself that it will not easily be forgotten. My consciousness is cluttered with memories of memories and half-memories of endless pilafs garnished with a variety of sautéed vegetables and scrapings from roast chicken or game carcasses—or combined with *ragoûts* concocted from leftover roasts or firm-fleshed fish stews, heightened perhaps with butter-stewed onion, saffron, mushrooms, dried or fresh, one or several of the garden's native and

denizen herbs; of *cromesquis, crêpes,* raviolis, or cannellonis stuffed
with refrigerator remainders become soufflé mixtures, mixtures cheese-
bound or *béchamel*-bound, held together with mushroom purée,
stiff *soubise,* egg and breadcrumbs or rice (a recent and happy
memory in this vein is that of cannelloni stuffed with a mixture
of braised sweetbreads and braised fennel, each drained, coarsely
chopped, mixed with chopped *fines herbes* and bound with fresh
sheep's milk cheese, egg and Parmesan, the cannelloni moistened
with the braising liquids, sprinkled with Parmesan, and gratinéed);
salads and soups; myriad vegetables sweated in butter, herbs, and
their own vapors; vegetable gratins, puddings, hashes, stews, and
daubes.

Certain of these terms suggest "extemporaneous" or "makeshift."
Daube, for instance, means (approximately) "a mess," the origin of
the word being presumably the same as that of "daub" in English.
I have executed, with loyal respect, printed formulas for *daubes* in
the interest of analysis and comparison but, left to my own devices, a
daube is never twice the same. One of the best I've ever made (my
judgment confirmed by a group of friends, all experienced and im-
passioned *daube* eaters) consisted of . . . several pounds of *entrecôte*
and rumpsteak parings and a leftover roast put to marinate with a
half-dozen ends of bottles (some flat Champagne, remainders of
Brane-Cantenac, Beaujolais, Bandol rosé, and a local white wine)
for a morning, then hastily assembled at lunchtime with leftover
roasting juices, a remnant of *demi-glace,* a handful of herbs scattered at random through the layers of meat along with dried cèpes,
soaked, rinsed, and chopped, and the usual aromatic vegetables. The
daube was left at a murmur for an afternoon, skimmed of its fat
the following morning, gently reheated and escorted by the inevitable *macaronade;* the sumptuous luxury of the slap-dash thing
astonished my guests, wary of the results of such methods (leftover
daube is, in Provençal cooking, after first being savored cold in its
jelly, traditionally made into ravioli stuffing, much as the sweetbreads above were described, often with cooked, chopped chard
or spinach—try it).

The approach to improvisation must vary with the individual. I
have to see everything before me: The refrigerator is emptied out,
down to the last drop of a jellied roasting juice or dribble of rice and
the cupboards and vegetable bins are examined; all possible ingredi-

ents are lined up on a table. From a given line-up a number of possibilities will always present themselves and, when one's path has been
chosen, the rejects may of course be removed and examined anew
for some other course for the meal . . .

The following recipe, which friends begged me to record, is
reproduced merely for the purposes of illustration, the likelihood of
the various ingredients reuniting under other circumstances being
slight; this ham, pathetically banal, had been purchased in error by
an innocent guest, and its urgent need of a camouflaging cloak was
the motivating force behind the dish's conception:

GRATIN OF LEEK AND HAM ROLLS
(Roulades au Gratin)

12 medium leeks (about 2 pounds)
1 pound small zucchini, coarsely grated or passed
   through medium blade of Mouli-juliènne, salted in
   layers, and squeezed free of all excess liquid
½ pound mushrooms, passed through medium blade of
   Mouli-juliènne or coarsely grated
1 heaping tablespoon chopped parsley or fines herbes
1 medium onion, finely chopped, stewed without coloring
   in butter for about ½ hour
Lemon, salt, pepper, butter
6 slices cooked ham

Béchamel   3 tablespoons flour
2 tablespoons butter
1 quart milk
Bay leaf, thyme
Salt, pepper, hint of nutmeg
½ cup heavy cream

1 heaping tablespoon green peppercorns (parboiled for a
   few seconds if fresh vacuum-packed or frozen)
3 ounces (1 cup) grated cheese (half Parmesan, half
   Gruyère)
Butter, well chilled

Trim the tough extremities from the leek greens, slit several times from the white section, piercing at point just below the formation of the leaves up through the leaves, soak, cut white and light-green sections into lengths corresponding to the size of the ham slices, tie into a bundle (the green tops will serve for soups or bouquets garnis) and cook in lightly boiling salted water until barely tender—about ten minutes. Drain thoroughly.

Sauté the zucchini in butter over high flame, tossing often, for 7 or 8 minutes. Set aside. Sauté the mushrooms, lightly salted, in butter over high flame, tossing constantly, for about 3 or 4 minutes or until all their liquid has evaporated and they begin to cling to the pan. Add the chopped herbs a few moments before removing from the heat and, at the moment of removing, grind over a bit of pepper and add a few drops of lemon juice. Mix together zucchini, mushrooms, and stewed onion.

Prepare the *béchamel* in the usual way (see page 164), cooking it gently for ½ hour; discard the thyme and bay leaf and add the pepper, the nutmeg, and the cream upon removing it from the heat.

Roll two leeks coated with a heaping tablespoonful of the vegetable mixture into each of the slices of ham and arrange them, flap side down, in a buttered gratin dish of a size so that they barely touch. Scatter over the green peppercorns. Stir half of the grated cheese into the sauce and spoon it regularly over the ham rolls, sprinkle on the remaining cheese, distribute paper-thin sheets of chilled butter over the surface, and bake for ½ hour at 375° to 400° or until the sauce is bubbling and the surface is richly golden.

Improvisation is at war with the printed word. It either defies analysis or, in accepting it, finds its wings clipped. The classroom facilitates things; with one's hands deep in the mixing bowl, eliminating a chosen ingredient, deciding to add another, tasting, altering, discussing, the spontaneity is alive and contagious and the result is there to be tasted.

My recent venture into teaching led the class progressively toward experiences of this nature. At first there was a certain amount of panic among the students—there were no more neatly transcribed recipes to be studied in advance and even note-taking was robbed of its solacing teaspoons, tablespoons, and cups. But distress rapidly succumbed in most instances to enthusiasm and I was delighted at the general excitement when, one day, weary of presenting time-

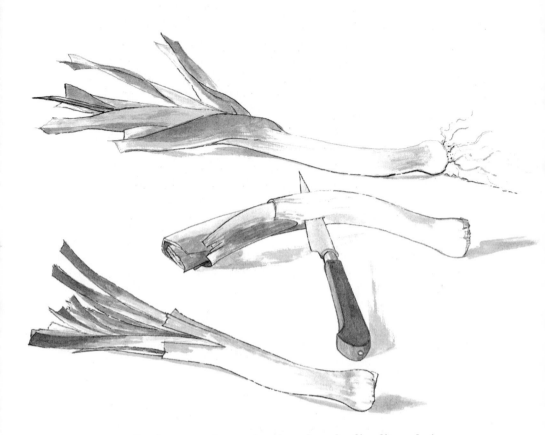

Leek, unpared; pared and ready to be slit; slit ready for washing

worn formulas, I cleared the market of the freshest and most attractive produce on display, lined it up along with all the classroom leftovers and we began to invent: a playful selection of vegetables thrown together more or less *à la Grècque* and others *en estouffade;* eggplant gratin; *crêpes* soufflés; ravioli stuffed with a concoction of leftover frogs' legs *poulette;* salads, composed and simple; braised red cabbage and, with a fish soup cooking, more frogs (boneless) wrapped in *crêpes,* moistened with the saffroned rich essence and gratinéed; a series of flat omelets, potato straw cake, grilled peppers, cucumbers in dill cream, and I know not what.

18

Another day we were faced with leftover braised lamb shoulder and a quantity of generously truffled fresh egg noodles. After taking an inventory of the larder, several pounds of zucchini, a quart of heavy cream, and a block of Parmesan were retained. A heavy round copper utensil some 6 inches high and 2½ feet in diameter was unearthed and in it were thoroughly mixed the noodles (already freely buttered), the slivered meat and its juices, the zucchini, first coarsely grated, salted, squeezed, and tossed in butter, a healthy amount of freshly ground pepper, a memory of nutmeg, the whole smoothed down, smeared thick with cream, and thickly dusted with Parmesan. An hour later the vast expanse of golden crispness was glorious to behold. The zucchini juliènne, imitating the form of the noodles, was meltingly different in texture and its delicate flavor fused happily, holding its own with the penetrating heady truffle, providing a unique taste experience that is stamped the more clearly in my memory thanks to the class's enthusiasm.

HERBS

For my part, the classroom has been instructive in many ways. One forgets so easily and I had long since come to think of herbs as an unquestioned presence in the kitchen. I discovered that, for the students, the summer course was a revelation in "herb cookery." The "recommended improvements" forms filled out at the end of the course nearly all suggested a series of herb lectures, and many of my students returned home to plant herb gardens.

Interesting books on herbs are not lacking, although a number of them are better informed in the ways of religious rites, witchcraft, and medicine than in those of the kitchen. For practical purposes, Tom Stobart's *The International Wine and Food Society's Guide to Herbs, Spices and Flavorings* (London: David and Charles; 1970) seems particularly good. *Of Herbs and Spices,* by Colin Clair (London: Abelard-Schuman; 1961) I have enjoyed for its historical and anecdotal content and another, *Les Soleils de la Cuisine* by Robert

Landry, is, in French, amusingly but seriously written. It has recently been translated into English, published by Abelard-Schuman under the title of *The Gentle Art of Flavoring*.

Herbs most often suffer from underuse (in bouquets garnis) or from overuse (with grills and roasts), and of course from emasculation—one must, above all, not think of all those little canisters of powdered condiments, vaguely peppery and dusty to the nose, as herbs. Even those herbs that are as good (or, as in the case of oregano, better) dried as fresh should be (relatively) freshly dried. Dried on the branch, the perfume holds best, and certainly the leaf holds better than a powdered version (I have, however, kept herbs I had ground for up to a year in glass jars without their suffering greatly).

Few are those who cannot permit themselves at least a few pots or a window box of herbs; and in a garden, borders, hedges, and clumps of herbs, in particular the labiates (rosemary, thyme, hyssop, savory, etc.—all have flowers of varying blues and lavenders that resemble, although minuscule, the snapdragon in form, the word itself describing the lip-like formation of the flower) can be of great beauty. Many of the herbs of this family, taken as infusions, have a relaxing and cleansing effect on the system. They are mostly vermifuge and antiseptic. Strong infusions added to a bath are also tonic and relaxing.

It is useful to keep a pot of mixed herbs at hand's reach for use in marinades, rapid stews, and grilled meats and poultry. Some may prefer to add a bit of rosemary or sage—I content myself with approximately equal quantities of thyme, oregano, and winter savory, adding fragments of marjoram from time to time.

BASIL *(Ocimum basilicum)*. French: *Basilic*. Labiate.

Annual. Easily raised from seed and may be kept as a potted plant. There are many varieties, ranging from tiny leaves hardly larger than pins' heads to large lettuce-like leaves. The small-leafed varieties tend to be more peppery in flavor and somewhat less characteristic. They can be an attractive addition to salads, but the large light-green leaves are preferable for general use.

As usual an element in bouquets garnis as thyme or bay in pre-Carême French cuisine, basil disappeared almost completely and, even today, its only common use is in the Provençal *soupe au pistou*. The author of a booklet on rabbit cookery, dating from the early part of this century, in which some of the recipes were culled from antique sources, notes that he has eliminated such bizarre herbs as basil, leaf thyme, rosemary, and marjoram, "aromatic plants employed in olden times, the taste of which would seem strange to us today." That attitude was and remains very general in France today (the Italians have never faltered in their loyalty, basil-flavored tomato sauces and the Genovese pesto having been borrowed into many an American kitchen as well).

Basil has a natural affinity for tomatoes, both raw and cooked, sweet peppers, olive oil, saffron, garlic—in short, for most things Mediterranean. In salads, it will lift certain lettuces from the realm of banality and forms an exciting alliance with a number of other herbs and salad greens—rocket, purslane, dandelion, leaf thyme, hyssop . . . Tarragon and dill should be kept out of its reach. It is only marvelous fresh and, in cooking, its qualities are best served as a terminal addition to a sauce. It is addictive, and few who form the habit of using it can do without it. By all means use the flowers as well as the leaves and, rather than chopping, tear the latter into fragments; then they won't blacken.

B A Y *(Laurus nobilis)*. French: *Laurier*. Laurel.

Perennial small tree or bush. Cannot survive severe winters but, in Europe, is a common potted plant used widely as a geometrically pruned decorative element on café terraces or in hotel lobbies. Sacred to Apollo, it crowned the heads of poets, heroes, and warriors and was chewed by the Bacchante and the Delphic pythoness to hallucinogenic ends.

Imported bay will serve you better than the harsh and aggressive California bay leaf. Bay (with thyme and parsley) belongs to the basic trinity of the bouquet garni, and it alone rarely finds other uses (see *Daube de pommes de terre* [p. 223]. Pieces are sometimes alternated with skewered meats and vegetables. In prolonged cooking processes, the fragment of bay leaf used in a bouquet garni is insufficient, its initial self-assertion being attenuated and refined over a period of several hours.

CELERY (*Apium graveolens*). French: *Celeri*. Umbellifer.

Biennial. The small dark-green garden celery looks like a large version of common parsley and is easily grown from seed. Slightly bitter, with a more concentrated flavor than cultivated branch celery, it is commonly grown in French gardens for use in bouquets garnis and is a more interesting herb for bouquets, but may be replaced by the branch celery.

CHERVIL (*Anthriscus cerefolium*). French: *Cerfeuil*. Umbellifer.

Annual. It should be seeded in rich earth every three weeks or so throughout the summer in order to have a constant supply. During the heat of the summer a shady spot should be chosen for seeding; watering is essential.

The most delicate of the *fines herbes*. It may be used alone in quantity, its light anise flavor, unlike that of tarragon, remaining discreet, or in combination with parsley, chives, tarragon, hyssop, leaf thyme, lemon thyme (but not all at the same time). Omelets and scrambled eggs, salads of all kinds, and certain cream soups or consommés most often receive its benediction. Its flavor dissipates rapidly in cooking and it should be added to soups only at the time of serving.

CHIVES (*Allium schoenoprasum*). French: *Ciboulette*. Lily.

Perennial. Tiresome to grow from seeds and hardly worthwhile in view of its widespread availability as a potted plant. It is useful to have several clumps, as it should be cut back to the ground regularly to keep the new leaves growing. It is so easily found that many people content themselves with replacing the plants.

Its role is identical to that of chervil.

DILL (*Anethum graveolens*). French: *Aneth*. Umbellifer.

Annual. Easily grown (the seeds keep badly and should be used as fresh as possible) but goes to seed rapidly and, if raised for its feathery foliage, should be sown several times during a season. The ancient Greeks admired it for its magical and medicinal qualities and it has often served to thwart witches' curses.

Dill is used abundantly in northern European countries and, in particular, in Scandinavia for quantities of fish preparations. It is practically unknown in France and, when found, is often confused with fennel, which bears a strong physical resemblance to it.

The fresh leaves, chopped, seem predestined to flavor cucumber (cream and lemon sauce, not vinaigrette) and fish—it is divine with crayfish. Good also whipped into fresh curd cheese or as a replacement for parsley with steamed and buttered potatoes. Although the perfume is attenuated by drying, it is not altered, and the dillweed of commerce is a useful addition to the kitchen shelf.

FENNEL *(Foeniculum vulgare)*. French: *Fenouil*. Umbellifer.

Perennial. May be grown from seed. Not to be confused with the cultivated bulbous or Florentine fennel, whose flavor is similar but less intense.

Wild fennel, in Provence, flavors a host of fish preparations with, sometimes, a bit of pastis being added to a marinade or a soup to reinforce its native liquorice-tinged taste. Bouillabaisse and snails' court bouillons cannot do without it, and it perfumes most grilled fish—famously the Mediterranean sea bass *(loup de mer)*. The feathery leaves can be chopped and added to salads or vegetable preparations. The flowers and stalks are dried for winter use.

HYSSOP *(Hyssopus officinalis)*. French: *Hysope*. Labiate.

Perennial. Easily grown from seed and may be raised in pots. A small bush whose dark-green leaves resemble those of tarragon, it is one of the sacred herbs of the Ancients, an obligatory element in the monastery gardens of the Middle Ages and much used in medieval cooking. Hyssop today is to most people only a word with vague Biblical associations—a pity, for it is an exquisite thing.

It shares a refreshing light bitterness with many of the labiate herbs but its perfume is apart. Writers mostly claim that it is too strong for the modern palate, but I love it and have never known it to trouble my guests, who regularly insist on eating "hyssop salad" at my table and have returned home to plant it in windowboxes, pots, or gardens. The tiny intense blue flowers, scattered over a background of varied greens and sliced hard-boiled eggs, are ravishing but, if the salad has been sprinkled with the chopped leaves as well, one is hardly aware of the more delicate flavor of the flowers.

LOVAGE *(Levisticum officinale)*. French: *Livèche*. Umbellifer.

Perennial. Easily grown but needs garden space. Just as celery looks like a large version of parsley, lovage resembles a large version of garden celery (and a small version of angelica) in appearance. Like hyssop, it was much used in the past and its name is known to many, but few know the herb.

The flavor recalls that of celery but is more penetrating and "wilder." It may be added, chopped, to vegetable soups—try it in small quantity at first; but its logical place is in a bouquet garni for a preparation—*pot-au-feu, poule-au-pot,* or a long-cooking stew—whose unhurried development permits the lovage to refine and fuse with the other aromatics, its own slight arrogance dissolving into the whole.

CULTIVATED MARJORAM, called also Sweet or Knotted Marjoram *(Majorana hortensis)*. French: *Marjolaine cultivée, marjolaine vraie, marjolaine à coquilles*. Labiate.

Perennial, but usually considered annual because of its fear of frost. Easily grown from seeds and may be cultivated in pots. Its confusion with oregano or the various oreganos (wild marjorams) in literature is extremely frustrating and, in Provence, the oregano that grows wild on the hillsides is called *marjolaine,* its correct name, *origan,* being generally unknown and *la marjolaine vraie* being equally unknown although another variety of oregano is often called *marjolaine cultivée* . . . Most books, French or English, claim that cultivated marjoram is widely used in Provence, but I have never encountered anyone from the region who was familiar with the herb. Its appearance—the tiny shovel-shaped velvety blue-green leaves and the miniature white flowers half lost in the shell-like geometric construction of surrounding leaves—is totally unlike that of oregano, as is its heavenly fragrance. Many authors pretend that its perfume is akin to that of thyme and that the two herbs are interchangeable—they who claim that have never tasted the herb. The commercialized versions are not even parodies of the real thing, no memory of the original perfume remaining.

The contrary of oregano, marjoram is marvelous in all sorts of preparations fresh, the tender young leaves and flowers finely chopped, and less interesting than its wild cousin dried, although still a valuable addition to a bouquet garni. It marries caressingly with eggs and many vegetables and, in the event that I failed to express myself strongly enough in the discussion preceding the omelet loaf (see page 88), I can but insist here also that the zucchini-marjoram omelet be extracted from the whole and tried once alone.

MINT *(Mentha viridis)*. French: *Menthe*. Labiate.

Perennial. There are endless varieties of mint—and subvarieties, hybrids, etc. The variations of spearmint are the most interesting in the kitchen—the French hardly use it except as a tea for tired stomachs; they consider the English affection for this herb an aberration. Arab and Middle Eastern cooking often makes interesting use of mint.

OREGANO *(Origanum vulgare)*. French: *Origan*. Labiate.

Perennial. Apparently seeds are available, but it is likely that the bundles of dried oregano available in Italian shops will be more interesting than the seeded product (Southern California might lend itself to a production of good quality). There are endless varieties (according to Tom Stobart, there are at least ten varieties in Greece alone, of varying flavors and intensities, all known indigenously as *rígani*). The Cretan oregano is so different from the others that it takes a different name—in English, that of "dittany"—and it is said that Mexico adds to the confusion by applying the name to other herbs as well . . . In my own experience, the Greek varieties are by far the most powerful, that of southern Italy (apparently *Origanum onites*) is still more pungent than the French varieties, but that which I know from the hillsides here is the finest —the same, however, growing wild in other parts of France, under another sun and from an earth less rude, is of relatively little interest. Oregano grows wild in England as well, but the quality corresponds to the climate.

Oregano must be dried to give of its perfume, but a few days' drying will bring it all out. In the south of France it comes into flower in July and, thanks to the dryness and the heat, is finished by the first week in August. Elsewhere in France one finds it in full but unfragrant flower through September. It must be picked in flower and dried, preferably in tied-up bouquets. I begin using it a week after picking, but at times bouquets remain in storage for up to two years and the full power of the perfume remains. The finest fragrance is in the flowers, but the leaves crumble and mingle with them automatically in usage and lend their perfume as well.

Oregano's use in France was restricted to Provence and the Côte d'Azur (and even there surprisingly little used in view of its natural abundance) until the international pizza movement swept the country some years ago; it is now known to many, but only as *l'herbe à pizza*. In Italy it is used more than thyme and deserves a place of importance in any kitchen. Alone or in combination with thyme and savory, it is a valuable flavoring for grilled and roast lamb, certain game birds (of those available in the United States, quail in particular), and no other herb so effectively flatters guinea fowl. It is useful in fish soups and sauces and with cooked tomato preparations...

P A R S L E Y *(Petroselinum sativum)*. French: *Persil*. Umbellifer.

Biennial. Grows easily from seed, flowers in its second year and dies. Should, therefore, be planted every spring in a garden. Parsley roots, scraped and well washed, lend a very particular and delicate flavor to stews or court bouillons and, if possible, should be included in all bouquets garnis. The second-year plants, destined, in any case, to disappear, should be dug up for this use. The stems, whose presence adds nothing to chopped parsley, should also be added to bouquets garnis rather than being discarded.

Parsley is too often thought of merely as a decorative element and showered in tasteless quantity over everything—it is true that the bundles of curly parsley bought in the market have little other quality. The common, flat-leafed, or Italian, parsley has a much finer flavor but, curly or flat, parsley must be freshly picked, its perfume disappearing rapidly. Deep fried (a handful of leaf clumps, each attached to a fragment of stem) for a few seconds in hot oil, it is the perfect garnish for fried whitebait or any nonsweet fritters —vegetable, brains, squid . . . The Provençal *persillade*—garlic-flavored chopped parsley—which is sautéed at the last minute with a ream of preparations is, if the garlic is not left coarsely chopped and in too great an abundance in the mixture, an attractive method of throwing into relief the parsley's particular perfume. A garnish of golden, butter-crisp croutons rapidly sautéed with a *persillade* can enhance many a stew or certain scrambled eggs.

PURSLANE *(Portulaca oleracea)*. French: *Pourpier à salade.* Portulaca.

Annual, self-seeding. A small ground-spreading midsummer garden pest with rounded fleshy leaves. The French have developed cultivated garden varieties that may be more interesting for their larger leaves, but are not otherwise noticeably different in flavor.

Braised as a vegetable or added, chopped, to an herb or a vegetable soup, it is mostly a curiosity, its great value being as an addition to a salad where, in combination with bitter herbs and flavorful lettuces, its different texture and separate flavor serve a real purpose. Cooked, its raw, mild taste turns sharp and bitter.

ROCKET *(Eruca sativa* or *Brassica eruca)*. French: *Roquette.* Crucifer.

Annual, easily grown from seed. Its use is almost entirely limited to salads, but for that purpose, it is one of the most exciting green things I know. Most people assure me that it is the same herb as that known as arugula in the Italian-American markets. My memory is of a less distinctive flavor, but growing conditions may be responsible. Rocket does take a number of other names in Italy: *Rochetta, ruchetta, ruccola, rughetta,* some suspiciously resembling arugula in sound.

The deeply cut-out dark green leaves look somewhat like an elongated oak leaf. The flavor may be described as lightly bitter and peppery, but such general adjectives are helpless to touch the personality of that lovely weed. In the south of France it is not happy with the dry heat of summer and begins to flourish only in autumn. Both the wild and the cultivated varieties are common in meridional markets.

ROSEMARY *(Rosmarinus officinalis)*. French: *Romarin*. Labiate.

Perennial. More practical to buy the plants than to attempt seeding, although in its natural habitat it is self-seeding. Little used except in Italy, where sprays of fresh rosemary are often tied up with a roast before being sold from the butcher's (and, today, in France where the meats of the modish restaurants specializing in charcoal grills with Provençal herbs are often thickly coated with rosemary). It is among the most exhilarating of all garden scents, but, brought to the kitchen, rosemary turns troublesome and aggressive. It can be good with pork, lamb, and certain strongly flavored, oily fish (such as sardines, smelts, mackerel, eel), but it is wiser to leave these in contact with branches of the fresh herb in a simple olive oil marinade, removing the herb before cooking (unless, for instance, a branch is placed inside a fish's abdominal cavity before being grilled and removed before serving).

Its greatest virtue lies in the gentle beauty of its smoke—totally different from its green presence—whose caress, when a branch is thrown to smolder on the hot coals a few seconds before removing any fish, fowl, meat, or vegetable from the grill, is subtle and genial.

SAGE *(Salvia officinalis)*. French: *Sauge*. Labiate.

Perennial. Easily grown from seed and, whatever its eventual use in the kitchen, it is a glorious addition to a garden. Its bluish-purple flowers share the beauty and the form of those of the other labiates but, larger than most, are particularly spectacular against their gray-green background of soft downy leaves. Its name and its history are synonymous with good health—sage has often, during the last couple of millenniums, been considered a cure-all and sometimes been thought to beget immortality.

It is now snubbed in America, no doubt because of its once abusive use in poultry dressings and probably justly also, for, dried, it acquires an unpleasant musty flavor. Fresh, it should be used with discretion—but it should be used. The French use it sometimes with pork, and a leaf of fresh sage in the stomachic *aïgo-bollido* is obligatory. The Italians use it often and often to excess with veal, but always fresh. One of the best ways I know to critically enjoy the qualities of the fresh sage leaf is as a (sparse) element, finely chopped, in a basic ravioli farce of ricotta, butter, egg, and Parmesan, the cooked ravioli simply sprinkled with Parmesan and brown butter.

SAVORY (*Satureia hortensis:* summer savory and *Satureia montana:* winter savory). French: *Sarriette*. Labiates.

The summer savory is annual; winter savory is perennial. The former is easily grown from seeds, but it is more practical to buy plants of winter savory, which, in a garden, may be reproduced by dividing and transplanting the roots in early spring.

Most authors agree that the summer savory is the more interesting of the two. I do not share their opinion and, although I regularly plant the annual variety, many a summer passes without its ever being touched, whereas the borders of winter savory find abundant use: in the spring the tender young leaves, chopped, transform a salad, and tradition justly renders them obligatory with cooked broad beans; later the leaves become too tough and brittle to be pleasant in salads, but they remain, fresh, a superior flavoring agent, and, in full late-summer flower, the branches are cut back to serve throughout the winter in herb mixtures and bouquets garnis.

The perfumes of the two savories are somewhat alike, but that of the summer savory seems to me to have an unclean edge of kerosene, its wild parent being stronger but purer. In Provence the perennial savory (known only as *pèbre d'aï* or *pèbre d'ase: poivre d'âne,* or "donkey pepper") always replaces thyme in rabbit stews and often is wrapped around fresh white goat cheeses, its fragrance penetrating. Useful also for grilled meats and poultry.

SORREL (*Rumex acetosa*). French: *Oseille*. Polygonum.

Perennial. Easily grown from seed (slow to sprout) and the plants continue to produce plentifully for easily six or seven years. Requires practically no care but for superficial weeding and continued use—the leaves should be cut back regularly, inciting the tender young leaves to grow anew (and flower stalks should be removed as they appear). There are a number of varieties of large-leafed cultivated sorrel. A tiny-leafed wild sorrel grows in the United States.

Too little known outside of France, sorrel's refreshing acidity can enhance endless meat, fish, poultry, egg, and vegetable preparations used in small quantities as a flavoring herb, as the principal element in a soup or sauce, or as a vegetable garnish in itself. A graceful and welcome change from the sempiternal lemon.

TARRAGON *(Artemisia dracunculus)*. French: *Estragon.* Composite.

Perennial. Reproduction by breaking up and separating the roots before the shoots begin to appear in the early spring. In any case, for the plants to remain healthy and vigorous, the roots must be dug up every two years, cleaned of any rotted ones, and then transplanted.

Tarragon is quarrelsome in the company of the bitter herbs and, but for its role among the *fines herbes,* is best used alone. Very pleasant when handled with discretion, it can become repellent— and this is especially true in cooked dishes—if too liberally dispensed; in combination with parsley, chives, and chervil, a few leaves, finely chopped, bring sufficient flavor to a full tablespoon of each of the others. It often flavors chicken preparations, either hot or cold, rabbit stews, and accompanying sauces for grilled or poached fish and grilled meats. Crustaceans welcome its presence.

THYME *(Thymus vulgaris)*. French: *Thym.*

LEMON THYME *(Thymus serpyllum citriodorus)*. French: *Thym à l'odeur de citron.*

LEAF THYME (Serpolet): *(Thymus serpyllum)*. French: *Serpolet.* All labiates.

Perennial all three. It is probably easiest to buy plants, although with ordinary thyme, even though but a few seeds from a packet will sprout, it may be worthwhile to prepare a bed and sow them in the early spring. Germination is very slow. There may or may not be a number of subspecies of ordinary thyme—it is certain that, from one climate and soil condition to another, thyme differs greatly. The garden thymes of the Parisian region and of England are, in appearance and in fragrance, of another world from that which grows wild in Provence (as, in a very different way, is that of the Peloponnesian hills). I have sown both here (one package labeled "Thym des Jardins" and the other "English Thyme") and both produced identically the same plant that grows wild in profusion on the hillsides and that I have planted in borders throughout the garden. It was an interesting experiment, in no way disappointing, for the Provençal thyme has much more character than that of more northern climates and richer soils—no doubt but that a poor rocky, limey soil and arid summers produce the best thyme. The garden thymes have more fragile stems and the vegetation is thicker, bushier, and greener. Provençal thyme is straggly, its leaves silver-gray-green and its stems heavy and gnarled in microscopic imitation of the proximate olive trees.

The best for drying is picked at the moment of flowering—April in Provence and somewhat later in other regions, but no doubt the best habit elsewhere is to keep one's garden thyme for uses fresh and buy dried Provençal thyme for bouquets garnis.

It may be the only altogether indispensable herb in French cooking. It is a pity that other herbs do not more often share the honors of the bouquet garni but, of them all, thyme, while positive and personal, is the most discreet, the least eccentric, harmoniously binding disparate savors with no self-assertion—this is true of preparations that require long cooking—stews, *potées,* etc. Grillades require the light touch; a little thyme, as with other herbs in this case, goes a long way.

Lemon thyme and leaf thyme are both most interesting fresh. Leaf thyme has the slightest of odors, but a light, bitter, refreshing taste and its tiny leaves may be scattered in quantity over green salads—or over lentils, grilled peppers, tomatoes, etc. It is agreeable in combination with hyssop. Lemon thyme is there mostly to touch and smell—and it is a lovely scent. It *is* useful in salads or omelets. A friend who is an herb-tea enthusiast claims that lemon thyme is the most beautiful of all.

WINE IN COOKING

I do not want to suggest that cooking with wine is a special kind of cooking in a world apart—it is not (any more so than cooking with onions, cooking with herbs, cooking with carrots, eggs, or bread). It is as natural and as logical a moistening agent in viticultural country as is milk in dairy country or water the world round. And yet, be it the responsibility of innocence, cynicism, or a super, but questionable refinement, the concept seems sometimes hopelessly clouded.

In innocence, many believe that a product designated as "cooking wine" has a place in the kitchen (nor are foreigners the only sinners —many a Frenchman is convinced that if a recipe calls for "very good wine," it means a cheap wine that titles 12 or 13 percent alcohol rather than a meager 10 or 11 percent). To taste a dish in which a dishonest wine has been used is conclusive, but that should not be necessary; it is only too reasonable to assume that a wine not good to drink can bring no positive quality to a cooked preparation. There should be no question of using a wine in the kitchen that one does not consider good enough to serve at one's table (which is not to say that wine should not be kept in the kitchen for cooking purposes—ends of bottles should certainly be kept, wines of a color poured together and corked in bottles or half-bottles, protecting them as nearly as possible from contact with the air).

The cynic—he whose chicken boiled up in *gros-rouge* is labeled *coq-au-Chambertin*—may really believe that it makes little or no difference, finding it more practical to pay lip service to a "noble" tradition that he privately believes to be a lot of pretentious hocus-pocus, but, more often, his own palate is not that naïve; he is convinced that the client (alas, he often wears chef's clothing) cannot tell the difference. In any case, if a restaurant menu lists *coq-au-Beaujolais* (or *coq-au-vin de Chinon, de Nuits,* etc.), it is a near certainty that it will be prepared with a wine superior to the one used in the *coq-au-Chambertin,* for no restaurant owner is crazy enough to pour a ruby fortune over an old cock.

Super refinement, whose seat is more often cerebral than "palatial," is peopled by a number of precepts, some of which are valuable and many of which are deceptively plausible: Good wines are rightly used in cooking, but great wines are often recommended, and repeated insistence is placed on the importance of serving the same wine at table that has been used in the confection of a dish, an eminently artistic conceit, mainly unrelated to the palate, although it is often possible to respect the form without inconvenience. Few, however, are those who would complain if their lobster, poached in a Pouilly-Fumé, were accompanied by a Montrachet; few, on the other hand, would willingly drink a white wine with a pheasant *salmis* or with beef braised in white wine . . .

One may respectfully find a place in the kitchen for a great wine only if heat never comes into contact with it, the wine's unique personality defining a dish—sparking its general character with a personal note in much the same way that a slight detail in a sketch may rescue it from impersonal abstraction (meat jellies, fresh fruits macerated in wine, and dessert jellies are cases in point, and it is to avoid the blunting effect of heat that the chosen wine should never be added to a jelly until it is nearly cold but before the jell stage).

Heat cannot efface the offensive qualities of a bad wine and it can, indeed, put to good use those of a robust and honest wine with a frank fruit, a solid structure, and a firm, uncomplicated bouquet, but, depending on the length or the intensity of the cooking process, it nonetheless alters or completely transforms the wine's original nature.

If one refuses to judge a wine's greatness by the dent it makes in one's purse, it is not easy to find a satisfactory yardstick: What precisely differentiates a perfect bourgeois growth in Pauillac from its seignorial neighbor—or a Vosne-Romanée from La Tache? It is the same thing that separates de Hooch from Vermeer. It can only be sensed, but one knows that between the two is an abyss; the one is terrestrial, the other divine. And the mystery remains intact.

The mystery has it, also, that a good wine, loyal and solid, will remain exactly that in our memories whereas a great wine will continue to evolve, barely perceived nuances and, if it is a very old wine, distant associations taking fuller form, unveiling fragile complexities —and that without bringing the slightest deception to a subsequent tasting.

Relegated to the kitchen, all wine becomes earthbound; the mystery is erased. If a great wine is thus sacrificed, we have destroyed a marvelous thing.

The eye often betrays the palate and preconceived ideas confuse it. A system of rules has been more or less consciously elaborated concerning the roles of red wine and white wine in the kitchen that is more closely allied to a cerebro-visual aesthetic than to a sapid reality.

Classical recipes for fish cooked in red wine (one of the most celebrated being *sole au Chambertin*—the word's consonance must surely be the main factor in its choice) are well known but usually considered as curiosities (the uses of white wine in the preparation of meats—red and game—are far more common but less known, simply because the eye fails to detect the presence).

Among the whites and the reds alike, each, after all, runs the gamut from light-bodied, fruity, and refreshing to muscular, chewy, powerful, and richly bouqueted. Yet, in a general way, and above all when we think of wines for cooking, the first run of adjectives means "white wine" and the second "red wine" and the laws are smugly laid down: Fish and white meats should be treated with white wine, red meats and game with red.

But, as a matter of fact, any dish traditionally prepared with white wine can as well be prepared with red and conversely; depending on the qualities of the chosen wine (assuming them to be positive) the result will be different but good. The only real reason—and it is valid—to insist absolutely on a white wine, for instance, in a creamed sauce bound by egg yolks is to avoid the dull and shadowy, violet-brown cast lent by the red wine—nor, even with the blood, will one ever have a richly velvet, nearly black civet with white wine.

BREAD

Apart from its importance at table, bread, in many of the recipes in this book, has an important place: Stale or completely dried out, it accompanies soups; crumbs, soft or dried, are used for certain gratins and for breading; soaked and squeezed dry, it is a major element in other gratins and a minor but vital one in many *pâtés* and stuffings; it is cooked crisp in butter for croutons and *croûtes* and baked in puddings.

For our purposes, the best of American breads are less than ideal because of over-sweetness and their much-admired soft and tender texture. The long loaves marketed as French bread in American bakeries leave much to be desired, as do the plastic-wrapped, preservative-drenched baguettes flown in from France, but I have found very good bread in Italian neighborhood bakeries in New York—large, round, crusty loaves reminiscent at the same time of Tuscan country loaves and of French peasant bread.

Superior-quality commercialized American breads—those with a firm-textured, heavy crumb—can be serviceable for croutons, for breading, or as crumbs for gratins, the native flavor and texture being sublimated to nutty, butter-flavored crispness and, when soaked in small quantity to lend smoothness and consistency to the body of well-seasoned stuffings or terrines, the disagreeable sweetness is imperceptible.

The dried crusts in a soup, on the other hand, should resemble, as nearly as possible, rough, tough old slices of peasant bread—the result, otherwise, will simply not be good. Many people think of bread saved and used in this way as a foolish, skinflintish economy measure and a repellent idea. They do not know and refuse to believe that it is, in fact, not only delicious but often integral to the soup's character.

Good bread is increasingly difficult to find in France, although sentimental memories of that of the past abound—of the great sourdough loaves prepared in the homes and brought to the village ovens, brick igloos preheated with the coals of wood fires. Anecdotal tradition claims that, during the winter, the bread dough often shared the honors of the conjugal bed, thus profiting from body heat to raise during the night while gaining in homely flavor as well.

I gave a recipe in *The French Menu Cookbook* for an approximation of the French country loaf of bread which I continue to find adequate. Instructions for oven temperatures and lengths of cooking times vary greatly among authors (and so they should, depending on the size of the loaves and the desired thickness of the crust). Any of the recipes, either for American white bread or for French bread, to

35

be found in American cookbooks (French cookbooks simply don't give bread recipes—they expect you to buy your bread at the baker's) will give good results if you cut out the milk, shortening, and sugar and bake the loaf on a flat surface rather than in a bread tin (my oven contains a heavy plaque rather than the grill to be found in most kitchens and I have taken to the habit of putting the loaf to raise on a sheet of aluminum foil that has been sprinkled with semolina, a stiff cardboard beneath it, and, with an abrupt motion, slipping the aluminum foil directly onto the hot oven plaque). A pan of water should be kept in the bottom of the oven. It is valuable to experiment with different flours (I have had interesting results with small additions of barley flour—about ½ cup to 3 or 4 cups of regular flour) and, in particular, one might profit from the current health food fashion to use the unbleached, stone-ground flours available. Those I have found in France have a fine flavor—they raise less than the more highly refined flours and give a heavier crumb.

CHAPTER ORGANIZATION

The chapter organization in the following pages has strayed but little from that usual to French cookbooks, respecting in its progression the traditional concept of a menu: Salads have been placed at the beginning because those considered are all conceived as first courses; soups are a bit tardily presented because so many serve as an entire meal. The only major displacement—that of the vegetables—is designed to emphasize the importance that vegetable preparations may—and too rarely do—assume in a menu. In France, only Provence has conceded to vegetables a placement on the menu worthy of their possibilities, giving them the opportunity to expand in beauty as a first course or to provide a light interlude between a fish and the roast in a more formal context. Elsewhere they are apparently considered as a banal, but necessary, accompaniment to meats and are loyally treated in manners contrived to reinforce that gray vision. Even vegetarians expend most of their ingenuity trying to destroy the vegetableness of the poor fresh things, welding them into horrible imitations of meat dishes in pathetic compensation for self-imposed deprivation.

Treated with respect, a vegetable can undermine the single-mindedness of the most bloodthirsty of carnivores. There is, moreover, no reason to take seriously the French claim that vegetables and wine do not go together.

MISCELLANEOUS THOUGHTS

OVEN TEMPERATURES

It is more important to know your oven—to understand its faults and its eccentricities—than to blindly respect the instructions of cookbooks concerning precise thermostatic regulations. Electric ovens act differently from gas ovens. Thermostats are not always accurate. Ovens in professional kitchens are usually kept at a higher temperature than that recommended for most preparations in cookbooks (say, at a guess, 425°) and nearly everything is cooked at that same temperature (the bakery ovens are a different matter). Those that are heated by a system of hot air circulation around the outside of the oven cavity can cook at higher temperatures than those that receive heat from a direct source. Throughout the preparation of this book I have kept two American thermometers in the oven and, inasmuch as they agree, I believe them to be accurate. But I know from experience that, when working with ovens in friends' kitchens, I must usually work with lower temperatures than at home. Oven temperatures here have often been altered in view of this experience.

BUTTER

When possible, use sweet (unsalted) tub butters—the taste is quite different from that of French butters, but they do have a taste and, often, quite a good one. "Lightly salted" packaged butters are, but for their heavy saltiness, disappointingly flat.

37

Mouli-juliènnes

"Mouli-juliènne" is the trademark name for a simple gadget manufactured by the French "Moulinex" company. It is equipped with a series of removable discs for slicing and shredding. They are exported to America and there are also American equivalents. The electrical "robot-cutters" have attachments that will do the same work. The "medium blade" that is repeatedly recommended here transforms vegetables into cylindrical threads of about 1/10 to 1/12 of an inch in diameter.

A "vertical cutter mixer" is useful in a kitchen for the rapid reduction of raw flesh to a purée in the fabrication of *mousselines,* for reducing soft bread crumb to fine crumbs with a whir, etc. It has a number of attachments for cutting, slicing, shredding, juliènning, etc. The manufacturer is:

Robot Coupe, U.S.A.

P.O. Box 10131

Jackson, Mississippi 39206

The machines are quite expensive, but solid: The smallest (2½-quart capacity) is priced, as of this writing, at 219 dollars.

Chopping

Chopping means cutting cleanly into minuscule fragments. Grinding, crushing, and puréeing, for all their apparent similarity, physically change the structure of a material, releasing the juices that are held within it. The particles of a correctly chopped article remain unbruised and intact, their primitive structure unaltered, their juices and, in the case of herbs, their perfumes retained. Machines and dull knives bruise, wound, bleed . . . Only with sharp knives and an absolutely plane and smooth wooden surface can one chop without damage. It is a gentle and a rational act; violence will get you nowhere. Use a so-called "chef's knife," the blade of which is wide enough to prevent your knuckles from rapping against the chopping board. First slice thinly, if the material calls for it, fingertips of the guiding hand turned inward out of reach of the blade, knuckle against the side of the blade to guide it. Cross-slice, then chop, keeping the fulcrum point of the knife always in contact with the board by a light pressure from the flat of your non-chopping hand,

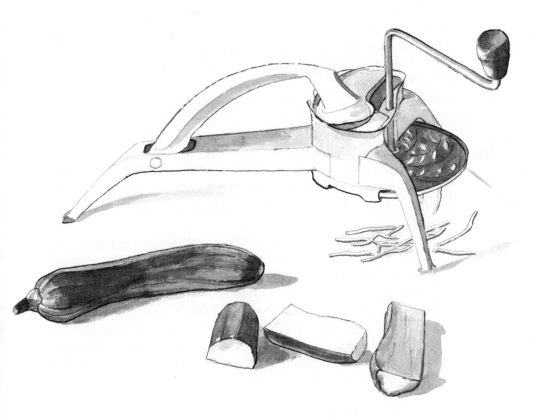

Mouli-juliènne *and* zucchini

an inch or two back from the point of the knife blade. An excess of enthusiasm can only lead to an erratic result and, very disagreeably, to a certain amount of chopped chopping board incorporated into the product. Have at least three or four good sharp knives and always keep a sharpening steel within reach. There are very good stainless steel knives on the market today; they sharpen well, are easy to care for, and will not blacken artichokes and certain other vegetables as will carbon knives.

Apart from the slicing and cubing, meat requires a different approach that, when necessary, is discussed in the text.

Tomatoes

Fresh tomatoes are good only in season and marvelous only at the height of the season, when they are also at their cheapest. Throughout some nine months of the year, they are perhaps the only canned product indispensable to a kitchen. Some commercially canned tomatoes are quite good, but all contain too many seeds and often there is a slight edge of the unpleasant metallic taste that, in tomato pastes, is so aggressive as to ban them from the kitchen. Peeled, halved, and seeded, home-canned tomatoes are always the best. Sterilizers carry their own instructions, which vary with the method. Season only with salt, count a pound of tomatoes for a pint jar, cover them with a purée of rapidly boiled and sieved tomatoes, leave a good inch of space at the surface, and sterilize for forty minutes.

To peel and seed tomatoes, cut out a conical shape to remove the core from the stem end, dunk them into boiling water for a couple of seconds, slit the skin at the flower end (or bottom), and peel, holding sections of peel between thumb and knife blade and pulling toward the stem end. Cut in two horizontally and either squeeze each half in your hand, shaking abruptly to extract seeds and water or, preferably, loosen each seed section with your little finger or with a teaspoon handle and shake gently to remove the seeds without crushing the tomato half.

Green Olives

The delicious *olives cassées* that garnish Provençal luncheon tables during several months of the year (put into their brine the first part of October, they are best from the end of October to mid-January, but will last through March or April), slightly bitter, refreshing, with a flavor that is nervous and exciting, resemble in no way olives commercially available in the United States. During early autumn, fresh green olives are sold widely in Italian neighborhoods for home preparation.

Each olive should be given a brisk tap with a wooden mallet—just forceful enough to split the skin without crushing the olive or breaking the pit. They are then put into a large basin of cold water and kept for ten days, the water being changed each day. This draws out their excessive bitterness. Rinsed well and well submerged in an herb-flavored brine, one may begin eating them two weeks later (any drained for serving and not consumed should be returned to the brine—they spoil in contact with the air).

The Brine: For each quart of water mix in 2½ ounces coarse salt (just under ¼ cup), bay leaf, thyme, several branches of fennel (or fennel seeds), a tiny bit of rosemary, 2 or 3 sage leaves (if fresh), oregano, savory, ½ teaspoon coriander seeds, a strip of dried orange peel.

Thyme and fennel should dominate. Bring the salted water to a boil, add all the other ingredients, boil for 10 minutes, and leave to steep until completely cold. Strain and pour the herb brine over the olives. Keep in a covered stoneware, porcelain, or earthenware jar. A scummy, mucous substance may form eventually on the surface of the brine—it is in no way harmful and should be left there, disregarded.

CHEESES

Compose your cheese platters with care—and, particularly, if you plan to serve a fine wine as an accompaniment. Strongly flavored fermented cheeses, very sharp cheeses, or heavily salted cheeses will annihilate a wine with any delicacy. If they are generally admired as companions to wine, it is because nothing else so effectively masks the negative qualities of a bad wine. Roquefort is a wine killer, as are most of the indifferent Camemberts found on the market today. Among the fermented cheeses, Reblochon and Pont l'Evèque are probably the safest, but only if they have been well cared for and remain delicate—almost sweet in flavor, soft, creamy, and uniform of texture. A Pont l'Evèque, even at best, has an astonishing perfume that belies its natural elegance. Good English Cheshire is a splendid cheese wine, as is Swiss Gruyère. Fresh chèvres, if properly drained and not oversalted, number among the truly sublime things of the table—it is rare to find decent examples outside of their areas of production. Some thirty-five or forty years ago, the general store in Marathon, Iowa, used to keep giant wheels of a Cheshire-Cantal type of cheese which I still remember very sentimentally. The only name we ever gave it was "rat cheese," and it wouldn't harm a Lafite.

Wine Vinegar

Wine, during its life in a barrel, must be regularly replenished from smaller containers—bottles or barrels—of the same wine to compensate for loss by evaporation, because if the wine is left in contact with air, an insidious culture in the form of a frail, white powdery veil will develop on the surface, eventually transforming the entire body of wine into vinegar. The same detested *fleur blanche,* for the fabrication of a good vinegar, must be pampered, kept at room temperature (60°F.–75°F.), a body of air always in contact with the surface, which should not otherwise be disturbed; the mold lives only in contact with air and, if submerged, is transformed into a heavy viscous matter called colloquially *mère de vinaigre* ("mother of vinegar"), which settles, harmless but inactive, to the bottom of the container.

A number of folklorique misconceptions, built largely around "mothers of vinegar," their various qualities and their care, have made the whole business of vinegar-making seem more complicated than it really is: Pieces of mother are lent out or exchanged to be dropped into vinaigriers (for it is believed that mothers differ greatly, one from the other, and that the vinegar culture resides in the mother). Odds and ends of wine are usually poured in daily—or at least with varying regularity—and vinegar is drawn from the spout as needed so that at times the mother is blamed for having nurtured an excessively strong vinegar and at others, if a large quantity of wine has been recently added, it is said that the mother has been drowned (and one must hasten to a neighbor or friend to borrow another piece of mother).

Le Cuisinier Parisien (1833) gives the following instructions for making vinegar:

> Have a keg containing 30 litres more or less, depending on your consumption. A hole 1 inch in diameter should be bored at one end as closely as possible to the border joint. Place the keg in such a way that the hole will be at the highest point. At the same end a wooden spigot should be installed 2 inches from the bottom. The cask should be placed in a warm place. It will be well off in a corner of the kitchen.

Vinaigrier *with spigot, screened aeration hole and glass funnel*

Heat 1 or 2 litres of good vinegar and pour it, boiling, into the barrel through the hole at the top of the end. Agitate the barrel so that all surfaces are impregnated with vinegar; then pour in five litres of good wine. Always leave the hole to the top uncovered.

Eight or ten days later add five litres of wine and continue, thus, every eight or ten days until the barrel is filled by two-thirds. Then (after another eight or ten days) you may begin to draw off the vinegar and, by always adding an equal quantity of wine, you will have a constant supply

43

of vinegar of the same quality, assuming the wine employed to be of unchanging strength.

No mention is made of the bond hole to the top-center of the staves (before being put into service, a new keg should have the hole bored for the spigot and the spigot pounded into place with a wooden mallet, but the aeration hole should not be bored until after the keg has been filled with water through the bond hole and left to soak for a day or two—there are always minor leaks until the wood, both of the keg and of the spigot, swells by soaking). A hole bored through the cork with a long-necked glass funnel (from a laboratory supply house—the length of the neck somewhat shorter than the width of the barrel) fixed through it so as to keep the neck tip in a stationary position well beneath the vinegar's surface permits wine to be fed in from the top without disturbing the surface—a dab of cotton closes the funnel entrance when not in use and a bit of plastic screen can be tacked over the aeration hole to discourage insects.

It is best to draw off large quantities at a time, replacing them with the same quantity of wine, and not to disturb the vinaigrier in between major operations except to occasionally draw off a few drops to check on its progression—if left for a long period, vinegar will become very strong. Leftover bottles of wine that have begun to turn, filtered dregs from decanted wines, and, notions of decorum and hygiene notwithstanding, undrunk glasses from the dinner table should all be joined together and stored in filled corked bottles to prevent further alteration until they are added as a lot to the vinaigrier. All wine that is added should be limpid, any containing sediment being first filtered. Use only dry wines.

It is important to start out the life of a vinaigrier with the addition of a certain amount of good vinegar to make certain that noxious cultures other than the acetic fermentation do not attack in its place. No metal should contact vinegar and, when heating it, earthenware, enamelware, or stainless steel should be used. I am not convinced that heating the vinegar to season a keg serves any purpose—the fumes may more rapidly penetrate the fiber of the wood—but, having started out my own vinaigrier that way and being satisfied with the results, I have preferred to quote my source. Friends have small earthenware or stoneware vinaigriers—approximately one-gallon jars with a hole toward the base into which a cork-tipped wooden spigot is fitted—and produce good vinegar; the top should be covered only with a cloth or other arrangement to keep out dust and insects while permitting a free passage of air.

The acid fermentation of vinegar, although it may be incomplete, is arrested when the vinegar is drawn off and bottled up, tightly corked, out of contact with air, but the vinegar itself, like the wine from which it is made, then takes on a life of its own, its aromas expanding, aggressivity succumbing to nuance with age; the difference between a freshly drawn vinegar and one that has two or three years of bottle is quite astounding—and perhaps even more marked with specially prepared vinegars into which other flavors have been suffused. Vinegar, although less temperamental than wine, should also be stored in a dark, cool place, the bottles on their sides. It is worthwhile labeling different vinegars and their vintages.

The vinegar I use to the near exclusion of all others is made by boiling down a large quantity (in enamelware or stainless steel) of vinegar by half, throwing in an abundance of garden and mountain herbs—oregano, savory, thyme, marjoram, bay leaves, hyssop—and a few crushed but unpeeled garlic cloves, leaving it, covered, to cool and to steep for several hours or overnight before straining it (funnel lined with a towel) into bottles.

A wonderful and unusual vinegar is prepared by steeping a large quantity of elder flowers (rapidly dried in the sun and crumbled free of the stems) in vinegar for 3 or 4 weeks, covered or corked, before straining and bottling it. Elder vinegar seems particularly suited to meat salads; cold sliced or diced *pot-au-feu,* in particular, is never as good as when marinated in an elder blossom vinaigrette with finely sliced sweet onions or scallions (elder grows wild throughout the United States—even if one does not make one's own vinegar, there is nothing to hinder one from transforming a good commercial wine vinegar into elder vinegar). Tarragon vinegar is prepared in the same way, using, preferably, fresh branches.

Charles Barrier (Chez-Barrier, Tours) prepares a very pretty raspberry-perfumed vinegar which I have never attempted to concoct myself. (Prosper-Montagné: "Pour 2 litres of vinegar into a stoneware jar and as many picked-over raspberries as the jar can contain; leave to macerate for 8 days; strain, without pressure, through a horsehair [nylon] drumsieve.")

Any of these vinegars, if kept for some time on the kitchen

shelf in a partially emptied bottle, may form the familiar white surface veil—and, as it is submerged while bits of the contents are
being poured out, a viscous mother occasionally forms, as well.
Neither affects the quality of the vinegar but, for aesthetic reasons,
the vinegar might be filtered. In home preparations, a certain
amount of eau de vie is sometimes added to vinegar at the moment
of bottling to stabilize it; commercial vinegars are undoubtedly
stabilized in less innocent ways.

SALADS

F<small>RENCH</small> dressing is vinaigrette sauce. As I understand it, it is
made of salt, freshly ground pepper, good red-wine vinegar, and
first cold-pressing olive oil. It is so easy to make that to prepare a
quantity in advance to be stored is risibly impractical. Its commonest
faults are: An excess of vinegar; poor oil; poor vinegar.

The flavor of good olive oil is rich, clean, clear, and fruity. There
should be no muddy, acid aftertaste. It belongs to the realm of
voluptuous experience. Good olive oil (that commercialized in
France as *"Extra-Vièrge"*) contains less than 1 percent oleic acid.
The oil has been extracted from healthy, ripe olives by purely mechanical means with no application of heat or intervention of
chemicals.

The light-bodied, light-colored olive oils preferred by some for
their minimal flavor are, although sometimes deceptively labeled,
almost certainly not pure olive oils. Even the better of commercialized French olive oils are blends (usually of Tunisian, Spanish, and
Provençal oils), but they are pure olive oil. The best I have found on
the American market is labeled "James Plagniol." It carries only the
designation "Pure Olive Oil," but the quality corresponds to that of
"Extra-Vièrge." The New York distributors are: M. H. Greenbaum,

47

Green Tree Bldg., 165 Chambers Street, New York, N.Y. 10013; the New Orleans distributors are: Gerde Newmann & Co., P.O. Box 30.310, New Orleans, Louisiana 70130.

Walnut oil is also a natural product and may, in some salads, be used to very good effect, but its very personal and powerful flavor radically limits its use and a tendency to turn rapidly rancid discourages its purchase.

The light-bodied, lightly colored vegetable oils, extracted from a variety of different seeds—peanut, corn, sunflower, grape, etc.—do not usually taste bad. Some have a vaguely bitter aftertaste, but most have no taste at all. They do, however, "feel" bad in the mouth and their lack of taste is disconcerting—nor is it particularly comforting to know that most have been submitted to a series of violent chemical treatments (the addition of solvents for the extraction of the oil, the addition of other chemicals to neutralize the effects of the solvents and to render the oil odorless and colorless—and, finally, for most, a further treatment designed to give a yellowish tone to the emasculated product).

Quite apart from the excessive acidity lent a salad by an overdose of vinegar, the resultant wateriness of the sauce is unpleasant. Vinegars have different strengths and certain salad materials require more or less vinegar than others (pungent greens support more vinegar than sweet lettuces, for instance). A good mean ratio is about one part of vinegar to four or five parts of oil.

A vinaigrette may often be enhanced by a suggestion of garlic and, in many fewer instances—with cold meats, for instance—by the addition of some Dijon-type mustard (whose strength smothers the lovely fruit of the oil, but is welcomed by the meat). If garlic is used, it should be pounded to an absolute purée with the salt and pepper before being dissolved into the vinegar; mustard also should be mixed first with the seasoning and then the vinegar and, in any case, the oil should always be added after the perfect dissolution of the other ingredients into the vinegar.

A lettuce salad or one of varied greens without any other garnish most often finds its place following the main course, serving as a weightless and cleansing pause before the cheese and, perhaps, between two wines, but it may, as well, provide a happy prologue to a simple supper. The salads suggested or discussed here are all conceived as overtures to a meal.

CRUDITÉS

An extremely attractive way to begin a meal—or to form the main body of a hot summer day's luncheon—and one that always creates a particularly sympathetic atmosphere at table consists of presenting a large and colorful still life of seasonal vegetables, whole and raw when possible, peeled, sliced, grated, or chopped if necessary, garnished with peeled hard-boiled eggs and bouquets of fresh herbs— basil, dill, chervil, tarragon, hyssop, lemon thyme, leaf thyme (parsley and chives should be chopped and served in dishes apart). Oil, vinegar, lemon halves, a pitcher of heavy cream, mustard, and seasonings are served apart, and each guest fabricates his own salad or series of salads, seasoned to personal taste or whim (the lemon, cream, and dill are for small, firm cucumbers, the seeds still unformed, peeled and split in four, the sticks to be dipped in the sauce). The vegetables, depending on the season, may be chosen from tender young broad beans and young artichokes, quartered bulb fennel, celery hearts, Belgian endives, tomatoes, cucumbers, scallions, Italian sweet green peppers, cauliflower (raw if tiny and sweet), parboiled green beans (which, like parboiled cauliflower, are marvelous rapidly drained and served alone, hot, accompanied by olive oil and lemon), freshly parboiled asparagus . . .

ASPARAGUS

But, it may be a sacrilege to eat asparagus any other way than alone, barely cooked, the head of each stalk delicately limp but firmly intact, warm, but not boiling hot, well drained and accompanied by olive oil, vinegar, salt, and pepper—and good sweet butter to be eaten in chunks on rough country bread.

It does no good to scrape or thinly peel asparagus with a vegetable peeler; they should be peeled with a sharp knife, starting at the cut end and terminating at the point where the skin becomes tender, so that all the fibrous material is removed and the entire stalk of tender asparagus can then be eaten, dipped repeatedly in its sauce. No cutlery is needed.

Many people suffer torture trying to tie up bundles of asparagus with a tiny length of string wrapped once around the bundle: Arrange the stalks carefully so that they form a neat and compact bundle held in the cup of your hand, the end of the string held firmly against the bundle with your thumb, and wrap the string tightly and repeatedly around, spiraling downward and back up to meet the string end, clipping the other end with plenty of length to permit easy tying; they are not only tied with no difficulty but, with strings wound the length of the bundle, they are easily lifted from their cooking water with the prong of a large kitchen fork. Cooking time may vary from 8 to 20 minutes, but for large, tender asparagus 12 minutes is a good mean to observe, testing the stems for firm doneness with the tip of a knife after 8 or 10 minutes. Drain the bundle first on a towel and transfer it to a platter containing a folded napkin (which absorbs further draining liquid and, at the same time, folded over the surface, prevents them from cooling too rapidly) before clipping the strings and arranging the asparagus.

I think one owes it to oneself in a restaurant never to accept a ready-made vinaigrette (nearly always muddied up with mustard and vegetable oils) and, unless it is particularly unmanageable, one owes it to one's guests to present salt, pepper, vinegar and olive oil at table, never imposing a prepared vinaigrette, however pure, with asparagus. Restaurants often serve warm asparagus that has been cooked, refrigerated, and dipped into boiling water—it is repellent; if asparagus is left over, do anything but that: Eat it cold, toss it in butter, throw it into a salad or an omelet, cover it with *béchamel* and buttered breadcrumbs and gratiné it, purée the stems and mix with the tips into a soufflé batter ...

IMPROMPTU COMPOSED SALAD
(Salade Canaille)

To baptize this kind of salad *canaille,* underlining the French affection for the delinquent and the demi-monde, is to suggest a quality of refreshing vitality allied to insolence—a certain flaunting refusal to respect accepted formulas. And, indeed, one need not often respect any of the endless and precisely defined classical recipes for composed salads (Niçoise, Waldorf, Andalous, Mimosa, Francillon, Bagration, and so forth interminably) to be struck with the puerility of such a pastime and to realize how much more valuable and exciting is the imaginative and playful, self-renewing invention of a giant composed salad, never once repeated, its composition dictated by the materials at hand. And, given the fanciful but far from frivolous presence of flowers and a sufficient variety of green things, presented in a vast, wide ceramic or earthenware vessel (you need the space for easy tossing and the large surface for decorative effect), nothing in the entire repertory of food possesses the same startling, vibrant visual immediacy—the same fresh and casual beauty. It is a concentrated, pulsating landscape of garden essences and must absolutely be tossed at table, for, no matter how delicious, the visual explosion of joy, mixing intricately and lastingly with your guests' memories of mingled flavors, adds a dimension.

This salad, in the seasonal round of my own life, symbolizes the happiest time of the year—that which is lived almost entirely out of doors with the table set daily on the terrace in the shade of a grape arbor, the sparkling play of light heightening the effect of the table display of variegated greens and bright-colored punctuations. Alternating the honors of the summer luncheon table with the earlier-mentioned *crudités,* it serves sometimes as an hors d'oeuvre; often, preceded by melon or figs with ham in the Italian manner and followed by cheeses, it is the principal course, and sometimes it represents the entire meal.

Aside from those elements listed under *crudités,* possible ingredients may include leftovers of all kinds: Meats, poultry, game or fish, the flesh carefully separated from bones and fat and cut into cubes, thin slices or rough juliènne, flaked or broken up, depending on its nature; boiled potatoes, macaroni, rice, white, kidney, or flageolet beans, chick-peas or lentils; peas, leeks, spinach, or beets; sautéed zucchini, mushrooms, raw or cooked, or grilled sweet peppers. Anchovies may be incorporated into the sauce or used as a garnish and, in the absence of more amusing leftovers, tinned tuna, crab, or lobster can be useful. Leafy things may include tiny tender leaves of borage or sorrel, purslane, arugula, rocket, chicory (the tiny, richly dark red heads of Italian chicory add wonderful color to their bitter freshness), watercress, field cress, young dandelion, and any of the lettuces—with the possible exception of the ignoble iceberg. The herbs I choose from among basil, parsley, chives, chervil, tarragon, hyssop, dill, lemon thyme, leaf thyme, fennel, marjoram, and, if it is young and tender, savory. The decorative splash of nasturtiums, calendula petals, or ultramarine hyssop is supplemented by delicate peppery savors, that of the nasturtium being particularly attractive and highly personal.

Roasting juices, carefully cleansed of all fat, or the syrupy liquid from grilled sweet peppers may be added to the vinaigrette or, for variety's sake, it may be replaced by a cream and lemon base.

In the face of so many possibilities, special care must be taken to avoid unhappy marriages between flavors that are either quarrelsome or tend to cancel each other out: It is wise not to mix up fish, meats, and poultry (even cured anchovy—which, in meridional France, is as common a flavoring agent as garlic—seems often to muddy a total effect and is probably best used either by itself or in combination with tuna); the peculiarities and the preferences of the various herbs have been discussed in the preface; tomatoes and beets clash ...

Few of the other possibilities mentioned will cause any trouble, but one should not attempt to pack too many things into a single salad and each should be chosen for the unique texture and flavor it lends to the whole: One starchy element is usually enough (although it is true that beans and rice or lentils and macaroni are common and good combinations); celery and bulb fennel are too similar in their crunchiness and sweetness to logically share a salad; too many herbs will confuse the palate; avocado and cooked artichoke, both delicately flavored and soft of texture, are also confusing together, whereas raw artichoke may be perfectly allied to avocado. A salad of this sort need not necessarily comprehend a meat or a fish, but, if it does, that ingredient should be thought of as holding a star part, everything else relating to it, lending it relief.

Consider, decorative effect apart, the roles of each of the ingredients in the following recipe: Raw onion is always a useful accompaniment to cold boiled beef—it, the garlic, the herbs, and the flowers are essentially seasoning agents; the potatoes attenuate some of the stronger flavors and, at the same time, lend body and a unifying effect; the lettuce also, although not absolutely essential, acts as a buffer for the bitterness of the rocket and the hyssop and the spiciness of the basil and nasturtium; the hard-boiled egg's gentle presence is always welcome among sharply flavored green things; the celery lends crispness and sweetness; and the remaining vegetables, each distinctly different in texture and flavor, complement one another. And, bearing these specific roles in mind, try to imagine a number of replacements: The *pot-au-feu* replaced by tuna and the potatoes by white beans; the bitter herbs and greens replaced by a handful of chopped *fines herbes* containing tarragon; in place of the meat, a remainder of squid braised in tomato and white wine, the sauce incorporated into the vinaigrette, tomatoes and eggs eliminated and the potatoes replaced by rice; mussels, fennel, and rice, eliminating meat, hyssop, basil, and potatoes; or, replace the meat with shrimp or crab, the potatoes with macaroni, the vinaigrette with lemon and cream, the herbs with dill, the tomatoes with cucumbers . . . One could go on forever, and, in practice, one does.

It is important to remember that many ingredients gain, and give, flavor by macerating some time in the sauce. Others are indifferent to this treatment and certain ingredients—leafy greens and green beans in particular—should only be tossed at the last minute. Tomatoes, if used as surface garnish, may simply be cored and cut into sections, but if they are to join in the maceration, they should be peeled, seeded, and coarsely chopped, sliced, or cut into small sections. Not only does the proportion of vinegar to oil vary depending on the ingredients, but the amount of seasoning necessary is also greatly elastic: A vinaigrette that is perfectly seasoned for a simple green salad will require a bit more salt in the presence of most starchy products—and a great deal more for grilled sweet peppers, for instance. The only way to satisfactorily prepare a sauce for a compound salad is to begin with the basic sauce, taking care not to oversalt—an irremediable error, and then season progressively, adding oil and vinegar also, if necessary, as the various elements are added.

It goes without saying that the following recipe is an example and that neither proportions nor specific ingredients need be strictly respected.

> 3 medium firm yellow potatoes
> ½ cup dry white wine
> 3 or 4 large, regularly formed sweet peppers (the yellow
> are the sweetest, the red are the richest in flavor)

53

3 medium artichokes
1 lemon
1 branch thyme

Vinaigrette 1 small clove garlic
Salt
Freshly ground pepper
About 1 tablespoon red wine vinegar
About ½ cup olive oil

8 to 10 ounces pot-au-feu meat (cooled out of its bouillon), slivered, cubed, or cut into rough juliènne strips
1 small heart of celery, sliced thinly crosswise
2 or 3 scallions (or 1 small sweet onion), finely slivered
1 small lettuce (Boston, romaine, or escarole)
1 handful each of purslane leaves, rocket or arugula, and fresh basil leaves and flowers
6 to 8 ounces tender young green beans, parboiled (8 to 10 minutes), drained, but not "refreshed," preferably still tepid
2 or 3 medium tomatoes, firm and ripe
4 hard-boiled eggs
2 teaspoons finely chopped hyssop leaves
12 to 15 nasturtium blossoms and buds plus small tender leaves

Boil the potatoes in their skins, peel them while still hot, holding them in a towel, slice them into a bowl, pour over the white wine and leave to cool.

Grill the peppers, preferably over hot coals, or in the broiler, turning them regularly until evenly grilled on all sides, the skin charred and the flesh softened. Leave them to cool on a plate, peel them, slit them, and discard all seeds, but carefully collect all the juices. Tear them into strips lengthwise.

See the section on artichokes for methods of paring (page 173). If they are young and tender enough to be eaten raw, prepare the vinaigrette first and then slice or cut them into quarters or eighths and stir them immediately into the sauce to prevent their blackening through contact with the air. Otherwise rub them with lemon and cook in salted boiling water with a branch of thyme until only just done, leaving them to cool in their cooking liquid.

Slice the clove of garlic into the salad bowl, add salt and pepper, and work vigorously with a wooden pestle until the garlic is completely puréed and forms a dry paste with the salt and pepper. Add the vinegar, stir until dissolved, and stir in the olive oil. Add the peppers with their juices and stir vigorously, taking care not to crush the peppers, until the sauce is in a state of semi-emulsion; taste for seasoning and rectify with salt, if necessary.

If using cooked artichokes, drain them, remove the chokes, leaving the edible base attached, slice them, and add to the peppers. Drain the potatoes and add them (the wine may be used for cooking), along with the meat, the celery, and the scallions. Stir everything well together, but gently so as not to crush the potatoes, and taste again for seasoning—add more oil or vinegar also, if necessary.

The lettuce and other greens should be gently but thoroughly dried between two towels after being washed. Place the serving fork and spoon crosswise in the bowl to help protect the salad greens from contact with the sauce, prop a few of the larger leaves between the service and the sides of the bowl and tumble the rest of the salad greens loosely on top, distributing the green beans over the surface. Decorate with tomato sections and quartered hard-boiled eggs, sprinkling with hyssop, and finish with the nasturtium flowers and their leaves. Present the salad in this state, tossing only at the moment of serving, turning all the ingredients thoroughly and repeatedly (few people toss a salad well and it is a matter of no small importance—if you are not sufficiently adept with fork and spoon, do not hesitate to use your hands to arrive at a loose but intimate intermingling of elements).

SALADS WITH HARD-BOILED EGGS

The hard-boiled egg is not simply another salad ingredient that may or may not find its place depending on the demands of décor or supplementary flavor. Its function, residing largely in the yolk, is, like that of salt, fundamental. It is a dulcifying agent, suavely veiling the bitterness or acerbity native to numerous leafy vegetables or bitter salads. With a vinaigrette or, more rarely, with cream and lemon, alone or in combination, chicory, endive, escarole, dandelion, parboiled spinach (rinsed in cold water, squeezed, and coarsely chopped), lambs' lettuce, or cress expands in its presence, mollified or flattered by the union. A salad for which I have a particular affection is that of rocket and hard-boiled eggs sauced with a vinaigrette. A breath of garlic may be welcome and the fantasy of scattered calendula petals is amusing. The eggs may be halved, quartered, sliced, chopped or, as in the following recipe, incorporated into the sauce:

LEEKS IN VINAIGRETTE
(Poireaux à la Vinaigrette)
(for 4 or 6)

3 pounds small leeks

Vinaigrette   Salt, freshly ground pepper
½ teaspoon Dijon mustard
About 1 tablespoon wine vinegar
About ½ cup olive oil

3 hard-boiled eggs
1 handful chopped parsley

See page 17 for paring and cleaning leeks. Use only the white and very light-green parts of the leeks. Tie them into bundles as for asparagus, plunge them into salted, boiling water, and cook, covered, at a simmer for about ten minutes or until they are only just done, the flesh offering but the slightest resistance to the point of a small sharp knife. Drain well before transferring to a serving platter, remove the strings, arrange the leeks, and spoon over the following vinaigrette: Mix the mustard with the salt and pepper, add the vinegar, stirring until the mustard is completely dissolved, mash in the egg yolks coarsely, without reducing them to a purée, stir in the oil and, finally, the finely chopped whites of the eggs and the

56

parsley. Taste for seasoning. For the sake of a prettier presentation, half of the chopped whites and parsley may be mixed together and kept apart for sprinkling the surface. Serve tepid.

SALAD OF HOT CHICK-PEAS
(Salade de Pois-Chiches)

Chick-peas, even more than dried beans or lentils (also delicious served in this way), are extremely sensitive to hard waters. I usually soak them overnight with sifted wood ashes and rain water. Most people substitute a healthy pinch of bicarbonate of soda for the wood ashes and do not bother with the rain water. They should, in any case, be well rinsed after either treatment, largely covered with cold water (rain or not), an onion stuck with a couple of cloves, a carrot, some thyme, and a bay leaf added, the water brought slowly to a boil and kept, covered, at a barely perceptible simmer until done (salting only toward the end of the cooking)—about two hours, or less if they are from the year's crop. A good idea is to save spinach cooking water, only lightly salted, in which to cook them.

Serve them drained, hot, accompanied by olive oil, vinegar, salt, pepper grinder, and dishes of finely chopped onion and parsley, each guest preparing his own salad to taste. The immediate explosion of perfume when good olive oil is added to any hot vegetable is always exciting.

WILTED CABBAGE SALAD
(Salade de Choux à l'Alsacienne)
(for 4)

In Alsace this salad, accompanied by potatoes (boiled in their skins or sautéed) would most often represent the body of a family supper. In Lyonnaise country, a certain amount of chopped, hard-boiled egg and potato (boiled in the skin, peeled, then sliced hot) might be tossed with the salad, and it might preface a lovely mess of tripe. In the first instance, it would be washed down with a Zwicker or a

Sylvaner and, in the second, with a young and light-bodied, cool Beaujolais.

If slab bacon is not easily available, use lean packaged bacon, taking care to cook it slowly until semicrisp—neither flabby nor crumbly.

1 cabbage, about 2 pounds
About 12 ounces lean slab bacon, rind removed, cut into ¼-inch wedges
Salt, pepper
¼ cup wine vinegar
½ cup olive oil

Remove the outer leaves of the cabbage, slice off the ribs of the visible remaining leaves, wash, cut in half vertically, remove the core, and shred the two halves as for coleslaw. Pick out and discard thick sections from inside ribs. Pack into the salad bowl, pour over boiling water, and leave, covered, to steep for ten minutes or so.

Cook the bacon wedges, with a spoonful of olive oil to start them off, over a moderate heat, tossing regularly until lightly crisp on all sides.

Drain the cabbage, pressing to extract the maximum of liquid, return to the hot salad bowl, season with salt, grind over a generous amount of pepper, pour over the bacon and its fat, the vinegar, and the oil, and toss rapidly but thoroughly. Serve on preheated plates.

FRESH FIG AND MINT SALAD
(Salade de Figues Fraîches à la Menthe)
(for 5 or 6)

The most successful of a number of experiments purposed to rescue the great wines of Sauternes from the dessert quarantine; the association is of the happiest, but the Sauternes' rich caress increases the difficulty of choosing a succeeding wine. If you prefer not to begin a meal with a Sauternes, a white wine with a certain roundness and depth of fruit is, nonetheless, indicated—one of the Côte de Beaune growths or perhaps the usually impossible-to-place Gewürztraminer (above all, oyster wines of the "bone-dry, flinty" category should be avoided).

French friends find the recipe bizarre, but all who have tasted it have been delighted by the clean, clear, surprising combination of flavors and fragrance. It is a refreshing summer day hors d'oeuvre. The only pity is that figs, even more than most fruit, suffer from being picked unripe; the fragility of the tree-ripened product precludes its commercialization.

2 pounds ripe figs, freshly picked, if possible
3 thin slices prosciutto, fat removed
12 to 15 leaves of fresh mint
Juice of 1 lemon
Salt
¾ cup heavy cream, unpasteurized and thick, if possible

Note: I have found unpasteurized cream on the market in Iowa—it may be illegal in some states. Cartons of pasteurized "heavy" cream contain a certain amount of milk. If poured into a bowl and kept, covered, in the refrigerator for 2 or 3 days, the surface will thicken and may be skimmed off for use in sauces of this kind. Otherwise, half-whipped cream will give a mousseline effect with more body.

Peel the figs and cut halfway down from the stem end, making two incisions in the form of a cross. Press gently from the sides to open them slightly (as one does with a baked potato). Arrange them closely on a serving dish and chill for about one hour in the coldest part of the refrigerator (not the freezer).

Cut the ham into fine juliènne strips (about 1-inch lengths, matchstick width).

Crush about half of the mint leaves in the lemon juice and leave to macerate for 20 or 30 minutes, then discard them. Dissolve the salt into the lemon juice and slowly stir in the cream—the acid of the lemon will thicken it somewhat and its addition in small quantities at a time with continued stirring encourages the thickening. Taste for salt.

Sprinkle the figs with half the ham juliènne, spoon over the cream sauce, distribute the remaining ham on the surface, and decorate with the remaining mint leaves.

COLD TERRINES, PÂTÉS, MOUSSES

MEAT AND POULTRY TERRINES AND PÂTÉS

T H E only rational translation of *pâté* into English is "pie": A *pâté de foie gras* is not liver paste. It is a whole, fat goose liver enclosed in pastry. A *terrine de foie gras* is whole liver prepared in a terrine without pastry. In serious restaurants, *pâté* on a menu still means "enclosed in pastry." Outside of that rarefied atmosphere, the confusion is so total—*pâté* can mean meatloaf, liver paste, or dog-food, and *pâté en croûte* means *pâté*—that it is not worthwhile even to attempt to respect the terminology.

To me, a true *pâté* represents an excessive amount of work to produce something that is no better than—and rarely as good as—a terrine. French puff paste (*pâte feuilletée,* not *pâte à choux*), in fact, does not rank among the foods I most worship—but, in fairness to the thing, it should be noted that it is rarely made with pure butter, often with none, and almost never with an unpasteurized, absolutely fresh, delicately perfumed, sweet butter of irreproachable quality. It is not only cheaper, but also much easier to work with margarine or other laboratory fat products and the visual result is handsomer. The taste is horrid. Furthermore, in the instance of *pâtés,* the essential spread of firmly bound forcemeat—*mousseline* or other—that rapidly

60

forms a seal, preventing the meat juices from penetrating to the pastry and transforming it into a soggy mess, is often forgotten. A *pâté,* correctly prepared, belongs strictly to the realm of professional *grande cuisine* (interested visitors to Paris should visit the young chef Claude Peyrot in his restaurant, Le Vivarois. He is a great *saucier* and a great pastry chef—a practically unheard-of combination—and, unlike a number of world travelers, never leaves his kitchens).

The complexly organized *pâtés* and terrines of *la grande cuisine* (and largely of the past) are composed of a variety of different meats, each of which is often marinated or precooked in a different way to underline differences in character and then layered in a variety of interrelationships, alternating with two or more forcemeats, also of markedly separate characters. These *pâtés* depend, for their particular refinement, on the fine balance of intermingling and separation of flavors and textures. Typical and, perhaps, the most celebrated of its type—Dumaine revived it—is Lucien Tendret's *L'Oreiller de la Belle Aurore,* or Lovely Aurora's Pillow (Claudine-Aurore Récamier was Brillat-Savarin's mother). This dish takes its name from the pillow-like form of the *pâté,* but, in passing, may be thought to harbor a mute reference to the lady's disinclination to leave her bed where, but for the hours of sleep, she spent most of her time eating. Upon a rectangular base of puff paste, the basic dough of which has been flavored with Cognac and strengthened by the addition of egg white, two forcemeats (one identical to that of the following rabbit terrine recipe; the second, but for the addition of finely chopped mushrooms sautéed in butter, finely chopped truffles, and the stronger-flavored partridge livers, similar to the following chicken-liver terrine recipe), beginning and finishing with the first, are alternated with layers in varying combinations of strips of partridge, hare, duck, chicken, veal, and pork fillets and parboiled sweetbreads (truffle pieces, pistachios, and slivers of raw, cured ham being packed into each of these layers). The pillow covering is formed by another sheet of the same pastry (in which small, circular air vents have been cut) sealed to the borders of the basic rectangle. The "pie" is baked for two hours, and a firm meat aspic, enriched with the partridge, hare, and poultry carcasses, is poured in through the air vents while the *pâté* is still hot. It is served chilled.

A simple terrine, based on a single forcemeat and a single meat garnish, is never so good as when prepared in the easiest possible way, all of the ingredients of the composition mixed, pell-mell but intimately, together.

CHOPPING

Meats that are ground or chopped mechanically are always crushed. The fibrous structure of the flesh is broken, the succulent juices originally imprisoned within this structure escape, and therefore the forcemeat is always pastier in texture and drier than when composed of meats chopped by hand. The forcemeat, moreover, gains in character when the different meats in its composition are chopped more or less finely, lending a varied texture to the whole.

To chop meat by hand, scrape it free from all fragments of tendon, nervous tissue, or skin, cut it first into thin strips, cut the strips crosswise into tiny cubes, then chop, carefully and slowly at first, keeping the point of the knife in fulcrum-contact with the chopping block. When the meat is reduced to small enough pieces to form a cohesive mass, fragments of which will not fly in all directions, begin chopping more rapidly, using, preferably, two large "chef's" knives of the same size and weight, one in each hand, held somewhat above the board, chopping firmly, but not violently, with alternate knives in a rhythmic, loose-wristed motion. As the chopped mass is flattened out, regularly fold it over on itself with the blade of a knife, turn it over on the board, and begin again, continuing to fold, turn over, and chop until the desired degree of fineness is achieved. If you do not have knives of the same size and weight, chop with one hand only—the rhythm is lost with unequal weights.

I have tried a number of alternatives to hand-chopping, but I can only say this: Mechanical chopping will produce good results (all restaurant terrines are, after all, made in this way) and, I confess, some of my guests have been unable to discern the difference; the difference is, nonetheless, very marked. It is a question of whether you, the reader, will be satisfied with a decent product or whether you prefer something sublime . . . The poorest results are those of meat-grinders—a massacre—and, in my experience, the best are those of the electrical, whirring-bladed robot-cutters, although the violence of the latter tends to reduce a part of the meat to purée before the whole is sufficiently chopped—the work is done in the space of a few seconds.

GENERAL COMPOSITION

Meat and poultry terrines are all made in pretty much the same way: The tender pieces of meat are left whole or cut into relatively large pieces to lend variety to the texture and are usually marinated (very often in Cognac, which lends a false, slightly rotten, gamey taste and renders the terrine indigestible—a good *eau de vie* is a valuable flavoring agent but should be incorporated only just before cooking); tougher flesh containing tendons or nervous tissue is chopped and usually combined with a certain amount of blandly flavored meat—veal or pork or both—to form the base of the forcemeat; liver lends smoothness to the texture and support to the egg binding; chopped or cubed pork fat (often about three times as much as the proportions given in any of the following recipes) is incorporated to nourish the forcemeat and prevent its drying out; breadcrumbs are too often not added but, if measured discreetly— about one ounce of crumbs per pound of flesh—so that its presence is imperceptible, it will always lend a gratifying lightness to the body of the terrine; in addition to salt, spices, and herbs, garlic, onion, pistachios, truffles, and the currently fashionable green peppercorns may lend aromatic support. The tender, unripened peppercorns are available tinned, but they are much more interesting in their highly perfumed fresh state; in Paris, M. Paul Corcellet, whose exotic foods shop at 46 rue des Petits-Champs is probably the most fantastic of its kind in the world, flies them in fresh from Madagascar, vacuum packs them in plastic envelopes, and deep freezes them. If this has not yet occurred to an American packager, it will soon.

A terrine mixture should contain only that liquid rigorously essential to its flavor; soaking breadcrumb in milk, for instance, only adds to the liquid content and the milk adds nothing to the quality, whereas a highly reduced, gelatinous stock not only heightens the flavor, but also, when the terrine is cooled, lends binding support to the forcemeat. And when a marinade is called for, its quantity should be limited to just that necessary to moisten the surfaces of the meat pieces, well turned around in it.

The terrine is always lined and the contents covered with thin sheets of fresh fat pork, which, serving the same function as the chopped or cubed fat in the mixture, forms a wrapping that facili-

63

tates serving. The four-sided envelope of fat, however, should be removed from each slice at the time of serving. English and American cookbooks often recommend substituting slices of bacon for the sheets of fat pork, but, in fact, the quarrelsome, smoky presence will slur the clean definition of most flavors. I think of two exceptions: (1) *Guinea fowl* unites happily with bacon to the advantage of both (a terrine of guinea fowl may be prepared exactly like that of rabbit, the skinned breast being cut up like the rabbit fillets, the remainder of the flesh as well as a couple of supplementary chicken livers being passed into the forcemeat, the terrine lined with bacon strips); and (2) *Veal,* whose bland and impersonal, submissive character assumes and flatters that of many a more aggressive ally. (A number of years ago, M. René Viaux introduced at the Relais Paris-Est a veal and American-sliced bacon terrine baptized *terrine de body*—"body" being Berry dialect for veal—that has since become something of a classic. It consists in filling a bacon-lined terrine with alternate layers of very thin veal cutlets, rindless bacon slices laid lengthwise, and a mixture of finely chopped onions, chopped parsley, freshly ground pepper, and crumbled, dried herbs, finishing with a layer of bacon, dribbling a bit of white wine over the surface, and baking in a slow oven—about 1¾ hours at 325° for 1½ pounds each of veal and bacon. It is cooled under weight and, inasmuch as there is no forcemeat binding, it must be served well chilled to ensure the slices' remaining intact.)

With the exception of the so-called *pâtés de campagne,* which are usually baked, mounded up, like American meatloaves, often wrapped in pig's caul rather than sheets of fat (for a typical *pâté de campagne,* double the pork-fat content, limit the meats to two parts of cheap cuts of pork to one of veal plus a piece of pork liver, grind everything up together, season and bind as for the rabbit terrine—bake for two hours), these terrines are always cooked in a *bain-marie* and should be cooled under weight, the better to ensure a compact, non-crumbly body, easy to slice and to serve. No one has yet bothered to invent a terrine with a reversible lid that could serve as well to weight the contents; boards should be cut to the inside dimensions of each terrine for this purpose. For small terrines, a heavy piece of cardboard may be cut to the inside dimensions and wrapped in aluminum foil. Place unopened tin cans on top for weights.

64

RABBIT TERRINE
(Terrine de Lapin)

Any small game, furred or feathered, may replace the rabbit in this recipe—with glorious results. The ham, although still welcomed by wild rabbit, pheasant, partridge, or wild duck, no longer plays an essential supporting role in relation to those flavors, all more distinctive than that of domesticated rabbit, and it could be replaced by a supplement of pork, veal, or the primary element. Rabbits have large livers; terrines made of game birds or duck need the addition of a couple of chicken livers.

Of domesticated breeds of ducks, the barbary duck or one of the sterile hybrids is the most interesting. Our dependence on freezers has all but wiped out, on the American market, any competition to the depressingly fat, deep-frozen Long Island ducks. They are, happily, serviceable in the fabrication of a terrine: All of the fat is contained in the skin itself or, loose, in the abdomen; the flesh is lean, but, once the skin has been peeled off and discarded, there is not much of it. Two ducks should be used to replace the rabbit in this recipe, the breasts being cut up, the legs and flesh scrapings chopped for the forcemeat, and the carcasses converted into a stock. The livers of deep-frozen Long Island ducks have an inexplicably strong and acrid taste and should be discarded, only chicken livers being used in the forcemeat.

The marination of game or duck is a question of personal taste; the bland flavor of domesticated rabbit can ill do without it, but I, personally, prefer not to marinate meats of more pronounced character. Any of these terrines will gain in depth by the addition of cut-up truffles or chopped truffle peelings. They should either be marinated with the meats or mixed with the basic forcemeat (eggs and Cognac added later) and refrigerated overnight, covered by plastic, to permit the maximum penetration of their perfume before cooking. If they are conserved, add their liquid to the stock while reducing it.

This recipe will fill 2 quart-sized terrines and will provide about 20 servings—or, perhaps, a great deal less if the guests are left to their own devices.

65

I rabbit, approximately 3½ pounds, skinned and cleaned

Marinade
⅓ cup dry white wine
1 tablespoon olive oil
1 healthy pinch finely crumbled mixed herbs (thyme, oregano, savory)
Bay leaf
Salt, pepper

Stock
The rabbit's bones, neck, and head (split)
Rinds from fat pork and ham
1 quart water
1 onion, finely sliced or coarsely chopped
1 carrot, sliced or chopped coarsely
Thyme, bay leaf, salt, branch celery, parsley

Forcemeat
1 large clove garlic
2 ounces stale bread, crusts removed, crumbled
2 ounces shelled, unroasted pistachio nuts
10 ounces firm fresh fatback, cut into tiny cubes
7 ounces lean veal (all fat and nervous tissue removed), chopped
7 ounces lean raw ham (prosciutto type), finely chopped
The remaining rabbit flesh—about 14 ounces (the flesh from the saddle and the tender white meat from the hind legs removed), finely chopped
The rabbit's heart, liver, and lungs, finely chopped
2 eggs
⅓ cup Cognac
Seasonings: 1 teaspoon mixed herbs (same as marinade), 3 heads of cloves, allspice, and a suspicion of nutmeg, all ground to a powder, freshly ground pepper to taste, a pinch of cayenne, salt

About 8 ounces thin sheets of fresh fat pork
Imported bay leaves
Melted lard (optional)

Make an incision the length of the rabbit's back to each side of the spinal ridge and carefully remove the filets (the elongated mus-

66

cles stretching from the beginning of the rib cage to the tail), loosening them with a sharp paring knife, following closely the contours of the vertebrae. Remove the filets mignons (much smaller corresponding muscles clinging to the inside of the spinal column). Detach the tender, fleshy white meat from the bones of the hind legs. Cut the filets crosswise into slices of from ⅓ to ½ inch thick and cut the meat from the legs into similar-sized pieces. Mix well with the elements of the marinade and leave, covered, in the refrigerator overnight.

Remove the remaining flesh (except for the neck and the head) from the bones, scraping with a knife, and put it aside, along with the heart, liver, and lungs, to be chopped. Break or cut up the carcass and add it, along with the head, the neck, and the rinds, to the water, bring slowly to a boil, skim off the foam, add all the other ingredients, and cook, the lid slightly ajar, at a bare simmer, for from 2½ to 3 hours. Strain the liquid, leave it to settle, carefully skim off the fat, bring back to a boil, and, keeping the saucepan a bit to the side of the flame so that a light boil continues only at one side of the surface, remove the fatty skin that forms, drawing it to the far side with a tablespoon; repeat this action several times over a period of 20 minutes or so. Turn the flame high and reduce rapidly, stirring, and, at a halfway point, transfer to your smallest saucepan. Reduce until the stock has passed the foamy boil and begins to make slurry sounds, the body noticeably thick and sticky. A scant half cup should remain.

Pound the garlic to a purée in the mortar, mix with the breadcrumbs, pour over the boiling stock and work to a thick sticky paste with the pestle.

Parboil the pistachios for a couple of minutes, rub them vigorously in a towel to loosen the skins, peel and chop them coarsely.

Combine all of the elements of the forcemeat and mix thoroughly with your hands, squeezing the mixture through your fingers. Then add the pieces of rabbit meat and continue to mix and squeeze . . .

Line the sides and bottoms of the terrines with the sheets of fat pork, pressing them firmly, fill with the mixture and tap the bottom of each terrine, smartly, two or three times against a wooden table top (or other surface softened by a couple of layers of towel) to be certain that the contents are well settled. Place one or two bay leaves on the surface of each, gently press a sheet of fat pork over all, cover, and cook in a *bain-marie* (the terrine placed in a larger receptacle—a cake tin, for instance—which is filled with boiling water so as to immerse the terrines by about two thirds) in a 325° to 350° oven, counting 1½ to 1¾ hours. The terrines are done when the center is firm to the touch and when, if pierced by a trussing needle, the juice that appears is completely transparent.

Remove the lids, place boards cut to the inside dimensions on each surface with approximately 1½ pounds of weight on each. Juices may run over the sides, so it is best to place the terrines in a shallow container while cooling. Allow to cool completely—several hours or overnight—before removing the weights and, unless the terrines are to be consumed within two or three days, pour a layer of melted lard over the surface of each, return the lids, and refrigerate. The flavor will improve if they are left for at least three or four days and, protected by the layer of lard, one may be kept, uncut, for a couple of weeks.

TERRINE OF VEAL SWEETBREADS
(Terrine de Ris de Veau)

The mode is now on the decline (chicken in vinegar, bass in pastry, and duck with green peppercorns having risen to stardom) but, during the 1960's, sweetbread terrines proliferated on the menus of France's fashionable restaurants. They were all poor, vapid things, underseasoned (except for one master who leant heavily on the cayenne) but, otherwise, mysteriously defying analysis: white, parboiled sweetbreads trapped in a white and remarkably insipid sort of *panade*—wrapped in their white cloaks of pork fat; the only relief for the eye was the caramel color of the chopped commercial jelly garnish and, for the palate, there was none.

Finally, I think that sweetbreads lend themselves best to hot preparations, but the idea of a sweetbread terrine has always appealed to me—it still does—and I am convinced that a respectable result depends on their being first braised in a richly flavored stock. The fragility of sweetbreads cannot permit their being mixed roughly into the general composition as one does with the rabbit. For variation, add to the forcemeat a handful of chopped spinach (first parboiled for a couple of minutes, refreshed under cold running water, and squeezed repeatedly to rid the mass of all possible liquid) or a half cup of stiff *duxelles,* a chicken breast, skinned and cut into pieces, or, as in the preceding recipe, skinned and coarsely chopped pistachios. A sweetbread terrine is accompanied to perfection by a sorrel mousse.

Tinned truffles, the container of which is filled to the brim with a brownish liquid, have been boiled in water before being sterilized and rarely retain much perfume. The best conserves contain very little liquid—the fresh truffles are sterilized directly with only a small addition of fortified wine, usually Madeira.

The following proportions will give two 1-quart terrines.

2 lobes (about 1½ pounds) veal sweetbreads

Forcemeat	4 ounces veal, all fat and nervous tissue removed, finely chopped
	2 ounces fillet of pork, finely chopped
	5 ounces fresh fatback, cut into tiny cubes
	2 chicken livers, finely chopped
	1 small tin truffles or truffle peelings, chopped (liquid added to stock)
	Salt, pepper, nutmeg, cayenne
	2½ ounces stale bread, crusts removed, crumbled
	2 eggs
	⅓ cup Madeira (or good sherry or port or Cognac)
Braising elements	Mirepoix (4 ounces finely chopped carrots, small branch finely chopped celery, 4 ounces finely chopped onion, 1 ounce butter, 1 teaspoon dried, crumbled, mixed herbs, ½ bay leaf, finely crumbled or chopped, salt)
	2 cups gelatinous veal stock (see page 103)
	1 bay leaf for each terrine
	About 8 ounces thin sheets fresh pork fat
	Melted lard (optional)

Soak the sweetbreads in cold water for 2 or 3 hours, changing it a couple of times. Cover them well with cold water in a large saucepan, bring to a boil over a medium flame, simmer for 5 or 6 minutes, drain, and plunge them into a basin of cold water. Peel off the loosened surface membrane, all fat, and the tubelike cartilaginous material, but leave the connecting membranes that hold the sections together. Arrange the sweetbreads flat, side by side, between two towels placed on a board. Place another board on top, weight it (3 or 4 pounds), and leave for several hours.

Mix together all of the elements of the forcemeat except for the breadcrumbs, the eggs, and the wine, and leave, covered, for several hours (or refrigerate overnight), permitting the truffles' perfume to permeate the mixture.

Choose a heavy pot, preferably copper or earthenware, just large enough to contain the sweetbreads arranged side by side on the bottom. Cook all the elements of the *mirepoix* in butter over low heat, stirring from time to time, for about ½ hour; they should not brown. Arrange the sweetbreads on the bed of vegetables, pour over the stock (which has been melted with the truffle juice), bring to the boiling point, and cook, covered, at a bare murmur for about 45 minutes. Remove the sweetbreads to a plate and pass the sauce through a strainer, pressing well to extract all cooking juices, but without passing the vegetables into the sauce. Lift off any fat on the surface, return to a boil and, over a period of from 10 to 15 minutes, keep at a light boil to one side of the saucepan, pulling the fatty skin that forms on the surface to the other side with a tablespoon and removing it. Reduce over a high flame, stirring constantly, to bring the liquid to the consistency of a heavy *demi-glace*—about ½ cup or slightly more should remain; then add the breadcrumbs and work into a firm, sticky paste.

Add the crumb-stock paste, the eggs, and the Madeira to the forcemeat mixture and mix thoroughly, using your hands. Spread half the forcemeat into the bottom of the fat-lined terrine (or terrines). Press the sweetbreads regularly into place. Fill the terrines with the remaining forcemeat, tap to settle the contents, place a bay leaf on the surface, press a sheet of fat over the surface, and cook in a *bain-marie* as for the rabbit terrine, but counting only about 1¼ hours, the sweetbread core being already cooked. Cool under weight and, if to be kept for more than 4 or 5 days, pour melted lard over the surface.

PORK AND HERB "MEATBALLS"
(Caillettes)

A recipe typical of the Vaucluse and Ardêche country, the area west of the Rhône valley stretching from Avignon to Lyons. The mixture may also be poured into a fat-lined terrine, baked for 1½ hours in a 350° oven, and cooled under weight. It becomes *la terrine aux herbes,* a specialty of Chez-Hiély-Lucullus in Avignon, one of the finest restaurants in France for the appreciation of regional cooking (and, among restaurants of quality, probably the least expensive).

The spinach is sometimes replaced, in part, by the green parts of the leaves of Swiss chard, also parboiled (10 minutes), pressed, and chopped. Caul *(crêpine)* is the thin, fatty, weblike membrane surrounding the pig's intestines. You may have to go to a specialty pork butcher for it or ask your butcher to order it especially. If you cannot find caul, substitute a couple of thin strips of fatback or bacon, wrapping each *caillette* so that they cross on the top surface, the ends being tucked beneath.

Caillettes are nearly always eaten cold as a first course, but, traditionally, they are served hot at Christmastime, accompanied by a truffle sauce.

1 medium onion, finely chopped
1 tablespoon olive oil
2 pounds spinach, well picked over and washed in several waters
2 large cloves garlic, crushed, peeled, finely chopped
8 ounces fresh fatback, chopped or cut into tiny cubes
10 ounces pork variety meats (liver, lungs, heart, spleen, in approximately
   equal quantities of those that you are able to find—sometimes only liver
   is used, but the result is less interesting), finely chopped
5 ounces chopped chicken livers
8 ounces lean, fresh salt-pork (uncured bacon), chopped
1 handful chopped parsley
1 teaspoon crumbled thyme
½ bay leaf, crumbled and finely chopped
2 eggs
Salt, freshly ground pepper
Caul

71

Gently cook the chopped onion in olive oil, stirring from time to time, for from 15 to 20 minutes—until yellowed and soft, but not browned.

Parboil the spinach for a couple of minutes in a large quantity of salted rapidly boiling water, drain, refresh under running cold water, squeeze the mass repeatedly in your hands to rid it of the maximum liquid, and chop it well.

Combine all of the ingredients except the caul and mix thoroughly with your hands. Form handsful of the mixture to the approximate size of a small orange and wrap each in a 5- or 6-inch square of caul (it is not always possible to cut it so mechanically—pieces may be spliced together). Pour about ½ cup water into the bottom of a shallow baking dish, cake tin, or anything that is just large enough to hold the *caillettes* placed side by side; arrange them in the pan and bake in a hot oven (450°) for about 25 minutes. Leave to cool and refrigerate. They are better served close to room temperature, so it is wise to remove them from the refrigerator an hour or so before serving.

LARDED PORK LIVER IN ASPIC
(Foie de Porc Piqué)

In view of the number of friends who nourish a passion for this preparation—a passion I understand intellectually but nonetheless fail to share (perhaps simply because pure liver I like only pinkly cooked and, in its unadorned state, pork liver does not number among those foods I most love), an unselfish impulse has banished my hesitation to give the recipe.

You will need a highly flavored, richly gelatinous stock. If you have veal stock on hand, use it—or a leftover *pot-au-feu* or *poule-au-pot* broth. Otherwise, make up a solid, vulgar stock out of pork and veal bones, beef, pork, and veal parings, chicken backs and necks, etc. A veal knuckle will lend sufficient gelatinous content or, lacking that, add a pig's foot. Prepare it as usual, the meats and bones covered with cold water, brought slowly to a boil, skimmed several times. Add a pound of carrots, an onion stuck with a couple of cloves, a head of garlic, and a big bouquet garni packed with leek greens, celery, thyme, bay leaf, any other herbs that meet your fancy, and, by all means, if available, a branch of lovage, and coarse salt. Cook at a bare simmer, lid ajar, for about 4 hours, and strain.

To make it in larger quantity, the proportions need not be respected to the letter, the precise quantity of liquid necessary depending on the size and form of the cooking vessel in relation to the liver.

Old bed sheets (cotton or linen), torn into squares, are useful both for wrapping the meat and for straining the jelly.

> 1 teaspoon mixed herbs (thyme, savory, oregano, sage, marjoram), ground to a powder
> Salt, pepper
> 5 ounces fresh fatback, cut into approximately 8-inch lengths, ¼ inch square
> The large lobe of a pork liver (something over 1 pound)

Marinade
> 2 cups dry white wine
> 1 head garlic, cut crosswise in two
> ⅓ cup sliced shallots
> Parsley stems and root, if possible
> Thyme
> 2 bay leaves
> 2 cloves
> Several grains allspice
>
> ⅓ cup Cognac
> 3 cups gelatinous stock

Mix the ground herbs, the salt, and the pepper in a bowl with the strips of fatback, tossing and turning until they are evenly coated with the seasonings. Using a larding needle (not a butcher's larder, which would tear the liver to shreds), thread the strips of fat repeatedly through the length of the liver, leaving ½-inch protrusions at either end. Work gently and unhurriedly so as not to damage or tear the liver. Marinate, covered and refrigerated, overnight or for up to 24 hours, turning the liver around in the marinade two or three times during this period.

Wrap the liver firmly in a square of cloth and tie it tightly.

Place it in an oval *cocotte,* pour over the marinade, including the solid elements, the Cognac, and the melted stock—the liver should be largely submerged. Bring to the boiling point, skim, and cook, the lid slightly ajar, at the slightest suggestion of a simmer, for about 1¾ hours (2 hours or slightly over for a larger bulk of liver). Leave to cool until tepid, then remove and unwrap the liver and place it in a terrine just large enough to contain it. Pour the liquid through a strainer lined with a tightly woven cloth; it will take its time and should not be forced, but, as the weave becomes clogged with sediment, rearrange the cloth slightly so the liquid contacts new areas. Skim off any fat that may have settled on the surface. The jelly will probably have to be reduced a bit—taste for seasoning and put a teaspoonful in a small container in the coldest part of the refrigerator to check its firmness in gelatin. If, after reduction, the stock seems still somewhat troubled, pass it a second time through a cloth—the jelly should be limpid but, for a preparation of this kind, it need not be crystalline. When you are satisfied with the stock, pour it over the liver. Chill for a day before serving. If traces of fat appear on the surface, they may be wiped off with a cloth dampened in hot water. Serve sliced, the cross-sectional view studded with the squares of fat.

CHICKEN LIVER TERRINE
(Terrine de Foies de Volailles)
(8 to 10 servings)

It was the beauty of a terrine Chez-Barrier in Tours that launched me on the series of experiments that have resulted in this recipe—totally different, however, from M. Barrier's. His, which he calls a mousse, contains, I suspect, proportionately more cream and egg and certainly no marrow (another fatty substance—probably grated pork fat—is surely present). It also contains dried currants, soaked, I think, in port wine. Chez-Barrier, the raisins seemed to me to lend an exciting note, but, on the two occasions that I attempted to introduce them into my own experiments, I found the result distinctly disagreeable.

Lucien Tendret is responsible for the marrow, which lends a rich suavity that could be gained in no other way. I have noted earlier that the second forcemeat of the *Oreiller de la Belle Aurore* is similar to this recipe. In fact, Tendret's only indication is that it should be composed of chicken livers, marrow, *panade,* and egg. The present mixture, uncooked, is completely liquid, which, when prepared as a terrine, presents no problem, but if it were to be a workable element in the mounting layers of a *pâté,* it would have to be much firmer. Eliminate the cream and Cognac, add proportionately more marrow, and make very stiff *panade.* Finally, chill the mixture well to give it body.

About 5 ounces beef marrow (that contained in one leg bone)
1 cup rich, gelatinous stock
3 ounces stale bread, crusts removed, crumbled
1 small clove garlic
1 pound chicken livers
Salt, pepper, cayenne
Large pinch powdered mixed herbs (thyme, savory, oregano, marjoram)
3 eggs
½ cup heavy cream
2 tablespoons Cognac
Butter for mold

Ask your butcher to saw the marrow bone into sections. They may be cracked open to remove the marrow or it may be removed from the sections with the help of a small knife.

Combine the stock and the breadcrumbs in a small saucepan and reduce, stirring with a wooden spoon, until the consistency of a firm paste. Pound the garlic to a paste in a mortar and mix with the *panade.*

Put the livers, the marrow, and the *panade* through a grinder, (or electric cutter), season, and pass the mixture again, this time through a fine sieve, a ladleful at a time, discarding the fragments of nervous tissue that remain in the sieve. Whisk in the eggs, the cream, and the Cognac, pour into a buttered 1-quart mold or terrine, and poach in a *bain-marie,* immersed by three quarters in hot but not boiling water, in a medium (350° to 375°) oven for about 1 hour or until the center is firm to the touch. The water of the *bain-marie* should not be allowed to come to a boil. The loaf shrinks slightly while cooling; unmold it when only tepid, pressing a sheet of plastic wrap around it to protect it from contact with air. Serve well chilled. It may, once chilled, be simply decorated and coated with a chicken or veal jelly. But for the beige exterior, the terrine should be a uniform and delicate rose throughout.

VEGETABLE TERRINE
(Terrine Verte)
(15 to 20 servings)

For the quantities given, a 2-quart terrine is necessary. The dish may easily be kept a week, refrigerated and protected by plastic wrap. The green body in cross-section is very pretty, with its mosaic accents of carrot and green-bean dice and little white macaroni discs, and the intermingling flavors of virgin vegetable things will surprise and please many an unwary palate.

1 cup duxelles
1 large onion, finely chopped
2 tablespoons butter
8 ounces mushrooms, finely chopped or passed through fine blade of Mouli-juliènne
Salt, pepper, lemon juice
Handful chopped parsley

10 ounces fresh, young sorrel, shredded
2 tablespoons butter
2 ounces stale bread, crusts removed, soaked in hot water, squeezed dry
3 cloves garlic
1 pound spinach, parboiled for 2 or 3 minutes, rinsed, squeezed dry, and chopped
1 pound Swiss chard, green parts only, parboiled for 10 minutes, rinsed, squeezed dry, and chopped
8 ounces green beans, cut into ½-inch lengths and parboiled for 8 minutes
6 ounces carrots, split, woody cores removed, if necessary, diced, parboiled 10 minutes
1 pound (unshelled) fresh white beans (or the equivalent

dried—enough to make 1½ cups stiff purée), well
cooked, drained, puréed

3 ounces elbow macaroni, cooked (still slightly firm) and
well drained

1 teaspoon mixed fresh savory and marjoram, finely
chopped (or finely crumbled dried herbs)

Salt, pepper, pinch cayenne

3 eggs

½ cup butter, softened

The duxelles: Cook the chopped onion gently in the butter without permitting it to color for 20 minutes or so, add the mushrooms,
turning the flame high and tossing and stirring until the mushrooms'
moisture has been evaporated, season, add parsley, and cook for a
couple of minutes still over low flame. Stir in a few drops of lemon
juice.

Stew the shredded sorrel in butter, stirring occasionally, for 10
minutes or so—longer, if necessary, until all excess moisture has been
evaporated and the sorrel is reduced to a purée.

Mix the squeezed breadcrumb paste thoroughly with the garlic,
which has first been pounded to a purée in a mortar.

Combine all the above with the remaining ingredients in a large
mixing bowl, mix thoroughly with your hands, turn out into the
buttered terrine, tapping the bottom of it several times against a
table top, the blows muffled by the intervention of several layers of
towel, to settle the contents, and poach for about 1½ hours in a
medium oven (350° to 375°), the terrine put into a *bain-marie*. Cool
under pressure as for the rabbit terrine and refrigerate for a day
before serving.

FISH TERRINES
(Terrines de Poisson)

Fish terrines are deservedly fashionable in France today. The formulas, but for the garnish, vary little, the basic forcemeat being
nearly always a *mousseline* of pike or whiting, sometimes of
salmon (raw flesh pounded in a mortar or reduced to a purée in
an electrical robot-cutter, egg whites and seasonings worked in,

passed through a fine sieve, chilled on cracked ice, heavy cream worked into it vigorously and in small quantities at a time, the last part of the cream being lightly whipped before being beaten in—for cold terrines, about 12 ounces flesh, 2 egg whites, and 1½ cups heavy cream are good proportions, and a pinch of cayenne will give it a lift); chopped truffles, chopped pistachios, poached cubed or cut-up scallops, lobster, or shrimps, or skinned and rapidly sautéed eel filets are common internal garnishes; sorrel or tomato mousses are good accompaniments. The Haeberlin brothers (the Auberge de l'Ill in Ill-haeusern, Alsace) serve a terrine of sole filets enveloping a pike *mousseline* studded with truffles and lobster that is of great delicacy; Michel Guérard accompanies an eel *pâté* with a watercress mousse that forms an original, and happy, alliance; a terrine of mine I particularly like consists of adding a healthy cupful of puréed raw sea-urchin coral to a basic whiting forcemeat before sieving it and incorporating a handful of chopped pistachios at the same time as the cream. The terrine is lined with sole filets as in the following recipe, and the clean but fragile note of urchin sweetness proscribes any accompaniment other than a trembling fish jelly.

None of these preparations is complicated in execution, but the reader may feel that the following recipe is still less demanding; it involves neither sieving nor working over cracked ice, and the slight coarseness of moist texture, the directness of taste, and the separateness of flavors have a charm that may please those who weary at times of ultimate refinements.

This terrine need not necessarily be masked in jelly, in which case the preparation of a fish *fumet* may be eliminated (the breadcrumbs being merely soaked in hot water and squeezed thoroughly dry).

FISH TERRINE, WHIPPED TOMATO CREAM

(Terrine de Poissons, Crème Mousseline Tomatée)
(about 10 servings)

Fish fumet	Several heads and carcasses of non-oily, white-fleshed fish, of nonaggressive flavor (whiting and sole if possible), cleaned and cut up, eyes and gills removed

Water to cover
1 large carrot, finely sliced
1 large onion, finely sliced
Thyme (or mixed herbs), bay leaf, parsley, fennel
  branches (or pinch of seeds), branch of celery, leek
  greens (if available)
Salt
1 cup dry white wine

Forcemeat   Duxelles: 1 medium onion, finely chopped
                          1 tablespoon butter
                          ½ pound mushrooms, trimmed, rinsed rap-
                            idly, passed through medium blade of
                            Mouli-juliènne or finely chopped
                          Salt, pepper
                          Small handful chopped parsley
                          Lemon juice

             Panade: 3 ounces crumbled stale (but not dried out)
                            bread, crusts removed
                          1 cup fish fumet

1 pound spinach, parboiled for 2 to 3 minutes, drained,
  refreshed in cold water, squeezed repeatedly, and
  chopped
1 pound whiting filets, all tiny bones removed, chopped
Salt, pepper, small pinch cayenne
A tiny pinch of freshly grated nutmeg
2 eggs
1-pound slice of fresh salmon, flesh separated from bones
  and skin, dark, brownish, oily flesh next to skin pared
  off, all tiny bones carefully removed, cut into ½-inch
  cubes
10 to 12 sole filets
Butter for the mold

Fish jelly   Fish fumet
              Gelatin (about 1 teaspoon per cup of fumet)
              Salt (if necessary)

79

        About ¼ cup fine sherry
        Chopped parsley

Whipped   1 cup preserved tomatoes (not tomato paste)
tomato cream   Salt
        ½ teaspoon mixed dried herbs
        Pepper
        Juice of ½ lemon
        1 cup heavy cream

The Fumet

Cover the fish carcasses well with cold water, bring slowly to a boil, skim off all the gray scum that rises to the surface, add the remaining ingredients, except for the white wine, and simmer, the lid slightly ajar, for about 15 minutes. Add the white wine, return to a boil, and continue to cook, lid ajar, at a simmer for another 20 minutes. Pour the contents into a large sieve, straining thoroughly, but without pressure, and reduce the liquid over a medium-high flame by about one third. Set aside the cup necessary for the *panade* and refrigerate the remaining *fumet* until the following day.

The Forcemeat

Stew the chopped onion in butter, over very low heat, stirring occasionally, for 20 or 25 minutes, until soft and slightly yellowed. Then add the mushrooms (which have been chopped or put through the Mouli-juliènne only the moment before) and seasonings, turn the flame up, and toss regularly until the mushrooms have lost all their water and the mixture has returned to a dry, firm consistency, stir in the chopped parsley, cook for another minute or so over a low flame, remove from the heat, and stir in a few drops of lemon juice.

Boil the cupful of *fumet* with the breadcrumbs, stirring vigorously with a wooden spoon, until reduced to a consistent, fairly stiff paste.

When the *duxelles* and the *panade* are sufficiently cooled to be handled, combine them with all the remaining ingredients of the forcemeat, except for the salmon cubes, working them together with your hands. Then mix in—gently, so as not to break them up—the cubes of salmon flesh.

Assembly

Soak the sole filets for a few minutes in ice-cold water, spread them out on paper toweling, sponge them gently dry and press each firmly, but without violence, with the side of a large knife blade to slightly flatten it out. Make several shallow incisions diagonally on the skin side of each filet with a sharp knife. Line a generously buttered, rectangular, 2-quart terrine (the bottom and sides, but not the ends) with the filets, slightly overlapping, the flesh side pressed into place against the buttered sides of the terrine, the skin side visible, the tips of the filets hanging over the edges of the terrine sides, and spoon in the forcemeat, spreading it evenly and mounding the surface. Rap the bottom of the terrine smartly several times against a towel-muffled tabletop to settle the contents and fold the filet tips, one by one, over the surface of the forcemeat (depending on the proportions of the terrine, they may or may not completely enclose the forcemeat; if not, several filets should be halved at a sharp bias and pressed into place to complete the enclosure, their tips tucked down inside those of the other filets, against the body of the forcemeat, before the other tips are folded into place).

Press a sheet of buttered parchment paper or aluminum foil over the surface, cover with the lid, and cook in a *bain-marie* (using a fairly deep container, which should contain enough hot, but not boiling, water to immerse the terrine by three quarters) in a medium oven (about 350° to 375°) for approximately 45 minutes, or until the surface of the terrine is firm and springy to the touch. Leave to cool until only tepid and unmold, first placing a pastry grill over the surface and turning it and the terrine upside down as if to unmold the contents (this is in order to drain off loose liquid) and turning it right side up again after draining, before unmolding onto the serving platter. Press plastic wrap over the entire surface to protect it from contact with air and refrigerate until the following day.

The Jelly

The fish *fumet,* depending on the varieties of fish used in its confection, will be more or less lightly jelled and the sediment will have settled to the bottom of the bowl. Carefully remove all traces of fat from the surface of the *fumet* and from the sides of the bowl and spoon the lightly jelled *fumet*—only that part which is limpid (about two thirds) into a saucepan. (It may be clarified by whisking it with beaten egg whites until a boil is reached and simmering it for a quarter of an hour before straining it through a tightly woven towel but (1) clarification tends to somewhat emasculate the jelly; (2) there should be enough limpid *fumet* without having recourse to clarification; and (3) the troubled *fumet* remaining in the bottom of the bowl is perfectly good for the confection of a fish sauce for another preparation.) Dissolve the gelatin in a small amount of warmed *fumet* in a small saucepan, heat it, stirring, until a boil is reached, and incorporate it into the remainder, also first warmed. Test it for firmness by placing a spoonful in a small container (metal will take faster) in the coldest part of the refrigerator for 10 minutes or so (or on cracked ice in the refrigerator); it should be fairly firm in view of the fact that sherry will be added to it. Taste the jelly for salt and, when it is only barely tepid, stir in the sherry, adding it in two or three doses and tasting before adding more—its presence should not be aggressive.

Pour about ¼ cup of the liquid jelly into a small bowl, preferably metallic, embedded in cracked ice, stir with a tablespoon until it begins to turn syrupy, and spoon it rapidly over the fish loaf, returning it then to the coldest part of the refrigerator for from 5 to 10 minutes, or until the film of jelly has well set. Begin again and, when a well-set film covers the entire surface, mix a tablespoonful of liquid jelly with the chopped parsley, form a ribbon of parsley the length of the loaf, return until the jellied parsley is set, and continue coating with jelly and returning to the refrigerator until all of the jelly has been used. Keep well chilled until serving. The loaf will not only be masked in jelly but also surrounded by a mirror of jelly over which may be scattered a *chiffonade* of tender lettuce leaves for the sake of presentation. Serve the tomato cream in a sauceboat apart, placing a spoonful to the side of each slice of terrine when served out.

The Whipped Tomato Cream

Stew the tomatoes, salted, and herbs over a low flame, stirring to prevent sticking, until all superfluous liquid is evaporated. Pass through a fine sieve, leave to cool, stir in the pepper and lemon juice and mix thoroughly with the cream, which has been first whipped until nearly stiff. Taste for seasoning.

THREE MOUSSES
(Trois Mousses)
(for 8 to 10 as a first course)

Mousses lend themselves to an infinity of combinations—among themselves and with other elements as well—that are not only flattering to the eye but, through the juxtaposition of similarly smooth textures that are sharply different in their flavors, are very exciting to the palate. The following recipe is a case in point.

A mousse may often provide an interesting method of using up leftover boiled or roast poultry, but none of the supple succulence of a chicken freshly roasted and only half cooled can be achieved from cold cooked flesh.

Note that in the following recipe you will need about 1 quart of firm meat jelly and 1 pint of heavy cream in all.

Chicken mousse 1 good-sized roasting chicken
Butter (for roasting)
1¼ cups firm meat jelly (see page 103)
Salt, pepper, nutmeg
1 cup heavy cream

1 recipe for Sorrel mousse (see page 105)

Tomato mousse 1 medium onion, finely chopped
1 tablespoon butter
⅓ cup white wine
1¼ pounds firm, ripe tomatoes, peeled, seeded, and chopped (or canned tomatoes, drained of their liquid)
½ teaspoon sugar
Salt, pepper, pinch cayenne
⅔ cup firm meat jelly
½ cup heavy cream

About 1 cup meat jelly (for masking the surface)

Roast the chicken, seasoned and basted with butter, for about 45 minutes or until the legs are only just done (the point at which, if the thigh, at the thickest part, pierced with a trussing needle, exudes a transparent juice) and leave to cool until only warm. Remove the skin from the legs and breast and scrape the bones free of the flesh (this should leave a good pound of flesh—the remainder of the carcass and the cooking juices may enrich a pilaf). Pound the flesh in a mortar (or purée it in an electrical robot cutter), adding in small quantities at a time about half of the meat jelly (melted, but not hot). Season (only a suggestion of nutmeg, freshly ground) and put through a food mill (the cooked flesh offers too much resistance to be passed by hand through a sieve), work in the remaining jelly, beating the purée vigorously, and, finally, incorporate the cream, half whipped (if whipped until stiff, the mousse will have a dry, cottony quality). Spread into the bottom of a glass or crystal bowl designed to throw into relief the bands of rose, pale green, and white of the tiered mousses and refrigerate.

Spread the sorrel mousse over the surface of the firm chicken mousse and refrigerate again until it, in turn, is firm.

Cook the chopped onion gently in butter for 15 to 20 minutes, until soft and lightly yellowed, add the white wine, reduce over a high flame until nearly dry, add the tomatoes, sugar, and seasonings, and cook at a simmer for about ½ hour, stirring occasionally. Then add half of the meat jelly, reduce the mixture by half at a rapid boil, stirring, pass it through a fine sieve with a wooden pestle, and stir in the remaining jelly. Place the bowl over cracked ice and stir the contents until they begin to turn syrupy; then, just before the jelling point, fold in the cream, half whipped. Pour over the surface of the sorrel mousse and return to the refrigerator to set completely before gently pouring over a layer of liquid, room-temperature meat jelly. Leave to set for several hours or overnight before serving.

EGGS

OMELETS

Were one to launch a "Demystification of French Cuisine" campaign, the rolled omelet should certainly mark the point of departure. There are no secrets, no special talent is required, and no method is any better than any other. Its execution demands less than a minute's time from the breaking of the eggs to the presentation at table. (I was asked recently to demonstrate an omelet to a group of American high-school girls, come to France to study the language. After the demonstration, I gave them several trays of eggs and told them to go to work. Their teacher later told me that the omelet session had been the high point of their summer, simply because each girl, in a relaxed atmosphere and with no previous experience, had produced an absolutely correct omelet.) And, in any case, it is only as good as the butter and the eggs with which it is made; it shares neither creamy suavity with scrambled eggs nor homely wit with many a flat omelet.

Standard professional-weight iron omelet pans need not be reserved for omelets alone, but they must be well cared for, the surface kept silk-smooth and oiled; if nothing has stuck, they need only be wiped with a clean dry rag or paper toweling (not the rumpled piece of old newspaper preferred by professional chefs); if something sticks but slightly, rub the inside with salt and wipe with oil, being certain to leave no trace of salt (which encourages rust), but if anything has stuck badly or if the pan has been used for deglazing, it should be scrubbed thoroughly with scouring powder and a fine abrasive pad or fine steel wool—nothing coarse enough to scratch—rinsed well, wiped dry, heated over a flame, and rubbed with oil. By all means, use them for small deep frys—it is good for them.

Filled and sauced omelets do not appeal to me as being very interesting. Finely chopped fresh marjoram will fuse with eggs to produce an omelet of singular fragrance. A handful of tender young sorrel leaves, raw and finely shredded, will, on the other hand, permeate the eggs with none of sorrel's qualities, but, because of its disposition to "melt" instantly in contact with heat, the effect of fragile, disembodied sourness laced in suspension through the body of the omelet is not less exciting.

ROLLED FINES-HERBES OMELET
(Omelette aux Fines Herbes)

3 eggs
1 tablespoon finely chopped parsley, chervil, and chives in equal quantities
    plus 3 or 4 leaves of finely chopped tarragon
Salt, pepper
2 tablespoons cold butter

Break the eggs into a soup plate, add herbs, seasonings, and 1 tablespoon of the butter, cut into small pieces. While the pan, containing the other piece of butter, is heating over a high flame, beat the eggs lightly with a fork—just enough to combine yolks and whites. Turn the pan, tilted, in all directions in order to evenly coat the sides and bottom with butter, and the moment the butter has stopped foaming and the slightly nutty odor of brown butter is perceptible, pour in the eggs, stir rapidly (without scraping the tines of the fork against the bottom of the pan)—a couple of turns only—to disperse the heat through the mass, and gently lift the edge of the omelet with the tines of the fork at two or three points successively, tilting the pan at the same time to permit as much liquid egg as possible to run beneath. Start rolling it immediately, easing the edge nearest you over with the side of the fork (it will not actually "roll"; a turn and a half is all that is necessary). Tip the pan sharply, cradling the omelet at the far side, press the outer edge of the omelet against the rolled mass with the tines, hold the still tilted pan for another three or four seconds over the direct flame to lightly color the underside, and turn it out onto a warm (but not hot) plate, either by inverting the pan or, holding it in its tilted position, by encouraging the omelet with the back of the fork to roll over, colored underside up. You may, if you like, lend it gloss by dragging a piece of butter across the surface.

FLAT OMELETS

Flat omelets are begun in the same way as rolled omelets, the mixture being poured into a hot pan and, if its consistency permits, being stirred briefly and its edges lifted with the pan tilted. In many flat omelets, a proportionately small amount of egg serves as a binder rather than as the principal element—such is the case with the zucchini and spinach mixtures in the following recipe; these not only may not be stirred, but they are also too stiff to spread evenly in the pan without the aid of a fork and, though begun over a high flame, they must be cooked longer over a lower flame before being tossed. They are best only just done—tossed as soon as they are firm enough not to fall apart in the tossing—and, once turned, they should remain over the heat but a few seconds longer. Too fragile at the half-cooked stage to be turned with a spatula, these omelets must be tossed— unless, in frustration, you prefer to finish each in the oven (starting it over a high flame to ensure its not sticking, then putting the pan into a hot oven for a half-minute or so—until the surface is only just firm).

Tossing is a simple enough affair, but one must be relaxed; the apprehensive novice often fails to produce more than a stubborn shudder from the omelet—or it may take flight. Before tossing, always shake the pan to be certain that the omelet slides freely. If it sticks at some point, gently free it with a flexible spatula, slipping a small piece of butter beneath it at the same time, and shake again. The pan is propelled forward in a scooping motion, abruptly curving upward, then back. The omelet slips out from the far side and is picked up in its elliptic course, the contact having hardly been broken. One's entire body directs the pan's action and the only perceptible movement comes, rhythmic and liquid, from the shoulder.

Any of the omelets from the following recipe served alone, either tepid or cold, provides an agreeable, light first course. The spinach version, sometimes enriched with a handful of grated cheese and some chopped onions stewed in butter or olive oil (chard may replace part or all of the spinach, fresh basil may be added, etc.), is a typical Provençal hors d'oeuvre and is often made in large quantities (about three pounds of spinach to a dozen eggs), first siezed over a high flame in a large, preheated pan containing olive oil, baked in the oven, and unmolded.

The delicate flavor and moist, melting texture of the zucchini omelet (count 2 eggs to something over 1 pound of zucchini) I find particularly attractive. Served alone, it, like the simplified *pipérade,* is best tepid, prepared 20 to 30 minutes before serving it.

COLD OMELET LOAF
(Gâteau de Crespèus)

A *crespèu* (or *crespéou,* the Provençal tongue lending itself to a certain orthographic freedom) is, traditionally, a flat omelet containing pieces of fried salt pork, sautéed potatoes, or both—identical to an *omelette à la Savoyarde*. By extension, other flat omelets are often called *crespèus*. The Provençal *crespèu* and the Italian *frittata* are twins.

This *gâteau* of multi-tiered omelets was chosen from the repertory of a regional restaurant for demonstration purposes in the Avignon summer classes.

The original contains, in addition to those omelets in this recipe, artichoke, Gruyère, caper, and sorrel omelets, and the tomatoes, sweet peppers, and onions are conceived as separate omelets rather than being grouped together in a hamless *pipérade*. Parsley, tarragon, chives, and chervil are added to all of them and each is spread with a reduction of anchovy, canned tuna, shallots, and white wine, mashed into a paste. The original *gâteau* contains only one omelet of each flavor and the whole thing is bound with a *fines herbes* omelet mixture.

Such an orgy of different and sometimes contentious savors had, tastewise, pretty much the same effect as mixing together all the colors on a palette—a muddy grayness. And to the eye the cross-sectional pattern was only confusing: The presence of tarragon in all the omelets lent a sameness to everything; the fish paste dulled the clarity of the other flavors; the capers and the cheese lent disruptive support to the fish; the tomatoes, onions, and peppers, which fuse so beautifully into a single Mediterranean note, were senseless apart; the artichoke omelet, lovely in itself, was completely lost in the jungle and, although the whole business badly needed the sharp, clean relief of sorrel, the single little sorrel *crêpe* in the midst of all that was only frustrating. There were far too many things and not enough of any single thing.

I resolved to limit the flavors, repeating each; to eliminate the oppressive fishy presence, and to replace the repetitious *fines herbes* egg binder with a sorrel cream. As it stands now, I think the dish cannot fail to please, and the cross-sectional ribbons of repeated red, greens, beige, and black afford a very pretty presentation.

Use a small 7-inch omelet pan for the confection of these omelets. You will need an approximately 2½-quart receptacle of about the same diameter; a large charlotte mold or a round *cocotte*—a round, enameled ironware casserole—should be perfect. You will also need kitchen parchment paper.

Be organized: Prepare the five basic apparels plus the sorrel purée and line them up in bowls near the stove. Before preparing the omelets, line up five plates or a couple of large platters so as to be able to stack omelets of different flavors separately. Keep the salt and the bottle of olive oil within arm's reach, a small ladle in the mixing bowl of beaten eggs, a fork in a soup plate for mixing the individual omelets, and a small flexible spatula at hand just in case an omelet should stick (should this happen—and even though the omelet has been successfully turned out and the pan appears to be clean—rub the pan with salt before continuing to the next omelet). Count about 1 tablespoon of olive oil for the confection of each omelet and reheat the pan for a few seconds each time before beginning another. The omelets should be from ¼ to ½ inch thick, depending on the material (the zucchini and spinach omelets will be thicker than the olive and mushroom omelets; the tomato mixture is more flexible). Individual mixtures should be salted separately (the zucchini will need no salt; the quality of the olives will determine their seasoning . . .).

The recipe will serve 12 to 15 people. It is impractical to prepare it on a smaller scale, but it may be kept for more than one meal, protected in plastic wrap.

The Preparations

(1)   1 pound small, firm zucchini
Salt
2 tablespoons olive oil
1 teaspoon fresh marjoram flowers, finely chopped (or a pinch of dried marjoram or a bit of crumbled fresh oregano)

Rinse the zucchinis, wipe them dry, trim the ends but don't peel them. Grate them coarsely or pass them, cut into sections, through the medium blade of a Mouli-juliènne, arrange in layers in a mixing bowl, each layer sprinkled with salt, leave to stand for about ½ hour, press the mass together, squeezing to release the water, pour the contents of the bowl into a sieve and, taking the mass in both hands, squeeze tightly and repeatedly to rid it of all the liquid possible. Sauté in olive oil over a relatively high flame, tossing regularly, for 6 or 7 minutes. Add the marjoram after removing from heat.

(2)   1 medium sweet onion, halved and finely sliced
3 to 4 ounces sweet peppers (the elongated light green Italian variety, if possible), halved lengthwise and sliced finely crosswise
3 tablespoons olive oil
2 medium tomatoes, ripe and firm, peeled, seeded, and coarsely chopped (out of season, use canned tomatoes, juice strained off)
1 large clove garlic, crushed, peeled, and sliced thinly
Salt, pepper, large pinch sugar, small pinch cayenne

Stew the onions and the peppers gently in olive oil until soft, stirring regularly—10 to 15 minutes. Add tomatoes, garlic, and seasonings, toss for about a minute over a high flame, then cook gently at a simmer, tossing occasionally, for about 15 minutes. Toss another couple of minutes over a high flame until all liquid is evaporated.

(3)   **1 pound spinach, stems removed, washed in several waters**
Salt

Parboil the spinach in a large quantity of generously salted, rapidly boiling water—2 or 3 minutes only. Drain, rinse in cold water, squeeze tightly and repeatedly with both hands, and chop.

(4)   **4 ounces firm, fresh mushrooms**
1 tablespoon butter
Salt, pepper

Rinse the mushrooms rapidly or, if clean in appearance, simply wipe each with a damp cloth. Slice them as finely as possible and sauté in butter, seasoned, over a high flame, tossing repeatedly, until their liquid is completely reabsorbed (3 or 4 minutes—or more, depending on the size of the pan).

(5)   **6 or 7 ounces natural black olives (no vinegar)**

Pit the olives or remove the flesh with a small knife and chop them coarsely.

(6)   **10 ounces sorrel**
1 tablespoon butter
Salt

Pick over the sorrel, pulling the stems off backwards to remove stringy veins from the leaves, and wash in several waters. If young and tender, cut into a fine *chiffonade* and put directly to stew, salted, in the butter over low heat, stirring from time to time, for about 20 to 30 minutes, until all liquid is evaporated and the sorrel is reduced to a purée. If the leaves aren't tender, parboil first, plunging them into boiling water and leaving only long enough for the water to return to a boil. Drain in a sieve and stew in butter as before.

(7)   About 20 eggs
            Pepper, salt
            About ⅔ cup olive oil (for making omelets)
            ⅔ cup heavy cream
            About 1 tablespoon butter (for buttering mold and parch-
                ment)

Beat the eggs and pepper (no salt—or very little) with a whisk, only enough to mix them well. Make two omelets from each of the preparations, *excluding the sorrel,* putting half of the preparation into the soup plate and stirring in enough egg to bind well; the zucchini will take little—the equivalent of something less than 1 egg for each omelet; the tomato mixture will require about double that of the zucchini, etc. Salt each to taste, bearing in mind the amount of seasoning in the original preparation—it is possible that only the spinach will require additional salt.

Cut 2 rounds of kitchen parchment paper to the dimensions of the top and the bottom of the casserole or chosen mold, butter the mold liberally, butter both sides of 1 round of paper for the bottom and press it carefully into the bottom of the mold, leaving no air spaces or unstuck edges where the egg might run beneath.

Whisk together the sorrel purée, the ⅔ cup cream, and the remainder of beaten eggs, adding more eggs if necessary—there should be the equivalent of about 5 eggs in the mixture. Salt and pepper to taste.

Pour a small ladle of sorrel cream into the bottom of the mold and stack the omelets in alternating colors and flavors, pressing each gently into place and pouring a small bit of sorrel cream over each before placing another. Pour in enough sorrel cream to barely submerge the omelets, tap the bottom of the mold smartly against a muffled tabletop (a couple of folded towels to soften the blow) to settle the contents and chase out any trapped air bubbles, and add more of the sorrel cream if necessary for the top omelet to be only just covered (if any is left over, it can be poached in a small mold apart). Butter the other round of paper and place it, buttered side down, on the surface.

Cook in a *bain-marie,* the mold immersed to about two thirds its height in boiling water, in a medium (375°) oven for 45 minutes, making certain that the center of the loaf is firm and elastic to slight pressure before removing from the oven. Leave to cool for about 1 hour—until only just tepid. Lift the paper off the surface, run a knife all around the sides, and unmold onto the serving dish (placing the dish upside down over the mold and turning it and the mold over together). If not to be served immediately, press plastic wrap over the entire surface to protect it from contact with air and refrigerate. Just before serving, decorate it simply (a ribbon of chopped parsley or *fines herbes* strung around the edge and a rosette of finely sliced tomato in the center, for instance. Pitted black olives sliced into rings or chopped hard-boiled egg yolks are also good decorative elements). To serve, cut into approximately ½-inch slices, using a spatula to transfer them to individual plates.

A salad of cucumbers in a dill-flavored lemon and cream sauce is an exquisite accompaniment.

SAVORY TURNIP OMELET
(Omelette de Navets à la Sarriètte)

This is an astonishingly good thing with a surprising flavor. Chopped black olives may be added to the mixture.

1 pound turnips (young and tender—any with spongy or fibrous inclinations should be relegated to the soup pot)
Salt
¼ cup butter
1 teaspoon fresh savory leaves, finely chopped (if not of a spring tenderness, chopped to a near powder)
3 eggs
½ cup chopped parsley
Pepper
2 tablespoons olive oil

Peel the turnips, grate coarsely or pass them through the medium blade of a Mouli-juliènne, and leave in salted layers to disgorge their water as for the zucchini in the preceding recipe. After ½ hour, squeeze the mass of juliènne tightly and repeatedly and put to stew

93

gently in the butter sprinkled with the savory, tossing often, for about 15 minutes or until tender. Taste for salt and season the mixture accordingly.

Stir together the eggs, the parsley, and a generous grinding of black pepper. Add the turnips, a little at a time if they are still hot, beating them in with a fork.

Prepare this like the other flat omelets, stirring the mixture the moment it is poured into the hot oil, smoothing it out, and cook for about 5 minutes over a moderately low flame before tossing (or start it out on the high flame and finish in the oven, unmolding it for the service). Serve tepid.

HOT ONION OMELET WITH VINEGAR
(Omelette à la Lyonnaise)

Lyons, to everyone in France, is known as the gastronomic capital of the world. What that means depends on who mouths the words. For the guidebooks and the foreigners it usually means elegant pike *quenelles* in crayfish sauce, truffled chickens, artichokes stuffed with foie gras, salmon in Champagne, bass in pastry—the fare of the starred and sometimes very good restaurants, for instance, that of the famous *mères Lyonnaises* and their successors and that of Point and his successors. To others—*les vicieux*—it means the *mâchon,* a morning meal of hearty and attractively vulgar preparations washed down with a cool abundance of Beaujolais, vibrant in its tender youth. Typical of this food are boiled pigs' tails and rinds, quaint salads of lambs' trotters and testicles, agrestic terrines, sausages poached in white wine with boiled potatoes, tripes in every conceivable form—and the following omelet. Sautéed onions and a pan washed up with vinegar melt into a single recurrent theme in Lyonnaise cooking.

3 large sweet onions (about 12 ounces), halved and finely sliced
¼ cup butter
3 eggs
Salt, pepper
1 tablespoon wine vinegar

Choose a relatively small, heavy pan in which to cook the onions so as to have a thick layer of onions—scattered loosely over a large surface, even with the tiniest of flames, they color too rapidly, their moisture being immediately evaporated. Cook them for at least ½ hour in 2 tablespoons of butter over a very low flame, tossing or stirring from time to time. They should be yellowed and very soft, but not browned.

Beat the eggs lightly with the seasonings, stir in the onions and prepare the omelet (hot pan, pour in the mixture when the butter stops foaming, stir a couple of times, lift the edges to let liquid run beneath, toss and, a couple of seconds later, slip it onto a warm plate —just done), add a tablespoon of butter to the pan, return to the heat, and, when the butter has stopped foaming and starts to turn brown, pour it over the omelet. Add the vinegar to the pan, swirl it around, and dribble it over the omelet.

BREAD OMELET
(Omelette au Pain)

2 ounces stale but not dried-out bread, without crusts
½ cup heavy cream
⅓ cup freshly grated Parmesan cheese
Salt, pepper
2 eggs
2 tablespoons butter

Mash the bread with ¼ cup of cream until the mixture forms a consistent paste, add Parmesan, salt and pepper, the remaining cream, and work the mixture together until the consistency is smooth and creamy. Stir in the eggs, beating lightly, and prepare like other flat omelets. The bread and cream make a lighter and more tender mixture than that of the usual omelet and it is more difficult to toss it without splashing—it may be finished in the oven.

BAKED EGGS WITH ARTICHOKES
(Oeufs aux Artichauts)
(for 4)

This is a common dish in the southwest of France and, in Italy, the identical preparation is known as a Florentine specialty. It is, essentially, an omelet that, because it is started out in a cold dish, sticks. Its uniqueness depends on a juxtaposition of flavors and textures—the crispness and nutty taste of the golden fried artichokes baked into the mass of creamy, barely set eggs—that can be obtained in no other way.

The size of the dish is important to the success of this preparation: it should only just contain the fried artichoke quarters, scattered closely over the bottom, the beaten eggs achieving a depth that easily covers them.

8 or 10 small, tender artichokes
About 1 cup olive oil
8 eggs
Salt, pepper
2 tablespoons butter

Pull off the tough outer leaves of the artichokes, cut off the top third of the remaining leaves, and pare any remaining tough edges. Split into quarters (or eighths, depending on the size of the artichokes), remove chokes, if necessary, and add to a bowl containing about ½ cup olive oil, turning to coat them completely in the oil, thus protecting them from blackening on contact with the air. Heat the remaining olive oil in a frying pan and fry the artichoke sections, turning them regularly in the oil with the tines of a fork, until tender and golden, the leaf tips crisp and richly browned. Drain on absorbent paper, sprinkle on all sides with salt and freshly ground pepper, and arrange them in the bottom of a liberally buttered gratin dish (any low-sided, non-metallic oven dish). Beat the eggs lightly with about 1 tablespoon of cold hard butter, cut into tiny pieces, add salt and pepper, pour over the artichokes, and bake in a moderately hot oven (400°) for about 8 to 10 minutes, keeping a close eye on the eggs—they should be removed from the oven before the center of the dish is set. The exact cooking time depends on the size of the dish and the depth of the eggs. Overcooked, all of the delicacy is lost.

SCRAMBLED EGGS

Correctly prepared, the softest of barely perceptible curds held in a thickly liquid, smooth, creamy suspension, scrambled eggs number among the very great delicacies of the table. They, like omelets, should be beaten but lightly with an addition of butter and, whether they be prepared over low, direct heat or in a *bain-marie* (their cooking utensil immersed in another containing nearly boiling water), they should be contained in a generously buttered heavy pan, **preferably** copper, which absorbs heat slowly and retains it for a long time. It is not only easier to precisely control the heat in a *bain-marie,* but also the cooking time is shortened, thanks to the heat's being absorbed through the sides of the utensil as well as from the bottom. The eggs should be stirred constantly with a wooden spoon during their preparation, the sides and the bottom of the pan being repeatedly scraped, and they should be removed from the heat some moments before the desired consistency is achieved and stirred continuously for another minute or so, for they continue to cook from an absorption of heat contained in the pan. It is wise to remove them two or three times from the heat toward the end of the cooking to control more exactly the degree of creaminess and, once removed definitively from contact with heat, a small amount of heavy cream may be stirred in, arresting at once the cooking and underlining at the same time their caressing consistency. They may be served in butter-crisp containers carved out of crustless bread. Otherwise, if one is among friends, it is preferable to serve them directly from the cooking vessel onto warm, but not hot, plates and a wonderful additional garnish is the crisp, brown-butter note of croutons, either scattered over the surface or stirred into the eggs at the moment of serving.

The complication of such rich garnishes as foie gras, game,

crayfish, or lobster with their corresponding Périgueux, Salmis, Nantua, or Américaine sauces seems only to detract from the purity of the thing. But for truffles (the black ones incorporated, slivered, sliced, or chopped before the cooking; the fresh white ones sliced paper thin over the surface the moment the eggs are done) and morels (fresh or dried, stewed in butter before being incorporated into the eggs), scrambled eggs ally themselves the most beautifully with a single vegetable—be it tender asparagus tips, parboiled and sweated in butter (or, Oriental-wise, slivered, raw, on the bias, parboiled for but a few seconds, and tossed for no more than a minute in hot butter), artichoke hearts stewed in butter, finely sliced zucchini sautéed in butter or in olive oil, shredded sorrel stewed in butter, tender peas, rapidly parboiled . . . The same herbs that find a place in omelets are good, alone or in combination with vegetables, in scrambled eggs.

It is said that eggs and wine do not marry. I, personally, take great pleasure in drinking a young, light-bodied, relatively dry white wine with scrambled eggs.

Both the following recipes, though traditional, stray from the classical formula.

EGGS SCRAMBLED WITH TOMATO AND BASIL
(Brouillade de Tomates au Basilic)
(for 4)

3 or 4 medium tomatoes, peeled, seeded, chopped coarsely
Salt
3 or 4 cloves garlic, crushed
Bouquet garni (bay leaf, thyme, celery branch—or a pinch of crumbled mixed dried herbs)
½ teaspoon sugar
¼ cup olive oil
¼ cup butter
8 to 10 eggs
Pepper
Handful fresh basil leaves and flowers

Cook the tomatoes, salted, with the garlic, bouquet garni, and sugar in the olive oil over a low flame, tossing from time to time, until the free liquid is evaporated and the tomatoes seem only to be coated with oil. Discard the garlic and the bouquet garni.

Add the butter, cut into small pieces, to the eggs, season to taste, beat them lightly with a fork and, with a wooden spoon, stir them into the tomato mixture, keeping it over a low flame and continuing to stir constantly, adding when the eggs begin to thicken the basil, chopped at the last minute to avoid its blackening. Remove from the flame just before the desired consistency is achieved and continue stirring.

EGGS SCRAMBLED WITH CHEESE AND WHITE WINE
(Fondue à la Comtoise)
(for 4)

3 cloves garlic, crushed, peeled, chopped finely
1 cup dry white wine
¼ cup butter
10 eggs
5 ounces freshly grated Swiss Gruyère (it must be a dry and nutty-tasting cheese with only a few very tiny holes; Emmental-type cheese is too bland and too sweet)
Salt, pepper

Simmer the chopped garlic in the white wine, covered, in a small saucepan for about ½ hour. The wine should, at this point, be reduced to about ⅓ cup—if it is not sufficiently reduced, turn the heat up with the lid off for a minute or so. Strain, discarding the fragments of garlic, and leave to cool.

Butter liberally the interior of an earthenware casserole and cut the rest of the butter into small pieces. Add all the ingredients, grinding in a generous amount of pepper. Beat with a small whisk. Install the casserole over a fairly high heat, using an asbestos pad to protect it from the direct flame, and stir the mixture with the whisk, first slowly, then, as the pieces of butter begin to melt, more rapidly, scraping constantly the sides and the bottom. As soon as the mixture begins to thicken noticeably, remove the casserole from the heat and continue stirring for a minute or so. The consistency should be that of a thick, but "pourable" cream. Serve directly from the cooking utensil onto well-warmed plates.

POACHED EGGS

There is a puzzling cluster of rules surrounding the poaching of an egg: The water should be kept simmering; vinegar should be added to the water to hasten the coagulation of the white; salt should be added to reinforce the vinegar's work; salt should not be added because it toughens the whites or because it counteracts the vinegar's firming action; the eggs should always be broken first into a cup or saucer to ascertain their freshness; they should be poached one at a time in a simulated whirlpool to prevent the white from spreading all over the place and one should deftly snatch the escaping edges of white from the far reaches of the whirlpool, folding them back over the yolk with a spoon; the eggs should be fresh . . .

The freshness is of primordial importance: The yolk stands high; the white clings to it in a mass. You can tell simply by taking an egg in your hand if the white is turning liquid—and, if you are uncertain, shake it gently close to your ear; you will not only feel, you will also hear the yolk rattling around. The other rules, I think, one may take or leave—I prefer to leave them. Water kept at a simmer toughens the underside of the egg and encourages its sticking to the bottom of the pan; vinegar flavors the egg; I sometimes add salt and sometimes not and cannot see that it affects in any way the success of the venture; breaking an egg first into a saucer only encourages the spreading of an unfresh white, dirties a dish, and is a waste of time, encouraging greater separation in the time that the eggs will be cooked; the whirlpool method may be useful in rescuing tired old eggs from total collapse, but tired old eggs should really be relegated to pastry-making (pastry chefs claim to prefer them—the whites mount higher and firmer) or to the garbage pail.

Use the largest low-sided receptacle that you have; a skillet is fine—a still larger *plat à sauter* is better. The larger the quantity of water, the less heat loss is involved with the addition of each egg; don't try to poach more than 4 eggs at a time—the loss of heat will be too great. The low sides are necessary to facilitate the removal of the eggs with a skimmer and a lid is necessary to prevent loss of heat.

Bring the water to a rolling boil, turn the fire off, and break in the eggs, one after another, cracking each on a convenient edge and opening the shell only at the water's surface, permitting the contents to slip softly in. Cover and count about 3 minutes—but don't depend on your timer; check and remove with a large, flat slotted skimming spoon as soon as the white is obviously sufficiently coagulated to be easily handled. Large or very fresh eggs may have to be left for as long as four minutes.

To be served cold, transfer to a shallow pan of cold water and later to a damp towel for paring and draining. To be served hot, remove directly to a damp towel for paring or, if not to be used immediately, transfer to a pan of warm water until ready for use.

Mollet eggs (cooked like hard-boiled eggs but only for 6 minutes) may replace poached eggs in any recipe and, if the eggs are not absolutely fresh, may be preferable. From infinite possibilities (the first edition of *Larousse Gastronomique* lists 115 formulas for poached eggs and they may easily be multiplied by the imagination), the American fancy appears, incomprehensibly, to have settled "once and for all" on eggs "Benedict." Artichoke bottoms, in form and taste, provide a perfect vehicle for the presentation of poached or mollet eggs and one of the happiest methods of finishing the production—and among the simplest—is with a generous coat of Mornay sauce sprinkled with cheese and a bit of butter and then rapidly gratinéed. A bed of vegetable juliènne or purée spread in the artichoke bottom before placing the egg there is a lovely addition. Make one from mushrooms, *soubise,* carrots, zucchinis, turnips, peas, green beans, broad beans, white beans, lentils, chick-peas, sorrel, spinach, black truffle or morel (or, for economy's sake, add pounded truffle peel or chopped butter-stewed morels to a *duxelles* or a mushroom purée or juliènne). To avoid overcooking the eggs, all of the elements in this kind of preparation should be hot and the gratin conducted rapidly beneath a broiler flame.

EGGS IN ASPIC WITH SORREL MOUSSE
(Oeufs en Gelée à la Mousse d'Oseille)

Whatever the garnish, the quality of eggs in aspic depends absolutely on the quality of the jelly. And, however sapid the jelly, all of its delicacy depends on the precise degree of natural gelatin contained in it: The jelly must be only just firm enough to hold its form easily, once unmolded—and it should tremble. No matter how rich and pure the flavor, an excess of gelatin will produce a rubbery and distinctly unpleasant material. A trembling jelly melts luxuriously on the tongue; a rubbery jelly smears it with gum.

A jelly may be prepared exactly like a stock with the addition of a calf's foot (first covered with cold water, brought to a boil for 5 minutes, drained and rinsed before being added to the other ingredients), but the most succulent of jellies is essentially a by-product of several different preparations. A plentiful veal stock (the meat from which may be removed when done and put into a tomato sauce, sorrel sauce, *blanquette,* etc., or simply accompanied by boiled vegetables, like a *pot-au-feu*) can be subsequently used to moisten a *pot-au-feu* (including gelatinous cuts—shank, oxtail, shoulder) and, still again, to moisten a *poule-au-pot* (see page 283; or chicken parts may be thrown into the pot from time to time during the other preparations. For each subsequent preparation, the stock, completely cleared of all fat when cold, should be warmed only enough to melt before adding the meat; vegetables should be added to each new preparation, but the head of garlic and the cloves should be eliminated. You will judge from tasting whether a new bouquet garni should be added each time and what and how much it should contain. Water may have to be added to provide sufficient moistening. I often keep a stock of this sort for weeks on end, using it, supplementing it, and, when flavor and gelatinous content coincide in the correct degree of concentration (the jelly quite firm, inasmuch as it will be somewhat lengthened by an addition of wine, the flavor rich but not so concentrated as to resemble a *demi-glace*), profiting to prepare some eggs in jelly. Obviously, one need not piously await the ideal moment; reduction can bring it about. A stock that is to be kept, unused, for some time should be reboiled every 2 or 3 days, simmered for about 15 minutes with regular skimming, returned to a non-metallic (unless it be stainless steel) container, cooled, and kept uncovered in the refrigerator. Submitted two or three times to this purifying process, the stock rapidly bypasses the respectable meat-jelly stage, becoming a *demi-glace,* invaluable for enriching sauces but too rich and too gelatinous to serve as a jelly. (To prepare a *sauce demi-glace,* which is nothing more than an honest *Espagnole,* it should be thickened slightly with a flour and butter roux before arriving at the *demi-glace* stage, simmered, and skimmed—or "skinned"—for a good hour; a bit of tomato is often added to enrich the color and to hasten the purification. Reduced to a meat glaze [*glace de viande*] by progressive transferrals to smaller saucepans and continued reduction to the state of a thick syrup [cooled, it is the consistency of fairly hard rubber; it can be kept, refrigerated, almost indefinitely and is one of the sauce-enrichening standbys of classical cuisine]. It should not be imagined that it undergoes no physical change other than that of concentration: dilution cannot transform it back into what it once was.)

The veal- stock aspic	1 veal hock 2 pounds veal shank (chicken backs and necks may also be added) 4 quarts cold water 1 medium onion stuck with 2 cloves 10 ounces carrots, peeled
Bouquet garni	Thyme (several branches or a good teaspoonful tied into a bit of cloth) 1 bay leaf 1 branch celery 1 pound leeks (or the green parts of 2 pounds) 1 handful parsley, preferably Italian, including a root, if possible (a small parsnip can be added to the broth if no parsley root is available) (a bit of oregano and savory may be added) 1 unpeeled head of garlic Small handful coarse (or Kosher) salt

Cover the meats and bones with the cold water and bring slowly to a boil—it is best that the water take nearly an hour to arrive at the boiling point. Skim several times, adding a bit of cold water after each skimming, until no more scum mounts to the surface. Add all the other ingredients; the bouquet garni, which should be a good bit larger than one's fist, tied firmly with several rounds of string spiraled up and down its length. Return to the boiling point, skim once more, and regulate the heat so that, with the lid slightly ajar, the water's surface is sustained at a light shiver.

Veal shank, after 2 hours of cooking, will have given of its best while remaining still serviceable for a family dinner, whereas the hock will have only begun to render its gelatin. It may be left alone to cook longer or it may be cooled in the stock and recooked with an eventual *pot-au-feu.*

If the contents remain undisturbed throughout the cooking process, care being taken never to permit the broth to reach a full boil, and if the same respect is applied to succeeding preparations of *pot-au-feu* or *poule-au-pot,* the bouillon, carefully decanted, will be initially honey-toned and will subsequently become limpid caramel. Clarification enervates, sucking the vigor from a meat jelly or a consommé, leaving a certain flaccidity where before there was vibrance. Its only raison d'être is to redeem a transparency originally sacrificed to sloppy methods.

A jelly should be completely cleared of any trace of fat, the cold, jelled surface first cleared with a spoon and then wiped with a clean cloth that has been dipped into hot water and wrung out.

The eggs in aspic	2 to 3 cups meat jelly (depending on the size of the molds), slightly firmer than the consistency eventually desired
	Decorative elements (fragments of canned pimento, rings sliced from pitted black olives, chopped parsley, blanched tarragon leaves, etc.)
	Fresh tarragon (optional)
	3 or 4 tablespoons of a fine-quality fortified wine of your choice (port, Madeira, or sherry)
	8 poached eggs

Rinse the molds (porcelain ramekins, individual Pyrex custard molds, etc.) in cold water and pour a tablespoonful of melted jelly into each, adding at the same time whatever fragments of décor have been chosen. Put them to set in the refrigerator.

If the jelly is to be perfumed with tarragon, add a branch or two, bring the jelly to a boil, and leave to steep until almost entirely cooled before discarding the tarragon and adding the wine. Otherwise, heat it only enough to melt, leaving it to recool before stirring in the wine. Place a poached, cooled, trimmed egg in each mold and pour over jelly to completely cover. If you are in a hurry, place the molds on a bed of cracked or shaved ice before returning them to the refrigerator—never try to make them set in the freezer; the outside will begin to freeze before the center "takes."

Unmold by running the tip of a knife around the edges and jarring the mold, upside down, abruptly against the palm of your hand. Arrange the unmolded eggs in a shallow serving dish, the bottom of which is garnished with a bed of sorrel mousse.

The sorrel	10 ounces sorrel, picked over, washed, parboiled for a
mousse	couple of seconds, drained
	2 tablespoons butter
	⅔ cup firm meat jelly
	Salt, pepper
	½ cup heavy cream

Stew the sorrel in butter, gently, without salting, stirring regularly with a wooden spoon for 20 minutes or until fairly dry, add ½ cup of the jelly and reduce, stirring, by something over half—to a consistent, semiliquid purée. Grind in pepper, purée through a fine sieve, stir in the remaining jelly, and taste for salt, remembering that the addition of the cream will attenuate the saltiness. Embed the container in a larger bowl containing cracked ice and stir until the mixture shows signs of beginning to thicken. Stir in the cream, slightly more than half whipped, but not stiff (which would lend a dry, cottony quality to the mousse), and pour into the eventual serving dish. Refrigerate until firm before placing the eggs on top.

HARD-BOILED EGGS

Hard-boiled eggs should be at least 4 or 5 days old; too fresh (a rare circumstance), they are impossible to peel. It is said that they must be room temperature before being put to cook, but, inasmuch as they form a part very often of last-minute-decision preparations, this rule cannot always be respected and I doubt that the dish is the worse for it. Many claim that the only correct way to hard-boil an egg is to lower it into rapidly boiling water and cook it for exactly 9 minutes. I prefer to begin the eggs in cold water, bringing it to a boil over medium heat and leaving it just under a simmer for 10 to 12 minutes, depending on the size of the eggs, their number, the quantity of water, etc. (The quantity of water and the number of eggs affect the length of time necessary for the water to come to a boil, and the longer it takes to come to a boil the less time the eggs should remain at the boiling point.) It seems to me that, done this way, there is less danger of the shell's cracking (particularly should the egg be refrigerated) and that the white remains tenderer. Whatever your method, the important thing is to avoid overcooking, which dries and dulls the flavor of the yolk, coating it at the same time a disgraceful blackish green, and turns the white to rubber. If, through misjudging the time, the very heart of the yolk should remain slightly liquid, that is no problem—it is at least as good that way.

GRATIN OF HARD-BOILED EGGS IN CREAMED SORREL
(Gratin d'Oeufs Durs à la Crème d'Oseille)
(for 4 or 6)

10 ounces sorrel
½ cup butter (in all)
1 cup heavy cream
1 cup stale bread, crusts removed, crumbled
Salt, pepper
6 hard-boiled eggs, peeled and halved

Pick over the sorrel. If it is young and tender, cut it into a fine *chiffonade* (shred) and stew it gently, salted, in 3 tablespoons of butter (if older, plunge the leaves first into boiling water, drain them the moment the water returns to a boil, and then stew in butter), stirring regularly, for about 20 minutes or until the liquid has evaporated and the sorrel has melted into a purée. Stir in the cream, a little at a time, permitting it to absorb the sorrel and thicken before adding more; grind in pepper and taste for salt.

While the sorrel is stewing, put the breadcrumbs to cook in 4 tablespoons of butter over a low flame, stirring or tossing regularly until they are lightly golden.

Arrange the halved eggs in a buttered gratin dish just large enough to hold them, placed cut surface up, side by side. Spoon over the hot sauce, evenly masking all the eggs, sprinkle the sautéed breadcrumbs regularly over the entire surface, and bake in a hot (400°) oven for about 15 minutes or until well heated through and the surface is lightly browned.

EGGS STUFFED WITH SORREL
(Oeufs Farcis à l'Oseille)
(for 4)

¼ cup olive oil
6 ounces tender young sorrel, stems removed, washed, sponged dry in a
  towel, and finely chopped
6 hard-boiled eggs
1 cup freshly grated Parmesan
Salt, pepper

Oil the bottom of a gratin dish with 1 tablespoon of olive oil, line with a third of the chopped sorrel, and sprinkle lightly with salt. Halve the eggs and, with a fork, mash together the yolks, the remaining sorrel, three quarters of the cheese, and salt and pepper to taste; then work in 2 or 3 tablespoons of olive oil—enough to bind the mixture. Stuff the halved whites with the mixture, packing gently and mounding the stuffing with a teaspoon. Arrange them on the bed of sorrel, sprinkle with the remaining Parmesan, dribble over a bit of olive oil, and bake in a hot oven (400° to 425°) for about 15 minutes.

HARD-BOILED EGGS WITH POTATOES
(Oeufs Durs aux Pommes de Terre)
(for 4)

Coming upon this rough little dish brushing shoulders with the sometimes extravagant refinements of Ali Bab's monumental *Gastronomie Pratique* is a bit like being offered a beer to quench one's thirst after having spent days tasting in the cellars of Champagne. He notes, "This dish, which I had occasion to taste in the country, seemed excellent to me after a long walk." He apparently made no attempt to re-create the object of this sentimental memory in his own kitchen, for the proportions given are completely fantasist.

The preparation is typically Lyonnaise in spirit, heart- and soul-warming, but it should be thought of as a winter's supper dish, perhaps accompanied by a bitter green salad and followed by a cheese, with no further adornment.

2 pounds potatoes, boiled in their skins
2 tablespoons finely chopped shallots (gray, if possible)
½ cup butter
6 hard-boiled eggs
Salt, pepper
2 or 3 tablespoons wine vinegar (depending on strength)
⅓ cup chopped parsley

The moment the potatoes are cooked, put the shallots to cook with the butter over a very low flame—they should soften and yellow without the butter's browning.

Peel the potatoes, hot, the moment they are out of their water, holding each in a towel to protect your hand and slicing them onto a heated serving platter. Slice the eggs thickly and gently mix with the potatoes, breaking them no more than necessary.

When the shallots are soft, sprinkle with salt and pepper, turn the flame up a bit, throw in the parsley, and, a couple of seconds later, add the vinegar and pour the contents of the pan all over the potatoes and eggs.

GRATIN OF ARTICHOKES AND STUFFED EGGS
(Gratin d'Artichauts aux Oeufs Farcis)
(for 6)

8 medium-large artichoke bottoms (see page 173)
About ⅓ cup butter
10 to 12 ounces mushrooms, wiped clean or rapidly washed

Salt, pepper, lemon
6 hard-boiled eggs
1 cup freshly grated Parmesan and Swiss Gruyère
Béchamel (based on 1 quart milk; see page 164)

Put the two least attractive of the pared artichokes (they will be puréed) to cook 10 minutes before adding the others so that, when the others are barely done, all may be left together to cool in their cooking liquid. Remove the chokes and stew the 6 firm bottoms gently in butter, a dab of butter added to the inside of each, covered, in stainless steel or a large, low earthenware vessel. Keep the flame very low and turn them a couple of times over a period of about 20 minutes to ½ hour. Set aside.

Chop or pass the mushrooms through the medium blade of a Mouli-juliènne and toss them, over a high flame, in 2 tablespoons of butter, seasoned, for 3 or 4 minutes, or until they have reabsorbed all their essence, the liquid completely evaporated. Sprinkle over a few drops of lemon juice, stir, and divide among the 6 artichoke bottoms, spreading a layer into each.

Purée the two "unattractive," well-cooked bottoms through a fine stainless-steel sieve.

After peeling the eggs, choose the point at which the yolk, barely visible, has settled closest to the wall of the white (only absolutely fresh eggs retain the yolk in the center) and slice off, lengthwise, about one third of the egg, removing the thinnest section of the wall. Chop the white parts removed and add them to the artichoke purée. Sieve the yolks. Season and mash the egg and artichoke purées together, adding the brown butter in which the other artichoke bottoms have cooked. Taste for salt and fill the boat-shaped lower sections of the whites with the purée, molding it firmly, well mounded, with a teaspoon, into the original form of the egg and place each egg in an artichoke bottom, pressing it gently into the bed of mushroom juliènne. Arrange them in a lightly buttered gratin dish.

Stir about two thirds of the cheese into the hot *béchamel,* spoon it regularly over the eggs, coating them evenly, sprinkle the surface with the remaining cheese, and bake in a hot oven (400° to 425°) for 20 minutes, or until the sauce is bubbling and the surface well colored.

EGG AND TURNIP GRATIN
(Gratin d'Oeufs Durs aux Navets)
(for 4)

1 pound turnips, tender, firm, crisp, non-fibrous
Salt
¼ cup butter (for the turnips)
2 tablespoons flour
3 cups milk
1 cup stale but not dried-out bread, crusts removed, crumbled
¼ cup butter (for the crumbs)
Pepper
6 hard-boiled eggs

It is not through disdain that *oeufs à la tripe* are not presented here—they are very much in the spirit of the text and among the most wonderful of egg dishes. It seemed to me, simply, that the preparations are so nearly identical that it would be senseless to present both the turnip gratin and *à la tripe* and, whereas recipes for eggs *à la tripe* abound, this will be found no place else.

Peel the turnips thickly, grate coarsely or pass them through the medium blade of a Mouli-juliènne, salt them in layers, leave for ½ hour, squeeze, first in their liquid and then, drained, squeeze thoroughly and repeatedly to rid them of all water. Cook gently in butter, tossing or stirring regularly, until tender—about 15 minutes.

Sprinkle over the flour and continue to cook, stirring, for another 3 or 4 minutes, then add the milk slowly, stirring all the time. Bring to a boil and regulate the heat to a simmer, stirring occasionally over a period of ½ hour.

At the same time, cook the breadcrumbs gently in ¼ cup butter, tossing or stirring regularly, until lightly colored.

Taste the turnip sauce for salt, add pepper, and spoon over halved hard-boiled eggs arranged in a lightly buttered gratin dish. Sprinkle over the buttered crumbs and bake in a hot oven until the sauce is bubbling and the surface colored—15 to 20 minutes.

FISH

O F the hundreds of fish that issue from American waters, I
know most by name only, a shameful lacuna that I share with
most Americans. A livresque acquaintanceship breeds frustrations,
not only because a valuable judgment depends on getting ahold
of the thing, feeling it and tasting it, but also because of our
maddening habit of naming fish: A number of different fish may
share a single name or a single fish may be known by a number
of different names, some of which inevitably apply to other fish as
well. Webster defines "bass" as "any of numerous edible spiny-finned
fishes"—presumably the striped sea bass is that which most resembles
that French Atlantic *bar* or the Mediterranean *loup,* but there is, as
well, a fresh-water fish called striped bass and an ocean fish called
black bass (as a child I loved a lake fish that we called black
bass . . .); "sole" (genuine sole is called "Dover" and does not exist
in American waters) apparently means any flat fish of Picassoesque
profile; whiting, silver hake, sea mullet, kingfish, and Pacific hake
would seem, to some mysterious extent, to be interchangeable appellations—although silver hake, according to my sources, grows to a
size of 3 or 4 pounds (and is probably the whiting with which I am
familiar and which is nearly identical to the French *merlan*) and
kingfish to 30 pounds . . . And so forth.

The reputation of variety and goodness enjoyed particularly by the fish of Mediterranean waters may be justified: its fame is certainly indebted to a loyal folklorique tradition and literature, to a long and civilized culinary tradition that precisely defines the various treatments to which each species best responds; to the intimate acquaintanceship of the cooks with the local water life; and, finally, to a general insistence that fish be absolutely fresh—serious shoppers only buy fish that have been fished the same morning.

Our habits of merchandising, of buying, and of living unhappily preclude, for the most part, the possibility of a fish's leaping directly from its habitat into the frying pan—and to the extent to which this is true the subtlest and most important part of fresh (uncured) fish cookery is lost to us. All waters are peopled (or were, at least, until very recently) with a wonderful variety of good fish whose various qualities correspond closely to those in other parts of the world; I don't doubt that a greater practical experience would permit me to abandon the depressing habit of making constant comparisons in search of analogies or substitutions.

FISH STEWS

The line dividing a soup from a stew is often infirm; some of the preparations discussed here may belong in the soup chapter—I don't know.

Fish stews differ from meat stews (see pages 287–296) only insofar as most fish (octopus and squid excepted) require a very short cooking period, being, in fact, cooked when thoroughly heated through; eel *matelote,* octopus *daube, coq-au-vin,* and *Bourguignon* are but a few variations on a same theme; *tripes à la Niçoise,* veal *marengo,* lobster *à l'Américaine,* and *estocaficada* on another that differs essentially only in the choice of moistening agents.

The Mediterranean coast is particularly rich in fish soup or stew traditions. A number of them may be described as fish in tomato sauce or fish and tomato soup, depending on whether water or a *fumet* has been added or not. Such is an *aigo-sau* (literally "water-salt")—one or several "white" fish boiled in an onion, tomato, and potato soup, the Provençal fennel and dried orange peel added to the usual bouquet, accompanied by the tempestuous red pepper and garlic *rouille*. *Bouillabaisse* is never far from mind—the concept representing a sort of absolute value, a yardstick by which other fish stews may be measured. When it is said of an *aigo-sau* that it is a preparation for convalescents or persons with delicate stomachs, one may understand that, whatever its virtues, its personality is less startling than that of the *bouillabaisse* and its digestibility relatively greater. *Bourride* is an *aigo-sau,* potatoes eliminated, thickened by slowly stirring the broth into an *aïoli* and continuing to stir over very low heat until lightly thickened, then poured over the fish and crusts of bread (the fish may be poached in a light-bodied fish *velouté*— its initial body will discourage its breaking while being thickened with the *aïoli;* some people enrich it unorthodoxly with the addition of a certain amount of cream).

I have had my say about *bouillabaisse* in the *French Menu Cookbook:* the Toulonnais add potatoes and mussels to their version and, in Martigues, a "black *bouillabaisse*" is made by adding small cuttlefish with their ink; *Revesset* is chopped and boiled spinach, chard, and sorrel, small fish—sardines, fresh anchovies, etc.—added a few minutes before serving over garlic-rubbed dried bread slices; *catigot* is an inland eel and red wine stew that may or may not be tomatoed and in which the red wine is not cooked long enough—when corrected, it becomes, on the one hand, a simplified *matelote* or, on the other, eel in *raito*.

On the Atlantic coast, the fennel and orange peel disappear from the bouquet, butter replaces the olive oil, and a certain amount of white wine is a constant. The fish remain much the same—for any of these stews the choice may be made among hake, haddock, halibut, skate, lemon sole, grey sole, conger eel, fresh cod, mullets, ocean perch, black drum, fluke, perhaps shark and sea squab, and, undoubtedly a great many more. Given enough time to cook, cuttlefish or squid are always good in a stew, but you had best eliminate the strong-flavored and fatty fishes except when they are specifically recommended for a recipe. Mussels or clams may be added. They are all, originally, fishermen's stews, and one of the principles is the use of cheap fish. The Charentaise *chaudrée* is made by putting everything in the pot together—fish, water, white wine, salt (when sea water is not used), chopped onion, crushed garlic, and herbs—and then boiling until done, swirling in butter and serving over dried bread, of course. The Breton *cotriade* (recipe following) is a rough country potato and onion soup with a variety of fish thrown in when half cooked.

Matelote is the best known of fresh-water fish stews. It is usually made of eels, but sometimes with perch and carp or with all three. It is made exactly like a red-wine meat stew (except in Alsace, where the local white wine is substituted), with a Bourguignon (little onions, mushrooms, lardons) garnish. The presence of lardons makes no sense to me, and the traditional method of sautéing the fish, cooking it for a quarter of an hour in the red wine and then putting it aside for an hour or two while finishing the sauce, gives much less happy results than if it is prepared simply as a *raito* (see page 136), the olives and capers being replaced by butter-stewed little onions and rapidly sautéed mushrooms.

The Burgundian *pauchouse* is rather particular (restaurant versions often include salt pork, flour, and cream, all certainly heretical). It was traditionally made of a thin, nasty, extremely acid little white wine, the vines of which have long since been pulled up. Those who remember it claim the wine was practically undrinkable but that *pauchouses* are no longer the same: Pack fish heads and debris (bluegills, crappies, perch, carp, wall-eyed pike, etc.) into the bottom of a pot with herbs, salt, lots of crushed or broken-up pepper, a couple of heads of unpeeled garlic cloves, the pieces of fish on top, as little open space as possible remaining; pour over a light-bodied, young, very dry white wine to cover; cook at a rolling boil for about 15 minutes; remove fish pieces to a heated deep platter and keep them warm while passing the contents of the pot through a sieve with firm pressure from the pestle and reducing the liquid at a continuing rolling boil; whisk in a generous quantity of butter away from the heat and pour over the fish . . . All very well, but I am happier preparing a *fumet* with the heads and whatnot and poaching the fish, rather than boiling it at a roll.

BRETON CHOWDER
(Cotriade)
(for 4 or 5)

Any kind of fish may find its way into a *cotriade*. If small, tender-fleshed fish—pilchard, sardines, smelts—are included, they should be whole and added only 5 or 6 minutes before removal from the flame. Originally, the smoky flavor from the bonfire over which the kettle of fish was cooked no doubt enhanced the rough, direct, soul-warming character of the thing. Cider is the usual accompaniment—some readers may share my preference for a Muscadet or other light, dry, young white wine.

One of the particularities of a *cotriade* lies in the liquid's being undersalted. The fish, after being removed from the pot, is then salted by pouring over a ladle or so of the bouillon in which has been dissolved a handful of coarse sea salt. The heavily salted liquid is drained off immediately, and the process is repeated three or four times. The fish absorbs the salt with a certain avidity and must not be left long in contact with the liquid. I much prefer, rather than salting the fish before serving, to distribute small bowls or ramekins of the salty bouillon to each guest, along with others containing the vinegar-crushed pepper mixture; the ritual aspect is attractive and the individual may, dipping first in one, then in the other, season to taste, biteful by biteful.

> 1 pound sweet onions, peeled and quartered
> 3 tablespoons olive oil (or, for authenticity, a handful of chopped fat salt pork)
> 2 pounds firm-fleshed potatoes, peeled and cut into large pieces
> Thyme, bay leaf, oregano
> Salt (lightly)
> 2 quarts boiling water
> 2 pounds fish (2 or more varieties, large fish cut into approximately 1-inch slices)

Accompani- ment	Dried bread slices
	2 tablespoons peppercorns, coarsely crushed in a mortar and mixed with 1 cup red wine vinegar
	A handful of coarse salt dissolved in 2 or 3 ladles of the broth

Cook the onions in a large, heavy saucepan with the oil (or the half-melted chopped fat) over medium heat for a minute or so, add the potatoes and herbs and continue cooking, stirring regularly, for 8 or 10 minutes or until the onions begin to color lightly, salt, pour over the boiling water and, as the potatoes begin to turn tender— about 15 minutes—add the fish (holding back the soft-fleshed varieties). Continue to cook at a light boil for another 10 or 15 minutes. Remove the fish and vegetables to a hot serving platter, prepare the accompanying salted broth, and serve the rest of the broth apart. Pour the broth, over the crusts of bread first placed in the soup plates, then the fish and vegetables served atop after the bread has been soaked.

POACHED FISH *(POISSON POCHÉ)*

Rules vary depending on the lawmakers; some claim that only fresh-water fish should be treated in court bouillon, salt-water fish being poached in salt water; furthermore, different court bouillons are often recommended for different fish. As far as I'm concerned, fresh fish of any sort is good poached in salt water; it is better if a bay leaf and a branch of thyme are added; and it is best if treated in a wine court bouillon, the specific proportions of the ingredients not being important. Onion, thyme, bay, white wine, and water are the constants (if dill is used, I prefer to eliminate other herbs); fennel and oregano are also particularly good fish herbs. The following recipe should be considered symbolic—don't bother to weigh vegetables or measure liquids (fill the saucepan a third or half full with water and when the vegetables are half cooked, pour in as much

wine as you like). Leek or celery may be added; add 10 or 15 peppercorns if you like, but only a few minutes before straining—or, if the
court bouillon is not strained, add them only when the fish is put in
to poach.

[handwritten: + perfection! prep: ~25 min. 1/24/15 w/ Winston. Start to finish, incl. beurre blanc, ~1/2 hrs. st recipe made from this cookbook. We poached petrale sole, w/ beurre blanc (see next page). I'd do swordfish next time.]

6 cups water
Salt
3 or 4 cloves of garlic, crushed
4 ounces carrots, peeled, thinly sliced
4 ounces sweet onions, peeled, thinly sliced
Parsley (including root), bay leaf, thyme, fennel (good handful of
  branches, leaves, flowers, depending on season), oregano
2 cups white wine *[handwritten: try Atalon Sauv. Blanc.]*

[handwritten: Try 1 sliced leek, too.]

Bring the water to a boil, add all the ingredients except the wine
(whose acidity will prevent the vegetables from cooking and per-
fuming the liquid to the fullest degree), simmer, covered, for about
15 minutes, then add the white wine, return to a boil, and continue
to cook, covered, for another 20 minutes or so. *[handwritten: or at a simmer]*

A court bouillon in which fish has been poached is a light *fumet,*
which may form a splendid base for a soup or a sauce.

Crayfish (if you can find them—they are often sold in the United
States for fish bait, the only drawback being their smallness) are never
so good as when simply cooked in a court bouillon, *à la nage,* the
central tail flap of each being first dislodged, the attached thread of
intestine gently pulled out (an hour's milk bath is said to remove the
intestinal bitterness, but I have not been happy with the results),
plunged alive into the boiling liquid, cooked, covered, at a simmer,
for no longer than 5 minutes, and left to steep, covered, for another
quarter of an hour before serving. The same observation is valuable
for lobster, which, in the face of recent prices, one can hardly afford
to treat otherwise lest its flavor dissipate in a sauce or its flesh turn
coriaceous beneath the broiler flame (for 1½-pound lobsters, simmer
for about 10 minutes once the court bouillon has returned to the
boiling point, then leave to half cool in the liquid). Both crayfish
and lobsters are (to me) better warm than either cold or hot; drawn
butter may be added to their court bouillon accompaniment.

Crustaceans aside, poaching means cooking, not at the boiling
point or at a simmer, but at a temperature slightly below that of a

117

simmer. Fish slices (no less than an inch thick) are immersed in the hot court bouillon and, if the container is large and heavy, retaining heat well, heating may be discontinued as soon as the liquid approaches the boiling point, the pan kept tightly covered until the poaching time is up. Large whole fish or fish sections are covered with tepid court bouillon, which is slowly returned to a near boil, the heat radically adjusted so that the boiling point may not be reached.

An explanation of timing for poached fish seems always to have frustrated cookbook writers, even such masters as Prosper-Montagné and Escoffier slyly sidestepping the issue and contenting themselves with the observation that the cooking time should be shortened for those fish destined to cool in their court bouillon. I am the more impressed by a note in James Beard's *American Cookery* (he gives credit to the Canadian Department of Fisheries): "Measure the thickness of the fish at its thickest point and estimate ten minutes cooking time per inch, whatever the cooking method. Thus, if you are poaching a whole salmon that measures 4 inches at its thickest point, you will poach it forty minutes. If a fillet is half an inch thick you will sauté it or poach it 5 minutes. To broil a steak of salmon or halibut 1½ inches thick, allow 7½ minutes a side."

Restaurant habits of tangling up a variety of fish, forcemeats, and sauces (sole, lobster, pike *quenelles, sauce vin blanc,* and *sauce à l'Américaine* is one of the most often found combinations and is named variously) rarely fail to confuse and tire the palate; a perfectly poached fish accompanied by a single and uncomplicated sauce is always more exciting.

A *sauce bâtarde* (see page 326) may be prepared rapidly at the moment of serving; replace the water in the recipe by the fish's poaching liquid. Capers are often added.

The following green sauce is beautiful with either cold or hot poached fish.

GREEN SAUCE
(Sauce aux Herbes)
(for 4 to 6)

1 tablespoon (or more to taste) capers, rinsed, drained
Salt, pepper
6 anchovy filets (preferably 3 whole anchovies in salt, soaked, fileted, rinsed well, sponged dry, then chopped)
1 teaspoon finely chopped fresh tarragon
Handful finely chopped parsley
½ pound each spinach and the green parts of chard leaves (parboiled together, the chard put to cook 5 minutes earlier, counting 7 or 8 minutes in all, then squeezed dry and chopped)
2 ounces stale bread without crusts, soaked in warm water, squeezed thoroughly
3 hard-boiled egg yolks
⅓ cup olive oil
1 teaspoon (or more to taste) vinegar or lemon juice

A large marble mortar is much the easiest to work with—lacking that, use a wooden bowl. Pound the capers to a paste with the seasonings, add the anchovies, pound, add the tarragon, the parsley, and the greens, pounding to a purée. Pound and stir in the soaked bread, then the egg yolks, and, when the mixture is absolutely smooth and uniform, begin dribbling in the olive oil, stirring vigorously and uniformly with the pestle as if mounting a mayonnaise. Taste for seasoning and stir in the vinegar or lemon juice to taste. If prepared ahead of time, the emulsion may not hold, traces of oil separating and appearing at the surface; give it a rapid beating with the pestle just before serving.

NANTAIS BUTTER SAUCE
(Beurre Blanc)

A good sauce for all poached fish. In the region of its origin it classically accompanies poached northern pike and is made with Breton salt butter (unsalted butter of the best quality is always superior to

119

salted butter in France and I have never made it with salted butter—
were one to use it, the salt should be eliminated from the recipe). If
using the reduced herb vinegar recommended on page 45, add a little
more white wine and a bit less vinegar. The color of the vinegar is
not specified—if red vinegar is used, the sauce will have a vaguely
violet cast, displeasing to some, but good red wine vinegar is usually
of better quality than the white vinegars. The quality of shallots is
not mentioned either, because the common, or gray, shallot, despite
its name, is hard come by. If you can find them (smaller, more
warped in shape, the skin a hard shell of a pale gray-beige with a rose
cast), don't hesitate to replace the harsh red shallots by these in any
recipe calling for shallots.

The utter simplicity of the thing, the paucity of elements, the
absence of a binder . . . have engendered a wariness, distrust, or un-
belief, than which there are no solider foundations on which to con-
struct a myth. The story goes that only a very special kind of culinary
genius with an inborn and mysterious twist of the wrist can produce
a successful *beurre blanc;* the fact appears to be that few have ever
tried, assuming it to be a lost cause. And restaurant *beurres blancs*
suggest that the infidel ranks count a heavy professional population,
for many are really light *sabayons,* an egg yolk having been sneaked
in to hold the thing together or a few breadcrumbs added to the reduction to reinforce the body.

For years, La Mère Michel, who is now retired, was the undis-
puted *beurre blanc* queen of Paris (for a time there was a pretender
whose version I tasted only once—it was a *sabayon*). Her little *beurre
blanc* temple in the rue Rennequin could seat but twenty-odd clients;
the menu was short (I only remember pike, turbot, and a couple of
other poached fish, all accompanied by the famous *beurre blanc,* a
tarragon chicken sauté, and a kidney sauté—a good Muscadet and a
good Beaujolais) and the kitchen, visible from the dining room, was
a cubbyhole most of whose space was consumed by an antique range.
Throughout the service, Madame Michel stood just inside the entrance to the kitchen whisking up *beurre blanc* after *beurre blanc,*
each impeccable, in a small, chipped, and battered saucepan of the
trashy, enameled, dimestore variety. I believe that she was quite
proud to be able to exhibit this bit of hardware, for it lent force to the
legend of her magic wrist (about which much was written in those
years). To suggest that her secret lay elsewhere than in her wrist is

not to detract from a very genuine talent and taste: She knew every square inch of her stove by heart—the precise quality of heat emanating from any given point of its surface; when working with a cast-iron kitchen range that is also an old friend, ambrosia may be concocted in tin cans.

With a less loyal stove surface, the qualities of the saucepan assume greater importance (small and heavy—copper, enameled cast-ironware, earthenware . . .) and one's control of the heat must be precise; use an asbestos pad if working over a naked gas flame. Work in a relaxed manner—use a small whisk, holding it casually, as a pencil is usually held (thumb and index outstretched, the whisk stayed by the knuckle side of the third finger, the two others curled out of the way). The sauce will break only if the heat is too high. The proportions given produce a fairly strong sauce whose flavor may be attenuated by the addition of a couple of ounces more butter.

Leftover *beurre blanc,* chilled, can satisfactorily replace a *marchand de vin* butter, chunks served over grilled steak—or it may be transformed into a *sabayon,* crumbled into a saucepan with a bit of cold water and one or two egg yolks, depending on the amount of butter, whisked until mounted in a *bain-marie,* the water kept beneath a boil.

1/24/15 divine ante! no need to add more butter at end.

¼ cup very finely chopped shallots (lightly measured—not packed)
¼ cup wine vinegar
¼ cup dry white wine
Salt
½ pound unsalted butter (or more), cut into tiny cubes

Combine the shallots, vinegar, wine, and salt in a small, heavy saucepan, bring to a boil, and reduce at a simmer until no more free liquid is in evidence, only the heavy film of moist and slightly mushy shallots lining the bottom of the pan (if working over a gas flame, use the asbestos pad during the reduction—it will then be tempered by the heat). Remove the pan from the heat for a half minute or so— long enough to cool slightly. Regulate the heat to *very* low, add about an ounce of the cut-up butter to the pan, and return it to the heat, whisking. Add more butter, approximately an ounce at a time (7 or 8 additions) as each addition begins to disappear, only a trace of solid butter in sight. As the last addition disappears into the sauce, remove the saucepan from the heat, continuing to whisk for a few seconds. The sauce is a rich, creamy emulsion—not thick but with a distinct, firm body. It is only warm and, to avoid loss of heat, is best served directly from the saucepan. If form dictates the use of a sauceboat, warm it first to the approximate temperature of the sauce—no more.

"FISH IN SAUCE" *(POISSON EN SAUCE)*

The term is arbitrary. It is most often used in a discussion of wine and food marriages to embrace a preparation-type that best accompanies a nervous and fruity, but full-bodied white wine—one of the white Burgundies, for instance. In that context, it nearly always means a sauce with a *fumet* and/or *velouté* base.

Fumet (see page 78) is stock; it is the preceding court bouillon packed full of fish carcasses and strained when finished. *Velouté* is *fumet* lightly bound with flour and butter roux and cooked gently, reduced and skimmed, over a period of ½ hour.

Most preparations in this category are fish (filets best lend themselves) poached in a relatively small amount of *fumet,* whose reduction then serves as the base or as an enrichment for the final sauce. (Fish loaves, *mousselines,* turbans, molded *paupiettes,* "poached dry" in a *bain-marie,* may be accompanied by the same sauces, prepared separately, reduced *fumet* replacing the reduced poaching liquid. A *velouté,* sometimes creamed, often combined with a certain amount of *duxelles,* is the usual sauce for fish gratins—raw filets arranged in buttered gratin dish either on a bed of the sauce or of a garnishing element such as stewed sorrel, mushroom purée, etc., sprinkled often with white wine or sherry, covered with the hot gratin sauce, sprinkled with butter-cooked breadcrumbs, baked in a hot oven until sauce is bubbling and surface lightly colored—about 15 minutes.)

The sauces are of three kinds: (1) The poaching liquid is drained into a saucepan, reduced over a high flame to a syrupy consistency, and butter is whisked in away from the heat—there is no *velouté,* only the gelatinous reduction and the emulsion of butter forming the body of the sauce; (2) The poaching liquid is reduced and added to a *velouté* (heavy cream may be added to taste), the sauce may be reduced if necessary, and butter—a couple of tablespoons or 4 or 5 times that much—is whisked in away from the heat; the procedure is identical to that of a *sauce suprême* for poached chicken; (3) The sauce is thickened with egg yolks, either (a) whisked into the partially cooled reduction of *fumet* poaching liquid and mounted (like a hollandaise) with butter in a *bain-marie* or over very low heat, or (b) diluted with a certain amount of partially cooled *velouté,* stirred back into the *velouté* and reduced poaching liquid and finished like a *blanquette,* stirring constantly over low heat and removing from the heat well before the boiling point is reached. (Egg yolks enrich a sauce, but that need not necessarily mean that they improve it. With these fish sauces, egg yolks make the first two less easily digestible while also masking the quality of the *fumet.*)

Mushrooms, if included in the garnish, are usually precooked with a bit of lemon juice, a couple of spoonsful of water, seasonings, and a dab of butter for a couple of minutes, and their cooking liquid may be added to the fish's poaching liquid. Mussels are also a common garnishing element and a part of their liquid (see page 143), the quantity depending on its saltiness, may be joined to the basic *fumet* poaching liquid. Occasionally, as with the *Dugléré* preparations, no *fumet* is used for poaching (the fish is poached with chopped shallots, chopped *fines herbes,* peeled, seeded, chopped tomatoes, and white wine) and a fairly stiff *velouté* is joined to the reduced poaching liquid to add it body before whisking in butter away from the heat. A handful of shredded raw young sorrel leaves added to the sauce a minute or so before it is finished will give a completely different effect than the incorporation of the butter-stewed and puréed sorrel of the following recipe ...

Play around; with the above *données* and your own imagination endless recipes can be created. As long as you remain fearful of the boiling point (don't boil the fish or it will dry out; don't try to incorporate butter into a boiling sauce or it will turn to oil; don't let a sauce containing egg yolks approach a boil or it will break), nothing can go wrong.

FISH FILETS IN CREAMED SORREL SAUCE
(Filets de Poisson à la Crème d'Oseille)
(for 4)

No fish sauce is subtler or more exciting than a creamed *velouté*-sorrel sauce—and it is not fragile; the novice need not be intimidated by a threat of collapse. The initial *velouté* should be very lightly bound with flour (most people overthicken sauces); subsequent reduction and the sorrel purée will give it needed body and the terminal incorporation of butter will suffuse it with velvet. When saucing poached filets, one must naturally profit from the enriching virtues of their poaching liquid to reduce it and add it to the sauce, but a simple *velouté* combined with a sorrel purée, creamed and buttered, remains an exquisite sauce and a perfect accompaniment to fish preparations poached in a *bain-marie* that offer no supplementary cooking liquid of their own.

	About 1 quart fish fumet (see page 78)
Roux for	2 tablespoons flour
velouté	1½ tablespoons butter
	12 grey sole or lemon sole filets
	Salt, pepper
	½ pound sorrel, parboiled for a few seconds, drained, stewed gently in butter for 15 to 20 minutes, and sieved
	About ⅔ cup heavy cream
	About ¼ cup butter cut into small pieces

Put aside about 1 cup of the *fumet* in which to poach the filets and, with the rest, prepare the *velouté* so that it will be ready when the fish is poached: Add the flour to the melted butter in a saucepan and cook gently, stirring, for about a minute without letting it color. Add the *fumet* slowly (away from the heat if it is hot), stirring all the while, and then cook at a very light boil, the saucepan pulled a bit to the side of the heat, for about ½ hour, skimming (skinning) from time to time.

Soak the filets in cold water for a few minutes, sponge them dry, flatten them slightly with the side of a large knife blade, and, skin side up, slit the thin surface membrane of each, diagonally, at approximately 1-inch intervals. Sprinkle lightly with salt, grind over a bit of pepper, and fold each filet in two, membrane inside (slitting and folding prevent deformation while poaching). Choose a low-sided heavy cooking vessel just large enough to hold the folded filets placed side by side; a copper *plat à sauter* is perfect, but a cast-iron enamelware frying pan or an earthenware *poëlon* will do. Arrange the folded filets in the bottom and pour over *fumet* to barely cover (if the quantity has been underestimated, make up the difference with a bit of white wine; if some *fumet* is left over, add it to the *velouté*). Press a buttered round of parchment paper over the surface, cover the pan tightly, and bring to the boiling point, shaking the pan gently from time to time to ensure the liquid's regular absorption of heat and lifting the lid to check progress. As soon as the boiling point is reached, turn off the heat and leave, tightly covered, to poach for about 8 minutes.

While the filets are poaching you should whisk the sorrel purée into the *velouté,* adding as much cream as the sauce can support without becoming too thin, and return it to a boil, reducing a bit, if necessary—more cream may be added along with the reduced poaching liquid if the body will then support it.

Drain the poaching liquid into a saucepan, keeping the filets in the pan or transferring them to a heated serving platter. Reduce the liquid over a high flame to a syrupy consistency, add it to the sauce, remove the sauce from the heat, and whisk in the butter. Pour it over the filets (or simply mask them and serve the remaining sauce apart).

STUFFED BAKED FISH *(POISSON FARCI AU FOUR)*

A fish like the sea bass, with relatively firm flesh and an uncomplicated bone structure, is best for stuffing. It is possible simply to stuff the gutted cavity and sew it up, lace it up with the help of toothpicks or leave it open, but it seems a pity that the stuffing isn't more of an integral part of the preparation as a whole; there is little interpenetration of flavors when a fish is stuffed in this way, and serving it is messy, the stuffing being separated from the flesh by the ribcage-like skeletal structure—the filets must be separated above and below from the backbone and the stuffing spooned out apart. When it is possible to obtain fresh ungutted fish, I prefer to bone it from the back (the bulk of the guts may first be drawn out with one's fingers through the gills, tearing the gills loose first and gently pulling out all attached material), slitting down to each side of the backbone, keeping the blade of the knife in touch with it, cutting through the bone near the base of the head and at about an inch's distance from the tail and working the bone structure free without piercing the abdomen. Boned in this way, the fish may be stuffed, the flesh molded around the stuffing, and baked, back up and open, boat-like.

If the fish has already been gutted and the abdomen slit, carefully work all of the curved bones surrounding the abdominal cavity free, one by one, with your fingers, breaking them loose at their point of attachment to the backbone, then free the backbone from the flesh, slitting to each side of the anal fin and using your fingers and the tip of a small sharp knife to loosen the bones from the flesh toward the back; clip through the bone at the base of the head and near the tail as before and remove it. Tear out the gills. Boned in this way, a fish is cooked on its side.

To stuff a flat fish of the sole or flounder variety, leave the white, underside skin (it protects the flesh while cooking), scraping it well to remove the tiny scales. Rip off the dark topside skin, removing the eyes with it (or ask your fishmonger to do it): Hold a towel or paper towels in each hand to keep the fish from slipping; slit the skin across the base of the tail, start tearing it loose carefully from the flesh in one piece, then grasp it firmly and pull, holding the fish's tail firmly against the tabletop with the heel of your other hand. Keep the fish white skin side down and operate as if you were going to filet it, using, preferably, a sharp, slender, flexible-bladed knife: Cut the length of the lateral line (describing the path of the vertebrae) with the tip of the knife to begin loosening each filet; then, holding the knife firmly and almost flatly against the bone, slice the filet free, down its length, leaving it attached to the flesh and small root bones of the fins. Break the spinal bone at four points by bending the body of the fish (folding it, white skin inside) and free it from the fish, section by section, with fingertips and knife tip. The presentation of

126

a stuffed flat fish is of the prettiest; the form resembles somewhat a partially opened coin purse.

STUFFINGS

The different mixtures suggested for "Stuffed, Split Baked Chicken" (page 382) serve fish well also. An egg-bound bread and butter stuffing generously flavored with chopped *fines herbes* is good. Variations on the classical *mousseline* forcemeat apart, I was surprised, upon gathering together my notes on fish stuffings, to realize to what extent they resemble one another, an abundance of green stuff, in particular, marking each. The following three are characteristic.

(1) For a 2½-pound sea bass: ½ pound chopped whiting filet; green parts of 1 pound chard, parboiled, squeezed dry, chopped; ¼ pound mushrooms, chopped or passed through Mouli-juliènne, and sautéed in butter till dry; 2 ounces crumbled crustless stale bread soaked in ½ cup heavy cream; 1½ ounces finely chopped green onions; 1 teaspoon finely chopped fresh marjoram; handful chopped parsley; 1 egg; salt, pepper, nutmeg. Buttered gratin dish, white wine in bottom; dabs of butter on stuffed fish, covered loosely with aluminum foil; baste regularly after 15 minutes; 35 minutes in 400° oven.

(2) For a 10- to 12-ounce sole: Open 1 quart mussels with white wine, herbs. Stuffing: 2 chopped sole filets; handful parboiled, squeezed, chopped chard; handful finely crumbled soft, crustless bread; finely crumbled oregano; 1 egg; salt, pepper; heavy cream. Buttered gratin dish scattered with chopped shallots, white wine; 20 minutes, hot oven, aluminum foil, basted; reduce basting juices and mussel liquid to syrup; add butter away from heat, add mussels, pour over fish.

(3) For 6 *paupiettes*: 6 sole-type filets, soaked in cold water, sponged dry, flattened, skin-side membrane slit at intervals (as in preceding recipe), each fitted into its own round, buttered ramekin, skin side facing in, forming a circular wall, the bottom of the ramekin remaining uncovered. Stuffing: ½ pound fish filets chopped; 1 pound spinach, parboiled, squeezed dry, chopped; 3 tablespoons softened butter; 3 egg yolks; salt, pepper. Pack stuffing into lined

ramekins, poach in *bain-marie* covered with foil, 375°, 10 to 12 minutes or until centers are firm to the touch; unmold, first onto flat wire or slotted skimming spoon to drain, then slip each onto a bed of creamed mushroom purée, creamed sorrel, or a *velouté*-based sauce (with peeled, seeded, chopped, butter-stewed tomato added, for instance)—or serve them ungarnished, a *beurre blanc* apart.

It is gratifying to note that the cooking times all correspond very closely to the 10-minutes-per-inch theory. The quality of all these rustic stuffings depends on the fish and the green stuff being chopped by hand (2 or 3 minutes' work, in all); puréed mechanically, the fish will be dry and the pleasant, coarse texture of the greens will be destroyed.

HERB-STUFFED BASS IN LETTUCE CASING
(Bar aux Herbes en Chemise)
(for 4 as preliminary course)

Stuffing
½ pound spinach, parboiled, squeezed dry, chopped
2 ounces stale but soft bread, crusts removed, finely crumbled
2 tablespoons softened butter
Handful finely shredded young sorrel leaves
Handful finely chopped parsley
1 teaspoon finely chopped fresh tarragon
Salt, pepper
1 egg

1 sea bass about 1½ pounds, fins clipped at base of flesh, scaled, gutted, gills torn out, boned
1 large head Boston lettuce
Salt, pepper
2 tablespoons butter
2 tablespoons finely chopped shallots
2 tablespoons dry vermouth
⅓ cup dry white wine
⅓ cup heavy cream

Mix the spinach, the bread, and the butter together well first, mashing with a fork, before adding the other ingredients of the stuffing and stirring well. Stuff the fish, pressing filets and stuffing firmly together so as to re-form the fish in the original shape. Place it on its side on the tabletop.

Arrange about 20 of the largest and most perfectly formed lettuce leaves in a saucepan, add salt, pour over boiling water, return to a simmer for a minute or so, and drain, pouring carefully into a sieve or colander so as not to damage the leaves or bunch them up into a mass. Run a bit of cold water over to cool them and delicately, one by one, lift them out and spread them on a towel to drain.

Wrap the fish from head to tail (muzzle and tail tip remaining exposed): First salt and pepper the fish's surface; arrange overlapping leaves of lettuce the length of the belly section, the rib ends gently tucked beneath the fish and the fragile leaf extremities pressed to the surface. Repeat the process along the length of the back, tucking rib tips under and pressing the leaves well into place. Turn the fish over, placing it in an elongated buttered gratin dish, the bottom of which has been scattered with chopped shallots; salt and pepper the newly exposed surface and repeat the performance with the lettuce leaves so that, when finished, the fish is firmly wrapped, mummy-like.

Dribble the dry vermouth over its surface, pour the white wine into the bottom of the gratin dish, adding the section (or broken sections) of bone that was removed from the fish, line the surface of the fish with dabs of butter, press over lightly a sheet of aluminum foil (or buttered parchment), and bake for about 30 minutes at 400° to 425°, basting regularly during the last 15 minutes. Transfer, with the help of spatulas (first detaching muzzle and tail tip from sides of dish if they are touching) to a heated serving dish, discard the bones, pour the juices into a small saucepan, reduce to a light syrup, add the cream, and reduce at a high boil, stirring, by approximately half or until the liquid takes on the consistency of a light sauce (whisk in a couple of tablespoons of butter away from the heat, if you like), and pour it over the fish. Cut into cross-sections for serving.

GRILLED FISH *(POISSONS GRILLÉS)*

Any fish can be rubbed with oil or brushed with melted butter, seasoned and grilled, served simply with lemon. A sauce, cold or warm, served apart—like the green sauce (page 119), one of the mayonnaise derivatives or béarnaise, choron (peeled, seeded, chopped tomato, butter-stewed until all liquid has disappeared, incorporated into a béarnaise), hollandaise, etc.—is particularly good with grilled slices of large fish.

To me—and to a great many people—grilled fish is associated with the Mediterranean, with a fairly limited variety of fish, with olive oil, fennel, and, of course, with wood coals. On the French Mediterranean coast, the fish most admired for this purpose are the *rouget de roche,* the *loup de mer,* and the various *dorades* (and closely related *sars, pageots,* etc.). Their near equivalents in American waters are red mullet, sea bass, and the porgies.

In the droll world of fish grillery, passions are easily aroused in defense of principles: The purists proclaim it criminal to scale, gut, season, or oil a fish before grilling it. Assuming the fish to be of the morning's catch, that might be all right were one permitted to season it at the table, but the high priests of the order are an unbending lot (a whole family of them operates a celebrated and very silly restaurant in Marseilles); and then there is the incendiary school, whose fish, after being grilled, must be offered up in a holocaust of brandy and fennel branches.

Hinged, double-faced grills are practically essential because of the fragility of the flesh, which would otherwise stick and tear in the turning. Those for small fish or flat fish are square and flat; for large fish they are oval and swelled, describing the form of the fish, and they exist in different sizes.

The fish gains from marinating, but involved marinades do not seem interesting to me. Fennel is a perfect herb for delicately flavored white-fleshed fish; sardines, fresh anchovies, mackerel, or herring are better with a stronger herb (of which my own choice is usually oregano). Enough olive oil to coat the fish well, salt and pepper, and either a bit of white wine or lemon juice are all that is necessary. If fish is prepared with fennel, a tablespoonful or so of pastis (Pernod 51 or Ricard) in the marinade will reinforce the slight anise flavor. The abdominal and head cavity of a large fish may be stuffed with a healthy bouquet of fennel branches, which helps perfume the flesh while lending the fish a full, attractive form.

Small fish (2½ to 3½ ounces), gutted but unscaled and well coated in their marinade, profit from being rolled, each, into a large (grape) vine leaf before being grilled over intense red coals for only a couple of minutes on each side—long enough to char the leaf, which, when unrolled and discarded, takes the skin of the fish with it, leaving moist and flavorful filets exposed. When small red mullets neither scaled nor gutted (or, if gutted, the liver left intact and inside) are marinated in olive oil and quantities of fresh feathery chopped fennel leaves and grilled this way, they are among the very sublime things of the sea. Olive oil is the only sauce necessary—the liver may be mashed with it at table to serve as a heavier sauce.

Before marinating a large fish, score the flesh diagonally at intervals (or cut a serpentine design to the bone at the thickest part of the fish) so that it will cook more evenly and, if the unaggressive fennel weed is an element in the marinade, be certain that the scored parts are well garnished with it. To grill a large fish, the bed of coals should be fairly deep and well sustained, but their intensity should have died somewhat, a gray film of ash masking the red glow. The fish should be at a 3- to 4-inch distance from the bed of coals; it should be turned every 4 or 5 minutes; and, after having been turned once, it should be basted often but not abundantly (to prevent the oil from dropping onto the coals and flaming up) with its marinade, adding more olive oil if necessary. A 1- to 3-pound fish will generally require a corresponding 10 to 30 minutes' cooking time, depending on the relative thickness of the fish. It is done when the flesh at the thickest point—behind the abdominal cavity and an inch or two below the base of the head—has turned from slightly translucent to milky-opaque next to the bone and is easily detachable, no longer clinging stubbornly; test with a knife tip—the flesh should not be "flaky." Olive oil is the best sauce.

FISH IN ALUMINUM PAPILLOTE
(POISSON EN PAPILLOTE D'ALUMINIUM)

More interesting for larger fish, I think—I have most often prepared salmon-trout and bass in this way. The aluminum casing is not
particularly attractive from the point of view of serving but, apart
from being easy to arrange, it has the advantage over parchment
paper of permitting the enclosure of a certain amount of liquid with
the fish. The fish may be marinated as for a grilled fish and enclosed
in the *papillote* with its marinade; it may be simply enclosed with a
scattering of chopped shallots and 2 or 3 tablespoonsful of white
wine, plus a handful of shredded sorrel; it may be placed on a scattering of *mirepoix* or *duxelles,* with more of the same spread atop and
a bit of white wine added—and so forth. Allow a generous amount of
foil—about 4 inches at each end of the fish. Place the foil on the
baking sheet before garnishing it: Put the dry materials and the seasoned fish in place, slices of butter atop, and pull the borders of the
foil up gently, boat-like, around the fish before pouring in the bit of
wine. Fold the edges together, doubly or triply, pinching tightly, beginning at the summit and working first to one end and then to the
other—it must be airtight and plenty of space should be left inside
the sealed *papillote*. Bake in a 400° to 450° oven, using the 10-min-
utes-per-inch time measure. Transfer the package to a heated serving
platter, slitting it open at table. The juices are sauce enough.

SALT COD (MORUE)

Salt cod is sold in filets or in sections cut from the filet. The abdominal section, although passable in recipes calling for poached,
flaked cod, is often discolored and, in any case, is inferior in quality
to the thickest part of the tail section—it is altogether unsatisfactory

for preparations requiring pan-fried pieces. Buy, preferably, high up on the tail and choose that which is whitest. The Icelandic salt cod is the kind most often used in France.

Salt cod is considered a vulgar thing by most people, which does not prevent a great many from adoring it—those who do not may always have tasted it boiled, dry and woolly, or have never tasted it at all. In those parts of the world where it forms an important part of the diet, it is rarely soaked long enough for the unaccustomed palate. (Some Provençal cookbooks offer, as a sort of folklorique curiosity, a recipe for unsoaked salt cod, wiped free of surface salt and grilled over hot coals, accompanied by potatoes in their skins and whole heads of garlic roasted in the ashes. Plenty of chilled rosé is necessary to wash it down, and it is much more current fare than one might imagine.)

All salt cod, even of the same origin, is not salted to the same degree, and it is difficult to give precise instructions for soaking. Written instructions usually call for an overnight soaking; many readers may prefer to put it to soak the morning of the day preceding its preparation—from 24 to 36 hours, in all. Place it in a colander immersed in a large basin of cold water, changing the water regularly —at least four or five times. The volume doubles approximately during the soaking, and one may tell by pinching if the structure of the flesh has more or less returned to its original undehydrated state.

For many preparations, it is first poached—and it must not boil: Cover the piece of cod generously with cold water, bring slowly to a near boil, turning the heat to a bare minimum the moment the water's surface shows signs of movement, and poach in the hot but not simmering water for from 7 to 10 minutes—or sometimes for as long as 20 minutes, depending on the thickness and the length of soaking time—or until the flesh at its thickest point shows little resistance to the tip of a sharp knife (for an *aïoli,* it may remain a couple of minutes longer in the poaching water). It should be only just done. When recipes call for "flaked" poached cod, it is not literally flaked—or, at least, no more than necessary to remove all the bones, and it must, above all, not be shredded or crushed; the fatty skin is removed and all the bones are removed; try to damage the flesh as little as possible, keeping it in the largest possible pieces.

Flaked salt cod is sometimes warmed up in an egg yolk–thickened *sauce bâtarde* (see page 326) made from the poaching liquid (assuming it's not too salty, which it would be if the cod were under-soaked) and served with boiled potatoes; it is often associated with cut-up hard-boiled eggs in a *béchamel* or, which is better, prepare eggs *à la tripe,* incorporate flaked cod, and scatter with butter-crisp croutons. Or, still with hard-boiled eggs, prepare a gratin, the gratin dish lined with generously creamed, butter-stewed sorrel, a layer of cut-up eggs or egg slices and flaked cod, creamed sorrel on top, sprinkled with lightly buttered-colored breadcrumbs, gratinéed in a hot oven—or replace the creamed sorrel with Provençal spinach sauce (parboiled, squeezed, chopped spinach, finely chopped garlic, chopped or pounded anchovy filets, seasonings, cooked for a few min-utes, stirring, in an olive oil and flour roux, milk stirred in, cooked gently for 15 to 20 minutes) and replace the buttered crumbs with dry crumbs and a dribbled crisscrossing of olive oil. Chopped leeks, first parboiled for 10 or 12 minutes and squeezed free of excess liquid, mixed with an egg and cream quiche mixture, a layer in the bottom of a buttered gratin dish, a layer of flaked cod, another of the leek mix, sprinkled with grated Parmesan and baked until swelled and browned is another happy gratin.

À la Provençal, the flaked cod is simmered for a few minutes in the standard stewed tomato mixture (chopped onion cooked in olive oil, peeled, seeded, chopped tomato, white wine, *persillade* added—strips of sweet pepper may be first cooked with the onion, a pinch of saffron may be added, black olives may be added . . .). Better, however, are sections of lightly floured cod pan fried in olive oil, as for the *raito,* and simmered gently in the tomato sauce for a few minutes; a pilaf is a good accompaniment. *À la Lyonnaise,* the flaked cod is tossed at the last minute with sliced boiled potatoes and sliced onions, each sautéed separately in olive oil, and chopped parsley—the pan is rinsed with a couple of tablespoons of vinegar, which is dribbled over the mixture.

A *bouillabaisse de morue* is a soup prepared like that for *bouilla-baisse Borgne,* in which cod sections are poached for 15 minutes (but more often they are deliberately overcooked at a rolling boil).

Many consider *brandade* to be salt cod's essential raison d'être; I have never understood the common passion for it. If you want to prepare it, the proportions are about 1½ cups olive oil and ½ cup boiling milk per pound (weighed unsoaked) of slightly under-poached, flaked cod: Add a clove or two of puréed raw garlic to the cod and beat it with a wooden spoon in ½ cup hot olive oil over a high flame until reduced to a purée; remove to very low heat, continue beating and incorporate the remaining oil at a dribble, alternating additions of hot milk; season to taste, peppering generously, and scatter with croutons. It looks like mashed potatoes.

COD, POTATOES, AND EGGS
(Estofinade à la Rouergatte)
(for 4)

Stockfish is at the origin of the preparation—but stockfish requires a number of days more soaking than salt cod . . . A glance at the list of ingredients may not be very inspiring, but the result may surprise you. It is a nourishing dish that does not lend itself well to a first course (unless followed by no more than a light vegetable preparation), and a cool (about 50° Fahrenheit) young red wine will accompany it better than a white.

The cod should be poached (its water perfumed with herbs) and the potatoes and eggs boiled so that all are still hot when assembled together.

2 or 3 cloves garlic, peeled, pounded to a purée in a mortar
Large handful chopped parsley
4 hard-boiled eggs, cut into pieces
1 cup olive oil
2 pounds firm-fleshed potatoes, boiled in skins, peeled, and thickly sliced
1½ pounds soaked salt cod, poached (as described earlier) in water containing bay leaf and thyme, and flaked (bones and skin removed)
Pepper (salt depends on the saltiness of the cod—it may not be needed)

Mix the garlic purée and parsley together well, add the eggs, and stir gently with half of the olive oil. Add the potatoes to the remaining oil over medium heat, toss with the flaked cod, and gently stir in the egg and *persillade* mixture, peppering generously; turn out onto a heated platter.

135

COD IN RED WINE SAUCE
(Morue en Raito)
(for 4)

Raito is the name of the sauce in which any number of fish—eel, conger eel, whiting, halibut, fresh haddock, sliced, fileted, or cut into sections, may be gently stewed after having been lightly pan fried. Salt cod, alone, is prepared in a *raito* (or sometimes in a *capilotade*—chopped onions cooked in olive oil, flour stirred in, moistened with water and vinegar to taste, bouquet garni, and a handful of capers; in parts of the Var, the vinegar is replaced by a glass of *vin cuit,* a homemade sweet wine, reserved usually for Christmas and prepared at the time of the grape harvest from the unfermented grape must reduced and skimmed—a certain amount of marc or distilled alcohol is often added to it) as one of the traditional dishes of the Provençal Christmas Eve *gros souper.*

Raito
½ pound onions, chopped
¼ cup olive oil
3 tablespoons flour
3 cups red wine
2 cups water
1 pound canned tomatoes (Italian plum tomatoes) or 1 pound summer-ripe tomatoes, cut up
6 cloves garlic, crushed
1 teaspoon crumbled dried herbs (thyme, oregano, savory)
Bouquet garni (fennel branches, bay leaf, parsley and parsley root, celery branch, leek greens, branch of lovage, if available)
Salt

Garnish
Handful (3 or 4 ounces) pitted black olives (Niçoises are the best—if available, don't bother to pit them)
2 tablespoons (more or less to taste) rinsed capers
1½ pound tail section salt cod, soaked, cut into 4 sections
Flour
Olive oil

Stew the onions in the olive oil for 20 to 30 minutes, stirring from time to time, until softened and yellow, but not browned. Stir in the flour, cook, stirring for a couple of minutes, then add the wine, slowly at first, stirring all the while. Stir in the other liquids, add all the other ingredients, salting lightly; bring to a boil and regulate the heat so as to maintain the sauce at a very light boil, uncovered, for some 2½ to 2 hours—it should, finally, be reduced by about two thirds. Discard the bouquet and purée the sauce. Add the olives and the capers and leave to simmer gently for another 15 minutes.

Flour the cod sections lightly and fry them in hot olive oil for a couple of minutes on each side, coloring the surface but slightly. Drain them on paper toweling. Pour a bit of the sauce into the bottom of a wide earthenware dish (or other fireproof deep serving dish just large enough to hold the cod pieces placed side by side), arrange the pieces of fish, and pour the rest of the sauce over them. Heat and simmer gently for about 10 minutes before serving. Sprinkle with parsley, if you like.

AÏOLI
(Aïoli)

Aïoli is garlic mayonnaise. Poached salt cod is its constant companion, and around it is built another of the sacred Provençal mystiques. It crowns village festivals: Each summer Provençal villages organize festivals lasting three or four days each, involving orchestras, dancing, music-hall attractions, local talent shows, and fireworks, the final day winding up with an *aïoli monstre* in the public square, the entire population turning out to pile plates high with boiled salt cod, potatoes, carrots, green beans, artichokes, chick-peas, beets, hard-boiled eggs, snails, squid stew, and huge globs of garlic mayonnaise, liberally moistened with the local rosé. And it is the unquestioned Friday luncheon for countless Provençaux: The local shops in the villages of the Var soak quantities of salt cod on Thursday and sell it the following morning for the luncheon *aïoli*. In Solliès-Toucas, the local butcher prepares *aïoli,* boils up salt cod, potatoes, carrots, and snails and portions them out to long waiting lines, each person with an empty dish in hand, between 11:30 and

12:30 every Friday. Snails alone are accompanied by *aïoli* for the Christmas Eve supper, no doubt because that evening the cod finds itself obligatorily stewed in a *raito* or a *capilotade*.

To most outsiders, how the mere thought of boiled salt cod, boiled vegetables, and garlic mayonnaise can transport a solid block of the meridional French population to heights of ecstasy must remain forever incomprehensible; and after having shared an *aïoli* at a Provençal table, one may find puzzling the medico-analeptic, stomachic properties so earnestly claimed for it (I have read in one of the Marseilles newspapers that, if certain persons find *aïoli* indigestible, it is simply because too little garlic has been included in its confection, a minimum of four cloves per person being necessary . . .). The combination of raw garlic and an egg yolk emulsion is not particularly digestible and, allied to the inevitable chilled rosé wine, the effect can be deadly (certain non-indigens pretend that only red wine may be drunk with an *aïoli* and others dismally, but perhaps correctly, assert that only water is possible).

A good *aïoli* is made with good olive oil. It is, traditionally, prepared in a marble mortar with a wooden pestle; the weight of the mortar prevents it from slip-sliding around as one turns the pestle with one hand while dribbling the oil with the other. I know of no other method as easy or as successful—and certainly no other receptacle from which to serve can be as handsome as the marble mortar. A good *aïoli* should be mounted slowly, rhythmically, and regularly, the pestle turned always in the same direction (clockwise is easiest for me) and, when finished, should be stiff and heavy, with a sweaty surface. The blender has now invaded the Provençal kitchen, and few *aïolis* are now mounted by hand; a blender *aïoli* is lighter, air having been whipped into it, and the flavor is altogether different, the violence—how, I do not know—destroying the fruit of the olive oil; nor is the body voluptuously oily, as in the hand-mounted product, but dry and flat.

Avoid any garlic cloves that are not firm and crisp or at the heart of which a green germ has begun to form. The oil and the egg yolks should both be room temperature to discourage the *aïoli*'s breaking. It is easy enough to control the flow of oil with one's thumb held over the bottle top (beginning drop by drop, moving into a tiny but continuous thread until the body is firmly in control and continuing with a heavier thread)—or a narrow V-shape may be cut from the length of a cork before corking the bottle, thus leaving a tiny opening for the dribbling process.

Some people pound a lump of crustless bread, soaked and squeezed dry, into the garlic and egg-yolk mixture before beginning to add the oil. A more easily digestible but less silken *aïoli* may be prepared by substituting a boiled potato (about 3 ounces—cooled until only tepid) for the egg yolks.

Most French authors content themselves with quoting Reboul's recipe from *La Cuisinière Provençale;* I can do no better (although I think it wiser to begin with 2 egg yolks rather than 1 and to turn them until their yellow pales before beginning to add the oil; and, for my own purposes, I am content to use no more than 3 or 4 cloves of garlic for this batch of *aïoli,* presumably destined to serve 7 or 8—garlic cloves in the south of France do tend to be about double the size of those in the United States):

> Take two cloves of garlic per person, peel them, place them in a mortar, reduce them to a paste with a pestle; add a pinch of salt, an egg yolk and pour in the oil in a thin thread while turning with the pestle. Take care to add the oil very slowly and, during this time, never stop turning; you should obtain a thick pommade. After having added about three or four tablespoons of oil, add the juice of a lemon and a teaspoonful of tepid water, continue to add oil little by little and, when the pommade again becomes too thick, add another few drops of water, without which it falls apart, so to speak, the oil separating itself from the rest.

> If, despite all precautions, this accident should occur, one must remove everything from the mortar, put into it another egg yolk, a few drops of lemon juice and, little by little, spoonful by spoonful, add the unsuccessful aïoli while turning the pestle constantly. This one calls "reinstating the aïoli" (*relever l'aïoli*).

> An aïoli for seven or eight persons will absorb something over two cups of oil.

EEL *(ANGUILLE)*

The eel's serpentine form apparently offends many people. There can be no other explanation for its lack of popularity. It is no rarity in American waters but, because of the little demand for it, one may have to order it in advance. Eels live for a long time out of water and should be alive when purchased. Gutted, cut into sections, skewered with alternate slices of lemon and grilled over hot coals, they need not be skinned; the fatty skin protects the flesh while cooking, the excess fat drops into the coals, and the skin is easily removed at the table (the Bordelais sauté them as in the following recipe, cut up but unskinned—the result is unpleasantly fatty). For all other preparations, they should be skinned: Rap the back of the head sharply against the edge of a table to knock the eel unconscious, cut a circular incision all around the base of the head, cutting slightly into the flesh, grasp the head firmly in one hand, holding it in a towel to prevent its slipping, and peel the skin, glove-like, from the body, turning it inside out; it is difficult to get it started and pliers can be useful, but once begun, it slips off easily (Midwesterners will recognize the process as identical to that of skinning bullheads and catfish). Slit the skin-like flesh the length of the abdomen, gut the fish, cut off the head, and rinse thoroughly (for the sake of presentation, the head is usually left attached, the tail in the mouth, if the eel is to be braised whole on a bed of *mirepoix* and moistened with white wine and *fumet*).

The nineteenth century gave a large place to eel dishes, probably because, apart from the real delicacy of the flesh, whole, boned, stuffed (usually with a pike or whiting *mousseline* base, *duxelles* often added, sometimes truffled), and braised large specimens lend themselves to spectacular presentation.

Today most larger eels end up in red wine *matelotes*, occasionally in *fricassées* (the Alsatian *matelote* is a *fricassée,* white wine and *fumet* moistening, garnish of mushrooms and little onions, egg yolk and cream terminal binder), and small eels are usually sautéed like that in the following recipe, but for the presence of grated lemon peel. In recent years, eel terrines and *pâtés* have become one of the trademarks of fashionable restaurants (alternating layers of eel filets, rapidly sautéed in butter, and *mousselines,* often one of salmon and another of a white-fleshed fish; pistachios, chopped truffles, etc.)

A French version of the delicious cold Flemish hors d'oeuvre, *anguille au vert,* is sometimes prepared with small, sectioned eels— butter-stewed with an abundance of fresh herbs (recipes call for sorrel, nettle, parsley, tarragon, chervil, fresh sage, savory, burnet, and a bouquet—or a sprinkling of thyme and a loose bay leaf; sorrel dominates and, in practice, shredded spinach usually replaces nettle; burnet, the most boring of herbs, and chervil, whose fragile beauty is lost in such a rough and tumble mixture, may both be eliminated), moistened with white wine and water (beer in the Flemish original), cooked for 10 minutes and thickened with egg yolks (2 yolks per cup or so of liquid, with usual precautions: Cool a bit, stir some of the liquid into the yolks first, then stir back into the stew, stir over low heat until slightly thickened—do not approach the boiling point), lemon juice to taste.

SAUTÉED EEL
(Anguilles Sautées à la Grémolatte)
(for 4)

> 3 or 4 small eels (about 20 inches long), skinned, cleaned,
>   cut into 1-inch lengths
> Salt, pepper
> Flour
> Olive oil (to generously cover bottom of pan)

Mixture
> Handful chopped parsley
> 2 large cloves garlic, pounded to paste in mortar
> 1 teaspoon grated lemon peel

Season the eel pieces on all sides, shake them with a handful of flour in a closed paper sack to cover well with flour, transfer them to a large sieve, and toss repeatedly to rid them of all excess flour. Heat from $\frac{1}{16}$ to $\frac{1}{8}$ inch olive oil in a large heavy pan over a high flame—

the eel pieces should be held in it side by side—and sauté for 6 or 7 minutes, turning those that don't toss with the tips of fork tines. The surfaces should be slightly crisp and of a light golden color. Pour off the excess oil, add the *persillade*-grated lemon peel mixture, toss for another minute, and serve.

MACKEREL IN WHITE WINE
(Maquereaux au Vin Blanc)
(for 6)

A cold hors d'oeuvre that should be prepared at least 1 day in advance and that will continue to improve over a period of 3 or 4 days.

> 2 pounds small (Boston) mackerel, cleaned, heads removed, rinsed, left whole if no more than 6 inches long, cut into 2-inch lengths if larger
> 1 tablespoon olive oil

Marinade
> 1 bottle dry white wine
> Handful branches and fragments of fennel (or healthy pinch of fennel seeds)
> Several branches of oregano and thyme (or large pinch crumbled dried herbs)
> 1 bay leaf
> Small bouquet parsley (including scraped parsley root, if possible)
> Slight teaspoon coriander grains
> Salt
> 4 or 5 unpeeled, crushed garlic cloves
> 1 large onion, sliced into fine rings
> 2 medium carrots, peeled and finely sliced
> 15 to 20 peppercorns

Arrange the mackerel in a large oiled saucepan or *plat à sauter*. In another saucepan bring the white wine to a boil, add all the other ingredients except the peppercorns, and simmer, covered, for about 15 minutes. Add the peppercorns, pour the boiling liquid over the mackerel, return it to a boil, and maintain at a bare simmer, covered, for 10 to 12 minutes. Transfer the fish to a non-metallic container (an earthenware gratin dish is a logical and attractive container for conserving and serving), discarding all or most of the parsley and fennel branches. Refrigerate, covered, after cooling. Serve chilled.

MUSSELS *(MOULES)*

Brush or scrape mussels (Americans brush, French scrape), pulling out the fragment of seaweed, or beard, that protrudes from the back. Discard any whose shells are cracked or broken and test each between your fingers to be certain of its live resistance to opening (occasionally a mud-filled shell, heavier than a live mussel, turns up). Soak in a generous quantity of salt water for 15 or 20 minutes so that they may disgorge much of the sand contained in them.

To open mussels, put them into a large saucepan or pot, throw in a handful of chopped onion, 3 or 4 crushed cloves of garlic, thyme, bay leaf, a handful of parsley (whole or chopped), and some white wine—a half cup, more or less. Cover tightly and place over a high flame, shaking and tossing the contents (while holding the lid tightly in place) from time to time over a period of from 3 to 4 minutes to 10 minutes or so, depending on the size of the container and the quantity of mussels. Remove from the heat as soon as most of them are opened (the remainder can be forced open with a knife—and are often the best). With a chunk of butter and a healthy grinding of pepper added before heating, this is the simplest version of *moules marinières* and the one that is served in small restaurants throughout France, the mussels piled high in soup plates and the liquid ladled over.

As a preliminary preparation for other recipes, the mussels are removed from their shells (unless destined to be sauced and served on the half-shell) and put aside and the liquid is strained through finely woven cloth to eliminate any sand. It then serves as a stock—it should be tasted and its saltiness taken into consideration for eventual use.

STUFFED MUSSELS
(Moules Farcies)
(for 4)

Much more rapid than stuffed mussels and also a typically Provençal mussel and spinach preparation (and one which, to the ravishment of the restaurant's clients, never quits the daily menu at Chez-Hiély in Avignon) consists of stirring together a heavily creamed *velouté* made of the opening liquid (the basic *velouté* may be quite thick and relatively salty, the addition of cream attenuating the one and the other), parboiled, squeezed, and chopped spinach tossed rapidly in a bit of olive oil, and the shelled mussels; the mixture is then gratinéed in a hot oven or beneath high heat. *Palourdes* (which may be replaced by littleneck clams) are also prepared in this way.

When preparing stuffed mussels, the business of tying each mussel up is quite tiresome; those who are tempted not to bother will probably be happy with the results, but the stuffing and the sauce will have intermingled to form a general sameness of texture and taste and the mussels within the shells will have withered. When tied, the effect is very different: The fragile, membranous flesh of mussels opened alive clings, lining the inside wall of each shell half; when packed with the stuffing and tied firmly closed, the flesh has no space in which to shrink at contact with heat and gathers itself instead around the heart of stuffing, enveloping it in a neat sheath; the stuffing retains its own character, which forms a contrast to that of the sauce.

4 pounds mussels, scrubbed, prepared for cooking (of which only a part will be opened in the following ingredients)

For opening
½ cup dry white wine
3 cloves garlic, crushed
Thyme, bay leaf, parsley

Sauce
1 medium onion, finely chopped
2 tablespoons butter

3 tablespoons flour
The strained opening liquid, water
1 large ripe tomato, peeled, seeded, chopped, stewed
    in butter (or ¼ cup puréed canned tomato)
1 pinch sugar, small pinch cayenne

Stuffing   2 chopped hard-boiled eggs
               2 pounds spinach, parboiled, squeezed well, chopped
               The steamed mussels, chopped
               Salt, generous amount of pepper

Sort over the mussels, retaining the largest—about two thirds—for stuffing, and open the remainder (as described earlier) with the wine, garlic, and herbs. Remove the opened mussels from their shells, chop them and put them aside, strain the liquid, and put the sauce to work: Stew the onion for about 15 minutes in the butter, stirring, without permitting it to brown, stir in the flour, cook for a minute or so, slowly stir in the mussels' cooking liquid and water to attenuate the saltiness (if necessary—some water will be needed, in any case, to bring the sauce to the correct thin consistency; perhaps salt will have to be added), add the tomato, sugar, and cayenne, and leave to simmer gently while stuffing the mussels.

Open the remaining mussels by gently forcing a knife blade between the shells, opening them out but not separating them. Mix the elements of the stuffing together, spoon it into the mussels, forcing each closed, scraping free the stuffing that has been forced out while closing the mussel shells, and tying each firmly with a round or two of thread or kitchen string. Arrange them in a *plat à sauter* or wide earthenware *poëlon,* just large enough to hold them placed side by side, jointed edges down, crests in the air. Scatter over any remaining stuffing, pour over the sauce, and simmer gently, covered, for ½ hour.

SARDINES *(SARDINES)*

Sardines or pilchards, when absolutely fresh, are rigid, arched like a bow, and they glitter with reflections of a bright steel blue. Fresh anchovies, finer but rarer (in France they appear on the market during the month of May and I am told that it is only then that they surface to spawn and may be netted), may be subjected to any of the treatments normally dedicated to the sardine.

The Mediterranean *poutine* (or *poutina*), tiny minnows of a number of closely related fish, for the most part sardines and anchovies, may, for all practical purposes, be considered to be the same thing as whitebait, minnows of their more northern cousins herrings and sprats, dominating in the English version; it is reasonable to assume that American whitebait varies in composition depending on where it has been fished. Whitebait is nearly always deep fried (tossed, as is, in a paper bag of seasoned flour, tossed repeatedly in a sieve to rid it of excess flour, fried, small quantities at a time, in very hot olive oil for a minute or so, drained, and garnished with fried parsley, lemon apart—it may be lightly sprinkled with cayenne) or, sometimes, pan fried, the floured and seasoned mass being colored as a block on one side before being tossed (or unmolded onto a plate and slipped back into the hot pan, to which has been added a bit more oil).

Sardines, outside of the Midi, are rarely prepared otherwise than grilled or pan fried (not only are they much better grilled but, if pan fried, the kitchen risks being permeated with the odors for days). In the south, perhaps their most usual mode of preparation is stuffed with spinach and gratinéed (gutted, head and central bone removed, filets left attached at the tail and the length of the back, spread out skin side down, spread with parboiled, chopped, and seasoned spinach, rolled up and pushed into a bed of chopped spinach, one after the other, all the tails in the air, sprinkled with crumbs and olive oil, and put in a hot oven for 15 minutes; a Provençal spinach sauce —see page 134—sometimes replaces the bed of spinach). A Niçoise variation consists in sautéeing raw shredded chard and spinach with a couple of cloves of crushed garlic in olive oil, mixing with parboiled rice, grated Parmesan, and eggs, arranging sardine filets between thick layers of the mixture in an oiled gratin dish, finishing with crumbs, grated cheese, and a dribbling of olive oil—this needs about ½ hour in the oven; instead of sardine filets, whitebait is sometimes stirred into the mixture and transformed into a gratin. Or, whole sardines, seasoned and sprinkled with crumbs and oil, are gratinéed and sprinkled with a garlic *persillade* and lemon juice as they are removed from the oven; sometimes they are placed on a bed of chopped, stewed tomato mixture . . . Layers of artichoke hearts, finely sliced, seasoned, and coated with olive oil, may enclose one of sardine filets and be baked with a sprinkling of breadcrumbs until the artichokes are just tender—about ½ hour.

It is characteristic of most of these preparations that the fish, by other standards, be overcooked—they are sometimes cooked in a gentle oven (traditionally, they are prepared, taken to the baker, and picked up an hour or so later) for a much longer time than I have indicated, but are always better, to my taste, if cooked in a very hot oven for a minimum of time. One preparation, however, that is worth trying—and one had best count 1½ hours in a 325° oven—is sardines *en Chartreuse* (more often prepared with thick slices of tuna, the skin and dark parts removed and the flesh transpierced regularly with alternating strips of anchovy filet and of fresh fatback): a fairly deep, oiled oven dish lined with the outer leaves of a large Boston lettuce, a few leaves reserved to cover the preparation, the rest of the lettuce shredded and added to an abundant mixture of shredded sorrel, chopped or finely sliced onions, peeled, seeded, and chopped or sliced tomatoes, mixed crumbled herbs, *persillade* . . .; half the mixture packed into the lettuce-lined dish, sprinkled with salt and olive oil, peeled and seeded lemon slices atop, the fish, more lemon slices, the rest of the mixture, salt, olive oil, white wine, water, covered with the remaining lettuce leaves—a loosely placed sheet of aluminum foil may be set on top during the first part of the cooking to cut down slightly on the evaporation and to protect the surface lettuce leaves from drying and burning. Lower the heat if anything more than a very gentle bubbling is in evidence and check after an hour's time the liquid in the container. It is a sort of *confit* of fish and vegetables, everything intact but trembling at the brink of collapse.

SORREL-WRAPPED SARDINES IN WHITE WINE
(Sardines en Chemise d'Oseille au Vin Blanc)
(for 5 or 6 as a first course)

To clean the sardines, hold each under water and rub gently with fingertips against the grain of the scales to remove them, split open the abdomen with forefinger, empty it, and pinch off the head. Gently pull back the filets, forcing with fingertips to loosen them from the spinal column, starting at the head end, and break off the bone close to the tail, leaving the filets attached to the tail. Rinse and sponge dry between paper towels.

2 pounds fresh sardines, cleaned (above)

Marinade   **1 teaspoon each crumbled thyme and oregano**
                ¼ cup olive oil
                ½ cup dry white wine
                Salt, freshly ground pepper

                About ½ pound large sorrel leaves (enough to wrap all of the sardines), stems removed, well washed, and drained without damaging (or sponged dry between towels)
                1 large sweet onion, finely chopped

Marinate the sardines for a couple of hours, turning them gently from time to time in their marinade. Wrap each in 1 or 2 sorrel leaves, placing it in a large gratin dish, the bottom of which has been scattered with the chopped onions—the dish should be just large enough to hold them pressed without forcing side by side. Dribble over the marinade, adding a bit more white wine if the bottom of the baking dish is not completely moistened. Press a sheet of aluminum foil over the surface and cook in a 450° oven for some 12 minutes—or a bit longer—until the liquid has come to a bubbling boil and the sorrel has turned grayish, clinging, film-like, to the form of each sardine. Leave for another 10 minutes or so in a warm but not hot oven (remove the dish, turn off the oven, cool it for a few minutes, and return the dish to the oven, still covered with the foil) to steep, the liquid evaporating a bit more—only a spoonful or so of the cooking juices should remain for each guest.

SCALLOPS *(COQUILLES SAINT-JACQUES)*

The best part is thrown back to the fish, only the white muscle appearing on the American market. Americans writing of the food of France never fail to extol the delicacy of the lovely tongue of coral; untraveled readers are conscious of being deprived, stupidly and wastefully, of an exquisite thing. The deaf ear of the fishing industry is incomprehensible; how fine a thing it would be were the scallop-eaters of America to launch a well-publicized boycott so that a ray of light might pierce thick heads ...

French cookbooks of the nineteenth century are not lacking in recipes requiring scallop shells, silver imitations often replacing the real thing, but they contain no suggestion of what may have happened to their contents. By the turn of the century there are recipes to prove that the flesh was being eaten—whatever the final preparation, it was first parboiled, presumably to get rid of the taste, and then cooked for some 20 minutes in a court bouillon. Later the parboiling was abandoned, but a 15-minute passage in a court bouillon preceded all other preparations. Today large sea scallops are considered to be perfectly cooked when poached or otherwise exposed to heat for from 8 to 10 minutes, a proportionately shorter period, and as little sometimes as 3 minutes are counted for sliced sea scallops or bay scallops; they are done, in any case, when the grayish translucence turns to opaque white and the somewhat flabby flesh becomes firm and resilient.

Pétoncles are tiny—much smaller than bay scallops, their shells measuring an inch or so in diameter—and are often served several to a shell, a dab of snail butter on top, heated only long enough in the broiler or a hot oven for the butter to bubble. I have sometimes ordered *pétoncles* and been served cubed scallops in *pétoncle* shells, a not too distressing fraud in view of its goodness. The charm of the presentation is, of course, in the small shells but, just as snails, spread with their butter, often garnish half-grilled or broiled mushroom caps, which are then returned to the oven, raw cubed (¼ to ⅓ inch) scallops, several to a cap, treated in the same way could not help but be attractive and delicious. In their own shells, even thinly sliced and thinly spread, they would require too much snail butter, and, for a radically simple preparation, they are then best left whole or sliced in half across the grain, coated with olive oil, seasoned, sprinkled with crumbs (which may or may not be mixed with a clove of garlic pounded to a purée) and a dribble of olive oil and gratinéed.

The pre-prepared scallop gratin (a layer of sauce in the bottom of the shell, sliced poached scallops—and corals—often supplemented by a garnish, another layer of sauce, a sprinkling of crumbs, of grated cheese, or of both, surmounted by a scallop of butter, all ready to pop into the oven for 10 minutes and serve), one of the mainstays of the French charcuterie (a take-out shop that specializes in glorious window displays), can be very good: The scallops are best poached whole in a scant white wine court bouillon (2 parts wine to 1 water) before being sliced; the sauce may be a *velouté* prepared from the poaching liquid, a sauce gratin (mixture of *duxelles* and *velouté*), a mixture of *duxelles* and tomato sauce, a *béchamel* (to which the reduced poaching liquid has been added), or a *mornay*. Sometimes a *duxelles* lines the shell and a *béchamel* tops the lot. The scallops may be thinly sliced and added raw to the dish, in which case it should be assembled just before being put in the oven. The nature of the preparation demands that a prettily colored, crisp surface coincide with the heating through of the dish and the bubbling of the sauce; unless your oven is equipped with overhead heat, the only way to perfectly achieve this effect is to put the shells first into a 500° oven for 8 to 10 minutes or until the sauce bubbles and then transfer them to the broiler for something less than a minute—until the gratin is formed. If you cannot put your hands on scallop shells, do the whole thing in a gratin dish and serve it out; and if the notion of the charcuterie sauce seems tiresome, substitute creamed sorrel or Provençal sauce in abundance, use raw sliced scallops, and count 20 minutes in a hot oven . . . less if in shells.

Twenty years ago, half the restaurants in Paris offered *coquilles Saint-Jacques au gratin*. Those I best remember and liked best were composed of poached sliced scallops, mussels, and sliced mushrooms (cooked with water, lemon juice, and butter) in a *velouté* made of the cooking juices of all three. Often a fluted border of *duchesse* potatoes prevented the sauce from brimming over while being reheated, stamping the presentation, at the same time, with a certain mechanical beauty (neither restaurateur nor client conceived of it as sapid support and, like *pâté en croûte,* the heart of the thing was dug out, the trappings being returned automatically to the kitchen).

The world of food and fashion having proclaimed flour-thickened sauces coarse and unrefined, *coquilles Saint-Jacques sautées à la Bordelaise* (*meunière,* finished with a shallot *persillade* and a bit of lemon) took the ascendance (to confuse matters, a sort of *à l'Américaine* preparation—scallops sautéed with butter- or oil-stewed chopped onions, garlic, herbs, cayenne in the seasoning, moistened with blazed Cognac, white wine, and tomato, cooked 8 to 10 minutes, the scallops kept warm while the sauce is radically reduced, sieved, often creamed and, away from the heat, buttered—takes the name *à la Bordelaise* if a *mirepoix* replaces the stewed onions) and when garlic replaced the shallot, the scallops became inevitably *à la Provençale,* although they exist neither on the meridional market nor in Provençal cookbooks . . .

Recently, in the confused service of ultimate purity and snobbism, the mode has turned to *coquilles Saint-Jacques à la nage,* a sobriquet restricted until a few years ago to lobsters and crayfish poached in court bouillon. When applied to scallops, the court bouillon is usually very scanty, indeed, and almost always reduced and mounted with butter so that, finally, the appellation no longer means anything at all, the scallops being served in a *fumet*-based *beurre blanc;* the preparation itself is delicious.

Whatever their preparation, scallops should first be well rinsed and sponged dry. They are often treated as fritters, marinated with *fines herbes,* lemon juice, and a few drops of olive oil before being dipped in batter and deep fried, garnished with fried parsley. *Meunière,* they are good accompanied by a *beurre blanc* rather than the traditional splash of brown butter; and they may be treated in any of the ways suggested under "Fish in Sauce," pages 122–124. Saffron complements them nicely—try stewing little onions in butter, sprinkling with powdered saffron, adding the scallops and stewing, stirring, for another minute or so, moisten with mushroom cooking liquid and white wine (or fish *fumet,* if some is on hand), poach until done, add the mushrooms and thicken with egg yolks—saucepan removed from heat for a few minutes, part of the sauce stirred into the yolks, the mixture stirred back into the stew, stirred over very low heat until lightly thickened (or drain the liquid off, reduce by half, and whisk, like a *sabayon,* with egg yolks and a generous amount of butter in a *bain-marie* kept beneath the boil, until the sauce assumes the appearance of a light-bodied hollandaise) ...

SKEWERED SCALLOPS AND CUCUMBERS WITH DILL
(Brochettes de Saint-Jacques et Concombres à l'Aneth)
(for 4)

Normally a coral butter would accompany the skewered scallops: About 3 ounces of the corals (the remainder left attached to the scallops and skewered) poached for some three minutes in a dill-flavored court bouillon (⅓ cup each of water and white wine), the corals sieved, the court bouillon reduced to a spoonful, the two whisked into about 4 ounces softened butter, ⅓ cup heavy cream whipped and whisked into the mixture, seasoned to taste ... In the absence of corals, substitute a *beurre blanc.*

If using dried dill weed instead of fresh dill, soak it for ten minutes or so in the lemon juice before assembling the marinade.

	10 to 12 ounces Cucumbers
	Salt
	1 pound scallops, halved across the grain if very large, rinsed, sponged dry
Marinade	1 tablespoon fresh dill leaves and tender flower buds, chopped finely (or 1 teaspoon dried dill weed)
	The juice of 1 lemon
	¼ cup olive oil
	Salt, pepper

Peel the cucumbers and, if small, firm, the seeds still unformed, cut them into ½-inch sections. Split larger ones into halves or quarters, seed them, and cut into sections approximating the dimensions of the scallops. Parboil for about 1 minute in strongly salted water and drain.

Marinate the cucumbers and scallops for about 1 hour, skewer alternating cucumber sections and scallops, and grill them, using a double-faced grill, over a fairly intense bed of coals for from 8 to 10 minutes, basting regularly with the marinade (or cook in the broiler, basting).

FISH FILETS WITH ZUCCHINI
(Filets de Sole aux Courgettes)
(for 4)

1½ pounds small, firm zucchini, sliced coin-thin
¼ cup butter
Salt, pepper
1 large ripe tomato, peeled, seeded, chopped
8 grey, lemon, or Dover sole filets
1 lemon
Handful fresh basil leaves and flowers
Handful finely crumbled crustless stale bread, cooked until dried and
    lightly colored in butter, stirred often

Sauté the zucchini, seasoned, in butter over high heat for about 5 minutes, add tomato, and continue cooking and tossing for 2 or 3 minutes—the zucchini should remain somewhat firm. Line the bottom of a buttered gratin dish with the seasoned filets, squeeze a few drops of lemon juice over each, tear the basil into fragments, scattering it over the surface, cover with the zucchini-tomato mixture, spread smooth, sprinkle liberally with the buttered crumbs, and gratiné for about 15 minutes in a 450° oven.

CUTTLEFISH; SQUID; OCTOPUS
(SUPPIONS, SEICHES; CALMARS, ENCORNETS; POULPES, PIEUVRES)

Octopus must be beaten to tenderize the flesh—fishermen heave them roughly and repeatedly against rocks to this end. Squid and cuttlefish do not require such harsh treatment. Unless bought cleaned, the tentacles should be torn loose from the fleshy hood, the eyes removed, the little beak-like teeth squeezed free of the orifice and the hood cleaned out, the cuttlebone removed from cuttlefish and the corresponding transparent, celluloid-like bone slipped out of the squid's hood. The greatest care, it is said, should be taken not to break the ink sack but, in fact, unless one wants the ink for the fabrication of a black sauce of Spanish character, it could not make less difference. The fragile, viscous skin should be peeled off and discarded (large octopus may be parboiled to facilitate its removal), leaving only white flesh. Octopus, unless tiny, are always cut up; only squid is well adapted, by its form, to stuffing, the hood of the cuttlefish being shallower and that part of the wall from which the cuttlebone was removed being thin and easily torn.

Except for tiny little cuttlefish, cleaned—tentacles and hood separated but otherwise whole, dipped in batter, and rapidly deep fried, it is doubtful that those who claim for them a greater delicacy than that of squid could, at a blind tasting, distinguish one from the other. The octopus is, admittedly, a rougher beast, but certainly not indign of a serious and unprejudiced table. It requires from 1 to 4 hours' cooking (usually from 2 to 2½), depending on the size, and it is wonderful prepared as a *daube* (exactly like a beef or a mutton *daube*—see page 301: Eliminate the pork products and calf's foot, and a *mirepoix* may replace the chopped onions and red wine may replace the white, if one likes; sometimes it is served over semidried slices of bread thickly spread with *aïoli,* more *aïoli* served apart, a rich and heady thing of beauty for those with iron stomachs). Allowing for the difference in cooking time, it may be prepared like any of the squid stews. The Toulonnais, who share with the Neapolitans the reputation of being octopus-eaters (*mange-poulpes* is not intended as a compliment), often simmer it in a court bouillon (which may be no more than salted water with bay and thyme added) and eat it tepid, seasoned at table with olive oil, vinegar or lemon, salt, and pepper.

À la Tomate, à la Provençale, à la Sétoise, à l'Américaine, à la Niçoise . . . The assertive Mediterranean presences of the recurrent preparation-type tomato sauce (described in the discussion of scallops, page 151) seem to me better suited to squid, cuttlefish, and octopus than to other seafood (unless it be the peppery little crabs—*favouilles* —which, scanty-fleshed but rich in flavor, are pounded and puréed to form a soup or sauce base). The finesse of lobster and scallop are compromised and the fugacious charm of the crayfish is crushed in the encounter, whereas the sweet, herbal-spicy cephalopod autonomy is positively underlined, lent new dimensions, its primitive qualities at the same time suffusing, taming, and refining the sauce. The cooking time for squid or cuttlefish varies from 40 minutes to twice as long, depending on the squid and on the cook (20 minutes before serving, the stew may be smothered in freshly shelled little peas—an attractive supplement more Italian than French), and the sauce, whose body depends on the tomato alone, often needs to be drained off and rapidly reduced to a firmer consistency. A saffron pilaf is a perfect accompaniment, but buttered, fresh saffron egg noodles (a half teaspoon of powdered saffron stirred into—or sifted with—the flour before preparing the dough) are astonishing. In season, fresh and freshly torn-up basil, added a few moments before serving, will always complement these flavors.

Squid, if stuffed, should not be packed full—the stuffing swells while cooking and the hoods shrink; the chopped tentacles are always an element of the stuffing, and the opening is tacked with a couple of stitches of kitchen string.

A highly seasoned tomato and white wine sauce is a good braising liquid for a stuffing of finely chopped onions cooked in olive oil, the chopped tentacles sautéed with them, chopped *fines herbes,* parboiled rice, seasoned to taste.

The stuffing is often a tomato mixture—oil-stewed chopped onions sautéed with the chopped tentacles, crumbled oregano, peeled, seeded, chopped tomato, seasonings (including cayenne and a pinch of sugar), reduced and stiffened with a handful of finely crumbled semisoft breadcrumbs, a handful of garlic *persillade,* and an egg to bind—and, for the sake of contrast, is better treated in a non-tomato sauce—oil-stewed chopped onions, to which chopped anchovy filets are often added, a sprinkling of flour, moistened with white wine and water, seasoned, thyme and bay . . . Quartered artichokes may be tucked into all the interstices and the dish is usually, but not necessarily, baked, uncovered, and basted regularly rather than being braised, covered.

Squid may be stuffed with a stiff Provençal spinach sauce—or, better, with the same spinach, hard-boiled egg, and mussel stuffing as that used for stuffing mussels (page 144), a similar braising liquid to that above with the mussels' opening liquid added to it—a handful of the mussels may be kept apart and warmed up in the sauce just before serving. Saffron flavoring and egg-yolk terminal binding can lend variety for either braised squid or baked squid; if baked, the sauce will reduce a great deal.

One of the commonest of squid stuffings is based on sausage meat, chopped ham, or a combination; the intermingled flavors of pork and of the sea taste, to me, like mud.

SQUID AND LEEKS IN RED WINE
(Estouffade de Calmars aux Poireaux)
(for 4)

The white and pale green parts of 2 pounds leeks, cut into 2-inch lengths
¼ cup olive oil
Salt
2 pounds squid, cleaned, hoods cut into ½-inch widths
2 tablespoons flour
Pinch cayenne
1 teaspoon crumbled mixed dry herbs (thyme, oregano . . .)
1 bay leaf
About 8 peeled cloves garlic, sliced paper-thin
About 2 cups red wine
About 1 cup water (2 parts wine to 1 part water in quantity sufficient
   to cover)
Butter-crisp croutons, chopped parsley

156

In a heavy copper *plat à sauter* or a large, low-sided earthenware receptacle large enough to hold the squid and leeks gently packed in a single layer, stew the leeks, salted, in the oil for 10 minutes or so, turning them carefully so as not to damage them, remove them from the pan, and put them aside. Sauté the squid in the same oil, over a higher flame, salted, for several minutes, until the liquid they exude has been almost entirely evaporated, sprinkle over the flour, stir, and cook for another minute or so, add the seasoning, herbs, and garlic, and, stirring all the while, slowly add the red wine, then the water. Bring to a boil, gently slip the leek sections back into the pan, one by one, easing each into place between squid sections. Cook, covered, at a bare simmer, for something over 1½ hours—the sauce should be consistent and the squid and leeks of a melting tenderness, but absolutely intact. Scatter the surface with the croutons and chopped parsley at the moment of serving (in the cooking utensil).

FROGS' LEGS *(CUISSES DE GRENOUILLES)*

Fresh frogs' legs should be well rinsed and sponged dry. They are often only available deep frozen, a treatment from which they suffer less than most uncooked flesh; they may be plunged into cold water to be unfrozen and then sponged dry.

Frogs' legs occasionally take the quaint name of "nymphs' thighs," a designation imagined by Escoffier to shield the sensibilities of an English clientèle, who theoretically held frogs in horror. They are most often sautéed *à la Provençale; à la Lyonnaise,* the *persillade* is replaced by chopped or finely sliced onions cooked in butter apart, parsley is sprinkled over, and a bit of vinegar, heated in the pan, is dribbled over; *aux fines herbes,* they should be sautéed in butter and finished with chopped parsley, tarragon, chervil, and chives and a bit of lemon, but, in practice, it is usually an alternate appellation for *à la Provençale. À la Poulette,* the frogs' legs are poached in a white-wine court bouillon that is then transformed into a *velouté* and finished with egg yolks. They may be marinated with chopped *fines herbes,* a bit of lemon juice, a few drops of olive oil, and salt and pepper, then dipped in batter and deep fried.

Paul Haeberlin has created quite a wonderful frog fantasy, *mousselines de grenouilles* (a preparation that traditionally takes the pretty name of "zéphir"), which is always on the menu at l'Auberge de l'Ill (Illhaeusern in Alsace): Buttered *dariole* molds or custard cups lined with a ½-inch thickness of firmly bound pike *mousseline* (about 10 ounces fish flesh to 2 egg whites and 1 cup heavy cream), filled with a cooled mixture of boned, poach frogs' legs, chopped truffles, and just enough stiff *velouté* to hold it together, sealed with a layer of *mousseline,* poached in a *bain-marie* in the oven (about 20 minutes, water kept below boiling point), left to settle for a few minutes, unmolded, and accompanied by a light, creamed *velouté* (the chopped truffles may be replaced by a more economical *duxelles,* in which case a purée of butter-stewed sorrel incorporated into the sauce provides an attractive variation).

FROG RAVIOLI
(Raviolis aux Grenouilles)
(for 4, 60 to 70 raviolis)

In my own experience, the intensity of frog flavor and the size of the legs are directly, but inversely, related, the one diminishing as the other swells . . . Nonetheless, for recipes requiring boned frogs' legs, it is more practical to work with relatively large specimens (about 2 ounces per pair). The boning, itself, is very simple, the flesh being practically free of the bones except for the tendon attachments at the joints.

The form is a matter of personal preference; I prefer the *cappelletti* shape to the usual *ravioli* square. The buttered *fumet* is the simplest and most rapidly prepared of sauce possibilities; peeled, seeded, chopped, butter-stewed tomatoes may be incorporated into it—or sorrel—or the *fumet,* rather than being reduced, may be transformed into a *velouté,* creamed and/or buttered. Or the reduced *fumet* may replace the cream in the stuffing, the sauce being replaced by a brown butter.

1 pound frogs' legs, boned

Fumet (made like fish fumet, bones and aromatic elements simmered first in 2 cups water for 15 minutes, 1 cup white wine added, simmered for 30 minutes longer, strained)

Stuffing

2 ounces crustless, stale breadcrumbs

½ cup heavy cream

2 tablespoons softened butter

Handful chopped parsley

Handful chopped chives

1 teaspoon finely chopped tarragon

Salt, pepper

2 egg yolks

The poached frogs' flesh, diced

Noodle dough (see pages 253 and 254 and 258 for preparation)

3 to 3½ cups flour

Salt

4 eggs

2 tablespoons olive oil

Salt

Olive oil

¼ to ½ cup butter (more or less to taste) cut into small pieces (for the sauce)

Poach the frog flesh in the strained *fumet,* bringing the liquid to the boiling point over a moderate flame; if the saucepan is of a heavy material, the heat may be turned off the moment the boil is reached, the flesh being left to poach and to cool in the liquid, the pan covered; in a pan that loses heat rapidly, maintain the liquid at a simmer for one minute and then remove from the heat and leave, covered, to cool. Strain, saving the poaching liquid.

Soak the breadcrumbs in the cream, mashing with a fork, until all the cream has been soaked up, mash in the butter, add the herbs, seasonings, and yolks, stirring vigorously, then stir in the frog meat.

Check pages 253 and 254 and 258 for method of preparing and stuffing the dough; for cappelletti, prepare 3-inch-diameter rounds and form half moons, as for the *koldouny,* forcing the tips backwards to join and pinching them together.

Drop ravioli into a large pot of salted boiling water to which a spoonful or so of olive oil has been added and, when it returns to a boil, cook at a simmer for about 5 minutes. Drain and serve the sauce apart: Reduce the *fumet* to a syrupy consistency—until about ½ cup of liquid remains—and whisk in the butter away from the heat.

SAUTÉED FROGS' LEGS IN PERSILLADE
(Cuisses de Grenouilles Sautées à la Provençale)
(for 4)

If given a choice, use small legs for this preparation—they must be eaten with fingers, and finger bowls will be appreciated. Ordinarily, they are only floured before being sautéed—one must nurse them constantly and they still often stick (not that that is a disaster—they are still good). Dipped in egg, they will not stick while cooking and they are, I think, at least as good in their thin, batter-like crust. If you do not have a pan large enough to contain them all without crowding, side by side, you should use the two largest pans you have.

> 1½ pounds frogs' legs, rinsed, sponged dry
> Salt, pepper
> Flour
> 2 eggs, beaten as for an omelet
> About ¼ cup olive oil

Persillade   Handful chopped parsley mixed well with 2 or 3 cloves garlic pounded to a paste in a mortar (or very finely chopped)

> 1 lemon

Season the legs, dredge them in flour (tossing in a paper bag to save mess), toss them in a sieve to rid them of excess flour, dip each in beaten egg, and drop into hot oil. As they begin to color—they will cook rapidly and the flame should be kept high, or relatively so, depending on their progress—toss them, gently turning over those that do not flip with the tines of a fork. Continue tossing regularly until lightly colored and crispened—5 or 6 minutes in all, add the *persillade,* and toss repeatedly for another minute. Turn out onto a hot serving platter, leaving behind any excess oil, and sprinkle the surface with lemon juice (some people add a small handful of bread-crumbs just after adding the *persillade*—they soak up the oil and give more body to the dish).

VEGETABLES

BÉCHAMEL GRATINS

"A u gratin" has long since been adopted into English. It seems, at times, to be a precarious transplant, ill at ease in its surroundings, if not a hopeless case of lost identity. Some believe it to denote specifically a cheesy surface; others may be content with the international flair that it bestows on any appellation. Nor does it carry the same associations as in the past in its home tongue: At one time, for instance, a *poulet au gratin* was a roast chicken presented on a dish, the bottom of which had been spread with a forcemeat and baked; today, pieces of chicken masked with a sauce, usually sprinkled with cheese, and colored in a hot oven or beneath a flame are called *poulet au gratin*.

A gratin is the crusty material that forms on the bottom and the sides of a dish in which a preparation has been baked and must be scraped or scratched loose. Primitively, gratin means "scrapings," and, by extension, it refers to the crust that forms on the surface of either a baked dish or, in the instance of a "rapid gratin," a hot, ready-cooked preparation that is passed summarily beneath intense heat. Crumbs or grated cheese may lend their properties to the formation of the crust but neither belongs inevitably to the definition.

In the minds of many, a gratin is only one thing—a precooked material (which may be a collection of leftovers of all kinds, but which is most often a parboiled vegetable) over which is spread a *béchamel;* cheese or buttered breadcrumbs or a mixture of both is then sprinkled over the surface and 20 minutes or so later it leaves the hot oven bubbling and golden. All these preparations are not only of an exemplary goodness, but also very much of a kind, I think, that belong to sentimental childhood memories, and I wonder that those who share the fashionable distaste for flour-bound sauces suffer no pangs of regret for having banned the friendly *béchamel* from their tables.

Béchamel vegetable gratins are very usual American home preparations; the French consider them to be typically Lyonnaise. For the purposes of this book, a *béchamel* is a "white" or "cream sauce." If a certain amount of cheese is incorporated into it at the last minute, it may be rebaptized *mornay*. It is rare that it gains from meat flavoring but, in some instances, an herb or two or an onion cooked in it can do no harm.

Béchamel must not be undercooked or it will have an unpleasant "floury" taste (the scientific explanation for this I cannot give. If only brought to a boil, as for the thick soufflé or croquette bases, or in the final addition of a *beurre manié,* this quality is not in evidence; it begins to invade the sauce only after a couple of minutes' cooking and begins to disappear only after half an hour or so). In general, a minimum of an hour's slow cooking is best, but for masking a gratin which is subjected to supplementary cooking in the oven, 30 or 40 minutes will do. No more than the amount of butter necessary to absorb the flour should be used in the preparation of the roux (unlike the fat in other sauces, which may be skimmed, it is here held in suspension by the milk, never rising to the surface—butter added for flavor or smoothness should always be whisked or stirred in after removal from heat, and for a gratin, no additional butter is added) and the sauce should be only lightly bound with flour, its body depending, eventually, as much on reduction as on the initial binding.

BÉCHAMEL
(Béchamel)

3 tablespoons butter
4 tablespoons flour
1 quart milk
Salt

Melt the butter in a heavy saucepan, stir in the flour with a wooden spoon, and cook for less than a minute over a tiny flame before beginning to add the milk, very slowly at first, stirring rapidly the while to prevent lumping (should lumps form, it is no disaster: Finish adding the milk, bring it to a boil, strain it, whisk, and put it back to cook). After further additions of milk, turn the flame up a bit. Stir constantly, adding more milk only as the previous addition begins to thicken (remove the saucepan from the heat for a moment if thickening too rapidly). The last half may be poured in steadily while stirring. Bring to a boil and adjust the heat, using an asbestos pad, if necessary, to keep the sauce at the slightest suggestion of a boil. Undersalt—seasoning may always be rectified. Stir from time to time, thoroughly scraping sides and bottom, the sauce tending to settle and thicken there. After long cooking, this repeated scraping will make the sauce rather uneven, but that is unimportant for a gratin, and if you are using the sauce as a base for others, simply whisk it or strain and whisk it again. Nutmeg is sometimes added (it should be used so sparingly as to be nearly undetectable) and cream— as much as one likes—may be used to thin and to enrich the sauce.

Precooking, for most vegetables, means parboiling until barely done—(varying from a couple of minutes to a ½ hour or so and settling usually around the 10-minute mark)—Artichokes, asparagus, broccoli, cabbage, cauliflower, celery, chard ribs, Belgian endives, fennel, leeks, onions, small new potatoes, spinach, sprouts, turnips . . . And most gain from being dried out in butter, gently tossed over low heat for a few minutes before being sauced.

Zucchini, tender young artichoke hearts, and mushrooms are

better cooked raw in butter. Sliced eggplant will have more character if fried in olive oil and drained (in Provence, the butter would be replaced by olive oil in the preparation of the *béchamel*).

Celery hearts, fennel, or endives, after being parboiled, are sometimes braised until melting-tender in a rich stock; in that case, the *béchamel* (or *mornay*) is best transformed into something richer —stirring in, for example, a healthy quantity of mushroom purée (puréed raw and sautéed in butter until the liquid is evaporated), forming with the mixture a bed in the bottom of the gratin dish on which are placed the braised vegetables sprinkled first with their reduced braising juices and, finally, with Parmesan before they go in the oven.

Combinations of vegetables are attractive: Peas and green beans may be scattered through the thing; beds of juliènned, butter-cooked carrots, mushrooms, turnips, or zucchini (the last two first disgorged with salt) may receive other vegetables in other forms; parboiled but for a minute or two, well drained but not squeezed, spinach and sliced, sautéed mushrooms form an exquisite combination—and, if the mushrooms are replaced by sliced raw truffles (the sauce sprinkled with butter-cooked breadcrumbs—no cheese), words fail; leftover rice or pasta, cooked chicken, brains, sweetbreads or tripes may, of course, be added . . .

If the dish is to be sprinkled with breadcrumbs, alone or in combination with cheese, they are better first gently cooked in butter until lightly colored—and, although dried crumbs are most often used and are perfectly good, stale but still soft crumbled bread (crusts removed) gives a more interesting result.

VEGETABLE FRITTERS
(Beignets de Légumes)

The fritter batter recipe is given at the end of this chapter, on page 263.

Turned artichoke hearts (quartered, chokes removed, rubbed with lemon, raw if young and tender, parboiled if their first youth is past), *asparagus tips* (parboiled but firm), *cauliflower flowerets* (parboiled, firm), *2-inch lengths of the white parts of leeks* (sim-

165

mered for 10 minutes), *mushrooms* (cultivated—raw), *small spring or summer white onions* (raw), *green beans* (parboiled, firm), *young sorrel leaves* (raw), *small zucchini sliced lengthwise in ¼-inch thicknesses* (raw) are my fritter preferences. All, with the exception of sorrel leaves, should be first marinated with a bit of lemon juice and olive oil, salt, pepper, and a selection of finely chopped fresh herbs—parsley, chives, chervil, tarragon, lemon thyme, hyssop, marjoram. The best oil for frying is a good olive oil but, in the interest of economy, a tasteless vegetable oil may be preferred. Rather than dipping, one by one, each fragment in the batter, it is easier to dump them all in (with the continuing exception of the fragile sorrel leaves), turning them around gently to be certain that each is well coated, and to remove them one by one, either with a teaspoon or one's fingertips, depending on the form of the object, dropping each immediately into the hot oil (test it for heat by letting drop a touch of batter—when it sizzles at contact, the oil is ready; the heat may have to be turned up or down several times before all are finished). Don't try to fry too many at a time and keep those that have been removed from the oil, after draining rapidly in a towel or in paper towels, well covered in the folded napkin (placed on a hot platter) from which they will be served. A handful of tiny bouquets of parsley leaves plunged for a few seconds into the fat as the last fritters are removed provides, scattered over the surface, a most attractive and flavorful garnish. Serve lemon wedges at the same time; some like to serve a tomato sauce apart.

COLD MIXED VEGETABLE HORS D'OEUVRE
(Légumes à l'Orientale)
(for 8)

If the raisins seem bizarre to you, leave them out; if you have no taste for coriander, leave it out; the dish will lose its Oriental distinction but will not, otherwise, be the worse for the omissions. If the presence of crunchy, hot peppercorns is distressing, leave them out ...

At the height of summer, replace the preserved tomatoes by fresh, firm, ripe tomatoes, peeled, seeded, and coarsely cut up or chopped; replace the fennel by quartered celery hearts and the parsley by fresh basil leaves and flowers.

Slices of sweet pepper may be added, as may any of those vegetables normally prepared *à la Grecque*—small zucchini, quartered lengthwise and cut into 2-inch lengths; cauliflower flowerets; asparagus tips; chard ribs . . .

1 large sweet onion (4 to 5 ounces), chopped
1 cup olive oil (in all)
2 cups preserved tomatoes, juice drained off
4 large garlic cloves, crushed, peeled, finely sliced
Salt
1 healthy pinch cayenne
1 teaspoon sugar
1 mounded teaspoon finely crumbled mixed herbs (thyme, savory, oregano)
1 bay leaf
4 tender artichokes (2 pounds), pared (see page 173), quartered, chokes removed, immersed immediately in remaining ¾ cup olive oil
1 ounce dried currants (or other seedless raisins), soaked 1 hour in tepid water, drained
8 ounces small garnish onions (25 or 30), peeled
8 ounces whites of leeks, cut into 2-inch lengths
1 pound hearts of fennel bulbs, trimmed, quartered
10 ounces firm, unopened mushrooms (whole, halved, or quartered, depending on size)
2 cups dry white wine
1 large pinch coriander seeds (about 30)
Juice of 1 lemon
About 20 peppercorns
Chopped parsley

Cook the chopped onion with ¼ cup olive oil in a large, heavy copper saucepan or earthenware *poëlon* for from 20 to 30 minutes without permitting to color, add the tomatoes and the garlic, stew gently for about 10 minutes, stirring, until nearly all liquid has evaporated, salt lightly, add the cayenne, the sugar, the herbs, and the artichoke quarters with their olive oil. Stir well together, add the raisins or currants and, a handful at a time, the remaining vegetables, stirring so that all are evenly coated with the tomato mixture. Add the wine, the coriander, and the lemon juice, bring to a full boil

167

over a high flame, reduce the heat, and simmer, covered, for about 40 minutes (the acidity of the cooking liquids prevents the vegetables from softening—they will remain firm and even slightly crunchy despite the length of cooking time).

Remove the vegetables with a large wire skimming spoon to a non-metallic serving utensil, add the peppercorns to the cooking juices, and reduce at a high heat for 5 or 10 minutes, stirring all the while. About 1½ cups—or slightly more—should remain, just enough to barely cover the gently packed vegetables. Taste for salt (the vegetables will be somewhat undersalted if correctly done and the sauce should be relatively salty—without exaggeration). Leave, uncovered, to cool and then refrigerate, covered. Serve either chilled or at room temperature, generously sprinkled with parsley.

MIXED VEGETABLE STEW
(Ragoût de Légumes)

One thinks of a stew most often as a variety of foodstuffs cooked together in sauce; the Lyonnais *barboton,* whose preparation, but for the absence of meat, is that of a simple meat stew (potatoes lent relief by onion, garlic, often a bit of tomato, and a bouquet garni, gently cooked in a lightly roux-thickened bouillon), or the genial *ratatouille,* whose vegetables, intact but purée-tender, are cloaked in a syrupy reduction of their own abundant juices, correspond nicely to that concept.

The subtle structure of harmonies drawn from a combination of tender young vegetables cooked (or, to be more accurate, sweated) together with butter (or olive oil or a combination) in a heavy, tightly covered vessel, each added, raw or precooked, at a specific moment corresponding to its own needs, the complexity of savory autonomies butter-bound in an amalgam of their own fragrances, accented by the caress of an herb or two—a melting, shimmering balance of separateness and unity in fragile suspension—is quite another thing and many have claimed that it deserves to be dignified by another name: *estouffade de primeurs, potée printanière, jardinière à l'etouffé,* and I know not what have been suggested as possibilities. None, in any case, can touch the succulent beauty of the thing and *ragoût* it must remain.

168

Artichoke and heart

The composition of these stews depends on the season and on whim and, insofar as they are never twice identical, one must, each time, more or less "feel" one's way through the preparation, adjusting the heat, shortening or lengthening the cooking time, and, if the chosen vegetables fail to furnish enough liquid of their own, adding a couple of spoonfuls of water or white wine at one or several points. The cooking time may vary from about 45 minutes in all to 1¼ hours or so. Small whole onions (or, lacking that, 1 or 2 large sweet onions, finely sliced or coarsely chopped) should always be present (I always add unpeeled garlic cloves—some readers may prefer to overlook that ingredient). Tender young peas or broad beans—each bean peeled—are particularly attractive additions, and if savory is added, the combination will assume a special meaning (if only dried savory is available, add it to the bouquet—tender spring or early summer leaves may be finely chopped and mixed with the parsley garnish). Under different circumstances, *fines herbes,* fresh marjoram, or fresh basil are valuable additions. A garnish of artichoke bottoms, butter-cooked apart and filled with a fine, buttered purée of peas or broad beans, can lend variety to the textures and style to the presentation.

Young artichoke hearts, onions, unpeeled garlic cloves, lettuce or sorrel *chiffonade,* tender, crisp turnips, carrots, and cauliflower flowerets (if delicate enough to eat raw) count among the vegetables that should be added at the beginning. Mature artichokes or split hearts of bulb fennel should be first parboiled for about 10 minutes and added at this time also. Some 20 minutes before removing from the heat, add the raw peas or broad beans (but, if so tender as to be edible in their raw state, 10 minutes will do—in either case, a bit of water should be added at the same time and the heat intensified somewhat, for they cook by steaming), the parboiled flowerets of cauliflower that is too strongly flavored to be eaten raw, or the parboiled lengths of leek whites. Then, 5 to 10 minutes before, add the rapidly sautéed mushrooms; parboiled, but firm, asparagus tips; snow peas (their edges carefully trimmed to eliminate strings) parboiled for hardly a minute; small, firm zucchini, sliced coin-thin and sautéed for 5 or 6 minutes over a high flame. Small, fresh green beans should be cooked in a large quantity of rapidly boiling water for from 8 to 12 minutes—until barely tender—and tossed in with the other vegetables only at the moment the butter is swirled in just before serving.

The *ragoût* is perfect as a first course, an intermediate course, or a garnish. I usually serve it after a first course, first to be savored alone and uncomplicated by the presence of meat flavors; then it acts as either a unique or a supplementary garnish to a roast. A choice of from 5 to 7 vegetables is best—with too many, one tends to lose one's bearings. To attempt to serve such a stew otherwise than directly from its cooking vessel would only entail a loss of valuable heat without improving the presentation.

A large copper low-sided saucepan or an earthenware *poëlon,* these materials absorbing heat slowly, regularly, and holding it for long, are the ideal receptacles. If working with a direct flame, an asbestos pad should be used to disperse the heat. One may begin at high heat—no longer than the time necessary to heat the vessel—before turning it low.

The ingredients below would serve from 4 to 6 people.

½ cup butter (in all)
1 pound walnut-size white spring onions (or small garnish onions), peeled
1 head garlic, cloves cleansed of superficial loose husk, but unpeeled
6 medium-size tender artichokes, pared (see page 173), quartered, chokes removed
Bouquet garni (celery branch, parsley, bay leaf, thyme, other herbs to taste)
1 medium head tender, leafy lettuce (Boston, for instance), coarsely shredded
Salt
1 pound small firm zucchini, sliced thinly
Pepper
Chopped parsley (finely chopped fresh marjoram added if available)

Melt about 3 tablespoons butter, add the onions, the garlic cloves, and the artichoke quarters (they should be pared at the last moment and added as they are ready, turned around in the butter, coating all surfaces to protect them from contact with air, which rapidly blackens them—if you are not accustomed to working rapidly, best do them just ahead of time, adding the quarters immediately to olive oil and, subsequently, cutting down on the amount of butter used in the cooking), embed the bouquet at the heart of things, scatter over the lettuce *chiffonade,* sprinkle with salt, cover tightly, and leave to sweat, cooking ever so gently, tossing from time to time (or stirring with a wooden spoon), for about ½ hour. Check the onions and the artichokes for their degree of doneness and note the moisture—there should be just the suggestion of a slightly syrupy juice. If the heat has not been too high, the lettuce, normally, provides enough liquid without a further addition, but if the vegetables are cooking in fat only and in danger of coloring, add a couple of tablespoonsful of liquid, shaking the contents of the pan gently. Depending on the degree of doneness, the zucchini may be put to cook now or somewhat later: Sauté them, tossing very often, over a high flame, in a fairly large omelet-type pan with a couple of tablespoons of butter for 5 or 6 minutes—or until all are just tender and a number lightly colored. Add to the other vegetables when they are melting tender and leave, covered, for the flavors to intermingle for another 5 or 10 minutes. Taste for salt, pepper generously, and, away from the heat, add the remaining butter, cut into small pieces or dabs, swirling or gently stirring the contents until it is absorbed into the juices, forming a slight sauce. Sprinkle with the parsley and optional marjoram, return the lid, and serve. It is best to count an approximate hour for the cooking.

ARTICHOKES (*ARTICHAUTS*)

Unless they are boiled whole to be served hot, tepid, or cold with a melted butter or a vinaigrette sauce, artichokes must be pared or "turned," and every precaution should be taken to prevent their blackening: Contact with air discolors them and one should work as rapidly as habit permits, immediately rubbing them with lemon, thrusting them into acidulated water, or, preferably, coating them with olive oil, which, unlike lemon, will not alter their flavor. In addition, contact with carbon knives or with iron, steel, or aluminum cooking vessels not only blackens them but also lends them a harsh and disagreeable taste—they are best pared with sharp stainless steel knives and, if cooked in liquid, prepared in stainless steel or enameled ironware; for baking, use earthenware, enameled ironware, porcelain, or Pyrex and for sautéing use tinned copper or earthenware.

In professional kitchens absolute whiteness is considered essential to an elegant presentation of artichokes and, to that end, they are always rubbed with lemon and cooked—or precooked—in a *blanc* (acidulated water containing a bit of flour and a dribble of oil), producing one of the characteristic and recurrent flavors of international hotel cooking; the native qualities of the artichoke are hopelessly perverted. Even rubbed with lemon, an artichoke bottom cooked simply in salted water, a branch of thyme added if one likes, will be slightly grayish but far finer of flavor.

Artichoke pared to heart (in two different ways, depending on tenderness of leaves) and halved and quartered (one quarter freed of its choke)

It is said that the stem of an artichoke should always be broken off rather than cut in order to pull out the tough strings from those bottoms no longer in their first youth. Young or old, that is the easiest procedure, but one must not imagine that a tough old artichoke, even deprived of its strings, can ever be of any great interest.

Whether preparing hearts of artichokes, whose leaves are tender and whose chokes are barely formed or completely unformed, or bottoms of larger, mature artichokes, the procedure is the same: Break off the stem, tear off the tough outer leaves, pulling each first backwards, then downwards, in order to break the leaf on its inside

173

surface at the point of its becoming fleshy. Pull the tough part of the leaf loose from its fleshy base (which must remain attached to the artichoke bottom). This can be done very rapidly if the artichoke is fresh and the flesh crisp, but be careful never to break the leaf off at the extremity of the base, for each base of flesh forms a resistant, buttress-like support against the inner rows of leaves—once off to a bad start, all the leaves will tend to break off too far down. For tender hearts, cut off the top third of the remaining leaves; for bottoms, cut off a good two thirds. Pare the artichoke, starting at the point from which the stem has been broken, peeling spirally and removing dark green, tough parts all the way around. A finished bottom will take the form of a flattened sphere and, unless unusually tender, in which case its choke should be removed with the help of a vegetable ball-cutter *(cuillère à racine)* and it may be cooked directly in butter, it should be parboiled, the choke removed only after cooking. A finished heart will remain loyal to its primitive form in reduced proportions and need never be parboiled.

See also "Eggs," pages 96 and 98, for other recipe suggestions.

GRATIN OF ARTICHOKES
(Tian d'Artichauts)
(for 4)

1 onion (4 ounces), finely chopped
2 large cloves garlic, crushed, peeled, and finely chopped
⅓ cup chopped parsley
Salt, pepper
4 ounces dried-out bread, crusts removed, soaked in hot water, squeezed
    dry, and chopped (2 cups, loosely packed)
¾ cup olive oil (in all)
4 medium-size tender artichokes
⅓ cup freshly grated Parmesan
Lemon wedges

Mix and chop together the onions, garlic, parsley, salt, pepper, and soaked bread. Spread a bit more than half of the mixture in the bottom of a generously oiled gratin dish. Pour ½ cup of olive oil into a bowl, pare the artichokes to hearts, split each in two, remove choke, if necessary, and slice each half, in the sense of the leaves' length, into ¼-inch thicknesses, plunging the slices immediately into the olive oil and turning them around in it to coat them thoroughly. When all are finished, turn the mass well together with your hands and turn it out onto the layer of bread mixture, spreading it evenly over the surface and pressing it firmly into place. Spread the remaining bread mixture on top, pressing with the palm of your hand to create an even, smooth surface, sprinkle with cheese, dribble the remaining olive oil in a fine crisscross pattern over the surface, and bake in a hot oven (about 425°), turning it down to about 375° after 10 minutes or so. Count 1 hour to about 1 hour and 10 minutes; the surface, sides, and bottom should form a richly golden-brown, crisp encasement, easily detached from the dish and, within, the layer of artichoke slices should be of a white tenderness in their voluptuous and alliaceous sheath. Serve the lemon wedges apart.

STUFFED ARTICHOKES NIÇOIS
(Artichauts Farcis à la Niçoise)
(for 4)

8 medium-size tender artichokes
About ½ cup olive oil
4 slices dried-out bread
½ cup chopped parsley
4 garlic cloves, crushed, peeled, finely chopped
Salt, pepper

Break off the stems, tear off the hard outer leaves—usually 10 to 15—until arriving at those paler in color and tender at the base. Slice off the top half of the remaining leaves, slice off the broken stem end, leaving the base flat, and force the leaves outward, one at a time, working circularly toward the center until the artichoke resembles an opened-out old-fashioned rose. Put the prepared artichokes into a large mixing bowl and pour over the olive oil, turning them around so that all surfaces are covered.

Soak the bread slices for a few seconds in hot water—only until they have swelled and the crusts are completely soggy; squeeze them out in your hands and mix them with the parsley, garlic, salt, and pepper, mashing and stirring with a fork, adding a tablespoonful or so of olive oil while working to render the mixture less resistant. Hold each artichoke upside down for a moment to drain it of excess oil, sprinkle the interior with salt, and place a heaping tablespoonful of stuffing on top, forcing it into the crevices and smoothing the surface with the palm of your hand. Arrange them in a gratin dish just large enough to hold them without having to force them into place (enough space should be left to permit basting). Pour the oil that was drained from them over the stuffed surfaces—about 1 tablespoon per artichoke—and bake in a medium oven (375°) for about 1¼ hours, basting four or five times after the first 20 minutes. When done, the surface should present a firm, crisp, golden gratin, the outer leaves will be crisply browned, and a knife point run through the center should find no resistance in the bottoms. If the artichokes are advanced enough for chokes to have developed, each guest must remove his own.

COLD STUFFED ARTICHOKE BOTTOMS
(Fonds d'Artichauts Farcis)
(for 6)

Court bouillon
- 1 quart water
- 3 tablespoons olive oil
- Salt
- 10 to 15 coriander seeds
- 1 teaspoon mixed herbs (thyme, savory, oregano, marjoram)
- 1 bay leaf

- 8 large artichokes
- Lemon halves (for rubbing bottoms)
- 12 unpeeled garlic cloves
- ¼ cup rice
- 2 tablespoons olive oil
- Salt, pepper
- Lemon juice
- Chopped parsley

This dish makes an excellent hors d'oeuvre.

Combine the elements of the court bouillon, bring to a boil, and leave to simmer, covered, while turning the artichoke bottoms, rubbing each with lemon the moment it is turned. Add the bottoms and the garlic cloves to the court bouillon and simmer, covered, until the former are just tender, but still slightly firm (usually about 15 minutes, but the time may, depending on the age and initial tenderness, vary from 10 to 30 or 40 minutes). Remove the six handsomest specimens, put them aside on a plate to cool, and leave the two others to cook another 10 minutes or so until very tender. Pour the contents of the saucepan into a sieve, collecting the court bouillon in another saucepan, bring it back to a boil, add the rice, and cook, covered, at a simmer for about 40 minutes or until very soft. Drain well in a sieve.

Remove all the chokes, gently prying them loose with a teaspoon, squeeze the garlic cloves out of their skins, and purée the two well-cooked bottoms, the rice, and the garlic together through a stainless steel sieve (they may, first, be put rapidly through the coarse blade of a food mill—once cooked and not permitted to remain in contact with the metal, the artichokes will not be altered). Work the purée, using a wooden spoon, to a fine, firm, creamy consistency, adding the olive oil, salt, freshly ground pepper, and, a little at a time, the lemon juice until seasoned to your taste. Stuff the bottoms with this mixture, mounding it neatly with an inverted tablespoon; serve cold, but not chilled (fragments of pimento, stewed tomato, chopped parsley, or black olive may lend a decorative note).

ARTICHOKE HORS D'OEUVRE
(Artichauts en Hors d'Oeuvre)
(for 6)

Best served tepid or cool, neither hot nor chilled. Precise proportions are of little importance—count about twice as much white wine as olive oil and as much water as necessary to just cover; the choice and quantity of herbs may be varied, more or less garlic may be added; sliced or chopped onion may also be added . . . If, after cooking, the liquid seems overabundant, it may be rapidly reduced apart. These artichokes are eaten like boiled artichokes, their cooking liquid replacing the vinaigrette, and side dishes should be furnished to collect the debris. Finger bowls are useful.

6 medium artichokes
½ cup chopped parsley (freshly picked Italian, if possible)
1 teaspoon mixed herbs (thyme, savory, oregano)
1 bay leaf
10 to 12 unpeeled cloves garlic
¼ teaspoon fennel seeds
Salt, pinch cayenne
⅔ cup olive oil
1½ cups dry white wine
⅔ cup tomato purée (not tomato paste)
1 cup (more or less) water—to barely cover

Break off the stems, pull off those tough outer leaves that are not attached to a tender base of flesh, cut off the top third or half of the artichoke (depending on the variety, the form, and the tenderness), and pare off the dark green parts from the bottom. Arrange them tightly, bottoms down, in a vessel just large enough to contain them, fill the interstices with the dry materials, and pour over the liquids in the order in which they are listed. Bring to a light boil and cook, covered, for from 25 minutes to 30 minutes—or more, depending on the tenderness of the artichokes. They are done when the bottoms resist but slightly the thrust of a trussing needle or a sharply pointed knife (the acidity of the wine and the tomato slows down the cooking process so time may not be judged in the same way as for boiled artichokes).

ASPARAGUS *(ASPÈRGES)*. See "Salads," page 49.

GREEN BEANS *(HARICOTS VERTS)*

Stringless green beans picked immaturely with the flower still clinging should be cooked some 8—or, at the most, 10—minutes, uncovered, in a vast quantity of generously salted rapidly boiling water.

As a garnish, they are drained, tossed rapidly over a high flame to rid them of clinging liquid and bound, away from the flame, by tossing them in butter, first cut into small fragments. As a salad, they are best served only well drained, hot, accompanied by olive oil and lemon wedges. One of the finest accompaniments to a roast leg of lamb, *haricots panachés,* consists of tossing, away from the flame, equal parts of drained green beans and white beans, together with salt to taste, a liberal amount of freshly ground pepper, freshly picked, chopped Italian parsley, and lots of butter. Restaurants often parboil green beans, rinse them in cold water to prevent their turning gray from slow cooling, and reheat them at the last minute by tossing them in butter over a high flame. The color remains intact, but their integrity is, otherwise, seriously compromised.

Larger green beans—those picked at the moment of their greatest weight rather than at that of their highest quality—are usually neither of an exemplary tenderness nor delicacy of flavor, but they may, with a bit of pampering, be transformed into good, wholesome, and sympathetic nourishment (a recipe for a purée of green beans is given in *The French Menu Cookbook*). The following recipe may, depending on personal taste, be simplified by eliminating the tomatoes or altered by the addition of chopped bacon, by tossing in precooked white beans or sautéed little new potatoes . . . The butter may be replaced, in part or entirely, by olive oil.

SAUTÉ OF GREEN BEANS
(Haricots Verts Sautés à la Paysanne)
(for 4)

1 large sweet onion (4 ounces), halved, finely sliced
¼ cup butter
2 medium tomatoes, peeled, seeded, coarsely chopped (or the equivalent of canned tomatoes drained of their juices)
½ teaspoon oregano
1½ pounds green beans, parboiled (12 to 15 minutes—still slightly firm) and well drained
Salt, pepper
Handful chopped parsley

179

In a large heavy frying pan, skillet, *plat à sauter,* etc., put the onion to cook gently in half the butter for from 15 to 20 minutes, stirring occasionally, until soft and yellowed, but not browned. At the same time gently stew the tomatoes, apart, in the remaining butter, with a pinch of salt and the oregano, tossing or stirring to prevent their sticking, until nearly dry, all the excess liquid having been evaporated. Add the parboiled beans to the onions, salt, turn the flame up somewhat and toss regularly over a period of approximately 15 minutes—the beans and onions should both be lightly browned, but one must take care not to let the onions color too darkly. Add the tomatoes, pepper, and half the parsley, toss everything together for 5 minutes or so, sprinkle with the remaining parsley, and serve.

BROAD BEANS OR FAVE BEANS *(FÈVES)*

Broad beans pass through four distinct stages of development: (1) The downy pods, having attained some 6 or 7 inches in length, remain firmly cylindrical and regular in form and the tiny, newly formed beans, the flesh not yet firm beneath its bright, clear, green skin, are most often eaten raw, shelled at the table. The skins have a slightly bitter, pleasant, and refreshing flavor, and it is only at this early stage that broad beans may be cooked, each in its skin; (2) the pod has lengthened and flattened, swelling irregularly around each bean, the skin of each remains a clear green color but has thickened and toughened, the light bitterness turning acrid, and it should be removed. The bean measures from $\frac{1}{2}$ to $\frac{3}{4}$ inch in length and the flesh, bright green, is absolutely tender, requiring but a couple of minutes' boiling if the beans are to be served simply drained and tossed in butter. At this stage and prepared in this way, a sprig of savory boiled with them and a pinch of chopped tender young savory leaves tossed with them, they have a unique and subtle beauty; (3) the beans are nearly mature in size, measuring about 1 inch in length, the tough individual skins are paler but retain still a greenish color. The flesh beneath the skin is still a clear green but less intense than in the preceding stage, is hard to the touch but tender enough to offer little resistance to a piercing fingernail. Boiled, they will require from 8 to 12 minutes and, as such, are still a good vegetable, but puréed, reheated over a high flame, vigorously stirred, and beaten with a wooden spoon to prevent sticking or burning, a generous amount of butter stirred in away from the heat, they provide one of the most heavenly of all vegetable purées; (4) the skins have turned a dull yellowish white, the flesh is hard and has turned from a light green to a dull yellow-buff; delicacy no longer numbers among the broad bean's virtues at this point. Dried, the beans must be soaked overnight and the skins removed before being cooked.

CREAMED BROAD BEANS AND BACON
(Fèves au Lard Fumé)
(for 4)

5 pounds tender young broad beans
4 ounces lean bacon slices
1 tablespoon butter
1 branch fresh savory (or a pinch of finely crumbled dried savory)
About ½ cup water
Salt, pepper
⅔ cup heavy cream
3 egg yolks
Lemon juice
Chopped parsley (mixed with a bit of finely chopped fresh, tender savory
    leaves, if available)

Shell the beans and remove the skins from all except those that are tiny and bright green. Remove the rind from the bacon, cut the slices into ½-inch widths, parboil for a few seconds, and drain.

Cook the bacon in the butter in a heavy saucepan over a tiny flame for a couple of minutes—it should remain limp. Add the broad beans, the savory, just enough water to moisten lightly, salt, cover tightly, turn the flame high for a few seconds to launch the cooking and turn it low again so that the beans may sweat in their steam rather than boiling. Shake the pan gently from time to time and

181

count from 20 to 30 minutes—until tender. Remove the saucepan from the heat and leave to cool for a minute or so.

Mix together the cream, egg yolks, and pepper, stir gently into the broad beans, and return to a low heat, stirring until the sauce is only lightly bound, coating the spoon thinly. Above all, it should not approach a boil. Squeeze in a few drops of lemon juice to taste, sprinkle with chopped herbs, and serve directly from the cooking vessel.

CABBAGE *(CHOU)*

Cabbage, in French cookery, is always cooked for a relatively long time—often 4 or 5 hours—is, preferably, parboiled before being subjected to its final cooking process (which attenuates its often aggressive flavor and encourages its digestibility), is pared of the leaf ribs whenever possible, and, whether shredded, chopped, quartered, or stuffed—whole or each leaf individually—and is usually braised in stock or bouillon, often with lean salt pork (first parboiled to rid it of excessive salt), a bouquet garni, and aromatic vegetables (which always include carrots and onions), chopped or cut up and first cooked in fat—olive oil, pork, or goose. Red cabbage, usually coarsely shredded, is treated in the same way except that half of the stock is replaced by red wine; an apple, peeled, cored, and chopped, is usually added; and sometimes chestnuts are braised with it.

CABBAGE LOAF
(Pain au Chou)

If served hot, a cabbage loaf gains by being sauced—a creamed *béchamel* or a tomato sauce, buttered at the last minute. Cubes of boiled ham may be added to the mixture and it may be served cold, sliced, as an hors d'oeuvre.

½ cup flour
Salt, pepper
3 eggs
⅔ cup milk
1 tablespoon olive oil
1 medium cabbage (about 2½ pounds), quartered, core and ribs removed,
   parboiled 30 minutes, drained thoroughly, squeezed dry, and chopped
Butter (for mold)

Combine the flour, seasonings, eggs, milk, and olive oil in a mixing bowl, working from the center out, whisking until smooth, and leave to relax for half an hour or so. Stir in the chopped cabbage, pour the mixture into a generously buttered baking dish, and bake for from 30 to 40 minutes in a medium hot oven (400°) or until the center of the loaf is firm to the touch. It may be unmolded or served directly from the cooking dish. If to be unmolded, press a buttered piece of parchment paper into the bottom of the mold before filling it and run a knife around the edges before unmolding.

STUFFED WHOLE CABBAGE
(Chou Farci à la Grassoise: "Sou-Fassum")

Traditionally, this stuffed cabbage is one of the elements of the *pot-au-feu* native to Grasse, a Gargantuesque Sunday repast that is further distinguished by counting mutton among its meats. The integral preparation requires a 20- or 25-quart receptacle, but the stuffed cabbage alone provides a more than honorable supper and may be cooked in a large saucepan or *marmite* of a size to easily hold it submerged in liquid. Lacking stock or leftover bouillon, it may be cooked in salted water to which a couple of carrots, an onion stuck with cloves, and a bouquet garni have been added. In season, a handful of freshly shelled peas are a welcome addition to the stuffing.

The Grassois nourish a proud affection for the thing that, to me, seems justified, although a group of friends, all originally from the southwest of France, once surprised me by unanimously pronouncing it insipid and flabby. The cook had, admittedly, been overcautious with seasoning, but their common yardstick for judgment was the golden, firm, egg-yolk-bound *farci* of the next recipe—quite another thing, which, to my mind, may be as good but is certainly no better than the *sou-fassum*.

A net-like arrangement called a *fassumier* was, in the past, manufactured in Grasse. A string bag, the top of which has been cut off, permitting it to be opened out flat, is its most practical replacement. Lacking that, cheesecloth may be used.

1 large Savoy cabbage
The green, leafy parts of 2 pounds Swiss chard, parboiled for 5 minutes, squeezed thoroughly, and chopped
1 pound lean fresh pork, chopped
½ pound lean salt pork, cut into ¼-inch dice, parboiled a minute, rinsed, and drained, lightly colored in a few drops of oil (chopped bacon may be substituted and need not be parboiled)
1 large onion, finely chopped
1 tablespoon butter
1 clove garlic, crushed, peeled, finely chopped
2 medium-size, firm, ripe tomatoes, peeled, seeded, and chopped (or the equivalent of canned tomatoes, drained of their liquid and chopped)
½ cup rice, parboiled for 15 minutes, rinsed, and well drained
Salt, pepper, suggestion of nutmeg
1 teaspoon powdered, dried mixed herbs (thyme, savory, oregano)
Stock or bouillon

Remove the dark-green outer leaves of the cabbage, pare the stem end, and parboil the whole cabbage in a large quantity of just simmering water for from 10 to 15 minutes. Drain in a colander until cool.

Spread the prepared string bag (or cheesecloth) out on a tabletop or chopping board, place the cabbage in the center, carefully open out about twenty of the outer leaves, spreading them flatly without damaging them or detaching them from the core. Remove the heart, slicing across the core so as to leave a base to which the outer leaves remain attached and, after cutting out the core from the heart, chop the leaves, pressing the chopped mass well to rid it of moisture.

Mix thoroughly the chopped cabbage leaves and all the remaining ingredients (with the exception of the bouillon), using your hands, and form the mixture into a compact ball, placing it at the heart of the opened-out cabbage leaves and re-forming the cabbage by pressing the leaves, one by one, back around the ball of stuffing. Enclose it in the net bag or cheesecloth, drawing the edges up around the cabbage and interlacing a length of kitchen string through the holes (or, in the instance of cheesecloth, threading it through with a trussing needle) and tying tightly so as to make a compact package. Place it in the *marmite,* pour over enough bouillon to generously cover, bring to a boil and cook, covered, the lid slightly ajar, at a bare simmer, for about 3½ to 4 hours.

Present it in a large salad bowl (place the tied-up cabbage in the bowl, tied end up, undo it, spread the net out and away from the cabbage, "unmold" it onto a plate, placing the plate upside down over it and turning bowl and plate over together, remove the net, replace the bowl upside down over the cabbage and turn the lot over again to present the cabbage right side up in its bowl) and serve, apart, a sauceboat of the cooking liquid with which to moisten the servings.

STUFFED CABBAGE LEAVES
(Feuilles de Chou Farcies)
(for 4)

The stuffing in these leaves is the *farci* of the southwest, about which many a sentimental word has been written but for which one rarely sees recipes—and, in fact, to give a specific recipe is no doubt to falsify the spirit of the thing, for the only rule of its preparation is that it be based on bread *panade* thickened with egg. It is often only that with aromatic support and, when it contains meat, it can be a chopped mixture of any odds and ends of leftover roasts, boiled meats, or poultry giblets. Often a piece of chopped salt pork is the only meat ingredient. If the stuffing most often garnishes cabbage, either whole as in the preceding recipe, destined to serve as the principal element of the meal, or individual leaves, as in this recipe, sometimes serving as a garnish to soup, sometimes served by itself, the reason is economical—whenever something else is stuffed (veal or mutton breasts for braising, chickens for *poule-au-pot,* various vegetables . . .), the same *farci* finds its place there. The stuffed leaves of

185

the following recipe may be braised in stock or bouillon and will be the richer for it.

> 1 large Savoy cabbage
> 8 ounces carrots, peeled and sliced thinly
> 1 large onion, chopped
> 1 tablespoon goose fat or lard (or olive oil)
> Salt

Stuffing
> 1 thick pork chop, bone removed (about 7 ounces), chopped
> 3 to 4 ounces lean salt pork, rind removed, cut into tiny cubes, parboiled for a moment, rinsed, and drained
> 5 to 6 ounces lean veal, chopped
> 1 medium onion, finely chopped, stewed gently in goose fat, lard, or olive oil
> 4 ounces stale bread, crusts removed, soaked in hot water, squeezed thoroughly, and mixed with:
>> 2 cloves garlic, peeled and reduced to purée in a mortar
>> 1 teaspoon powdered, dried herbs (thyme, savory, oregano, marjoram, a tiny bit of sage)
>> 1 handful chopped parsley
>> 2 eggs plus 2 egg yolks
>> Salt, pepper

> Water to cover

Discard the dark outer leaves of the cabbage and carefully remove all the others without damaging them. Pare the rib of each, arrange them stacked in a large saucepan, pour over boiling, salted water, and simmer for about 10 minutes. Pour carefully into a colander and leave to cool.

Choose preferably a heavy, low-sided vessel just large enough to contain the stuffed leaves placed side by side—a 10-inch-diameter copper *plat à sauter* is perfect, as well as being presentable at table, eliminating the loss of valuable heat. Cook the carrots and chopped onion in the fat, salted, over a low heat, stirring occasionally for from 20 to 30 minutes, until lightly colored.

Mix all the ingredients of the stuffing into a completely homogeneous mass with your hands and roll heaping tablespoonsful—approximately ¼- to ⅓-cup portions—into the leaves, placing the stuffing in the center, folding the stem end of the leaf over, then the two side flaps and rolling the package into place over the extremity of the leaf to completely enclose the stuffing. When arriving at the smaller leaves, two may have to be used. You should have approximately 16 stuffed leaves in all, which should be placed, as they are finished, folded side down, on the bed of vegetables in the cooking utensil. Pour over boiling water to just cover, sprinkle with a bit of salt, and cook at a simmer, lid slightly ajar, for 1½ hours. Ladle a bit of the cooking liquid over the stuffed leaves when serving them out.

CARROT PUDDING
(Juliènne de Carottes au Gratin)
(for 4 to 6)

This mixture may also be baked in a precooked pastry shell if one likes.

2 pounds carrots, peeled and coarsely grated or passed through the medium blade of a Mouli-juliènne
⅓ cup butter
The juice of ½ lemon (or more—to taste)
Salt
1 teaspoon sugar
Water to cover
1½ cups heavy cream
3 eggs
Pepper
Butter (for the baking dish)

Combine the carrots, butter, lemon juice, salt, and sugar in a saucepan, pour over just enough water to barely cover, bring to a boil, and simmer, covered, for about ½ hour, then, over a high flame, stirring all the while with a wooden spoon, cook until the liquid has evaporated. Leave to cool for about 10 minutes. Whisk together the cream, eggs, and seasonings, stir into the carrots, pour into a buttered baking dish, and bake for about 35 minutes or until the surface is swelled and brown.

CAULIFLOWER *(CHOUFLEUR)*

Tender, small cauliflower may be broken into flowerets and cooked gently in butter until done, tossing regularly, but very often the larger cauliflower is too strong in flavor to permit this treatment. Parboiling attenuates the taste, but few people realize how little cooking is required—usually, if it has been broken into flowerets, simmering for 5 minutes is enough. A couple of minutes more and it is transformed into an unpleasant mush. Parboiled but kept slightly firm, well drained, flowerets sautéed in a generous quantity of butter over a brisk flame until well colored, a handful of chopped parsley tossed in a couple of minutes before removing from the heat, are delicious as a garnish for roast or grilled meats. Whole cauliflower steamed (about 20 minutes—kept slightly firm also) afford a very pretty gratin, first coated with *béchamel* and sprinkled with cheese on top.

GRATINÉED CAULIFLOWER LOAF
(Crème de Choufleur au Gratin)
(for 4)

2 small or 1 large cauliflower (enough to furnish 2 cups of purée), broken into flowerets and parboiled
2 eggs
⅔ cup heavy cream
Salt, pepper
½ cup freshly grated Parmesan
2 tablespoons butter

Coarsely purée the well-drained cauliflower through a vegetable mill, mix thoroughly with the whisked eggs and cream, salt and pepper to taste, pour into a buttered gratin dish, sprinkle the surface evenly with cheese, distribute paper-thin shavings of butter (taken from a cold block), and bake for about 20 minutes in a hot (450°) oven—or until the surface is nicely colored.

CELERY *(CÉLERI-BRANCHE)*

Celeriac more often serves as a cooked vegetable than branch celery (two parts of celeriac parboiled with one part of potatoes, well drained, puréed, and generously buttered, is a splendid accompaniment to roast lamb, beef, or venison—mysterious and exquisitely flavored white purées may be conceived by a judicious addition of onions and garlic cloves, parboiled with them, and turnips, parboiled apart and stewed in butter before being combined into the purée . . .), but hearts of the latter, braised, are among the more sumptuous of roast garnishes. The syrupy braising juices may, removed from the heat, be bound by whisking in butter or, once braised, the hearts may be transformed into a gratin with a sprinkling of Parmesan and some 20 minutes in a hot oven.

BRAISED CELERY HEARTS
(Coeurs de Céleri-branche Braisés)

1 celery bunch per person, outer stalks removed, bottoms trimmed, tops cut off to leave approximately 5-inch-length hearts, split in halves
Gelatinous veal stock or reduced pot-au-feu or poule-au-pot bouillon (See page 103)

Cook the celery heart halves in simmering salted water for from 8 to 10 minutes (they should remain firm), drain well, and gently pack them into a shallow, heavy cooking utensil large enough to hold them in a single layer. Pour over hot stock to barely cover and cook, covered, at the slightest simmer for from 1½ to 2 hours—or until meltingly tender, the braising juices reduced to a clinging syrup.

(SWISS) CHARD ("BETTE," "BLETTE," OR, RIB ALONE, "CARDE")

The wide, fleshy rib of the chard leaf is appreciated throughout France, usually parboiled in a court bouillon like that of the following recipe, drained, and gratinéed with a *béchamel* and cheese. Sometimes a simple white *(bâtarde)* sauce is prepared with a roux and a couple of ladles of the court bouillon and given a terminal egg-yolk binding (in which case it must not be permitted to return to a boil nor may it be submitted to a gratin process; the preparation is conveniently baptized *à la Poulette,* and it is best to omit the vinegar from the court bouillon and add lemon juice to taste at the last minute), or the ribs may be diced and added to soups.

La Mazille *(La Bonne Cuisine du Périgord)* writes, with a certain satisfaction (and an evident disdain for the eaters of chard greens), "In the country [of Périgord], one has no taste for them [the green parts]. The white ribs, which, when cooked, are tender and perfumed, are preferred." And, in fact, outside of meridional France, where they are an indispensable element in most stuffings, in many gratins, and in occasional soups, the green leafy parts of the chard are usually fed to the rabbits and the ducks. In Nice, however, they replace the Italian's spinach in the fabrication of green pasta, and the Niçois have a passion for a *tourte* of olive oil pastry containing a mixture of shredded chard greens, raisins, pine nuts, grated cheese and sugar, bound with egg. Sometimes a bit of marc is added and sliced apples may mask the filling before the top crust is sealed into place. Sugar is sprinkled on top as it is removed from the oven. It is a thing more often eaten in the streets than at table. Parboiled and served hot, tepid, or cold, seasoned at table with olive oil and lemon (or vinegar), the clean, uncomplicated, and uncompromising, healthy flavor of the chard green is an appreciable thing.

SAFFRONED CHARD RIBS
("Cardes au Safran" or "Côtes de Blettes au Safran")
(for 4, or, as a main course, for 2)

This, to me, has a great deal more spirit than most chard rib preparations. A robust and well-chilled dry white wine with no pretensions
to subtlety is its best accompaniment and, if serving as the main
course of a light supper, it cannot be better escorted than by an unadorned pilaf.

Court bouillon   2 quarts water
1 large onion, finely sliced
2 bay leaves, large branch thyme
1 tablespoon wine vinegar
Salt

The ribs of 2 pounds chard (about 1¼ pounds), trimmed,
strings removed as for celery branches, cut into sections
of approximately 1 inch by 4 inches
Pepper
2 anchovy filets
2 large garlic cloves, peeled

Roux   1 tablespoon olive oil, 1 tablespoon flour
Handful chopped parsley
Pinch cayenne
Knife tip of powdered saffron (to taste)
2 cups of the court bouillon

Bring the water to a boil, add all the ingredients of the court
bouillon, and cook, covered, at a light boil for ½ hour. Strain the
liquid, discard the solid elements, and cook the chard ribs in it, covered, at a light boil, for about 12 minutes—or until tender. Transfer
them with a large wire skimming spoon to a gratin dish and grind
pepper over the surface.

Pound the anchovy filets and the garlic cloves to a paste in a
mortar.

Cook the olive oil and the flour together for a minute or two over a tiny flame, stirring, add the anchovy-garlic paste, the parsley, the cayenne, and the saffron, stir well together, and add the court bouillon, the first cupful in small quantities at a time, stirring the while to avoid lumping. Continue stirring until the boil is reached and leave to simmer—or to boil very lightly at one part of the surface, skimming off the skin that forms two or three times over a period of 20 minutes. Taste for salt. Pour the sauce evenly over the ribs and put into a hot oven (450°) for another 20 minutes.

CHICK-PEAS *(POIS-CHICHES)*

GRATIN OF CHICK-PEAS WITH SPINACH
(Gratin de Pois-Chiches aux Épinards)
(for 4 to 6)

2 pounds spinach, picked over, stems removed, washed in several waters
2 quarts water
Salt
8 to 10 ounces chick-peas
½ teaspoon baking soda
Thyme, bay leaf
1 onion stuck with 2 cloves
1 (3- or 4-ounce) carrot, peeled
About ⅓ cup olive oil (in all)
2 medium tomatoes, peeled, seeded, coarsely chopped (or equivalent of canned tomatoes, drained of their liquid)
3 cloves garlic, peeled, sliced paper-thin
1 handful chopped parsley
1 teaspoon finely chopped fresh savory (or a pinch of finely crumbled dried savory)
10 to 12 almonds, blanched 2 minutes in boiling water, skins removed
2 hard-boiled eggs
1 pinch cayenne, ⅛ teaspoon saffron, freshly ground pepper
About ½ cup stale bread, crusts removed, crumbled

Cook the spinach for no more than 3 minutes in lightly salted, boiling water (the same water will be used for the chick-peas and later reduced, so excess salting must be avoided), drain it, saving the water, rinse in cold water, and press lightly—only to remove excess water. Put aside in a bowl, covered.

Pick over the chick-peas, looking carefully for small stones. Soak them overnight in a large quantity of cold water in which the soda has been dissolved. Rinse in several waters and put to cook with the cold spinach-cooking water, the herbs, the onion, and the carrot. Bring slowly to a boil, skim, and cook, covered, at a bare simmer, for about 2 hours—or until done. Drain the cooking liquid into another saucepan, discard the herbs, onion, and carrot, and put the chick-peas aside. Reduce the cooking liquid to about 1 cup (tasting for salt—if it risks becoming too salty, stop reducing), skimming off any scum that forms on the surface.

Stew the tomatoes gently in 2 or 3 tablespoons of the olive oil with the garlic, parsley, and savory, lightly salted, for about 15 minutes. Pound the almonds to a paste in the mortar, add the yolks of the 2 hard-boiled eggs, the cayenne, the saffron, and the pepper, and work together with the pestle into a consistent paste. Slice the egg whites thinly.

Combine the chick-peas, their reduced cooking liquid, the tomato mixture, the almond and egg-yolk mixture, and the sliced egg whites, bring to a boil, stirring—and, with the pestle, crushing some of the chick-peas to lend greater body to the sauce. Mix in the spinach, taste for salt, and pour the mixture into a lightly oiled gratin dish. Smooth the surface, sprinkle evenly with the breadcrumbs, dribble olive oil in a crisscross pattern over the entire surface, and bake in a hot oven (about 400°) for ½ hour or until the mass is bubbling and the surface is crisply golden.

EGGPLANT (*AUBERGINES*)

Eggplant has an important place in Provençal cooking and, as in Italy, tomato commonly assists in its preparation. Their affinity cannot be questioned, but it is sometimes good to savor an eggplant

alone. For instance, you can bake them whole. Use small eggplants—
5 or 6 ounces, baking them for about ¾ hour or until the flesh is
purée soft at the stem end—but don't test with the point of a knife,
for, while cooking, they swell, retaining the hot air in their skins and
each guest should have the pleasure of puncturing his eggplant at
table; accompany with olive oil, salt, pepper, lemon, and, if one likes,
finely chopped parsley, onion, and garlic. They may be eaten split
lengthwise and spooned directly from the skins or the contents
spooned out and mashed with a fork and the chosen seasoning.
They are also good grilled (split in two lengthwise, if they are small,
crisscross incisions made deeply into the flesh, taking care not to cut
through the skin, marinated in olive oil for 15 minutes or so, seasoned
and grilled over hot coals, flesh side first—until golden brown, finished on skin side until the flesh is completely tender at the stem
end). And, of course, they can be fried.

EGGPLANT CUSTARD
(Crème d'Aubergines à la Provençale)
(for 4)

10 ounces mushrooms, passed through medium blade of Mouli-juliènne
Salt, pepper
Olive oil (for mushrooms, tomatoes, eggplant)
½ lemon
2 large, firm, ripe tomatoes, peeled, seeded, coarsely chopped (or equivalent
  of drained canned tomatoes)
1 clove garlic, crushed, peeled, finely chopped
1½ pounds eggplant
2 eggs
1 cup milk
About ⅛ teaspoon powdered saffron dissolved in a couple of tablespoons
  boiling water

Sauté the mushrooms, seasoned, in a couple of tablespoons olive
oil the moment they have been juliènned, over a high flame until
their liquid is evaporated. Squeeze in a few drops of lemon juice.

Stew the tomatoes, seasoned, in 2 tablespoons olive oil until nearly dry, stirring in the garlic a minute before removing from the heat.

Cut the eggplant into slices of from ⅓ to ½ inch thick and put immediately to cook in a skillet or omelet pan containing a depth of about ½ inch olive oil. When golden on both sides and tender, remove to drain on absorbent toweling, sprinkle with salt and pepper.

Spread the mushrooms in the bottom of an oiled gratin dish, arrange half of the eggplant slices on this bed, spread them with the stewed tomato mixture, and arrange the remaining eggplant slices on top. Beat the eggs with a whisk, whisk in the milk, salting lightly, then the dissolved saffron, and pour over the vegetables, lifting them gently here and there around the sides with a fork, permitting the liquid to penetrate evenly. Bake for about 30 minutes in a medium (375°) oven or until the custard has only just set in the center.

EGGPLANT FANS
(Aubergines en Eventail)
(for 4)

3 medium elongated eggplant (1 to 1¼ pounds), rinsed, wiped dry, ends trimmed but unpeeled
2 large firm ripe tomatoes, core removed, unpeeled, split vertically, the halves sliced thinly
1 large onion, finely chopped
4 cloves garlic, peeled, finely sliced
⅓ to ½ cup olive oil
4 tender artichokes, pared to hearts, quartered, chokes removed
3 ounces black olives (preferably small "Niçoises")
2 bay leaves, broken into small pieces
1 teaspoon mixed herbs (thyme, oregano, savory)
Salt, pepper

If only the large, egg-shaped eggplant is available, split it and cut it into slices crosswise. Otherwise, split the small elongated variety, place the halves, split side down, on the chopping board, and cut each, leaving the slices attached at the stem end, into ⅓-inch thicknesses, forming "fans." Slip tomato slices into the slits of the sectioned egg-plant halves and arrange them, gently forced together, side by side, in a large, oiled gratin dish, on the bottom of which has been scattered half of the chopped onion and sliced garlic.

Pour the olive oil into a bowl and, the moment the artichoke quarters are pared, turn them around in the oil, coating them to protect them from contact with air. Force them and the olives (first rinsed) into the crevices or hollows left by the eggplant fans, fit in the bay fragments here and there, scatter the remaining onion and garlic over the surface, and sprinkle with the mixed herbs, salt, and pepper. Press everything into place to form as nearly regular surface as possible, and dribble the oil left over from the artichokes over the entire surface, adding a bit more, if necessary. Bake for about 1½ hours, a sheet of aluminum foil placed loosely over the surface, starting with a 450° oven and turning it down to about 350° after 10 minutes or so. When done, the stem ends of the eggplant should be perfectly soft to the touch. Serve as an hors d'oeuvre, either tepid or cold (but not chilled), sprinkled, if you like, with chopped parsley or fresh basil leaves torn into small fragments.

EGGPLANT GRATIN
(Gratin d'Aubergines)
(for 4)

Most Provençal gratins of eggplant consist simply of alternate layers of precooked eggplant slices and stewed tomato, the surface sprinkled with cheese, or, in some instances, there is only an intermediate layer of stewed tomato with *béchamel* poured over the surface and sprinkled with cheese. This recipe seems to me very much more interesting, both from the point of view of presentation and of flavor. Often the eggplant is parboiled rather than being precooked in olive oil, but the latter method lends a more exciting savor. In any case, the eggplant must be precooked and the usual reason for failure is insufficient precooking; the stem end is tougher than the rest of the flesh, requiring longer cooking, and the slices should not be removed from the olive oil until the stem end offers no resistance to a knife tip.

With any preparation involving eggplant precooked in olive oil, it is a mistake to add more oil, for the eggplant has, in its first cooking, absorbed a great deal of oil, which, even though the slices are drained on towels, is partly retained and exuded during the subsequent cooking process.

1½ pounds eggplant (preferably small, elongated variety) sliced lengthwise into ½-inch slices (or, if large, sliced crosswise)
Olive oil for frying

Stewed tomatoes
1 medium onion, finely chopped
1 tablespoon olive oil
1 clove garlic, finely chopped
1 pound tomatoes, peeled, seeded, cut into pieces
½ teaspoon sugar
Salt, small pinch cayenne

Cheese custard
4 ounces ricotta or other fresh white cheese
1 egg
Salt, pepper
About ½ cup freshly grated Parmesan
About ½ cup heavy cream

Pepper
Handful fresh basil leaves and flowers
About ½ cup freshly grated Parmesan

Cook the eggplant slices in hot olive oil (turning the flame up or down as necessary to achieve even coloring without burning) until golden brown on both sides and tender at all points. Drain on absorbent paper toweling (for this quantity, the slices will probably have to be fried in three batches, additional oil being added to the pan for each).

Cook the onion in olive oil for some 15 minutes until soft and yellowed, but not colored. Add the garlic and the tomatoes, season, turn the flame high, tossing several times, until well heated, then simmer gently—for 15 minutes or so—until the tomatoes' liquid is almost completely reduced. Taste for salt.

Mash the white cheese with a fork, mixing in the egg—first stir-

197

ring, then beating. Season and stir in enough Parmesan to bring the mixture to the consistency of a thick paste, then stir in cream until a heavy but easily poured creamy consistency is achieved. Taste for salt.

Line the bottom of a gratin dish or shallow baking dish with half of the eggplant slices, grind over a bit of pepper, tear the basil leaves into tiny pieces, sprinkling the surface evenly with leaves and flowers, sprinkle lightly with cheese, and spoon the tomato mixture evenly over the surface. Gently press the remaining eggplant slices into place and spoon the cheese-custard mixture regularly over the entire surface. Sprinkle generously with Parmesan and put into a fairly hot oven (425° to 450°), turning it down after some 10 minutes to about 375°, counting approximately 25 minutes or until the surface has swelled, no depression remaining in the center, and it is uniformly colored a rich golden brown.

(BELGIAN) ENDIVES *(ENDIVES)*

Endives are often parboiled, left to cool a bit, squeezed out, and sautéed in butter until lightly browned. Sometimes they are put to cook, raw, with a chunk of butter, seasoning, a bit of lemon juice, and a couple of tablespoons of water, barely simmered in a tightly covered vessel until tenderly done—45 minutes to 1 hour—and served as such, or they may be moistened with cream just before serving. Gratins are common, and the simplest consist of squeezing out parboiled endives, sprinkling with cheese, spreading butter shavings over the surface, and baking in a hot oven until a golden surface is formed; cream or a light *béchamel* may be poured over before sprinkling with cheese. They may be first parboiled, squeezed, then cooked gently until meltingly tender in a rich stock or reduced bouillon, arranged on a bed of mixed mushroom purée and fairly thick *mornay,* their cooking liquid reduced to a light syrup and poured over, Parmesan sprinkled over the surface, and gratinéed . . .

GRATIN OF ENDIVES AND BACON
(Gratin d'Endives au Lard Fumé)
(for 3 or 4)

6 medium endives (about 1 pound)
3 tablespoons butter
Salt, pepper
½ cup freshly grated Parmesan
⅔ cup stale (but not dried out) grated bread, crusts first removed
2 tablespoons chopped parsley
3 ounces lean bacon slices, coarsely chopped
¾ cup heavy cream
Lemon quarters (to be served apart)

Remove the outer, discolored leaves from the endives, trim remaining discolored edges, if necessary, and split each in two lengthwise. Pack them in a tight single layer, split side down, in a generously buttered gratin dish and sprinkle the surface with salt and pepper. Mix together the grated cheese, the breadcrumbs, the parsley, and the chopped bacon, pulling apart any fragments of bacon that stick together, and distribute this mixture evenly over the surface. Start in a 450° oven and, after a few minutes, reduce the thermostat to about 375°. After 40 or 45 minutes, remove and moisten with the cream, trickling it regularly over the surface, and return to the oven for another 20 minutes or so. Serve with lemon quarters.

CREAMED ENDIVES AND BACON
(Endives à la Crème)
(for 4)

2 tablespoons butter
1½ pounds firm, well closed endives, outer leaves removed, parboiled
15 minutes in salted simmering water, cooled, squeezed
3 ounces lean bacon slices, cut crosswise into ⅔-inch sections
Salt

Pepper
Juice of ½ lemon
⅔ cup heavy cream
2 tablespoons finely chopped fines herbes (or parsley)

Melt the butter in a heavy *plat à sauter* or an earthenware *poëlon* just large enough to contain the endives placed side by side, arrange them, and distribute the bacon pieces regularly in the crevices between. Salt lightly and cook, covered, over a low heat for about 45 minutes, shaking gently and turning the endives over from time to time, then turn the heat up somewhat, cooking uncovered for about 10 minutes more, surveying closely and turning regularly until they are lightly browned on all sides and the liquid is completely evaporated.

Grind pepper generously over the surface, sprinkle with the lemon juice, and pour over the cream, shaking the pan slightly to dislodge the endives and to equalize the distribution of the cream, and leave, covered, over low heat, without permitting the cream to come to a boil, for about 5 minutes—the time necessary for the flavors to intermingle. Sprinkle with the *fines herbes* and serve directly from the cooking vessel.

BRAISED FENNEL
(Fenouil Braisé)
(for 4)

2 pounds tender bulb fennel
10 or 12 cloves garlic, unpeeled
¼ cup olive oil
Salt
½ cup water
Pepper

Remove outer stalks from fennel bulbs, pull out the strings from those now at the surface of the bulb, split each bulb in two, and put, dry, along with the garlic cloves, to cook in the olive oil in a *plat à sauter,* large skillet, etc., designed to hold them placed side by side.

Salt them, turn occasionally over a period of about ½ hour until all are browned lightly, pour in the water, bring to a boil, and cook over very low heat, tightly covered, at the suggestion of a simmer, for about 1 hour. The fennel halves should be meltingly soft while still holding their shape and the water should have reduced with the caramelized material from the pan to a rich, deep brown syrup that coats the vegetables like a light sauce. The garlic cloves will be appreciated by some in themselves, but they will have done their delicate work for all in caressing ever so slightly the fennel and its juice. Pepper.

GARLIC *(AULX)*

GARLIC PURÉE
(Purée d'Aulx)
(proportions for about 1 cupful)

An extremely useful flavoring agent—as an addition to other vegetable purées, to soups, sauces, stuffings, terrine mixtures, *tapenades,* or the so-called *caviar d'aubergines*—it is also delicious spread on slices of bread with other hors d'oeuvres or mixed into a vinaigrette. The flavor is not aggressive, as many a novice might expect, and the self-appointed enemies of garlic will be unaware of its presence if it is used with discretion.

20 to 25 whole heads of firm, healthy garlic (avoid those which have begun to sprout or which contain in the heart of each clove a green germ)
Salt
About ¼ cup olive oil

Wrap the heads of garlic together in a large sheet of aluminum foil and bake in a hot oven—400° to 425°—for 1 hour or until the sharp point of a small knife passes through a head without resistance. Leave to cool until easily handled, undo all the cloves, tearing off the root attachment after the outer cloves have been removed. Remove

Garlic

superfluous parchment but don't try to remove the skins from individual cloves.

Place a fine sieve over a mixing bowl and, one at a time, squeeze each clove firmly, forcing the purée out of the root end (most will empty cleanly in a single mass or spiral out—occasionally a clove skin will split and the purée will exude in all senses). Pass through the sieve with a pestle, season to taste with salt, stir in 2 or 3 tablespoons of olive oil, and, if to be stored, pack into a small jar and pour another tablespoon of olive oil over the surface. Keep covered and refrigerated.

LENTILS *(LENTILLES)*

Lentils are a wonderful accompaniment to any of the various salted or smoked pork products, cooked apart in an herb and aromatic vegetable-flavored court bouillon. More often these meats are cooked together with the lentils, which, imbibing the fats and jealous flavors of the meats, lose their own pure autonomy, their digestibility being seriously compromised at the same time.

Check them carefully, spreading small quantities at a time out on a plate, to remove any tiny stones or foreign grains. Rinse in a couple of waters, drain them, and cook them in a heavy utensil—earthenware is perfect—covered generously with cold water, a carrot, an onion stuck with a clove or two, a couple of cloves of garlic, thyme, a bay leaf, and salt, the water brought slowly to a boil and reduced to the suggestion of a simmer, covered, for from 1 hour to 1½ hours (depending on their age and quality) or until purée soft but still intact. Drained (their cooking liquid saved for a soup), with butter and freshly picked, chopped parsley tossed in, peppered and salted to taste, they lend their best qualities.

A lentil purée, alone or as a companion to other vegetable purées (green bean, celeriac, mushroom, turnip, *soubise* . . .), is a classical and impeccable accompaniment to roasts of furred game, lamb, or beef: Cooked and drained as above, they should be first coarsely puréed through a vegetable mill, then, a few spoonfuls at a time, put through a fine sieve to produce a smooth, velvety texture from which all suspicion of skin fragments has been eliminated, seasoned to taste, reheated over a high flame, briskly stirred and beaten with a wooden spoon to incorporate the heat while preventing the purée from sticking, butter beaten in away from the heat in sufficient quantity to bring the purée to a nearly pourable state.

LETTUCE *(LAITUE)*

LETTUCE CUSTARD
(Pain de Laitue)
(for 4 to 6)

1½ pounds (4 heads) Boston lettuce
1 cup heavy cream
4 eggs
Salt, pepper, nutmeg
Butter (for the mold)

Pick over and wash the lettuce leaves as for a salad, parboil them, counting 3 or 4 minutes from the time that the water returns to a boil, drain, refresh beneath cold running water, and squeeze them free of excess moisture. Chop them.

Whisk together the cream, eggs, and seasonings, stir in the lettuce, taste for seasoning, and pour into a buttered charlotte mold or deep baking dish against the bottom of which has been firmly pressed a round of buttered parchment paper (to facilitate unmolding). Cook in a 375° to 400° oven in a *bain-marie* for 45 to 50 minutes or until the center is firm to the touch. Run a knife around the edges before unmolding, lift off the round of parchment, and, as a garnish, serve either as is or moistened with roasting juices. As a course apart, it is attractive with a lightly buttered tomato sauce.

MUSHROOMS *(CHAMPIGNONS)*

The steadily increasing number of adherents to mycological societies apart, most people still fear all but the widely commercialized cultivated mushroom. It is a pity, for, though a faithful standby, it knows nothing of the delicacy of certain of its wild cousins. Edible wild mushrooms are not all very good; to my way of thinking—a way perhaps at variance with that of the passionate mycologist—no more than a dozen or so are of real culinary interest. Some few are sublime and all grow wild in one part or another of the United States.

Two American field guides appear to me to be particularly serious and, at the same time, easy and enjoyable reading for the amateur:

The Mushroom Hunter's Field Guide by Alexander H. Smith
(University of Michigan Press, 1971)

The Savory Wild Mushroom by Margaret McKenny and
Daniel Stuntz
(University of Washington Press, 1971)

Dr. Smith's book is of the greater interest to the general reader, *The Savory Wild Mushroom* concentrating mainly on the mushrooms to be found in the states of the Pacific Northwest; both are replete with information that cannot fail to interest even the timid reader who would not trust himself to pick and eat a wild mushroom.

The greater a mushroom's delicacy, the simpler—and more respectful—should be its preparation (the morel and the Caesars' amanita are little appreciated by many Provençaux because of the autochthonous habit of sautéing all mushrooms *à la Provençale,* a handful of heavily garlicked *persillade* thrown in at the last minute; cèpes have a sufficiently bold presence to support this treatment, whereas chanterelles, milk caps, or trumpets of death are positively flattered by it). The Caesars' amanita, for instance, is never so good as when simply rolled in melted butter, seasoned, and grilled over hot coals, a few drops of lemon juice sprinkled over as it is served (these mushrooms, according to Dr. Smith, are found in the southeastern states; another closely related variety with which I am unfamiliar but which, apparently, possesses the same qualities, *Amanita calyptroderma,* is found along the Pacific coast, most commonly in northern California. These are autumn mushrooms. Both of the above-mentioned books concur in discouraging the beginner from collecting them because of the danger of confusing them with deadly varieties— so, under no circumstances should you try them without professional assurance of their identity; with this assurance, you may well agree with many a European lover of mushrooms—and with the Caesars before him—that they are the loveliest of all).

Morels (which are said to be poisonous if eaten raw) are best gently stewed and tossed in butter for some 10 to 15 minutes, finished or not with heavy cream (the stem ends must be trimmed and they should be split in two and well rinsed beneath a vigorous jet of water, then sponged dry before being put to cook; dried morels, after first being soaked in cold water until supple—usually for about 1 hour or slightly more—and drained, must also be trimmed, split, and rinsed and can then be treated like fresh morels). First stewed in butter, they provide a sumptuous addition to delicately flavored forcemeats—chicken *mousseline,* for instance—or to scrambled eggs. They are a spring mushroom; the state of Michigan is celebrated for its May morel festivals.

Despite the intellectualizing myco-hedonists' pretension that to wash a mushroom is sacrilege, the unpleasantness of grinding one's teeth into gravel, soil, or other foreign matter will proscribe such blind reverence to a rational palate unless the mushroom's firm smoothness permits its being, once the stem end has been carefully pared, wiped absolutely clean with a damp cloth. Of the noble varieties, only the Caesars' amanita and the cèpe *(Boletus edulis)* may successfully be cleaned in this way. The hearts of cèpe stems are sometimes worm-riddled—they should be pared clean or discarded, depending on the extent of the damage. Firm, healthy cèpe stems make the best of all *duxelles.* Cèpes may be creamed (thickly sliced, stewed with a bit of chopped onion in butter, submerged in heavy cream, reduced until they are coated with sauce, a bit of fresh cream and chopped *fines herbes* stirred in just before serving); to me, they seem best sautéed with olive oil either *à la Bordelaise* (with shallots) or *à la Provençale* (with garlic), or merely marinated in olive oil and grilled over hot wood coals, a few drops of lemon juice added as they are removed from the grill. Cèpes occasionally are found in the springtime but they are commonly an autumn mushroom. Dr. Smith notes that "collectors are not prone to give away information as to localities where this species may be found."

MUSHROOMS PROVENÇAL
(Champignons à la Provençale)
(for 3 or 4)

This is the easiest and best method of treating any number of mushrooms whose native flavors tend to be a bit flat, such as the milk caps (*Lactarius deliciosus* or *L. sanguifluus*), spreading hedgehog mushrooms (*Dentinum repandum*—known as *pieds de mouton* in France), or trumpets of death (*Craterellus cornucopioides*). Cultivated mushrooms are often prepared in this way also and, despite a more alluring personality, chanterelles (*Cantharellus cibarius*) are most commonly treated this way. They, unlike the others, must first be disgorged of their excess liquid (see page 208) before being sautéed.

The garlic is usually finely chopped, but its presence will be more discreet if it is puréed and mixed with the chopped parsley.

If, after carefully trimming the earthy stem ends, it is possible to wipe the mushrooms clean, do so—otherwise, plunge them into a large basin of cold water, swirl them around vigorously with your hands, and remove them immediately to a colander, lifting them with both hands, fingers splayed. Sponge them gently dry in a towel.

¼ cup olive oil
1 pound mushrooms, thickly sliced, cut into largish pieces, or, if tiny, left whole
Salt
2 cloves garlic reduced to purée in a mortar
1 handful chopped parsley
1 small handful breadcrumbs (preferably finely crumbled half-dried bread, crusts removed)
Pepper
½ lemon

Heat the oil in a large, heavy frying pan and toss the mushrooms, salted, over a high flame for from 5 to 10 minutes (the length of time depends on the size of the pan in relation to the quantity of mushrooms—the best results are had when the mushrooms only cover the bottom of the pan), or until their moisture has been reabsorbed and they begin to color lightly. They should be tossed every few seconds. Add the garlic purée and parsley, well mixed together, and continue tossing for a minute or two—until the mingled perfumes of the two explode—add the crumbs and toss for a few moments more, pepper generously, squeeze over a bit of lemon juice, toss again, and serve.

CRUSTS OF CHANTERELLES WITH FINES HERBES
(Croûtes aux Girolles aux Fines Herbes)
(for 4)

The bread and butter cases afford an attractive presentation but may be replaced by a scattering of croutons. To easily carve the cases, the bread should be of a relatively heavy, firm-textured body and not too fresh. Light-bodied loaves will have to be deep frozen to be workable.

Chanterelles throw off much more liquid in contact with heat than any of the other commonly used mushrooms and this liquid should be drained off. It is flavorful and may be added to soups or reduced to a syrup and added to sauces—in particular the butter-bound juices of sautéed chicken or rabbit that take the sautéed chanterelles as garnish. If the chanterelles were permitted to remain in their juices until those juices were reduced and reabsorbed, they would become tough and rubbery from overcooking. After having picked them over, discarding any spongy specimens and trimming earthy stem tips, wash them briskly, drain them, and put them, lightly sprinkled with salt, into a heavy, tightly covered saucepan over a high flame. Hold the lid tightly in place and shake the pan over the flame to prevent their sticking to the bottom. No sooner will the heat have thoroughly penetrated them than they will be completely submerged in their liquid. As soon as it reaches a full, foamy boil, remove the chanterelles from the heat, drain them in a sieve, pressing gently with the back of a wooden spoon, and put them aside. Raw, chanterelles should be absolutely fresh, firm, and dry, but, once heated and drained, they may be refrigerated for a day or so in a tightly covered bowl without suffering.

4 2- to 2½-inch thicknesses stale white bread, crusts removed, rounds or squares of approximately 3½ inches in diameter

½ to ¾ cup butter (in all)

1½ pounds chanterelles, cleaned, heated, and drained (as explained above)

Fines herbes (1 tablespoon chopped parsley, chervil, and chives in equal quantities plus a few leaves of finely chopped tarragon)

3 egg yolks

Salt, pepper

⅔ cup heavy cream

½ lemon

Use a sharp and sharply pointed paring knife to hollow out the bread cases, cutting downward to within about ½ inch from the bottom and forming ½-inch walls. Pierce the case ½ inch from the bottom and, cutting in a swivel-like motion without widening the point of entry, free the inside section of breadcrumbs, which may then be lifted out with little or no tearing. Spread all the surfaces, inside and out, with well-softened butter (or brush with melted butter) and dry them out on a baking sheet in a 325° oven, turning the heat up or down as necessary to achieve an evenly golden crispness on all of the exterior surfaces and, to this same end, turning them around, onto their sides, or upside down several times over a period of 25 or 30 minutes. Start to cook the mushrooms only when the crusts are nearly ready.

Stew the chanterelles gently in a heavy saucepan with about 2 tablespoons butter, tossing or stirring with a wooden spoon occasionally, for about 10 minutes, stirring in most of the *fines herbes* a couple of minutes before removing from the heat. Leave to cool for a couple of minutes. Whisk together the egg yolks, salt, pepper, and cream, stir it into the mushrooms and, stirring all the while, cook over a low heat until the sauce begins to perceptibly thicken, lightly coating the spoon—it must not approach a boil. Remove from the heat, taste for seasoning, stir in a few drops of lemon juice to taste, fill the crusts, and sprinkle a pinch of *fines herbes* over each.

STUFFED MUSHROOMS
(Champignons Farcis)
(for 4)

One of the nicest things one can do to a cultivated mushroom. Relatively small (about 3-inch diameter), firm, healthy cèpes are glorious prepared in this way; their heady and exhilarating flavor will not be improved by even the slightest addition of nutmeg to the *duxelles*. In either case, the flavor will be much the best if the mushrooms are cooked over a bed of hot coals, but the presentation will be prettier if they are prepared in the oven.

>1 pound large mushrooms, preferably unopened, stems firm and brittle (count 1½ pounds if using cèpes because of the weight of their stems), stem ends trimmed, wiped clean or rapidly washed, and wiped or sponged dry
>Olive oil

Duxelles
>1 large onion, finely chopped
>2 tablespoons butter
>The mushroom stems, finely chopped
>1 handful chopped parsley
>Salt, pepper
>Suspicion of freshly ground nutmeg (optional)
>½ lemon
>
>About ¼ cup dried breadcrumbs and butter shavings (if to be prepared in oven)

Break the stems free of the mushroom caps at their point of attachment, tearing gently first to one side, then to the other so as not to damage the caps (don't cut them—you will have no place for the stuffing). Put the caps into a bowl and sprinkle them liberally with olive oil, turning them around in it until they are well coated.

Stew the chopped onion, seasoned, gently in butter, stirring occasionally, for about 15 minutes or until soft and yellowed, but not browned. Add the chopped mushroom stems, turn the flame high, tossing and stirring until their moisture has been evaporated, stir in the parsley, turn the flame low again for a couple of minutes, and when the mixture begins to stick to the bottom of the pan, remove from the heat, taste for salt, stir in nutmeg (if desired) and lemon juice to taste.

Season the mushroom caps. If they are to be grilled over wood coals, place them on the preheated grill hollow face down for about 4 minutes or until that surface is lightly browned with just a suggestion of crispness here and there, remove from the grill, stuff them with the hot *duxelles* (rapidly reheated over a high flame, stirring the while, if necessary), packing it and mounding it with the hollow of a spoon, and return the mushrooms to the grill, rounded surface down, to finish cooking for another 4 minutes or so—the exact time depends on the size of the mushrooms and on the intensity of the heat; you must sense when they are ready.

If being prepared in an oven, put the seasoned caps, arranged in a shallow baking dish, into a hot (450°) oven for 8 to 10 minutes (or "broil" them for a few minutes on each side beneath a flame) before stuffing them, sprinkling the surface with breadcrumbs and a shaving of butter for each, and finishing them either in the hot oven until lightly colored or, preferably, beneath the broiler flame.

MUSHROOM PUDDING
(Pudding aux Champignons)
(for 4)

10 ounces cultivated mushrooms
2 tablespoons butter
Salt

Béchamel   1½ tablespoons butter
3 tablespoons flour
½ cup milk
⅓ cup heavy cream
Salt, pepper, nutmeg if desired

2 eggs
Butter (for the mold)

Chop or pass the mushrooms through the medium blade of a Mouli-juliènne and toss them, salted, in the butter, over a high flame until their moisture has completely evaporated—3 or 4 minutes.

Prepare the *béchamel* as indicated on page 164, adding the cream as soon as the milk has been added and removing from the heat as soon as it is thickened, a boil having been reached. Leave to cool for a couple of minutes, stir in the mushrooms, beat in the eggs, pour into a fairly deep buttered oven dish, and cook in a *bain-marie,* two thirds immersed in hot water, in a 400° oven for about ½ hour or until the very center of the loaf has just set.

ONIONS *(OIGNONS)*

ONION GRATIN
(Gratin d'Oignons)
(for 3 or 4)

1 pound walnut-sized onions (white spring onions, "silverskins," etc.—or, lacking those, large sweet onions, thickly sliced or coarsely chopped), peeled
Salt, pepper
Nutmeg
About ¾ cup heavy cream
Butter (for gratin dish)

Parboil the onions in well-salted simmering water, counting about 5 minutes from the time the water returns to the boiling point for tender spring onions or up to 10 minutes for certain winter onions —the flesh should be limp but not soft. Drain well and pour them into a buttered gratin dish large enough to put them in a single layer. Salt lightly and grind over pepper to taste. Stir a tiny bit of freshly grated nutmeg into the cream and pour it evenly over the onions, just to cover. Bake in a 350° oven for about 45 to 50 minutes.

STUFFED BRAISED ONIONS
(Oignons Farcis Braisés)
(for 4)

4 large (5 to 6 ounces) sweet onions, peeled
3 tablespoons butter (in all)
4 ounces lean bacon slices, rind removed, slivered crosswise
Handful finely chopped parsley
Handful finely crumbled stale bread, crusts removed
½ pound mushrooms chopped or passed through medium blade of
  Mouli-juliènne
Salt, pepper, nutmeg
1 cup stock or bouillon

Cut off about a quarter from the top of each onion and carefully empty it out, using a vegetable cutting spoon (melon-ball cutter) and leaving a double-walled thickness at the sides and an equivalent thickness at the bottom. Chop the tops and inside finely and stew them gently along with the slivered bacon in 1 tablespoon butter for 15 or 20 minutes, stirring regularly. The bacon should sweat, remaining limp, and the onions should be only soft and yellowed. Stir in the parsley and the breadcrumbs and remove from the heat a minute or so later.

Toss the chopped or juliènned mushrooms in 1 tablespoon butter, salted, over a high flame until their liquid is evaporated and combine with the other mixture. Season to taste and gently, but firmly, pack the stuffing into the onion cases, mounding it with the hollow of a tablespoon. Arrange them in a casserole or fairly deep oven dish just large enough to hold them, pour the stock into the bottom, bring to a boil on top of the stove, and cook, covered, in a 375° to 400° oven, basting regularly after the first quarter of an hour, for about 1 hour. The onion cases should be meltingly tender and, to be served out intact, a certain amount of care must be taken.

ONION PUDDING
(Battue aux Oignons)
(for 4)

Compare this with the cabbage loaf, page 182. The principle is the same: a *crêpe* batter combined with a precooked vegetable and baked. Without the vegetable, it is an English Yorkshire pudding; sweetened, with dried fruits added, it is a *flaugnarde* or, with fresh fruits, it becomes a *clafoutis*...

1 pound sweet onions, halved, finely sliced
2 tablespoons butter
2 eggs
Salt, pepper
⅔ cup milk
¼ cup flour
Butter (about 1 tablespoon for the gratin dish)

Stew the onions gently in butter for about ½ hour without letting them color. Add the eggs, seasonings, and milk to the flour, whisk until smooth, and stir in the onions (slowly if they are still hot). Pour into a liberally buttered gratin dish and bake in a hot (450°) oven for from 20 to 25 minutes or until swelled up and well browned.

POTATOES *(POMMES DE TERRE)*

We have nearly forgotten; good potatoes—like good rice—have an exquisite and delicate flavor, a flavor of such fragile purity that only a breath of salt, a turn of the pepper grinder, and a chunk of sweet butter can fail to mask it.

A reviewer of my last book, commenting on a recipe that called for a firm-fleshed, non-mealy type of potato, complained that it was hard enough to find an edible potato, let alone one of such specific attributes. I felt that the remark was unfair, for I remembered delicious potatoes from my childhood and, on recent visits to American markets, although the plethora of potatoes that had been dipped in a ghastly pink dye was depressing, a substantial choice of different types of potatoes was, nonetheless, in evidence.

I appealed to the U.S Department of Agriculture for all the information they could give me concerning different potato varieties, the specific qualities of each, and their general availability in different parts of the country. I described in detail those available on the French market, the qualities that each possessed, and, in particular, one hybrid variety, the "B-F-15," whose qualities I hoped to find duplicated in an American variety (small, in the form of an elongated kidney, with a dark, dull, dusty umber-colored thick skin, a firm, moist, compact, yellow flesh that remains intact even over a prolonged cooking period, and a good, clean taste. It is not a productive variety and the price is approximately double that of most others).

I received in gracious response, some months later, an impressive collection of literature. One pamphlet was devoted to U.S. grade standards for potatoes. I learned that, in order to meet the requirements of "U.S. Extra n° 1" (formerly "U.S. Fancy"): (1) size gradation is of particular importance; (2) soil clinging to the skins is considered a defect; (3) potatoes should not show more than slight shriveling; (4) artificial coloration is only considered a defect if it entails "more than 5% waste when discolored flesh is removed," is "unsightly," or is designed to disguise other defects (U.S. Extra n° 1 may be "8% defective"); (5) no more than 10% of the potatoes in any lot of "U.S. Extra n° 1" may have sprouts over ¾ inch long! The message, in short, would seem to be that, but for the cardinal importance of size gradation, mediocrity of appearance is tolerated and no qualities other than appearance are deemed even worth consideration.

The remaining literature consisted mostly of articles reprinted from recent years of the *Yearbook of Agriculture*. One opened with this puzzling statement: "In general, potatoes can be classed as long or round and white, red or russet. It would also be desirable to classify potatoes for use, as boiling, baking, or frying. Unfortunately this is not possible because of the wide range of growing and storage conditions as well as personal preferences." The nature of the potato, itself, is, apparently, the only thing that does not apply to its use in cooking. Most of the article is devoted to the potato's interest and versatility in its tinned, deep-frozen, or dehydrated forms.

Another article was, promisingly, actually consecrated to a potato variety—and, but for the previous suggestion that potatoes might be long or round, white, red, or russet, that was the only indication in the whole pile of stuff that a potato may possess any other quality than anonymous potatoness. The article is entitled: "An All Purpose Potato" (anyone knows—or should know—that an all-purpose anything can serve no single purpose well). The potato's name is "Kennebec" and the article opens with a charming verse dedicated to it:

> Some like it hot
> Some like it cold
> Some like it as a chip,
> Bright as gold.
> It may be baked,
> It may be fried,
> It may be mashed,
> Or even be dried.

"The American potato grower today (1968) grows about 50% more potatoes on only 44% of the land area used in 1930." And, thanks to Kennebec, yield trends are still soaring . . . Its qualities are fantastic: gigantic production, disease resistance, aptitude for dehydration . . . Only its taste and its texture are ignored in the eloquent little homage to Super-Potato. The last lines look brightly to the future: "The all-purpose Kennebec of today will most certainly be replaced by a still more superior potato of tomorrow. The future holds great promise for potato growers, shippers, processors . . ."

And so—I cannot help it—I shall continue to recommend potato types, but, if real potatoes cannot be found, substitute Kennebecs.

If you are fond of potatoes boiled in their skins, try, for a change, adding sliced onion, crushed garlic cloves, a couple of cloves, and a choice of bouquet garni elements (branches of parsley, celery, lovage, thyme, oregano, savory, marjoram, bay leaves . . .) to a pot of salted boiling water and leaving it to simmer, covered, for ½ hour before cooking the potatoes in it. Drain the whole lot together and serve with unsalted butter apart (and/or, for the meridional temperament, olive oil).

In America only cheap restaurants moisten mashed potatoes with their cooking water rather than with milk and cream. In France no self-respecting peasant would think of doing otherwise. But the greatest difference between American mashed or whipped potatoes and a French potato purée lies in the fluffy, white, firm, and slightly elastic body of the one—a result of the beating it is given—and the supple, relaxed, grayish, thinner body of the other. The potatoes, halved or quartered if large, should be only just cooked—usually 20 minutes, drained (cooking water saved), and gently pushed through a sieve with a large wooden pestle (with direct pressure—no grinding or mashing), a generous quantity of butter stirred, but not beaten, in and enough cooking liquid added to bring them to a barely pourable consistency, tasted for salt, and generously peppered. Try them on the family (guests might suspect that you had make a mistake—or that you had never read a cookbook). I love them. They are often served liberally onto a plate with a grilled sausage—*andouillette,* blood sausage, or other—plopped into their middle.

Try sautéing tiny new potatoes (scraped and rinsed—or merely scrubbed—and wiped dry) in butter, olive oil, or a combination with a handful of unpeeled garlic cloves thrown in: Use a heavy omelet pan, cook, covered, over a low heat for about ½ hour, shaking the pan often to discourage sticking and tossing them regularly (but never stir them, be it ever so gently—if one should stick, delicately pry it loose with the tip of a blunt knife). Cook another 10 minutes or so, tossing, with the lid off. Chopped parsley may be thrown in a minute or two before removing from the heat. The potatoes should be creamy soft inside, lightly golden outside, and the garlic cloves, if the heat has not been too high, will contain a creamy purée that may be squeezed out and spread on bread.

The question of rinsing potatoes or not is not one of personal preference; it is dictated by the type of a given preparation. One of my preferred garnishes for grilled or roast meats or fowl is a potato *paillasson* (sometimes called *pommes Dauphin:* a mass of potatoes passed through the medium blade of a Mouli-juliènne, well rinsed in a couple of waters, rapidly drained, spread out on a towel, rolled tightly up, squeezed dry, and packed into a heated omelet pan containing lots of butter, cooked covered over a low flame for 20 minutes or until the bottom is golden crisp, flipped—or unmolded onto a plate and slipped back into the pan to which a bit more butter has been added—and cooked, uncovered, for another 18 or 20 minutes before being slipped onto a hot serving platter). Repeatedly, friends who have asked for the recipe have complained that it does not work for them and repeatedly, after stubborn questioning, they have admitted refusing to rinse and dry the potatoes "because all that chi-chi doesn't really make any difference." In fact, that chi-chi is responsible for the voluptuous smoothness contained cleanly within the still sharply defined juliènne texture (assuming the potatoes to be not of an inferior, mealy, soup variety). Left unrinsed, the inside of the cake will be unpleasantly glutinous and the outside will stick to the pan (one friend, thanks to Teflon, had no trouble with sticking but the outer casing, falling short of golden crispness, seemed to be of gray leather). Any raw potatoes, cut to whatever form, that are destined to be sautéed should be well rinsed and wiped dry if only to prevent sticking.

That which mars the perfection of one preparation may reinforce the quality of another; the cooking liquids of a *gratin dauphinois* or an Irish stew are lent extra body by the superficial starch clinging to sliced potatoes and that of shredded potatoes serves the same purpose in the batters for *criques* or fritters . . .

CHIPPED SAUTÉED POTATOES
(Pommes de Terre Emincées Sautées)

An old-fashioned *mandoline* (an attractive wooden device recalling the musical instrument—now sometimes fabricated in stainless steel), by means of which slices of a regulated thickness—paper-thin if desired—may rapidly be obtained, is valuable for many potato and other vegetable preparations.

It is impractical to give precise proportions for this kind of preparation: Count approximately a pound of potatoes, preferably non-mealy and yellow-fleshed, to a third of a cup of butter, using a heavy 8-inch omelet pan and proportionately more for a 10-inch pan to serve for from 3 to 6 people. But for the less exacting method of preparation, these potatoes are, in effect, *pommes Anna.*

Use large potatoes; peel them and slice them lengthwise in order to obtain the largest possible slices, cut thinly as for potato chips, rinse in a large basin of cold water, rubbing them gently between your hands, drain rapidly, spread them out on a towel, and pat them dry with another towel.

Melt the butter, turning the omelet pan around in all directions in order to coat the sides as well as the bottom, add the potatoes, arranging those on the surface neatly in an overlapping design, press the mass compactly with the palm of your hand, season the surface, and cook, covered, over a low flame, gently shaking the pan in a to-and-fro motion from time to time to make certain that they are not sticking, for about 20 minutes or until the underside is crisp and forms a solid block. Turn the flame up or down slightly after 10 or 15 minutes if the potatoes seem to be coloring too little or too rapidly. Shake the pan to be certain that the mass slides freely and toss them over (or unmold them onto a plate and slip them back into the pan, to which has been added a small lump of butter). Finish cooking, uncovered, for another 15 or 20 minutes, seasoning the surface lightly just before slipping them from the pan to the serving dish.

POTATO CUSTARD
(Flan aux Pommes de Terre)
(for 4)

1 pound potatoes, sliced, rinsed, dried (as above)
⅓ cup butter
8 ounces sweet onions, thinly sliced
2 ounces thin slices prosciutto ham, rolled and shredded into a fine juliènne
1½ cups heavy cream
3 eggs
Salt, pepper, nutmeg

Sauté the potatoes in half the butter over a medium-low flame (somewhat higher than in the preceding recipe), salted, tossing them regularly after the first 7 or 8 minutes, until they are lightly colored and just cooked—about 20 minutes. Stew the onions in the remaining butter for from 20 minutes to ½ hour until melting soft.

Spread the shredded ham over the bottom of a lightly buttered gratin dish, the onions on top, then the potatoes, beat together the cream, eggs, and seasonings (only a breath of nutmeg), pour over the lot, and bake in a 425° to 450° oven for 20 minutes or until the cream has swelled and is barely solidified at the center.

POTATOES IN BEER
(Pommes de Terre à la Bière)
(for 4)

1½ pounds potatoes, thinly sliced (but not rinsed)
1 large onion, finely sliced
1 cup beer
Salt
2 tablespoons butter
½ cup heavy cream

Press alternate salted layers of onion and potatoes into a buttered deep baking dish, beginning with a layer of onion on the bottom and finishing with a layer of potatoes, arranging the layers of potatoes neatly overlapping so that they take up a minimum of space. Pour over the beer, distribute paper-thin shavings of butter over the entire surface, and bake for 1 hour, beginning with a hot oven and turning it down to 350° to 375° after 10 minutes. Ten minutes before removing from the oven, pour the cream evenly over the surface.

POTATO TART
(Tourte aux Pommes de Terre)
(for 4 to 6)

1 recipe for short paste (see page 247)
Salt
1½ pounds potatoes, finely sliced, wiped free of excess starch, but not
  rinsed
1 cup heavy cream
Pepper

Line a pie dish or other round mold with the pie dough, crimping the edge as for a single-crust pie. Fill with salted layers of overlapping potato slices, place a round of pastry cut to the inside dimensions of the mold over the potatoes, piercing it in several places with
the sharp tip of a paring knife, and bake for about 35 minutes at
375°. Remove from the oven, carefully lift off the pastry lid, pour the
cream evenly over the potato surface, pepper to taste, replace the
lid, and bake for another 15 minutes. If, toward the end of the
cooking, the pastry seems to be browning too much, place a sheet of
aluminum foil loosely on top.

SCALLOPED POTATOES
(Gratin Dauphinois)
(for 4)

A quarrel rages in France as to what may be the true *gratin dauphinois*. Egg and cheese are included in the recipes from old cookbooks
(too far removed from the sources, according to the purists). Nearly
every reputed restaurant has its celebrated *gratin dauphinois* and each
is willing to divulge its recipe, usually incomprehensible and conceived in the interest of mystification (I have eaten potatoes boiled
in milk and dryly reheated days later under a salamander in a restaurant whose publicly presented recipe pretends that they should be
poached in milk, the milk discarded, covered with heavy cream, and

gratinéed in the oven). When one gets rid of the nonsense, there is nothing very mysterious about this dish, suddenly become one of the masterpieces of *la grande cuisine;* but for the breath of garlic, it is the scalloped potatoes of our American mothers and grandmothers.

The quality of the dish depends on a number of different things (but not only one quality is the right one): The thinness of the potato slices as well as their breadth; the proportions of the dish in which they are cooked; the proportion of milk to cream; the heat at which they are cooked . . . Thickly sliced potatoes piled thickly into a deep dish, moistened only with milk, and cooked in a slow oven for 2 hours are neither less authentically *gratin dauphinois* nor less good (although a totally other experience) than paper-thin slices spread thinly in a wide and shallow dish, richly endowed with cream and baked in a hot oven for less than half the time . . . The most important factor remains the quality of the potato and it should not be mealy.

1½ pounds potatoes, sliced thinly lengthwise on a mandoline, wiped free of excess starchy liquid but not rinsed
2 cloves garlic
Butter
Salt
Milk
Cream

Earthenware will take the garlic better than other materials. Rub a large gratin dish with garlic (or, which is easier and more effective, put the peeled cloves through a garlic press, rubbing the purée and juices all over the sides and bottom of the dish and discarding any solid debris that remains), leave for a few minutes until the garlic juice has completely dried and is no longer tacky to the touch, butter the dish liberally, and pack in the potatoes in lightly salted layers. Pour over enough milk to just cover the potatoes, bring the liquid to a boil on top of the stove (using an asbestos pad to protect earthenware from the direct flame), dribble a thin layer of cream over the surface, distribute thin shavings of butter, and bake in a 375° to 400° oven for about 45 to 50 minutes or until the liquid has been nearly completely absorbed, the potatoes give no resistance to a knife point, and a richly colored skin has formed on the surface.

POTATO DAUBE
(Pommes de Terre en Daube)
(for 4 or 5)

5 cloves garlic, crushed and peeled
2 cups water
Salt
About ⅓ cup olive oil
2 pounds firm, yellow-fleshed potatoes, sliced to ¼-inch thickness, wiped
  dry
3 or 4 European (not California) bay leaves

Cook the garlic cloves in the salted water, at a simmer, covered, for about 15 minutes, then purée the garlic through a sieve back into its cooking water. Rub an oven casserole with olive oil, pack in half the potatoes, distribute the bay leaves, salt lightly (or not at all, depending on the saltiness of the garlic water), add the remaining potatoes, and pour over the garlic water and purée—the potatoes should be well covered with liquid, but not drowned. Dribble olive oil over the surface and cook in a 400° oven for 45 or 50 minutes . . .

POTATO FRITTERS
(Beignets de Pommes de Terre)
(for 4)

One may, eliminating the flour and the olive oil, make thin pancakes from this batter, cooking them as for flat omelets in butter, olive oil, or a mixture, as one prefers, but keeping them for longer over a lower flame, covered until tossing and finished uncovered, so that each side is crisply golden. They should be eaten hot from the pan and it is impractical to prepare them for more than 2 or 3 people. A salad of wild or other slightly bitter greens would complement them handsomely.

Poor-quality potatoes often exude a dismaying quantity of starchy liquid after being shredded in this way. Should this happen, press them against the side of the mixing bowl, pouring off excess liquid, before adding the other ingredients.

10 ounces potatoes, grated or passed through medium blade of Mouli-juliènne
3 tablespoons flour
Salt, pepper
1 egg
1 tablespoon olive oil (plus olive oil for frying)

Sprinkle the potatoes with the flour and the seasonings, add the egg and the oil, beat the egg with a fork, then stir thoroughly until the potatoes are in a suspension of well-blended batter.

Heat from ¾ to 1 inch olive oil in a large skillet until hot, but not smoking—a drop of batter should sizzle at contact. Slip in a heaping teaspoonful of the mixture, taking no care to form them neatly—a few straggling wisps only add to the charm, making the fritters crisply spider- or crab-like. Stir each time before taking up a new spoonful, don't try to fry too many at a time, and adjust the flame—repeatedly, if necessary—to prevent the oil from overheating or cooling. When the undersides are deeply golden, delicately turn each over with the tines of a fork. A flat wire skimming spoon *(araignée)* is the most practical instrument with which to remove them. Drain on absorbent paper for a few moments before serving.

STUFFED BAKED POTATOES
(Pommes de Terre Farcies au Four)

These potatoes are cooked "dry" and will be lightly colored and crisp-surfaced when done. Waxy-fleshed potatoes may also be stuffed with a mixture like that used for the stuffed onions (see page 213), the chopped or shredded hearts of the potatoes added to the stuffing, and braised in stock or broth.

The ingredients are for 1 person.

1 large, regularly shaped potato
1 clove garlic, finely chopped

1 tablespoon chopped parsley
Salt, pepper
Olive oil

Cut thin slices from opposite sides of the potato to form a flat base and top; hollow out the potato, using a vegetable ball–cutting spoon and taking care not to pierce the walls or the bottom. Chop the slices and the insides and mix with the chopped garlic, parsley, salt, pepper, and a few drops of olive oil. Wipe the potato cases dry, rub them with oil, pack them full of the stuffing, mounding it, arrange them in a lightly oiled casserole, dribble a few more drops of oil over the surfaces, and bake for about 45 minutes, covered, in a 400° oven, basting several times after the first 20 minutes and, if more coloring is desired, removing the lid during the last 10 minutes of cooking time.

SORREL *(OSEILLE)*

SORREL TART
(Tarte à l'Oseille)
(hors d'oeuvre for 4 to 6)

10 ounces sorrel, stems pulled off backwards, washed in several waters, drained
Salt
¼ cup butter
10 ounces sweet onions, halved, finely sliced
1½ cups heavy cream
3 eggs
Pepper
1 half-baked 9-inch pastry shell (see page 247)

Plunge the sorrel into salted boiling water and drain the moment the water returns to a boil and all the leaves have turned grayish. Put to stew gently in half the butter, stirring occasionally, until excess liquid has evaporated and the leaves have fallen into a complete purée—about 20 minutes.

Stew the onions, salted, in the remaining butter for at least ½ hour, covered, stirring or tossing regularly. The saucepan should be heavy and not so large as to impose a depth of less than 1 to 1½ inches on the layer of onions—they should sweat as much in their own humidity as in the butter, and, finally, should be translucid, un-colored, and melting on the verge of purée.

Mix together the sorrel and the onions in a bowl and, when no more than tepid, whisk or beat the cream, eggs, and seasonings apart; then pour the mixture slowly into the onions and sorrel, stirring all the while. Pour into the pastry shell and bake in a 375° oven for about 40 minutes or until swelled, firm in the center, and lightly col-ored. Serve warm 20 minutes to ½ hour after removing from the oven. A well-chilled, young, light, dry white wine with a suspicion of sparkle or a light-bodied Champagne are perfect companions.

SPINACH *(ÉPINARDS)*

If bought unpicked-over and unwashed, tear the spinach leaves free of the stems, soak them in a basin of water to dissolve clinging soil and then wash thoroughly at least three times, swirling them in a large basin of water and transferring them by handsful to another basin of water—don't pour the lot into a colander before transferring it to another basin of water; you will only collect all the dirt with the leaves. Lift the leaves from their final rinse water to a colander to drain.

It is often said that spinach should be cooked "dry"—that is to say, only in the bit of washing water that clings to the leaves or, at most, with a couple of tablespoonsful of water added—and that to cook it in a large quantity of water entails a serious loss of flavor and vitamins; this method requires a longer cooking time, a large part of the spinach is subjected to a sort of stewing process rather than to a rapid contact with boiling water, and, although the draining liquid may be relatively small in quantity, it will be a thick, black concentration of all the vegetable's goodness that is discarded.

When it is to be parboiled, plunge it into a large quantity of salted boiling water. As the water returns to a boil begin repeatedly forcing the mass of spinach back beneath the water with the back of a wooden spoon, counting no more than 2 minutes' cooking time— or, if its youth and tenderness are suspect, at most 3 or 4 minutes— from the moment the water has returned to a boil. Drain it, pressing lightly with the back of the spoon to rid it of excess moisture (drained and simply tossed for a moment over a flame with butter, it is delicious) or, for those recipes that call for it squeezed dry, refresh it beneath cold running water until cool enough to handle and take the mass in both hands, squeezing tightly and repeatedly. In this state it may be wrapped in plastic and refrigerated for use in days to come.

In Provençal cooking, spinach is often cooked directly, raw, in olive oil without a preliminary parboil. Sometimes, as for flat omelets, it is stewed gently over a low flame before being incorporated into the egg mixture, but most often, alone or in combination with other vegetables (mushrooms, sliced and oiled raw artichokes—Parmesan may be sprinkled between the layers), it is presented as a gratin. To be used in this way, the leaves must be young and tender or the flavor will be harsh and tannic. Tough, leathery-textured leaves are to be avoided. Light, clear-green leaves are dependably young and gentle of flavor, but, with certain varieties, the leaves are dark green in youth, as well. Spinach produced at the height of the summer is often strong. Prepared raw, it is always wisest to pick over the leaves, tearing the stems backwards, thus removing any tougher veining that runs into the leaf itself.

PROVENÇAL SPINACH GRATIN
(Tian d'Epinards)
(for 4)

2 pounds raw spinach, washed and well drained
Salt, pepper
3 tablespoons flour
⅓ cup olive oil

Hold the mass of spinach tightly together on the chopping board, cut it into a fine juliènne, using a large knife, then turn the mass around and chop it, cutting across the juliènne. Pack it into an oiled gratin dish, sprinkle the surface with seasonings and flour, dribble olive oil crisscrosswise over the entire surface, and cook for 1 hour in the oven, beginning at 450° and turning the heat down to 375° after about 10 minutes. No refinement could possibly improve it.

GRATIN OF SPINACH AND HARD-BOILED EGGS
(Roussin d'Épinards)
(for 4)

The *roussin* should be nursed gently all the way—it must take its own time. The good odor of a bread-and-butter gratin mingled with the browned edges of spinach and the homely marriage made in heaven of spinach and hard-boiled eggs cannot help but stir ancestral memories of farmhouse kitchens and meals taken at scrubbed wooden tables.

1 large sweet onion, finely chopped
2 tablespoons butter
2 pounds spinach, parboiled, squeezed, chopped
1 tablespoon flour
2 cups milk
3 hard-boiled eggs
Salt, pepper, nutmeg (optional)
Butter (for the dish and to top the gratin)
About ½ cup breadcrumbs

Stew the onion in butter in a heavy saucepan over low heat for about 15 minutes, stirring frequently, until soft and yellowed, add the spinach, continuing to cook over low heat, for 15 minutes longer, stirring and respreading the mass out on the bottom of the saucepan by tapping into it with the side of a wooden spoon. By this time all the moisture should have evaporated and only a hint of a delicate frying odor should be noticeable. Sprinkle with the flour, stir well, and begin adding the milk in small quantities at a time, stirring and waiting until it has been thoroughly absorbed by the spinach before adding more. Count another 15 minutes or so for the spinach to absorb all the milk, season to taste, and add the hard-boiled eggs, coarsely cut up. Stir well and turn out into a large buttered gratin dish, spreading the mixture smoothly to no more than 1-inch thickness. Sprinkle evenly and liberally with breadcrumbs, distribute paper-thin shavings of butter over the entire surface, and bake at 400° for about 40 minutes or until the surface is crisply golden.

GRATINÉED SPINACH LOAF
(Crème d'Épinards au Gratin)
(for 4)

1 cup heavy cream
1 egg
Salt, pepper, suspicion nutmeg
1 pound spinach, parboiled, drained well (but not squeezed dry), and
 chopped
Freshly grated Parmesan (or a mixture of Parmesan and Gruyère)
Butter

Beat the cream, the egg, and the seasonings together, stir in the spinach, pour into a buttered gratin dish, sprinkle with grated cheese, distribute shavings of butter over the surface, and bake at 450° for 20 minutes or until well colored.

SPINACH-STUFFED CRÊPES
(Gratin de Crêpes Farcies aux Épinards)
(for 3)

The cheese and spinach mixture is a traditional Italian ravioli filling. As it stands, it is of a gratifying versatility and it may, furthermore, be subjected to infinite variation (see page 382).

> 6 crêpes (2 tablespoons flour, 1 egg, salt, pepper, scant
> tablespoon olive oil, beer: See page 260 for method)

229

Filling   4 ounces ricotta or other fresh white cheese
2 tablespoons softened butter
Salt, pepper, nutmeg (optional)
1 egg
½ pound spinach, parboiled, squeezed dry, and chopped
1 ounce (about ½ cup) freshly grated Parmesan

Butter (for gratin dish and to top crêpes)
Parmesan (to sprinkle on surface)

Make the *crêpes.*

Mash together the white cheese, the butter, the seasonings, and the egg, then briskly stir in the spinach until well mixed but still mottled in appearance. Add the Parmesan progressively, stirring and mashing after each addition, until a firm paste is formed. Stuff each *crêpe* with a couple of mounded tablespoonsful of the mixture, rolling it like a cannelloni into the form of a thick cigar, and arrange them, flap side down, in a buttered gratin dish just large enough to hold them placed loosely side by side without packing. Sprinkle Parmesan over the surface, place a long thin strip of butter on each *crêpe,* and bake in a 450° oven for from 20 to 25 minutes or until swelled and golden brown.

BRUSSELS SPROUTS *(CHOUX DE BRUXELLES)*

For aggressiveness and determined lack of subtlety, sprouts have no peer. To be good—or so it seems to me—they demand shock treatment, a counteracting flavor to soften harsh relief without altering character—bacon, anchovy, vinegar, hard-boiled eggs . . . Mysteriously, those countries that appear to nourish the greatest affection for sprouts are usually content to serve them boiled to death, dribbling a gray liquid.

SPROUTS GRATIN
(Gratin de Choux de Bruxelles)
(for 4)

2 ounces lean bacon, cut into ½-inch widths
2 tablespoons butter
1 pound small, compact Brussels sprouts, outer leaves removed, parboiled about 12 minutes, drained, and coarsely chopped
Salt, pepper
½ cup heavy cream
⅓ cup breadcrumbs
Butter (for gratin dish and surface)

Cook the bacon gently in butter until limp but not crisp, add the sprouts, season, and toss over a medium-high flame for a minute. Spread into a buttered gratin dish, spoon the cream over the surface, sprinkle with breadcrumbs, and distribute paper-thin shavings of butter here and there. Count about 25 minutes in a 400° to 425° oven.

WINTER SQUASH *(COURGE; POTIRON)*

The French use a number of different varieties of squash interchangeably and to the same ends, depending on the season. The pumpkin and Hubbard squashes are the closest American equivalents—perhaps new varieties with which I am unfamiliar have appeared (one, in the south of France, recently transplanted from North Africa, which the natives frustratingly fail to identify more specifically than as *courge rouge,* seems to me particularly interesting; elongated in form, it attains about 1 yard in length and 8 inches in diameter, is seedless and solid throughout with a hard brownish skin, deep red-orange flesh, and a sweet, delicate flavor).

PROVENÇAL SQUASH GRATIN
(Tian de Courge)
(for 4)

2 pounds pumpkin or other firm, red-fleshed squash, well peeled of its
  hard rind, seeds and stringy flesh removed
7 or 8 cloves garlic, crushed, peeled, and finely chopped
½ cup finely chopped parsley
Salt, pepper
4 tablespoons flour
⅓ cup olive oil

Slice the squash into thicknesses of ⅓ inch and cut each
slice into ⅓-inch strips. Cut firmly held bundles crosswise into
tiny dice and toss them in a mixing bowl together with the garlic
and the parsley, seasoning several times while tossing so that the
cubes will be regularly seasoned and coated with the *persillade.*
Sprinkle over the flour and toss the contents of the bowl repeatedly
until each tiny cube is evenly coated with flour (adding a bit more
if necessary—excess flour will fall to the bottom of the bowl and
may be discarded later).

Generously rub the bottom and sides of a fairly deep earthenware gratin dish with olive oil, fill with the cubed squash mixture,
pressing gently and evening the surface, dribble olive oil in a crisscross pattern over the entire surface, and cook in a gentle oven (325°
to 350°) for from 2 hours to 2½ hours or until the surface forms a
deep, rich brown crust—falling just short of being blackened. Beneath the crust the squash should have melted to a near purée, the
cubes retaining perfectly their form but ready to collapse at the touch
of a fork or a tongue.

PUMPKIN SATCHELS
(Chaussons au Potiron)
(for 6—about 36 satchels)

Called, in Niçois dialect, *Barba Jouan* ("Uncle John"), these little pastry purses, served hot from the oven as an hors d'oeuvre and washed down with a well-chilled white wine redolent of the fruit of tender youth—Muscadet, Pouilly-fumé, Sancerre, for instance—are a joy and a perfect example of that which the meridional French like to describe affectionately as their *cuisine spirituelle.* They may also be served, apart, as an accompaniment to a bouillon or other relatively light soup to the advantage of both.

Sharp, powerful sheep's milk cheese—a local and noncommercialized peasant production—goes into the making of an authentic Uncle John. Roquefort provides an honorable substitute.

The pastry should be rolled out as thinly as possible and, to this end, a pasta machine is a great help; the dough should be kneaded, in this case, no more than absolutely necessary to render it manageable before being rolled out (I use the next to last notch on a machine whose rollers may be set at eight different thicknesses). Treated in this way, the pastry becomes more shell-like—much firmer and less tender—when cooked. To best make the comparison between this and tender olive oil pastry, it may be useful to prepare *Barba Jouan* with half of the following recipe and to transform the remainder into a *tourte,* following, except for the filling, the directions given for zucchini pie, page 240 (the resultant pumpkin pie may surprise many a compatriot).

Once having had some 2 cups of this leftover filling and a couple of lambs' brains (poached in court bouillon, sliced, breaded, and cooked in butter) remaining from the previous day, I distributed the brains, in a buttered gratin dish, beat 2 eggs, salt, pepper, and ⅔ cup of cream into the filling, poured it over the brains, sprinkled the top with Parmesan, and baked it in a hot oven for 25 minutes—until swelled and browned. So taken were friends and I with the result that I have often prepared it since. It may also be transformed, with or without brains, into an open *tourte* using either a half-baked butter pastry as for the sorrel tart or a half-baked olive oil pastry single shell. In subsequent preparations when the brains were used, they have only been cooked in court bouillon and sliced.

A 2½- to 3-pound slice of pumpkin or other red-fleshed squash (1½ cups baked and drained pulp), seeds and stringy material removed
Salt
1 medium (2-ounce) onion, finely chopped
1 tablespoon olive oil
2 ounces Roquefort
¼ cup garlic purée (see page 201)
1 slight teaspoon fresh marjoram, chopped powder-fine (or, lacking that, a healthy pinch of finely crumbled oregano)
1 egg
1 cup (2 ounces) freshly grated Parmesan
Pepper
⅓ cup long-grain rice, parboiled for 10 minutes, rinsed, thoroughly drained
Provençal pastry (see page 249)
Olive oil (to oil baking sheet and pastry surfaces)

Wrap the squash in aluminum foil and bake, skin side down, in a 375° to 400° oven for about 2 hours or until the flesh is purée tender. Leave to cool. Line a colander with a towel, empty out the squash shell with a spoon, placing the spoonsful in the towel and salting each layer, fold the towel edges over the surface, place a small plate upside down on top and, on it, a weight of some 10 pounds. Leave to drain for at least 3 or 4 hours.

Cook the onion in the oil in a tiny, heavy saucepan, over very low heat, for about ½ hour, stirring occasionally, without letting it color.

Mash the Roquefort to a paste in a mixing bowl, mash a bit of the squash with it, then stir in the lot, adding the onion, the garlic purée, the marjoram, and the egg, and beating well with the fork. Stir in the Parmesan, grind in pepper to taste, and, finally, add the rice. Taste before adding more salt (the pumpkin has already been salted as well as the garlic purée, Roquefort is often oversalted, and Parmesan sufficiently so . . .).

Using a cookie cutter, an empty tin can, a large highball glass, etc., cut rounds approximately 4 inches in diameter from the rolled-

234

out pastry, stacking them as they are cut and filling them and sealing them immediately afterward to prevent their drying out and becoming unmanageable: Hold a round in the flat of your hand, place a heaping teaspoonful of filling in the center (the amount should not be forced or the pastry walls will split during the baking), dip fingers of the other hand in a bowl of water, smearing it around the edges of the pastry round and fold gently closed, pinching the edges well together. As each is prepared, place it on an oil-filmed baking sheet and lightly crinkle the sealed edges, forming a ruffled crest. Place them an inch apart, one from the other, to permit even baking, brush the surface of each (or smear with your fingers) with olive oil, and bake for from 25 to 30 minutes in a hot oven (about 425°) or until the body of the pastry is lightly golden and the lacy edges of the crests are prettily browned, but not blackened.

ZUCCHINI SQUASH *(COURGETTES)*

Small and firm—almost crisp, zucchini can be a great delicacy, but to remain so they should never touch water in the course of cooking. Their skins are tender, flavorful, and attractive and there is never any reason to peel them. Large zucchini with well-formed seeds are not interesting fare and should not be considered as a possible replacement in any of the following recipes.

THREE ZUCCHINI GRATINS
(Trois Gratins de Courgettes)

Any of the following, if served as a course apart, may be accompanied either by a tomato sauce or, preferably, by fresh ripe tomatoes, peeled, seeded, chopped, and gently stewed in butter or olive oil, seasoned to taste, and finished with fresh chopped herbs of your choice.

(1) ZUCCHINI AND CHARD GRATIN
(Tian de Courgettes aux Feuilles de Blettes)
(for 6)

2 pounds zucchini, coarsely grated or passed through medium blade of Mouli-juliènne, salted in layers, and, 15 minutes later, squeezed free of water

2 medium onions (6 to 7 ounces), finely chopped, stewed gently in 2 tablespoons olive oil for about 20 minutes—until soft and yellowed, but not colored

½ cup long-grain rice, parboiled 15 minutes, rinsed beneath running water, well drained

The green leafy parts of 2 pounds Swiss chard (about 10 ounces), washed, drained, and shredded

3 ounces bacon slices, chopped or sliced crosswise into ⅛-inch ribbons

3 large cloves garlic, peeled, finely chopped

1 large handful chopped parsley

3 eggs

Salt, pepper

1 cup freshly grated Parmesan plus a handful for sprinkling over the surface

About ⅓ cup olive oil

Because of the bulkiness of the uncooked, shredded chard, you will need an unusually large mixing bowl, pot, or basin in which to combine the ingredients. Put everything, with the exception of the final handful of Parmesan and the olive oil, together, mix intimately with your hands, squishing the mixture repeatedly between your fingers, pack it into a large oiled gratin dish, pressing the surface smooth with the palm of your hand, sprinkle the remaining cheese evenly over the surface, dribble over olive oil in a crisscross pattern, and bake in a medium oven (350°) for about 1 hour, turning the heat up to 450° for the last 10 minutes or so to give the surface a rich gratin.

(2) ZUCCHINI GRATIN
(Tian de Courgettes)
(for 4)

1 cup milk

1 ounce (fist-sized piece) soft bread, crusts removed

¼ cup olive oil

2 eggs

¾ cup freshly grated cheese (Parmesan, Gruyère, or a mixture of the two)

Salt, pepper

1 pound zucchini, rinsed, wiped dry, sliced coin-thin (with mandoline, if handy)

⅓ cup long-grain rice, parboiled for 15 minutes, rinsed, and well drained

Pour ½ cup milk over the bread and leave to soak for a few minutes, add 2 tablespoons olive oil, the eggs, ½ cup grated cheese, salt, and pepper. Mash and stir with a fork until batter-like in consistency, add the sliced zucchini and the drained rice, mix well, and pour out into an oiled gratin dish. Press evenly all over, smoothing the surface with the tines of the fork, pour over the remaining milk (the contents should be bathing, the milk barely covering the surface), sprinkle evenly with the remaining cheese, dribble crisscross threads of olive oil over the entire surface, and bake in a 375° to 400° oven for 1 hour or until the surface is golden and the mass dry and firm to the touch.

(3) ZUCCHINI GRATIN
(Gratin de Courgettes)
(for 4)

1 pound zucchini sliced coin-thin (mandoline)

3 tablespoons olive oil

Salt, pepper

2 ounces stale bread, crusts removed, soaked in hot water, well squeezed

3 ounces Swiss Gruyère cut into ¼- to ⅛-inch dice

Persillade: 2 peeled cloves garlic pounded to paste in a mortar, mixed with a handful of chopped parsley

1 egg

Olive oil (for the gratin dish and the surface)

Toss the zucchini slices, salted, in the olive oil over a high flame (tossing every few seconds) for 5 or 6 minutes or until limp and but lightly colored.

Mix together the soaked bread, diced cheese, *persillade*, egg, salt, and pepper, beating with a fork. Stir in the sautéed zucchini and smooth the mixture into an oiled gratin dish, sprinkle a bit of olive oil on the surface, and bake in a hot (about 425°) oven for ½ hour.

TWO STUFFED ZUCCHINI GRATINS
(Deux Gratins de Courgettes Farcies)

Recipes for stuffed vegetables should not be taken too seriously—at least insofar as the ingredients for the fillings are concerned; vegetables may be stuffed with practically anything, and, if a bit of common sense is brought to the composition, they cannot help being good. Leftover roast, boiled or stewed meats or poultry often find their way, chopped, into these stuffings. Stock meats, although most of their goodness has been drained from them, may be ground or finely chopped—revivified by a larger than usual dose of herbs and a pinch of cayenne, they provide an absolutely respectable base. Something alliaceous always gives a spark of life; soaked, squeezed bread, precooked rice, leftover mashed potatoes, or chopped leftover pasta will lend lightness and consistency; egg is for binding and cheese both for sapid relief and textural coherence. Throughout this treatise, Parmesan and Gruyère have been recommended to the exclusion of other grating cheeses and there can be no doubt but that, along with aged Cheshire, they are the best—but other firm cheeses that may have become too unsightly, too dry, or too strongly flavored for continued use on the cheese platter should certainly not be discarded; the various *tommes* and related cheeses or Cantal serve this purpose well, and if American Cheddar continued to resemble its English parent, so would it. Dry goat cheese, become too sharp or too salty to be pleasant as an eating cheese, may, used discreetly, be an interesting and unusual flavoring agent.

(1) PROVENÇAL STUFFED ZUCCHINI
(Courgettes Farcies à la Varoise)
(for 4)

4 firm zucchini (5 to 6 ounces each)
1 medium onion (2 ounces), finely chopped
2 tablespoons olive oil
1 large clove garlic, peeled, finely chopped
Salt
1 large ripe tomato, peeled, seeded, and coarsely chopped
2 tablespoons chopped parsley
⅓ cup long-grain rice, parboiled 18 minutes, rinsed, and well drained

Pepper
¾ cup freshly grated Parmesan
2 thick slices (2 ounces) stale bread, crusts removed, soaked in warm
  water, well squeezed, and chopped
About ¼ cup olive oil

Trim the ends of the zucchini, split each in half lengthwise, and, using a vegetable ball–cutting spoon, remove the flesh from each half, leaving a wall of about ¼-inch thickness. Chop the zucchini flesh.

Cook the onion gently in oil without coloring for about 15 minutes, add the chopped zucchini, garlic, and salt and continue cooking over a slightly higher flame, tossing regularly, for another 10 minutes, then add the tomato and count another 10 minutes, tossing or stirring occasionally, for excess liquid to disappear. Mix with the parsley and rice, taste for salt, grind in pepper to taste, and stir in half of the Parmesan.

Rub the zucchini shells inside and out with olive oil and fit them into a lightly oiled gratin dish just large enough to contain them, forcing them gently if necessary. Spoon the filling into them with a teaspoon, spreading it, forming it, and mounding it with your fingers. Spread a layer of chopped soaked bread over the entire surface, pressing it gently into place, sprinkle with the remaining cheese, dribble olive oil regularly over the surface, and bake in a 400° oven for about 45 minutes or until the flesh of the zucchini shells is tender, lending no resistance to the point of a sharp knife, and a uniformly crisp and colored crust has formed on the surface.

(2) ZUCCHINI STUFFED WITH SORREL
(Courgettes Farcies à l'Oseille)
(for 6)

1 large onion, finely chopped
3 tablespoons olive oil
6 firm zucchini (2 pounds) split and emptied, flesh chopped, as in preceding recipe
1 cup loosely packed young sorrel leaves, stemmed, washed, drained,
  shredded
Salt, pepper
⅔ cup rice, parboiled 18 minutes, rinsed, and drained

1 teaspoon finely chopped fresh marjoram (or other herb)
½ cup water
Freshly grated Parmesan
Olive oil

Cook the onion gently in the oil until soft and yellowed, add the chopped zucchini flesh, and continue cooking, stirring or tossing regularly, until it is soft and its liquid reduced, add sorrel and seasonings, and cook for a minute longer—until the sorrel has turned grayish and begins to melt. Mix with the rice and marjoram; taste for seasoning. Oil the zucchini shells inside and out, pack them gently full of the stuffing, mounding with a spoon, and arrange them in a large gratin dish. Pour the water into the bottom, sprinkle the surface of the stuffed zucchini with cheese, dribble over oil, and bake for 40 to 45 minutes in a 375° to 400° oven.

ZUCCHINI PIE
(Tourte aux Courgettes)
(for 4)

10 ounces small firm zucchini
Salt
1 medium (2-ounce) onion, finely chopped
1 tablespoon olive oil
⅔ cup freshly grated Parmesan
1 tablespoon garlic purée (see page 201)
1 egg
Pepper
Provençal pastry dough (page 249, about ½ of the recipe)
Olive oil (for oiling baking sheet and pastry surface)

Cube the zucchini (sliced lengthwise into ⅛- to ¼-inch widths, each slice into narrow strips, the mass diced crosswise) and put it to disgorge in salted layers in a bowl for 2 hours. Pour into a sieve, rinse under running water, and pat dry in a towel.

Stew the onion gently in olive oil for about ½ hour without letting it color.

Form a paste of the Parmesan, the garlic purée, and the egg, stir in the zucchini and the onion, add pepper to taste. Roll out half of the pastry, trim to an approximate circle, and place on a lightly oiled baking sheet. Spread the filling evenly over the surface to within about ¾ inch of the border. Roll out the other half of the pastry—slightly wider than the first, fold it, cut a tiny "V" from the center to form a vent permitting steam to escape, moisten the edges of the bottom round of pastry and unfold and seal the top into place, pressing all the way around with your fingers. Roll the sealed edges upward and inward on themselves, forming a slightly thicker ribbon of dough surrounding the filled center, and press firmly all the way around with the back of a fork, forming a striated pattern like the rays of symbolic sun images (or press all the way around with the floured edge of your thumb). Brush (or smear) the surface with olive oil and bake at about 375° for from 45 to 50 minutes or until the pastry is richly golden, turning the heat up or down, if necessary, during the last 10 minutes or so to arrive at the correct coloration.

ZUCCHINI PUDDING SOUFFLÉ
(Pudding Soufflé aux Courgettes)
(for 4)

The traditional soufflé, raced from oven to table with, its lovely golden head bobbing precariously, is a pretty sight and may have evinced more gasps of admiration than any other single bit of culinary theater. Even served rapidly by an accomplished maître d'hôtel, it has already collapsed into an indefinable ectoplasmic stuff before the tines of one's fork can reach it (the uncooked heart of the matter, it is said, serves as the sauce).

A pudding soufflé and, in particular, one that has been gratinéed, being thus subjected to two separate cooking processes, is a sublimely different thing: It is first cooked gently in a *bain-marie* until done, then unmolded when slightly cooled; it settles somewhat, its volume diminishing, but, inundated with a light-bodied sauce (often simply heavy cream) and put to gratiné, it swells again, retaining its new-found volume. It is light—for it, too, is mostly air—but it remains,

241

nonetheless, firm. One of these little puddings, prelude to an amicable chunk of rare meat, might take many a jaded gastronome by surprise.

Soufflés à la Suissesse, the inspirational source for this recipe, are individual soufflés in which a cup of grated Parmesan replaces the zucchini. They are, otherwise, treated in the same way and are particularly exciting if unmolded onto a bed of parboiled, squeezed, and chopped spinach before being drowned in heavy cream, sprinkled with cheese, and returned to the oven. Of possible variations, I have found mushrooms to be the most interesting (about 10 ounces mushrooms—put through a Mouli-juliènne and sautéed in butter until their liquid is evaporated—replacing the zucchini). An addition of puréed, butter-stewed sorrel to the cream is an especially attractive variation on the sauce, in which instance I think that fresh crumbs, first lightly colored in butter, may be a better surface garnish than the grated cheese. The presence of the zucchini—or of mushrooms—in the mixture need not necessarily preclude the addition of cheese as in the *soufflés à la Suissesse;* try it both ways . . .

The *savarin* mold permits a strikingly handsome turban-like presentation. If you do not have one, use individual ramekins or custard molds rather than a large mold of unbroken form.

> 1 pound small, firm zucchini
> Salt
> 2 tablespoons butter

Béchamel
> 2 tablespoons butter
> 3 tablespoons flour
> ¾ cup milk
> Salt, pepper

> 3 eggs, separated
> Butter (for the mold)

Sauce
> ⅔ cup tomato purée (drained canned tomatoes or, in season, fresh tomatoes, stewed with a pinch of herbs, salt, a pinch of sugar, until thick, put through a sieve—don't use tomato paste)

1 cup heavy cream
Salt, pepper, pinch cayenne

½ cup freshly grated Parmesan, Gruyère, or a mixture

Coarsely shred or grate the zucchini or put through the medium blade of the Mouli-juliènne, reducing them to spaghetti-like shreds, arrange in layers in a mixing bowl, sprinkling each layer with salt, and leave to stand for half an hour. Squeeze the juliènne with your hands—in the bowl and in its liquid—until it is swimming. Pour into a sieve, press to rid it of flagrant moisture, then form the mass into a ball and squeeze tightly and repeatedly between both hands until no more liquid may be wrung from it. Sauté in the butter over a medium flame for from 7 to 8 minutes, tossing often and spreading the mass out again with a wooden spoon—until well dried and lightly colored.

Prepare the *béchamel* as usual, removing it from the heat as soon as it is stiff and allowing it to cool for a couple of minutes before adding the egg yolks, one at a time, stirring well after each addition. Salt and pepper to taste and stir in the zucchini. Beat the egg whites until they stand in peaks, incorporate about one third into the mixture, turning and folding gently, to render it more supple, then carefully fold in the remaining beaten whites.

Pour into a generously buttered quart *savarin* mold (filling no more than two thirds to three fourths full), smooth the surface with the back of a spoon, tap the mold lightly against the tabletop to settle the contents, and bake for from 20 to 25 minutes (until the surface is firm and springy to the touch) in a *bain-marie* (placing the mold into a larger pan and installing it at the entry to the oven before pouring in enough hot but not boiling water to immerse the mold by two thirds) at about 350°. Remove the mold from the *bain-marie* and leave to cool for 10 minutes or so before unmolding onto a large, round, shallow baking dish (porcelain tart mold, for instance—something presentable for serving).

Whisk together the tomato purée and the cream, season to taste, and pour slowly and evenly over the unmolded soufflé, masking it entirely (but permitting only as much as is necessary to coat the inner sides of the soufflé to run down into the well). Sprinkle cheese over the surface and return to a hot oven (450°) for 20 min-

243

utes or until the surface is richly colored and the sauce bubbling. Serve onto preheated plates, spooning the sauce to the side of the soufflé so as not to mask the gratin.

ZUCCHINI FANS
(Courgettes en Eventail)
(hors d'oeuvre for 4 to 6)

Thanks for this preparation are due Georges Garin. It has served well and rarely has a guest failed to ask for the recipe. It is good hot or cold, but it is only wonderful warm, accompanied by a cold and rustic, dry white wine.

9 or 10 small zucchini (2 pounds)

3 large, firm, well-ripened tomatoes, unpeeled, conical core cut out, halved vertically, each half sliced thinly

2 large sweet onions, halved and sliced as thinly as possible

4 or 5 cloves of garlic, peeled and sliced paper-thin

3 or 4 branches each of thyme, savory, and oregano (or a healthy pinch, dried, of each)

Something over ½ teaspoon coriander grains

Salt, pepper

⅓ cup olive oil

⅔ cup dry white wine

Rinse the zucchini, wipe them dry with a towel, trim the tips, and split each in two lengthwise. Place the halves, cut side down, on the chopping board and slice each lengthwise into ¼- to ⅓-inch widths without severing the slices from the stem end so that each half, remaining intact, may be spread slightly, fan-like. Slip one or two tomato slices into place between each of the fan sections.

Scatter half the sliced onion and sliced garlic over the bottom of a large, relatively shallow oven dish that has been lightly oiled, press the zucchini fans, cut side down, firmly into place, forcing them slightly, side by side, slip the branches of herbs here and there in the crevices (or sprinkle them over the surface), scatter the coriander evenly, sprinkle with salt and pepper, scatter the re-

244

maining onion and garlic regularly all over, press the surface firmly with the palm of your hand, dribble olive oil liberally all over and pour over the white wine (the contents should bathe by slightly over half). Press a sheet of aluminum foil over the surface and bring to a full boil on top of the stove (protecting the receptacle from direct heat with an asbestos pad if it is earthenware) before transferring it to a 375° to 400° oven for about ½ hour or until the zucchini is only just tender (it will remain slightly firm, thanks to the acidity of the white wine). "Cool" for a good ½ hour in a warm place (turned-off oven, for instance) before serving directly from its dish.

TURNIPS *(NAVETS)*

Tender, crisp young turnips may, thickly peeled, be gently stewed in butter without being parboiled. They may also be braised in stock or bouillon, and when their braising liquid has been reduced to no more than a veil cloaking them, a bit of heavy cream may be dribbled over . . . Grated into a fine juliènne, salted, squeezed, and stewed in butter (as on page 110), there may be many unexplored possibilities. Among those explored, a pound of turnips, first prepared this way, may replace the sorrel and onion mixture in the sorrel tart; I have also sometimes spread a half-baked pastry shell with the butter-stewed turnip juliènne and poured the sorrel-onion quiche batter over the top to the general ravishment of the guests. The same turnip preparation would almost certainly provide another perfect base for soufflé puddings gratinéed with cream and grated cheese. But, were one to chase each passing thought, crystallize it, and put it to the test, cookbooks would never get written . . .

TURNIP GRATIN
(Gratin de Navets)
(for 4)

Garlic
3 tablespoons butter (in all)
1½ pounds crisp, tender turnips, peeled thickly, sliced in ⅛-inch thick-
    nesses, parboiled 2 or 3 minutes, drained
Salt, pepper
1 scant teaspoon finely crumbled dried herbs
3 ounces thinly sliced prosciutto-type ham, cut into a fine juliènne
3 ounces Swiss Gruyère, cut into very thin slices
½ cup heavy cream
¼ cup breadcrumbs

Rub well a small gratin dish with garlic (or purée the garlic
and rub the dish with the juice, discarding all debris), let dry, butter
generously, and arrange the turnip slices, slightly overlapping, in
three layers, sprinkling with salt, pepper, herbs, and the juliènne
ham in between the two intermediate layers. Arrange the slices of
cheese on the surface, pour over the cream, sprinkle with breadcrumbs, cover with paper-thin shavings of butter. Bake 45 minutes
in a 400° oven.

STARCHY PREPARATIONS

SHORT PASTE
(Pâte Brisée)
(proportions for a single large crust)

I was taught, before anyone (at least, in northwestern Iowa) had ever heard of Spry or Crisco, that, if one liked tender pastry it should be made with lard and that, if one preferred crisp pastry, it should be made with butter. I have never liked lard (and it should be noted that lard pastry tastes like lard whereas pastry made with good, fresh unsalted butter tastes like butter), and I have never liked crumbly, fatty pastry, so my narrow path was, from the beginning, cleanly defined. For as long as I can remember, but for the occasional (and fairly recent) intrusion of olive oil, I have always prepared pastry with nothing but butter and, be it in America or in France, it has, to my taste, been perfect. But, of recent years, a great many people have assured me—with a distressing ring of authority (I have been away too long . . .)—that, whereas perfect pastry may, indeed, be made with pure butter in France, the flour in America does not permit it. I had, as recently as seven years ago, prepared satisfactory pastry from "all-purpose" flour in the United States, but, troubled (memory, they say, plays tricks), I asked friends to bring me American flours—"all-purpose" and "wondra" (which, except that it is bleached much whiter, corresponds closely to a type of flour that is now widely commercialized in France); with these flours, a pinch

247

of salt, a lot of butter, and a bit of water, one may make impeccable pastry; the "wondra" seems to require a bit more water and makes a slightly more "brittle" pastry, a quality that I appreciate and that, perhaps, everyone does not.

¾ cup flour
Salt
3½ ounces cold butter (7 tablespoons)
¼ cup cold water (for "wondra"; slightly less for "all-purpose")

For ease in working, use a fairly large mixing bowl; pour in the flour, sprinkle with salt, add the butter, cut into small pieces, and cut with table knives, one in each hand, blades crossed and touching, repeatedly and rapidly pulling the blades outward and away from each other and recommencing; gather the flour and the butter pieces back to the center of the bowl regularly with the knife tips. Work no more than a minute or so—the butter fragments need not all be as small as the traditional pea. Add the water (not all at once—you may need just a bit less . . .), stirring with a fork and mashing as little as possible to begin bringing the mass together; finish rapidly, working with the tips of your fingers—only enough to create a cohesive body that may be formed into a ball. Wrap in plastic and refrigerate in the coldest part (not the freezer) of the refrigerator for at least 2 or 3 hours.

The coldness of a marble slab—if you have one—facilitates one's work. Dust it generously with flour, flatten the dough with your hand—it should be quite hard—and give it a few gentle smacks with the rolling pin to flatten it more and render it more supple. Turn it over to be certain that both sides are well floured and roll it out rapidly. Fold the pastry round in two to facilitate draping it into the mold and gently fit it to the form, cutting off the excess pastry some ½ inch outside the border, rolling the ½ inch under, pressing it firmly into place, and crimping the border all the way around by pressing with the side of your repeatedly floured thumb while holding the inside and outside of the pastry rim in place with thumb and forefinger of the other hand. Pierce the bottom here and there with the tines of a fork or the sharp point of a knife.

To half bake an empty pastry shell, line it with a sheet of aluminum foil or kitchen parchment paper, pour in dried beans, split peas, or what have you (keep something around for that use—it can serve no other purpose afterwards; a litre of chick-peas has served me well for several years) and bake for 15 minutes at 375° to 400°, remove the paper and dried contents, and return the pastry to the oven for 5 minutes to let it dry out.

Short pastry, rather than being rolled out only once and fitted to its mold, may first be rolled to a length of about one foot by some 5 or 6 inches, folded in three and then rolled out to the desired form. This is the first step in the preparation of a somewhat simplified *feuilletée* and lends the pastry a bit of the *feuilletée*'s quality of flakiness. To transform the pastry into a simple *feuilletée*, roll the folded length again to the long rectangular form, fold the two extremities in to meet each other, then fold the two, this forming four layers, refrigerate for at least ½ hour, repeat, refrigerate again, repeat and roll out (or refrigerate again before rolling out).

Fold the trimmings into a many-layered stack (or roll them up), form into a ball, wrap in plastic, and refrigerate for another hour or so and you will have a *demi-feuilletée*. Roll it out (not too thinly; to about ⅛ inch) to a length about 4 inches wide, sprinkle each side very lightly with cayenne and generously with grated cheese, pressing it first into the surface with the flat of your hand, then with a cleaver, flat mallet, or the flat of the blade of a large knife, cut into ½-inch-wide strips, twist each gently—three or four turns—into a spiral, and place on a lightly oiled baking sheet, pressing the extremities lightly so that the form will hold. Bake for 15 minutes at 400° and serve with an apéritif . . .

PROVENÇAL PASTRY
(Pâte à l'Huile d'Olive)

Little distinction is made, traditionally, in the south of France between noodle dough and pastry dough. For many a housewife, a pound, more or less, of flour, an egg, and a dribble of olive oil brought to the desired consistency with tepid water serves indifferently for the fabrication of noodles, ravioli, pies, tarts, and deep-fried, stuffed little fantasies. As such, it is neither very interesting as

249

pasta nor as pastry. With a bit more olive oil, the pastry acquires personality and, for many, will be quite a new experience. It is best to prepare a relatively soft dough—it will absorb the necessary supplement of flour in being rolled out.

2 cups flour
Salt
1 egg
¼ cup olive oil
¼ cup tepid water
Flour (for rolling out)
Olive oil (with which to brush the pastry)

Add all the ingredients except the last to the flour in the mixing bowl, mix, first with a fork, then knead rapidly with your knuckles until consistent. Form into a ball, cover with a towel, and leave to rest for at least an hour before rolling out on a well-floured board or marble. Whatever the preparation, brush (in Provence, one smears with one's fingers) the surface with olive oil before baking the dough.

HERB PASTA
(Pâtes aux Herbes)
(for 3 or 4)

This dough should not be rolled out on a machine—the uncompromising rollers force it into an amalgam in which the singleness of the savors is lost and flour is absorbed to excess. Also, it is better to pound the herbs in a mortar rather than purée them with the liquids in a blender—they remain, pounded, distinct and multiflavored fragments.

The herbs mentioned should be considered as among the many possibilities—any wild salad greens may be used and other herbs, depending on personal taste; strongly flavored herbs such as rosemary, common thyme, sage, savory, etc., should be avoided or used with a fine discretion. If you can gather together but three or four elements, don't hesitate to try them; the spirit of the thing is just that —you put into it what you can find.

250

Lightness and delicacy are not among its attributes, so don't try it on difficult guests. It is delicious—perhaps better—leftover and transformed into a gratin: The squares stick together hopelessly, so they should be taken en masse and sliced thinly, noodle-like, then "crumbled"—to loosen as well as possible the little noodles one from the other—directly into a buttered gratin dish, the bottom of which has been sprinkled with grated cheese. If the quantity of pasta is large, sprinkle cheese also over an intermediate layer. Pour over heavy cream, sprinkle the surface with cheese, and bake at 400° to 450° for about 20 minutes; the exhilarating wild green flavors are thrown into even cleaner relief this way, thanks no doubt to the cream's sweet presence.

1¾ cups flour
Salt
1 egg
4 ounces green things, in approximately equal quantities, pounded to a
    paste in a mortar (about 1 cup, pounded): sorrel, wild chicory, dande-
    lion, rocket (or arugula), basil leaves and flowers, etc.—plus a leaf or
    two of lovage, purslane, leaf thyme, hyssop, fresh marjoram, burnet,
    young fuzzy borage leaves (before they become prickly) . . .
About 2 tablespoons warm water
Flour (for rolling out)
1 tablespoon olive oil (for the cooking water)

Add all the ingredients (except the water and the last two listed) to the flour, work together with a fork, adding a bit more flour if necessary, until fairly consistent—a slightly lumpy but single mass. Throw a bit of water in to bring it all together, work well with the fork, and turn it out onto a heavily floured board or marble. Roll in the flour to coat it and knead with the palm of your hand, turning it around and over and folding often. Work for some time as the herbs continue to bleed moisture into the mixture, which, finally, during the kneading, will absorb easily another ½ cup of flour from the board. As the paste becomes elastic, difficult to work, and stops sticking, flour it well, cover with a towel, and leave to rest for about an hour. It should remain quite supple—less firm than normal noodle paste.

Roll it out to about ⅛ inch, cut the sheet into 1½-inch ribbons,

251

cut each ribbon into squares, and drop them loosely into a large quantity of salted boiling water to which has been added the spoonful of olive oil (to discourage their sticking together). Move them with a wooden fork to make certain that none are sticking together and boil for about 6 minutes from the time the water returns to a boil. Drain and serve onto hot plates, sprinkled generously with grated Parmesan and bubbling brown butter.

BATTER NOODLES
(Nouilles à la Poche)
(for 3 or 4)

Treated as a gratin, these rich, round, tender eggy noodles are quite astonishing—simply drowned in cream and sprinkled with grated cheese (or liberally sprinkled with meat or poultry roasting juices and cheese . . .). Served as a garnish, they may also be tossed in butter and seasoned to taste, and a few chopped *fines herbes* may be added; or they may be tossed with fresh breadcrumbs that have first been cooked gently and tossed often in butter until lightly golden and crisp—more butter added at the moment the noodles are joined to the crumbs. They may, of course, be combined with other ingredients, either as a gratin or sautéed. With the former, it is a good way to stretch truffles, respecting their flavor. Or a bed of mushroom purée may line the gratin dish; or dried morels (soaked, trimmed, rinsed, and butter-stewed) may be mixed with them to the happiest of effects. Or rapidly parboiled little peas . . .

1⅓ cups flour (more or less; the "instant blending" variety is good for this)
Salt
1 tablespoon olive oil
4 eggs

Put 1 cup of flour in a mixing bowl and whisk the other ingredients into it. When smooth, add enough more flour, sprinkling it over the surface a little at a time and whisking it in, to bring the consistency to approximately that of a firm cake batter.

252

Roll a large square of kitchen parchment paper into a cone, flatten it and seal the length of the loose edge with a strip of Scotch tape, fold the tip to prevent loss of batter as the cone is filled, open the cone out again and place it upright in a tall vase, pitcher, or other article that will hold it still as it is filled (a pastry bag may be used, but, with the paper, the tedious, nasty job of cleaning afterwards is eliminated). Fill the cone with the batter, squeeze the top firmly closed, snip off the tip to leave a tiny hole something less than ¼ inch in diameter and, continuing to squeeze and hold the top part in one hand, squeeze the body of the cone with the other, holding the tip just over the surface of barely simmering salted water (the movement of boiling water would shatter the batter before it has time to set). The container should be the largest—with the largest surface—available; a large American roasting pan serves well. As you squeeze ribbons of batter, relax the pressure regularly to let them separate, forming lengths of from 3 to 5 inches. Move the tip over the surface, being careful not to squeeze batter onto already formed noodles. Cover and leave to poach for half a minute or so—until the water returns to a boil—and drain.

FRESH EGG NOODLES
(Pâtes Fraîches aux Oeufs)

Noodles, the dough of which has been rolled out by hand, well dusted with flour, rolled up, and sliced, have a charm apart, which depends largely on the slight variations of thickness and of width, but also, because the dough is worked less brutally, with greater suppleness, than by the machine, the fresh egg taste is more in evidence—or, in the instance of green noodles, the spinach flavor is cleaner. The quasi-miraculous little Italian pasta machines, however, turn the work into a fantastically effortless, amusing, childlike game, and with a smattering of experience or habit, splendid results may be had (mine bears the trademark "Titania" and is manufactured by the firm "I.P.S." in Turin; it is commercialized in the United States—as are several others with which I am unfamiliar). I willingly bear witness to the fact that, whereas, in the past, months at a time went by without my preparing fresh pasta, a week never passes now that I do not offer myself or guests fresh egg noodles, my funny little machine doing all the work.

The dough may be firmer for a machine than that which is to be rolled out by hand—and it is easier to work, but less good. It may also, if one is pressed for time, be worked immediately (although it tends to fall apart for the first two or three passages through the rollers during the kneading) rather than being left to relax, but, in that case, it must be kneaded longer before being rolled out thinly, and the result is very like that of commercial fresh pasta. For best results: (1) an "instant-blending" flour is easily superior to others; very fine semolina gives good results also—count about 3 minutes longer cooking time than for noodles made with flour; (2) the dough is much finer if forced in egg yolks—one made only of egg yolks is quite remarkable (count about 5 yolks to a cup of flour and 1 tablespoon of olive oil—soft or melted butter may be substituted); (3) the dough should be fairly supple and it should be left to rest, preferably for a good hour, before being kneaded in the machine; (4) it should be passed through the rollers, set at maximum (kneading) width, only the number of times—4, 5, or 6—necessary to render the sheet absolutely cohesive before being passed through at the desired thickness; (5) the sheets, if rolled out from a supple dough, will be slightly sticky and should be hung (over a broomstick suspended between two chair backs) to dry for 20 or 30 minutes before being passed through the noodle-cutting rollers.

Green noodles are traditional in Niçoise cooking, but they are more often made with parboiled, squeezed chard greens than with spinach as in Italy (2 cups flour; salt; 1 whole egg and 1 yolk; 1 tablespoon olive oil; ½ pound parboiled spinach or chard greens squeezed dry and chopped). The dough needs to be kneaded by hand before being put to rest, flour added as necessary, because of the green stuff's habit of releasing its moisture progressively; otherwise it is treated in the same way as that for egg noodles. Green noodles are perhaps best understood if served tossed only with grated cheese and butter, a generous amount of pepper ground over—but a pan of tiny zucchini, sliced paper-thin and sautéed over a high flame for 5 or 6 minutes with a couple of crushed cloves of garlic (discarded before serving) in olive oil, may be strewn over the lot without incurring the displeasure of a radical purist.

1¾ cups flour
Salt
1 whole egg and 3 egg yolks
1 tablespoon olive oil

Put 1½ cups flour in a mixing bowl with the other ingredients, work with a fork until consistent, adding a bit more flour if necessary, then knead with your knuckles just long enough to bring it all together in a firm, cohesive mass. Roll into a ball and leave, covered by a towel, to rest for about an hour.

Divide the dough into two or three parts, press one out flatly on a lightly floured board and turn it through the rollers set at the widest notch. Fold it in three and if it is sticky, drag the two sides over the floured board before passing it through again; fold again, in triple or double, and continue passing and folding until the sheet of dough is smooth-textured, consistent, and its width equals that of the width of the rollers. Adjust the rollers to the thickness desired (I prefer, for most purposes, the next to finest), pass it through, and hang it to dry while treating the other sections of dough in the same way. Pass the sheets through the noodle-cutting rollers and toss them lightly, sprinkled with a bit of flour, with splayed fingers, to keep them from sticking together while waiting to be cooked (for Alsatian noodles, use the finest rollers—spaghetti or tagliarini width—and keep a handful apart to be sautéed raw in butter until lightly colored and crisp; they are scattered as garnish over the remaining noodles, which are boiled, drained, and tossed in butter).

Cook them in a large quantity of salted, boiling water to which a dribble of olive oil has been added (an old Italian habit, which the French, mistakenly, do not always respect). The moment they are added to the water, gently shake them free of each other with the prongs of a wooden fork. Count 3 to 4 minutes' cooking time, surveying them closely—the time necessary may vary some 30 seconds, depending on the thickness of the noodles, the firmness of the dough, the extent to which the sheets of dough or the noodles have been dried before cooking, etc. Drain and, as a garnish, serve rapidly tossed with butter; tossed with butter and grated cheese; tossed with butter, cheese, chopped butter-stewed tomatoes (to which chopped *fines herbes* or fragments of fresh basil may be added) . . .

However served, freshly ground pepper is welcome and hot plates are essential. Note: Eaten in the Italian manner, the long strands twirled on one's fork are an integral part of the experience; outside of meridional France, noodles are conceived of as a garnish and, as such, it is wiser to cut the sheets of dough into 7- or 8-inch lengths before passing them through the noodle cutter.

Tender young peas require about the same length of cooking time as fresh noodles; throw them into the boiling water at the same time, drain, and serve with butter . . .

The two following recipes I have noted in the course of emptying out the refrigerator for my solitary needs. Each, in itself, is deliciously satisfying but should be entertained as a symbol of infinite possibilities; in the context, there is no reason ever to do precisely the same thing twice.

FRESH NOODLES WITH CHICKEN BREAST
(Nouilles Fraîches au Blanc de Poulet)
(for 4)

The breasts of 1 young chicken (or guinea fowl), skin, bone, and cartilaginous fragments removed, cut cross-grain into ¼- to ⅓-inch strips
3 tablespoons olive oil
Salt
Handful chopped parsley
1 teaspoon finely chopped fresh marjoram (or pinch finely crumbled dried oregano)
2 or 3 cloves garlic, peeled and finely chopped
1 recipe for fresh egg noodles (see page 253)
Pepper
½ cup freshly grated Parmesan, Gruyère, or a mixture of the two
¼ cup softened butter (or olive oil)

In a large, heavy receptacle, sauté the strips of breasts, salted, over a high flame for 1 or 2 minutes, until the flesh is firm and springy and all surfaces have turned milky and opaque in aspect; then add the herbs and the garlic and cook for a minute longer, the heat still high, stirring and tossing constantly. Add the drained noodles, toss well together with wooden forks, remove from the heat, grind over pepper to taste (add more salt, if necessary), add the cheese and the butter and toss, mixing well.

CREAMED NOODLES WITH HAM AND VEGETABLES
(Nouilles à la Crème)
(for 4)

10 ounces mushrooms, sliced paper-thin
1 pound small zucchini, sliced paper-thin
Salt
3 tablespoons butter
2 cloves garlic, peeled and finely chopped
3 ounces prosciutto-type ham, thinly sliced, cut into inch lengths of fine juliènne and mixed with the herbs (to keep the juliènne from sticking together)
Handful chopped parsley
1 teaspoon finely chopped fresh marjoram (or eliminate the garlic and substitute fresh tarragon)
1 cup heavy cream
1 recipe for fresh egg noodles (see page 253)
Pepper
⅔ cup freshly grated Parmesan

Sauté the vegetables, salted, in butter over a high flame until liquid is evaporated—6 or 7 minutes, adding the garlic after 3 or 4 minutes. Add the ham and herb mixture, continue sautéing for another minute or so, add the cream, reduce for a couple of minutes, still over high heat, and toss in the noodles. Remove from the heat, taste for salt, grind over pepper, add the Parmesan, and toss, mixing thoroughly.

RAVIOLI *(RAVIOLIS)*

See the preface (page 15) and stuffed *crêpes* (page 229) for further discussion.

The dough is the same as for egg noodles but, for ravioli, it must be supple and the rolled-out sheets should not be hung to dry.

The French usually cling to the classic square form of ravioli, but they do not distinguish the Italian tortelli or tortellini (filled rounds sealed into half-moon forms) by a different name. One rarely sees cappelletti in France (half moons, the tips forced gently backwards and pinched together), but the form, quite aside from its attractive and amusing aspect, is practical if the pasta is being served directly from the boiling water, simply sprinkled with cheese and brown butter. Its eccentricity prevents the cappelletti from sticking together both during the cooking and on the plates, but the same formal irregularity makes them impractical for saucing and gratinéing, for it takes up too much space, requiring an excess of sauce. Any of these ravioli-type preparations provides one of the more elegant means to disposing of leftovers.

BEEF AND MARJORAM RAVIOLI
(Koldouny)
(6 to 8 as a first course; 4 as a main course)

Apparently Tartar in origin, the two recipes with which I am familiar (Dr. de Pomiane and Ali Bab) are quite different, but the fundamental characteristics are the same. Both use crumbled or powdered dried marjoram (as will you if you have no fresh . . .) in staggering quantity.

Koldouny should be served instantly and directly from the vessel in which it is cooked, nakedly ungarnished (the flavor should all be on the inside—an addition of butter or cheese would only confuse the effect) onto well-heated plates, and it should be eaten with spoons. Knives and forks should be kept out of the reach of the guests for, in Ali Bab's quaint words, the *koldouny*'s basic quality (an astonishing explosion of imprisoned perfume in one's mouth) would be lost "were one to wound it by using a fork" (the surprise and the pleasure are renewed each time one is bitten into—and the temptation to continue eating them forever is sore). If serving as a main course, it is well to cook them in two batches to make sure they are hot at the moment they're served.

You will need a large marrow bone—ask the butcher to crack it open for you or to saw it into short lengths. Take care that no fragments of splintered bone remain clinging to the marrow.

The following proportions will produce 75 to 80 raviolis.

> 1 large onion (4 ounces), finely chopped
> About ⅔ cup water
> 8 to 10 ounces lean beef cut from a tender cut of steak, all traces of nervous material, membranes, etc., removed, chopped (see page 62 for hand-chopping method)
> 5 to 6 ounces beef marrow, chopped
> 2 tablespoons fresh marjoram flowers and leaves, finely chopped (to a near powder)
> Salt, pepper

Noodle dough
> 3 to 3½ cups flour
> Salt
> 4 eggs
> 2 tablespoons olive oil

Cover the chopped onions with water in your smallest saucepan, bring to a boil, skim off the gray scum that forms on the surface, and simmer for about 20 minutes, checking that they do not boil dry. Turn the heat up slightly and stir until all the water has been evaporated. Add to the other ingredients in the mixing bowl, peppering abundantly, stir first to disperse the heat of the onions, then work the stuffing with your hand, squeezing it repeatedly through your fingers until thoroughly homogeneous. Pick up dabs of the stuffing (each the equivalent of a slight level teaspoonful—or about the size of a normal olive) with the tip of a teaspoon and arrange them on a large platter. Put to chill in the refrigerator for an hour or so (just beneath the freezing unit, a ½ hour will do).

Prepare the noodle dough as in the preceding recipe, leaving it to rest. Don't roll it out until the stuffing dabs are firmly chilled.

Roll out the dough (if by hand, to about ¹⁄₁₆ inch or, if by machine, somewhat finer) and, using an inverted tumbler, tin can, or cookie cutter three inches in diameter, cut it into rounds and then stack them, undersides lightly floured, to prevent their drying out. Gather the cuttings together in a ball and roll them out again.

Form the ravioli into half moons, placing a dab of stuffing in the center of each, moistening a band all around the circumference, folding and pinching firmly all around the edge to be certain that the contents are tightly sealed in. Cook in the largest pot you have— in a large quantity of salted, boiling water, counting 4 minutes or slightly over from the moment the water returns to a boil.

CRÊPE BATTER
(Appareil à Crêpes)

Good *crêpe* pans are made of heavy iron. They differ from omelet pans only in that the sides are lower and more oblique; in their absence, small omelet pans will serve.

Like all flour-based batters or doughs, *crêpe* batter is usually left to relax, losing the elasticity that is developed to an extent relative to the length and violence of its beating; but the nature of *crêpes*—the simplicity and the rapidity of their preparation, their usefulness as an elegant means of disposing of leftovers or of tossing off a hastily improvised dessert—thrusts them often into the category of last-minute-decision preparations. Care should be taken to whisk the batter gently and no longer than necessary to perfectly combine the ingredients and they may, then, be prepared immediately.

The best *crêpes* are made with a proportionately high egg and low flour content. Cognac is a useful flavoring agent, and a certain amount of either melted butter or olive oil is necessary— otherwise it seems to me to make little difference what they are moistened with; good *crêpes* can be made moistened only with water, or only with beer, or heavy cream may be added to enrich the batter. The precise proportioning of ingredients is of little importance, but the consistency of the batter is of the greatest—its body should be approximately that of American fresh heavy cream (that is to say, very thin).

Sugar is usually added to dessert-*crêpe* batter; after years of dumbly respecting this rule, I realized that I preferred unsweetened *crêpes*; whatever their ultimate treatment, they will receive a large sufficience of sweetening. Recipes calling for an addition of chopped fruit, crumbled macaroons, or other cookie-like substance to the batter may sound attractive but, in practice, the added bulk necessitates the use of too much batter to make a *crêpe* and its finesse suffers greatly, thinness being part of its essential character.

For non-sweet preparations, finely chopped *fines herbes* are often added to the batter. Powdered saffron—as much as one can heap on a knife tip—may be dissolved in a bit of hot water and stirred into the batter. Saffron *crêpes* seem to me particularly useful as a wrapping for mixtures based on crustaceans or shellfish—shrimp, crab, lobster, scallops, mussels, clams . . . Spread with softened butter, rolled up, and eaten hot from the pan, they are sublime; buttered, folded in four, arranged overlapping in a buttered gratin dish, spread with stiff cream (or a small amount of stiff *béchamel* generously creamed), the surface sprinkled generously with grated Parmesan and put in a 500° oven for 10 minutes or until the sauce is bubbling and the surface colored, saffron *crêpes* cannot help but elicit admiration.

⅓ cup flour
Salt
3 eggs
Liquid (approximately 1 cup—milk, water, beer, enrichened or not by the addition of heavy cream)
1 tablespoon (or 2) Cognac
3 tablespoons olive oil or melted butter (butter for dessert)

Add the eggs to the flour and salt, whisk from the center of the bowl, working gradually out, until no lumps remain, then stir in (with the whisk) the other ingredients.

Use a small ladle to pour the batter into the pan; count (but do not measure) 1½ tablespoons for a small *crêpe* and 3 tablespoons for a large *crêpe*. The pan should be rubbed with a buttered or oiled rag only for the first *crêpe,* no more than a film of fat remaining in the pan—too much fat will make them buckle and cook irregularly (it is only possible to flip *crêpes* if there is too much fat in the pan—so don't bother).

Heat the pan—give it a high flame for the first few moments if you like—and then adjust the heat to medium-low. The batter should sizzle when it touches the pan. Lift the pan and, at the same time that the batter is poured in, give it a rolling motion, turning it in all directions so that the surface is coated as rapidly as possible. Add only enough to coat the pan—a bit more can always be added (or if you add too much, pour the excess immediately back into the bowl of batter). It is ready to turn when the surface becomes almost dry—tacky—and the edges curl. Turn it either by loosening it gently and picking it up with a round-tipped table knife or by picking it up by the loosened, curled edges with your fingertips. After the first 2 or 3 *crêpes,* the heat may have to be turned slightly up or down and, since the pan heats progressively, it should be removed from the heat for a very few seconds before each successive bit of batter is poured in. The batter should be stirred lightly each time it is used, as it tends to settle, becoming heavier at the bottom of the bowl. If not to be used immediately, stack the *crêpes* on a plate to keep them from drying out and, if to be kept for some time, wrap the stack in plastic and refrigerate.

FRITTER BATTER
(Appareil à Beignets)

Unlike *crêpe* batter, fritter batter must rest for an hour or so at room temperature before its beaten egg whites are gently folded in. The slightest elasticity will cause it to shrink, coating imperfectly the articles to be fried. Its thickness is, to some extent, a question of personal taste—a relatively thin batter will fry more crisply but a certain amount is inevitably dispersed in the hot oil; a thicker batter will produce a thicker and rather spongy coating on the material treated and there will be no loss in the oil. I prefer a thin batter.

¾ cup flour
Salt
2 eggs (separated, whites put aside)
2 tablespoons olive oil
¾ cup warm beer

Whisk the dry ingredients with the yolks, oil, and beer, working from the center out and whisking only long enough to produce a smooth batter. Leave in a warm place for at least an hour before using. Just before using, beat the egg whites until the peaks hold and fold them gently into the batter.

SOUPS

IT is impossible, in the context of this book, to list the soup possibilities whose preparations require approximately the same amount of effort as that demanded to open one of the famous and redoubtable tins, whose inimitable flavor remains always that of some metal which is not tin and which must, surely, be noxious, as well: Plunge, for instance, a handful or two of fresh and finely shredded spinach into salted, boiling water for 2 or 3 minutes and pour it over dried bread crusts that have been rubbed with garlic cloves and dribbled with olive oil; boil a lot of crushed garlic cloves with a leaf of sage and one of bay and strain the water over olive oil–soaked crusts; boil together practically any combination of vegetables, cut up, sliced, or diced, add a piece of butter, and it will be delicious.

Note: Soups peppered during the cooking process acquire an acrid taste; peppercorns of fine quality, ground in at the table, will perfume them agreeably.

PANADES AND ONION SOUP

Rational habits permit of discarding nothing left over, and the use to which leftovers (and their economic allies, the wild things of nature) are put is often at the heart of a cooking's character. Half-dried bread—that which is not reduced to crumbs or croutons or used in stuffings—is sliced (completely dried out, an attempt at slicing would break it into pieces) and put aside for soups. Many French peasants still begin every meal with a great tureen half filled with dried crusts of bread over which is poured a boiling broth. And a *pot-au-feu*, a *garbure*, a *bouillabaisse*, or an onion soup without crusts of dried bread is unthinkable. But the mere presence of bread in a soup does not constitute a genuine *panade*, which for most of the French, is but a memory and, for many a detested one, recalling the boiled bread and water on which, as children, they were nourished of an evening.

Soup *panades* have mostly disappeared from today's cookbooks. One, however (a curiosity published in 1907, entitled *Menus Propos sur la Cuisine Comtoise* and signed *"Une Vieille Maîtresse de Maison"* with no further attempt at identity), after attributing the extreme longevity of the author's grandfather to the daily consumption of *panade* and the local wine, contains a detailed exposé of the art of making a perfect *panade*. It is described as "the best, the cheapest, and the most digestible of all soups." Its preparation consists of pouring boiling water into an earthenware vessel filled with slices of dried-out bread, simmering for at least an hour and a half and, shortly before serving, stirring in a piece of butter. The secret to its success lies in not stirring it until that point. This, the primordial version, I have tried and I cannot claim to have been ravished by the result. Others, but slightly more elaborated, are sound and succulent fare. The Périgord peasants replace the water by a stout and richly saffron-flavored chicken broth—only enough to be completely absorbed by the swelling bread—and leave it undisturbed, but for an occasional and slight addition of boiling broth, in a gentle oven for an hour or so. It is delicious and they call it *mourtairol*.

An onion *panade* is surely the ancestor and still the best of all the onion soups. The French onion soup, to which a less sophisticated America once vowed a passionate loyalty—the same that has soothed generations of night-reveling kitchen-crashers on the French ships and has astonished others by its unfailing presence on the French Line's breakfast menus—is a good and comforting dish: onions browned in butter, cooked in stock, topped with bread and grated cheese, and rapidly gratinéed. In Lyons, the same preparation is enriched by an addition of beaten egg yolks and Port wine (a surprising variation, Gaston Dery's cinnamon-flavored fantasy in which the Gruyère is replaced by Camembert and the onions are moistened with Champagne, Port, and Armagnac, is more often assured a place in literature than in the kitchen). One sloppy version (hastily fried onions drowned in boiling water and crowned with a slice of *baguette* and a puddle of bubbling rubbery glue, the acrid taste of burned onions strangely wed to the flat sweetness of French Emmental) has attained mythic stature. For Parisians and world travelers it will be forever a symbol recalling a fantastic and beautiful surrealist world in the heart of Paris through whose glorious mountainous landscape of vegetables and fruits wandered the most extraordinary collection of night denizens, each in search of a last drink and the obligatory bowl of onion soup in one of the bistros animated by Les Halles' blood-smeared butchers.

ONION PANADE
(Panade à l'Oignon au Gratin)
(for 6)

Your dried-out bread should correspond, as nearly as possible, to the coarse, vulgar, compact, heavy loaf of sourdough peasant bread described on page 35.

The onions should be of tender-fleshed sweet variety, softening readily and uniformly in cooking—the large white summer onions or violet Bermudas. Some of the yellow-skins are sweet, other varieties tough and strong (if only the latter are available, don't renounce).

The cheese must be freshly grated and only two—either singly or together—are ideal; Swiss Gruyère and Italian Parmesan. The

Swiss cheese should never be soft and elastic—these are the qualities that transform the eating of onion soup into a taffy-pulling contest. A good Gruyère, less than half the size of the 200-pound wheels of Emmental, is aged for about 6 months. It is always firm and relatively dry without being hard—crumbly under firm pressure. It contains only a few, tiny holes, or none, and its color is darker and duller than the pale yellows of Emmentals and American Swisses. It is dry and nutty in flavor—sometimes lightly sharp but never biting.

Parmesans pose less of a problem. Cylinders of 50 to 80 pounds are aged for from 2 to 3 years, and even the freshest (which are also good table cheeses) are sufficiently ripened to cook properly without forming rubber ribbons.

A wide-mouthed earthenware vehicle, broader than it is high (leaving the largest possible surface for the gratin to form) is perfect and may be used, as well, for coloring the onions (protected by an asbestos mat from the direct flame). If enameled ironware is to be used, the onions should be colored in another heavy vessel— copper, earthenware, cast-iron, since an enameled surface does not color them correctly.

The mind rarely registers weights and measures in terms of visual bulk. The precision of the measures given here could not be of less importance; the thing to remember is that there should be lots of onion, lots of bread, and lots of cheese in relation to the (undetermined) amount of water. Just before putting the casserole into the oven, the surface may, if one wishes, be sprinkled with Cognac.

4 large onions, thinly sliced (about 1½ pounds or 6 cups)
Salt
4 tablespoons (¼ cup) butter
8 ounces dried bread, thinly sliced (about ⅓ inch)
6 ounces (3 cups) freshly grated Parmesan and Gruyère
Lightly salted boiling water

Cook the onions, lightly salted, in the butter over a very low heat, stirring occasionally, for about 1 hour, keeping them covered for the first 40 minutes. If the heat is low enough and the saucepan of a heavy material, there will be no problem of coloration—they should begin to caramelize lightly toward the end of an hour's time, at which point the flame may be turned up slightly and they should be stirred regularly until the entire mass is of a uniformly rich caramel color. Should there be signs of coloration too soon, the flame should be lowered even more, or the heat may be dispersed by separating the pan from the flame with an asbestos pad.

Spread slices of bread thickly with the onions, arrange a layer in the bottom of the casserole, sprinkle over a thick layer of cheese, and repeat the process, packing each layer gently and arranging the bread slices as well as possible to avoid empty spaces. The onions should be used up on the next to last layer of bread, the last layer being sprinkled only with cheese, and the casserole should not be more than two thirds full at this point.

Pour in the boiling, salted water, slowly and very carefully, at one single point against the side of the casserole, permitting the bread to swell and the mass to rise about 1 inch, or until obviously just floating, but no more (if you fear an unsteady hand, carefully ease the tip of a funnel down the side of the casserole to the bottom and pour the boiling water into the funnel).

Cook on top of the stove, uncovered, over a very low heat, the surface maintaining a light, slow bubble for ½ hour. Add, as before, just enough boiling water to be certain that the body of the bread is submerged, sprinkle a bit more cheese over the surface (sprinkle over Cognac now, if you like), shave paper-thin sheets from a firm, cold block of butter, distributing them over the surface, and transfer the casserole to a medium oven (325° to 350°) for 1 hour, raising or lowering the temperature, if necessary, after about 40 minutes' time, depending on how the gratin is developing. The soup should be covered with a richly colored crust of gratin and should be served out with a large spoon onto preheated plates.

GRAPE HARVESTERS' SOUP
(Tourain à la Bordelaise)

The various *tourains* of southwestern France are also onion soups. The onions are colored in goose fat, lard, or drippings and the simplest is moistened with water, simmered for from 45 minutes to 1 hour and served over crusts of bread. Garlic is sometimes added, often a spoonful of flour is stirred into the onions after they have been browned and before they are moistened, a handful of French thread-thin vermicelli may be added a few minutes before serving, and terminal egg-yolk bindings are not uncommon. The bread crusts may be rubbed with garlic, and certain households add a bit of vinegar at the last minute.

The following is a typical Bordelais *tourain* and is traditional at the season of the wine-grape harvest. A native may first eat his sopped bread crust, empty out his (red) wine glass into the soup, and drink the rest from the soup plate, a performance known as *faire chabrol* (or *faire chabrot*)—to act like a little goat—and which belongs more to the realm of folklore than to that of contemporary habit.

1½ pounds onions, thinly sliced
¼ cup olive oil
Salt
4 cloves garlic, peeled and finely chopped
3 medium firm, ripe tomatoes, peeled, seeded, and coarsely chopped
½ teaspoon sugar
½ cup dry white wine
6 cups boiling water
Slices of stale bread

Using a large, heavy saucepan, cook the onions gently in the oil, stirring regularly with a wooden spoon, until they are uniformly light golden and very soft. Add the salt, the garlic, the tomatoes, and the sugar and continue to cook gently, stirring from time to time, for another 10 minutes. Add the white wine, turn the flame up, reduce by half, stirring, and add the boiling water. Simmer, covered, for from 45 minutes to 1 hour before serving out the soup over crusts of bread placed in the individual soup plates.

POTATO AND LEEK SOUP
(Potage aux Poireaux et Pommes de Terre)
(for 6)

The *potage bonne-femme* of the cookbooks (finely sliced leeks and potatoes stewed in butter, moistened with consommé, usually but not always puréed, and finished with milk and either butter or cream—or with both)—that soup which, chilled and richly creamed, has become the American vichysoisse—would come as a surprise to the bearers of the tradition from which it is borrowed. The potato and leek soup that is prepared night after night in the kitchens of nearly every Parisian *concièrge* and in the kitchens of nearly every Île de France working family is nothing more than potatoes and leeks more or less finely sliced or cut up, depending on the *bonne femme*, boiled in salted water, and served, a piece of butter being either added then to the soup or being put to join the inevitable crust of bread in the soup plate before the boiled vegetables are poured over. It carries within it always the message of well-being and, were my vice and my curiosity more restrained, I, too, would adore to eat it every evening of my life.

2 quarts boiling water
Salt
1 pound potatoes, peeled, quartered lengthwise, sliced
1 pound leeks, tough green parts removed, cleaned, finely sliced
3 tablespoons unsalted butter

Add the vegetables to the salted, boiling water and cook, covered, at a light boil until the potatoes begin to cook apart—or, until, when one is pressed against the side of the saucepan with a wooden spoon, it offers no resistance to crushing—about ½ hour to 40 minutes, depending on the potatoes. Add the butter at the moment of serving, after removal from the heat.

BREAD AND SQUASH SOUP
(Pain Bouilli à la Courge)
(for 6)

A clean, invigorating flavor, exciting and subtle—perfect for a winter evening and a far cry from the banal Lyonnaise version, which is pumpkin boiled in water, finished with milk, and served with crusts and grated cheese apart (Bocuse has launched a rich and picturesque variation that involves cutting out a lid, seeding the pumpkin, filling it with alternate layers of grilled bread slices and grated Gruyère, salt, and pepper, pouring heavy cream to the brim and baking in the oven for 2 hours).

2 pounds pumpkin or other winter squash, peeled, seeded, and cut into small pieces
8 to 10 cloves garlic, peeled
3½ cups boiling water
Salt
2 ounces stale bread, crusts removed, torn into small pieces
Pepper
¼ cup olive oil
Parsley or fresh basil

Add the squash and the garlic to the salted, boiling water and cook, covered, at a light boil, for 25 or 30 minutes or until the squash is purée-soft. Throw in the bread, leave to simmer for a couple of minutes longer, put the contents of the pan through a sieve or vegetable mill, taste for salt, grind in some pepper, reheat, and stir in the olive oil at the moment of serving. The soup may be garnished with finely chopped parsley or, in season, fresh basil leaves, torn into tiny pieces.

RED WINE SOUP
(Soupe à la Bourguignonne)
(for 4 or 5)

Somewhat reduced, with an additional garnish of sautéed mushrooms and little butter-cooked onions, this soup becomes the basic Burgundy sauce in which beef is cooked for a *Bourguignon*, chicken for a *coq-au-vin*, eel for a *matelotte*; poached eggs, brains, veal, lungs, or a variety of river fish, thus sauced, are said to be *en meurette*.

The dried crusts and chopped herbs may be replaced by crisp little croutons cooked in butter and rapidly sautéed in a *persillade* at the last minute. Their charm, unlike the soaked crusts, resides in their crispness and their nutty, brown-butter separateness of flavor, so they should be added only as the soup is being served.

3 ounces lean salt pork (unsmoked bacon), cut into small (¼-inch) lardons, parboiled 2 minutes and drained
2½ tablespoons butter
4 ounces sweet onion, finely sliced
1 tablespoon flour
2 cups water
Salt
Bouquet garni: branch of celery, thyme, bay leaf, parsley (including root, if possible), fragment of lovage, if available
3 cups red wine
Slices of dried-out bread rubbed with garlic
Chopped parsley or fines herbes

Cook the lardons gently in ½ tablespoon butter, tossing, until lightly colored. Add the onions and cook over a very low heat, covered, stirring occasionally (add a bit more butter, if necessary) for about ½ hour, without permitting the onions to brown. Sprinkle over the flour, stir regularly for a couple of minutes, and add the water, slowly at first and in small quantities at a time, stirring the while and bringing to a boil before adding more, salt lightly, add the bouquet garni, and simmer, covered, for about 15 minutes. Add the red wine, return to a boil, and cook, covered, at a bare simmer, for about 1 hour, skimming two or three times during the last 5 minutes to remove any skin or traces of fat visible at the surface. Stir in the remaining butter at the moment of serving, pour the soup over the crusts, and sprinkle with the chopped herbs.

SORREL SOUP
(Soupe à l'Oseille)
(for 4)

A handful of shredded sorrel, young and tender, will brighten any vegetable or herb soup with its light, clean acidity. A recipe for the academic, but lovely, *Germiny*, rich, creamy, and egg-yolk-bound, is given in *The French Menu Cookbook*.

Hot, I prefer this soup unpuréed but, made into a fine purée, the terminal addition of butter eliminated, strengthened a bit in cream, and served chilled, it is another and equally good thing.

6 ounces sorrel (tender, newly formed leaves—if older, they should be
   parboiled for a couple of seconds before being put to stew in butter)
1 large sweet onion, finely chopped
6 tablespoons butter
1 pound potatoes, quartered lengthwise, finely sliced
Salt
1 quart boiling water
½ cup heavy cream
Pepper
Handful chervil leaves (if available) or chopped chives

Pick over the sorrel, pulling the stems off backwards, taking with them any stringy veins from the leaves, wash, drain, and cut into a *chiffonade* (coarsely shredded).

Stew the onions gently in 2 tablespoons butter, stirring, for 15 minutes, until melting-soft but uncolored, add the sorrel, continue cooking until it is "melted," add the potatoes, stir, and cook together for a few minutes, salt, pour over the boiling water, and cook, covered, at a light boil, for ½ hour. Uncover and continue cooking for

10 minutes, crushing regularly with a wooden spoon or pestle, until the potatoes are reduced to a coarse semipurée. Stir in the cream, return to a boil, remove from the flame, stir in the remaining butter and the pepper, and serve, sprinkled with chervil.

VEGETABLE SOUP WITH BASIL AND GARLIC
(Soupe au Pistou)
(for approximately 4 to 6)

The French have imposed their own pronunciation on the Italian *minestrone* to describe a hearty soup of boiled vegetables and pasta. The Provençal *pistou* is a garlic, fresh basil, grated cheese, and olive oil pomade, descendant of the Genovese *pesto,* which contains pounded pinenuts and most often sauces pasta. A *soupe au pistou* is a *minestrone* into which, at the moment of serving, a *pistou* is incorporated. Beyond that point of definition, no two are alike and, despite Italian antecedents, all are jealously Provençal.

Some people prefer to cut all the vegetables into tiny cubes and boil them rapidly for about 20 minutes; others cut them into chunks, adding certain at different times and cooking until the potatoes begin to disintegrate and the squash has melted to near dissolution. Some add chopped tomato to the soup and none to the *pistou.* The Varois consider white beans and squash essential to a smooth body (fresh basil and large squash, from which slices are cut, are stocked in all the local shops for 6 months of the year, both destined only for use in *soupe au pistou*); in the Alpes-maritimes, white beans are rarely added and the use of squash is either unknown or thought to be heretical.

Soupe au pistou has been fairly widely popularized in American kitchens—and American friends never fail to be astonished at the goodness of a *pistou* that has been patiently pounded in a mortar rather than violently emulsified in a blender . . .

The thing, in itself, is like some unleashed earth force, sowing exhilaration in its wake—but, in that wake, nothing else may be savored, for it has a distinctly paralyzing effect on the palate; one may as well make it in quantity and plan to make a meal of it . . .

And it is a sure wine-killer, so one may as well settle for a well-chilled, light-bodied, dry rosé.

The *pistou* is most often mixed into the soup before its arrival at the table, but, not only is it kinder to those guests who are shy of garlic to serve the fearful paste apart, but also the ritualistic aspect of each person's serving himself from the mortar deepens the joy and the group involvement; *soupe au pistou* creates an atmosphere that deserves to be pampered.

The soup

2 medium leeks, white and tender green parts finely sliced crosswise

6 ounces sweet onion, finely sliced

6 ounces carrots, peeled, split, woody core removed, finely sliced

12 ounces potatoes, peeled, quartered lengthwise, sliced

10 ounces pumpkin-type squash, seeded, peeled, coarsely diced

1 pound (before shelling) fresh white beans (or the equivalent of precooked dried beans)

Bouquet garni: celery branch, parsley, bay leaf, thyme

2½ quarts water

Salt

6 ounces fresh green beans, tips snapped, cut crosswise (a handful at a time) into approximately ½-inch lengths

2 or 3 small, firm zucchini (about 8 ounces), cut into ¼-inch slices

1 cup short or "elbow" macaroni

The pistou

4 large cloves garlic, peeled

1 packed handful fresh basil leaves and flowers

Salt, freshly ground pepper

About 1 cup freshly grated Parmesan

1 medium-sized, firm, ripe tomato, peeled, seeded, and cut into pieces

About 1¼ cups olive oil

Add leeks, onion, carrots, potatoes, squash, white beans, and the bouquet garni to salted, boiling water and cook, covered, at a light boil for about ½ hour; test the beans for doneness and, if necessary, cook a bit longer, or until they may be crushed with little resistance while remaining still completely intact. Add the green beans, the zucchini, and the macaroni and cook another 15 minutes (depending on the quality of the macaroni—it should be well cooked, but not falling apart—and on the tenderness of the green beans).

While the soup is cooking, prepare the *pistou*: Pound the garlic, basil, salt, and pepper to a paste in a good-sized mortar (a quart-sized marble *aïoli* mortar is perfect—use a wooden bowl if nothing else is available), using a wooden pestle and alternating between pounding and turning with a grinding motion. Work in some cheese until you have a very stiff paste, then add about one third of the tomato, pounding and grinding to a paste, more cheese, a bit of olive oil, more tomato, and so forth, the final addition of cheese bringing the consistency to that of a barely fluid paste. Add the remainder of the olive oil slowly and progressively, turning the while. It will not produce a genuine emulsion—and should not—and should be thoroughly mixed each time it is served out.

Serve the soup boiling hot, the mortar of *pistou* at the table. Each guest stirs a small ladleful (1 or 2 tablespoons—more or less, depending on taste) into his soup.

EGG "BOUILLABAISSE"
(Bouillabaisse Borgne)
(for 4)

The fabled and much fêted, saffron-robed Marseillaise legend and presence—arrogant, flamboyant, and insolent, with its crown of horny *rascasse*, its exotic suite of tropical-colored Mediterranean denizens, and its fiery red *rouille*—shares its special titles of nobility with only one other preparation, the Provençal fish soup *(soupe de poissons)*, which holds in its clear and essential broth the soul of *bouillabaisse*. The same sensuous warmth, the same sapid density, and the same limpid reflections of red-gold are only thrown into sharper relief by the absence—but for a few floating fresh egg noodles—of solid garnish. Outside of Marseilles, many a Provençal

276

native will insist that *soupe de poissons* is a much finer dish than *bouillabaisse,* whose "broth is underflavored and the fish overcooked" (an accurate description, in fact, of nearly all restaurant *bouillabaisses*): "The bore of dealing with the bones and the overcooked flesh is eliminated and, since *soupe de poissons* is only a first course, one can follow it with a correctly cooked fish" (meaning a grilled sea bass). However unflagging one's loyalty to a good *bouillabaisse,* there can be no doubt that a *soupe de poissons* numbers among the very pure and the very exciting things of the table. It is prepared like the following recipe (potatoes and eggs eliminated), an abundance of small fish, fish pieces, and fish heads (avoid oily, strong-flavored varieties, such as sardines, tuna, smelts, herring, mackerel) being added after the tomatoes have cooked awhile and before the water is added. They are stirred, crushed, and generally messed around for 15 minutes or so, until everything is cooked and supremely unsightly; then the boiling water is added, kept at a boil for ½ hour, and the liquid is put through a fine sieve, the solid material being pressed thoroughly to extract all juices, but not entering as a purée into the broth. The soup is reheated and fresh egg noodles, first parboiled for a minute and drained, finish cooking in it. It is, in Provence, traditionally made with several pounds of the minnows of *bouillabaisse* varieties—but that detail must, elsewhere, be ignored. Since the broth is strained, the contents of the bouquet garni may be added loosely (and, except for the orange peel, abundantly) and the refinements of peeling the tomatoes and chopping the garlic no longer have any meaning (the garlic should, nonetheless, be crushed—and several supplementary cloves may be added).

There are a number of poor cousins on which the name has been imposed—any soup, in fact, with the exception of *soupe de poissons,* that has been caressed by tomato, saffron, fennel, and garlic. Those of small interest (*bouillabaisse de sardines,* or the salt-cod version, *bouillabaisse de morue*) gratefully assume the splendid title. A *bouillabaisse d'épinards* is a pleasant thing and the Marseillais render it homage by calling it *épinards à la Marseillaise. La bouillabaisse borgne* ("one-eyed" *bouillabaisse*) is exquisite, and its very real qualities suffer from the imposition of the noble title. It can—in its own way—be bettered only by a *bouillabaisse de petits-pois* (identical preparation with a few potatoes less and a couple of handsful of tender, freshly shelled peas tossed in at the halfway point).

277

The bizarre name indicates the single egg in the plate of each guest. Lent normal vision, it may well serve as a relaxing and principal course for a light supper.

¼ cup olive oil
2 medium leeks, white parts finely sliced crosswise, green parts added to bouquet garni
1 large onion, finely chopped
3 firm, ripe tomatoes, peeled, seeded, coarsely chopped
3 large cloves garlic, peeled and finely chopped
Salt, pinch cayenne
¼ teaspoon saffron (or less—to taste)
Bouquet garni: the leek greens, branch celery, parsley, bay leaf, thyme, oregano, savory, fennel branches (or small sachet of fennel seeds), strip of dried orange peel
2 tablespoons pastis (Ricard or Pernod 51)
About 5 cups boiling water
1½ pounds non-mealy, yellow-fleshed potatoes, peeled, cut into ¼-inch slices, and rinsed
4 fresh eggs
Chopped parsley
Dried bread slices rubbed with cloves of garlic

Cook the leeks and onion gently in the olive oil, stirring occasionally, for some 15 minutes or until softened and yellowed, but not colored. Add the tomatoes, the garlic, and the seasonings, stir, and continue cooking for 5 minutes or so, add the bouquet garni and pastis, pour in the boiling water, and, when the boil returns, add the potatoes. Turn the flame high and cook, uncovered, for about 20 minutes, or until the potatoes are done. Discard the bouquet garni and, with the help of a large wire or slotted spoon, remove the potatoes to a preheated serving platter. Remove the pan from the heat and break the eggs, opening each just at the broth's surface and letting it slip gently in. Cover and, when the eggs are poached, remove them carefully to the potato platter. Sprinkle generously with parsley. Pour the broth into a preheated tureen and serve, a crust of garlic bread in the soup plate of each guest, the bouillon ladled over, potatoes and an egg served on top.

BOILED DINNERS *(POTÉES)*

Most of the regions of central and northern France claim their own *potées*, but they are all pretty much alike and a Bourguignon being served a *potée* in Auvergne, Lorraine, or Savoie might well mistake it for his very own. In addition to the usual *pot-au-feu* vegetables, white beans and cabbage often find their place in a *potée,* and the meats are usually chosen from a variety of pork products—sausages, salt or smoked slab bacon, ham, ears, heads, tails, feet . . . Cabbage should, for the sake of digestion, be first parboiled and drained and, to get rid of excessive salt, it is best to first soak salt pork and then parboil it and drain it. Otherwise, it is essentially a question of throwing everything together and cooking until done.

A *garbure* is a *potée* with a special personality and, although not made with pork, *pots-au-feu* and *poules-au-pot* are, generically, *potées.*

CABBAGE SOUP WITH PRESERVED GOOSE
(Garbure du Béarn)
(for 4)

In cookbooks of the nineteenth century, *garbures* are *panades*; thick soups, the body of which is often but not necessarily that of cabbage, baked with alternating layers of dried bread, producing something akin to a moist pudding containing no remainder of loose liquid. The only *garbures* retained in today's kitchens are those of the southwest; thick cabbage soups (to underline the importance of their consistency, it is said that a wooden spoon or a ladle thrust into the soup should stand erectly), which, although served over dried bread crusts, are not genuine *panades*. *Garbures* may contain little else than a piece of salt pork and some potatoes, but that baptized *béarnaise*, containing preserved goose and made, preferably, in the spring of the year, when a selection of tender young vegetables abounds, has a rich suavity unknown to the others. Preserved goose finds its two most celebrated roles in this *garbure* and a *cassoulet*. A variety of small, green-leafed cabbage, the heads of which are elongated, loosely formed, and picked before maturity, is shredded and added directly to the soup. This cabbage is not found on the American market and it is best to first parboil other cabbages. Replacing the white beans in the following recipe, tender but fully developed broad *(fave)* beans, shelled and individually peeled (each bean measuring a short inch at the widest part, the flesh still clear green and easily pierced beneath a somewhat leathery skin) lend a particularly sumptuous quality that is enhanced by the presence of savory in the bouquet. A couple of handsful of freshly shelled tender peas, added at the same time as the goose, are always welcome. A finely chopped mixture of fresh pork fat, garlic, and parsley is often stirred in at this time also; its value, I think, is more real in the absence of preserved goose.

1 medium cabbage (about 2 pounds), preferably of a green, crinkly-leafed variety

Salt

10 ounces carrots, peeled, split (if core is woody, pry it out and discard it), finely sliced

10 ounces tender, crisp turnips, thickly peeled and finely sliced

1 large, sweet onion, halved and finely sliced

1 large leek (6 to 7 ounces), white part finely sliced crosswise, greens added to bouquet

3 tablespoons goose fat (from the preserved goose)

Bouquet garni: celery branch, leek greens, bay leaf, parsley (plus root), large bouquet of thyme (or 1 teaspoon dried, tied in sachet)

Pinch of cayenne

A scant 2 quarts of water

1 pound (unshelled) fresh white beans (or 1 cup dried "Great Northern" beans: If the beans are fresh, add them directly, freshly shelled; dried beans should be washed, immersed largely in cold water, brought slowly to a boil, drained, covered again in cold water, brought again to a boil, and simmered, unsalted, covered, with carrot, onion, thyme, and bay leaf until tender, but intact—1½ to 2 hours)

12 ounces potatoes, peeled, cut into ½-inch cubes

12 ounces pumpkin or other "winter" squash, seeded, peeled, cut into
½-inch cubes
The legs and the split breast of a preserved goose (or, for a family dinner,
neck, feet, back pieces, etc.); see page 389
Slices of dried bread

Remove the outer leaves of the cabbage, split it, vertically, into
quarters, cut out the core, remove as many of the ribs as you can
easily get at, shred it coarsely, and parboil it in a large container
of salted, boiling water for 10 minutes. Drain well, pressing gently.

If possible, use a 5- or 6-quart earthenware vessel (protected
from the direct flame by an asbestos pad)—a deep *marmite*, Boston
bean pot, etc. Lacking that, a large, enameled ironware casserole
will do. Gently stew the carrots, turnips, onion, and leek in the
goose fat, stirring regularly, for about 15 minutes, add the drained
cabbage, continue cooking and stirring for another 10 minutes, add
the bouquet and the seasonings (salt lightly—the preserved goose
will add to the saltiness), pour over the boiling water, add the beans
(without their cooking liquid, if dried and precooked), the potatoes, and the squash and cook, uncovered, at a light boil for about
40 minutes, adding a bit of boiling water if necessary, scraping the
bottom from time to time with a wooden spoon to be certain that
nothing is sticking. Push the pieces of goose (with only a bit of the
goose fat clinging) into the soup, seeing to it that they are completely
submerged, and continue to cook for another ½ hour. Lift off any
fat from the surface and serve from the cooking vessel, over dried
slices of bread (rye bread is good in this instance), either serving,
first, only a bit of broth or, immediately after soaking up the bread
with a ladle of broth, placing a quarter of goose on top, surrounded
by a couple of ladles of vegetables.

"STEWED" CHICKEN AND VEGETABLES
(Poule-au-pot)
(for 4 to 6)

But for cooking times, a *poule-au-pot* is prepared like a *pot-au-feu*,
the hen or chicken being added an hour or so after the beef. The

chicken is sometimes stuffed, but the stuffing (*farce*—or, in the southwest, *farci*), delicious in itself, adds neither to the quality of the chicken nor to that of the bouillon. If a stuffing is to be part of the garnish, it seems best to stuff a cabbage and braise it apart (see page 185) in a few ladles of fatty broth skimmed from the pot, preserving the chicken bouillon both from the cabbage onslaught and the confusing flavors of the stuffing. Furthermore, a platter with a hen surrounded by *pot-au-feu* cuts of beef, another crowned with a whole stuffed cabbage escorted by the vegetables from the pot, is an impressive sight and a heartening experience.

An unstuffed chicken is often accompanied by a pilaf cooked in part of the chicken broth and a sauce *suprême* (chicken *velouté* reduced with more of the broth, cream added, and finished with cream and butter—an egg-yolk binding will transform it into an *allemande* or a *parisienne*), but one can, then, no longer take the same pleasure in the broth and the boiled vegetables.

Sometimes the bird is simply covered with water, brought to a boil, vegetables and bouquet added, and simmered until done. That is good agrestic fare, but the soup tends to be a bit lightweight. An old hen, sacrificed because of a diminished egg output, may take up to 3 hours to cook and will lend a fine flavor to the bouillon but one should not expect total satisfaction from the flesh. A young chicken (American fryers and French *poulets à rôtir* are killed at from 6 to 8 weeks) and, in particular, a commercially raised young chicken will lend little beyond a bit of gelatin to the bouillon and will, itself, have no taste—it will be cooked in ½ hour. A hen about 1 year old is ideal and should require no more than 1½ hours.

It is a Sunday meal and, traditionally, the bouillon serves throughout the week as a base for the evening soup or as stock.

Stock, meat jelly or aspic, bouillon, and consommé differ only in that: (1) Especially gelatinous cuts and bones are usually avoided in the preparation of bouillon or consommé, the quantity of gelatin essential to the structure of a stock's derivative silken sauces and to the physical integrity of an aspic troubling the clear definition of bouillon's flavor; (2) consommé is clarified (cooked for an hour with a paste of egg white and finely chopped lean beef, the albumen draining all solids in suspension from the liquid, to mark it with discrete sparkling transparency.

The slightest trace of fat on the surface of a consommé would constitute an offense to the world of hierarchical formal service and high social precepts that it so neatly symbolizes, whereas, a few glistening and anodyne pearls of fat on a bouillon's surface, supported by fragrant effluence, dispel tensions, transforming social contact into human communion. But the crystalline consommé's world now belongs increasingly to the realm of Proustian recall, the tiny *quenelles* and *royales,* the cocks' combs, truffle juliènne, and plovers' eggs that have garnished it, permitting it to assume a thousand denominations, having been relegated to gastronomic literature; and clarification is considered archaic in most professional kitchens (if cooking methods are respected, the bouillon will be sufficiently clear and of a warmer and deeper cast than a clarified consommé). It has never been current practice in home kitchens where leftover *pot-au-feu* or *poule-au-pot* broth, with or without the sliced leftover vegetables, may, when not accompanied by the recurrent dried crusts, be garnished with any of a variety of pastas, rice, tapioca, stuffed braised cabbage leaves, rolled and slivered *crêpes,* beaten egg threaded through a sieve into the simmering broth. Freshly cooked vegetables, diced or in juliènne, may also be added, or a handful of fresh peas, or one of shredded sorrel . . .

1 hen
Lemon (optional)
2 or 3 quarts veal stock, prepared without bones or knuckle; or leftover pot-au-feu bouillon; or a simple stock prepared with beef and veal parings, the chicken's neck and wing tips, plus a few pieces of cheap chicken parts
Water to cover
2 pounds leeks, green parts in the bouquet, white parts tied in a bundle
1 pound carrots, peeled, whole if small or cut into 2- or 3-inch lengths
½ pound small, tender turnips, thickly peeled
Bouquet garni: branch celery, leek greens, thyme, bay leaf, parsley (with root, if possible—or replace wtih a small parsnip), branch of lovage, if possible
1 head garlic, superficial husk removed, whole
Salt (depending on the quantity of water added and on the saltiness of the stock)
1 cabbage
1 pound small potatoes (preferably new)

Accompaniment: dried slices of bread, a dish of coarse (or Kosher) salt, freshly grated Parmesan (or a piece of Parmesan with grater at table)

Unless the chicken has already been badly mauled and slashed by the butcher, remove the neck by slitting the neck skin on the back side, carefully peeling it loose from the neck, cutting halfway through the neck at the point where it joins the backbone, and twisting it off, thus leaving an intact flap of skin which may be folded across the neck cavity and secured against the back, preventing the loss of valuable juices (and permitting a handsomer presentation). Remove all fat from body cavity. Loosen the skin from the upper part of the breast and remove the wishbone (this should be done with any poultry, poached, braised, or roasted, that is destined to be served whole and carved at table; the breast cannot, otherwise, be carved neatly and rationally): Slit the flesh the length of the two sections of the wishbone with the tip of a small sharp knife, work it loose with tips of thumb and forefinger, cut through the cartilaginous attachments to the breastbone, and gently pull the two branch bones backwards, tearing the summit loose from its attachment.

Truss the chicken (this, too, is not only a question of presentation; trussed compactly, a chicken cooks more evenly): If the feet have not already been removed, pass all parts of them over a flame at the same time that the chicken is singed, blistering the skin. Remove the skin, holding a towel or paper towel in your hand; cut off the "toes" except for the longest, central digit, which should be sectioned at the first joint, removing the claw tip. Cut off the wing tips (the second joint from the tip, leaving only the shoulder section attached to the bird). Fold the neck skin over the back, spreading it, and place the chicken on its back. Use two lengths of kitchen string and an approximately 6-inch trussing needle. Thread the first string, run it through the wing section just below the shoulder joint, the needle brushing the underside of the bone, bring it out through the back and the near edge of the neck flap, return it through the far edge of the neck flap, the back and, identically, through the far wing. Run the string back through the body of the bird, this time through the drumstick, just beneath its connection with the thigh, and tie the two string ends, pulling the strings gently, but tightly, before tying. Repeat the process with the other length of string, piercing this time the lower ends of the wing sections and the drumsticks. At this

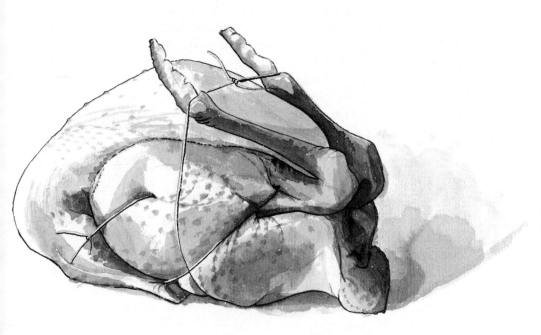

Chicken trussed for poaching or roasting, using three lengths of string: one run through upper parts of wing joints and drumsticks; one run through lower parts of wing joints and drumsticks; one tied loosely around the bird to hold the feet in place

point, the chicken may be rubbed with lemon juice, if one likes—it is a question of discouraging discoloration during the poaching. If the feet are attached, fold them over the breast and tie a length of string loosely around the girth of the bird to hold them in place.

Place the bird in its pot, pour over warmed stock and water to cover, bring slowly to a boil, skim as for a stock, add the vegetables, the bouquet, the head of garlic, salt (if necessary) and maintain the liquid, lid slightly ajar, at the slightest suggestion of a simmer until the chicken is cooked, tender, 1½ to 3 hours. Skim off the bulk of the fat.

285

Remove the outer leaves from the cabbage, quarter it, arrange the quarters in a large saucepan, pour over boiling water to cover, and parboil for 10 minutes. Drain, keeping the quarters intact and pressing them gently to rid them of the maximum of liquid, return them to the saucepan, and ladle over enough fatty bouillon from the surface of the pot to barely cover them, pressed well into place. Simmer, covered, until serving (in this case, a bare 1½ hours).

If the potatoes are young, they may, depending on taste, be cooked in their skins, first well washed and scrubbed. Cook them apart in salted water, putting them to cook ½ hour before serving the dish.

Serve first a tureen of the bouillon, crusts on the bottom of each soup plate. Those who wish may sprinkle the bread and broth with Parmesan. Discard garlic and bouquet. Clip and remove strings from chicken and leeks. Serve the chicken and the vegetables on separate platters (the latter interfere with carving). Keep the bouillon at table, pouring a ladle over each serving of meat and vegetables. Some people like to have Dijon mustard and horseradish handy as well as the coarse salt.

MEATS AND POULTRY

STEWS *(RAGOÛTS, DAUBES, SAUTÉS . . .)*

B RAISED meats are those which, discreetly moistened, cook slowly over a relatively long period of time. When the meat is cut into pieces, they are dubbed stews and may be said (without denying the *pot-au-feu* its importance) to form the philosophical cornerstone of French family cooking; they embody—or spark—something akin to an ancestral or racial memory of farmhouse kitchens—of rustic tables laid by mothers, grandmothers, or old retainers.

Les petits plats qui mijotent au coin du feu is a phrase that is used like a word and it rarely fails to garnish a conversation about food. It would be unfair to accuse those who use it—albeit at times as a crutch—of leaning on a vain cliché, for they know it—or sense it—to be a magical formula: the incantational touchspring that unites a diverse people in a single reaction. It means "slow-cooking stews," but it symbolizes "the good life" and somewhere, shadow-like, behind its words lies a half-remembered state of voluptuous, total well-being *("Là, tout n'est qu'ordre et beauté, luxe, calme et volupté").*

Le coin du feu is the hearth that, even for those who have never known it, recalls the security of the family united before it in warmth. But the magic word in the magical phrase is *mijoter*. It describes that condition of near suspension in which there is, nonetheless, a whispering movement, a tiny bubble rising here and there to break a stew's still surface—and it means, at the same time, a slow ripening. The comfortable satisfaction felt upon lifting a lid and glancing at a stew's surface—the sense that, merely because a liquid's surface is sustained at precisely the right point of hardly perceptible movement, all is well, the stew's progress out of one's hands and its success assured—is familiar to all cooks.

A stew that is boiled will cook no faster, but the meat will always be dry and stringy, the sauce muddy in aspect and in taste, and it will be indigestible, thanks to the emulsion of cooked fats contained in it.

It is a question of taste whether the meats be marinated for a few hours (or refrigerated—which greatly slows down the action of the marinade—overnight). Cognac or other strong alcohols may, during the cooking, intervene as flavoring agents but, in a marinade, they rapidly and insidiously render a meat indigestible, stamping it with a putrid, false high-gamy taste. Recipes involving prolonged marinations—3, 4, 5, or 6 days (depending on the season, it is said)—are not uncommon in cookbook literature; they are relics from an unrefrigerated past when marinades served as much to keep meat from spoiling as to heighten its flavor and, to me, they are simple abominations, trailing sleepless nights in their wake.

A stew without the aromatic support of onion is difficult to imagine—carrots and garlic are usual but not inevitable allies. Thyme, commonly assisted by bay leaf, celery, and parsley, is the constant of all bouquets garnis, but it need not be: oregano, savory, and marjoram are among the very useful herbs too often ignored in French kitchens. Nor is a bouquet, in itself, indispensable; its aim is to prevent the herbs from spreading through the sauce in fragments, making them easily removable in a neat bundle. A sauce that is strained will, in any case, eliminate them, and a simple stew with a rough sauce suffers in no way from finely crumbled herbs being scattered through it. A stalk of celery or a bay leaf is easily removed but, if bouquets of parsley or leek greens are used in quantity, it is obviously less messy to tie them up.

Water, stock, leftover roasting juices (fat removed—lamb or mutton juices should not be used with other meats), tomato, and wines are among the more satisfactory moistening agents (in Normandy cider, sometimes reinforced with Calvados, is often used and, in Flanders, beer). Wine may have transcendental powers but, if improperly treated, the sauce will be "winy" and the flavor raw and harsh—distinctly unpleasant. As the principal moistener in a *daube* that cooks for a number of hours (and may be further improved by being left to cool, gradually returning to a simmer the following day), it will eventually melt with the aromatic, succulent, gelatinous strains into a single languid and caressing note, but a stew that cooks for less than some 2½ to 3 hours should never be moistened with wine alone unless the sauce be subjected to a further slow cooking and reduction after the meats are removed (or unless the wine has been simmered apart with aromatics for an hour or so before being added to the meats initially). With tender meats—chicken or rabbit —that require no more than 30 or 40 minutes' cooking from the moment they are moistened, a relatively small quantity of wine should be used to deglaze the pan, and it should be almost entirely reduced before other less temperamental liquids are added.

Stews that involve neither an initial (flour roux) nor a terminal (egg-yolk, cream, *beurre manié,* blood . . .) binding are one-step affairs, and *daubes* are the prototype: The meats and the aromatic elements are united, moistened and cooked at a muffled simmer until done; the free-floating fat is lifted from the surface and that is all, the limpid, essential juices' only body deriving from the natural gelatin contained in the meats and the rinds.

The family contains a few eccentric members (the *blanquettes,* for instance, the first part of whose cooking is conducted like that of a *daube,* the juices being then transformed into a *velouté* and, finally, thickened with egg yolks . . .), but *daubes* apart, nearly all stews belong to the branch commonly (some say incorrectly) called *sautés* (other examples are *carbonnades, gibelottes, matelottes, navarins, boeuf Bourguignon,* and *coq-au-vin*)—meats and aromatic vegetables sautéed (which translates, in this instance, "colored in fat"), lightly sprinkled with flour (treated like a roux), and moistened. The sauce (of the radical sauté-type—many a stew, from this point on, is simply cooked until done and served) is strained, simmered, skimmed (or "skinned"—a process known as *dépouillement:* the combined slow reduction and periodic removal from the sauce's surface of the repeatedly formed skin into which are drawn the cooked fats and other impurities otherwise held in suspension in any flour-bound sauce), and reduced to a suave essence that is then returned to cloak the meat and its garnish (a choice of vegetables, sometimes in combination with lardons, each of which has been cooked apart in a manner conceived to respect its nature), the ensemble intermingling at a simmer for another quarter of an hour or so. Croutons, sometimes caressed with garlic or tossed in a *persillade*, as well as those vegetables that can support no supplementary cooking—green beans, little peas, or broad beans—are scattered about at the moment of serving.

Whereas the soul of a *daube* resides in pervasive unity—the perfect fusion or transformation of individual qualities into a single character, a sauté should comprehend an interplay among entities, each jealous of distinctive flavors and textures—piquant in their diversities—but united in harmony by the common veil of sauce.

The following is an attempt to present an abstract recipe that may successfully be adjusted to any meat or poultry—preferably gelatinous cuts or pieces, game birds being, for the most part, excepted. If they are young and tender, their flesh will remain moistly succulent only if roasted or grilled slightly underdone—older specimens may lend fine flavor to a stew, but the flesh will always be dry. Do not forget, meanwhile, that a stew—perfect of its kind—may always be made by throwing pieces of leftover roast or grilled meats or lean meat parings into a couple of spoonsful of hot fat, adding a few minutes later a handful of chopped onions, after another short interval a light sprinkling of flour, a minute later a healthy pinch of dried, crumbled herbs and liquid to cover—if you happen to have a wine glass in hand, empty it in first. Be certain to scrape the bottom well with a wooden spoon to dissolve all caramelized material and simmer for about an hour and a half, carefully removing any fat that appears on the surface . . .

SAUTÉ-TYPE
(Sauté-modèle)
(for 4)

Basics		2 pounds beef heel or chuck, cut into approximately 3-ounce pieces (count 2½ to 3 hours cooking from time of moistening)
	or	2½ pounds lamb shank (1½ to 2 hours from moistening)
	or	2 pounds boned veal shank (about 1½ hours)
	or	1 large frying chicken (or 5 or 6 thighs and drumsticks, attached or separated as preferred: 30 to 40 minutes from time of moistening)
	or	1 rabbit (see rabbit sautés, page 354, for method of cutting up: 30 to 40 minutes from moistening)

(optional) 2 ounces fresh fat pork (impractical with poultry), cut into strips about 1 inch long by something less than ¼ inch square

1 clove garlic, peeled

1 tablespoon finely chopped parsley

Healthy pinch finely crumbled dried herbs (thyme, oregano, savory)

Salt, pepper

Marinade
(optional) 2 tablespoons olive oil

1 medium onion, finely sliced

3 or 4 cloves garlic, peeled and crushed

Parsley, bay leaf, thyme (or mixed herbs)

Wine (about 1 bottle) to cover

(meats should be turned around several times in marinade—kept covered, a maximum of 3 hours at room temperature or, refrigerated, overnight)

About 3 tablespoons fat (olive oil is best; a tasteless cooking oil may be used; butter not to be recommended)

Aromatics	8 ounces onions, peeled, coarsely cut up
Vegetables	8 ounces carrots, peeled, split if large, cut into 1-inch lengths
	Garlic (same as in marinade—or the equivalent if meats not marinated)
Bouquet garni	Thyme, bay leaf, parsley (including root, if possible), branch of celery ...
	Plus a choice of leek greens, oregano, savory, marjoram, lovage

Seasoning	Salt
	½ teaspoon (or less) sugar (particularly useful in the presence of tomato)
	Pinch cayenne or a tiny fresh red hot pepper (more often with white meats than with red)
	Pepper (to be added toward the end)
	About 3 tablespoons flour

Moistening Agents (possibilities alone or in combination)	Water
	Wine (if marinated, the same)
	Stock or bouillon
	Leftover roasting juices
	Tomatoes (peeled, seeded, and chopped; canned out of season—in some instances tomato juice is possible; avoid tomato paste)
	Beer
	Cider
	Small amount Cognac or other eau de vie: marc, Armagnac, Calvados, etc.

Garnish (possibilities alone or in combination)	The following to be joined to the meat and gently stewed in the sauce during the final 15 or 20 minutes
	About 5 ounces lean salt pork cut into lardons (⅓-inch widths cut from thick slices), parboiled for a minute or

two, rinsed, drained, and cooked until superficially crisp with carrots and onions at the beginning, then put aside to be added with other garnish later on

20 to 25 whole onions the size of a small walnut, gently stewed, salted, in butter until just tender but not colored

The carrots from the stew—or 5 or 6 ounces peeled small carrots (or carrot sections) cooked with ¼ cup water, salt, pinch sugar, 1 tablespoon butter until tender and glazed, all liquid evaporated

8 ounces small mushrooms (or halved or quartered if larger), rapidly sautéed, salted, in butter over high heat

Tender artichoke hearts, whole, halved, or quartered, depending on size, stewed, salted, in butter until only just tender

1½-inch lengths of leek whites, parboiled at a simmer for about 5 minutes, drained, stewed, salted, in butter

Tiny new potatoes, scraped, rinsed, wiped dry, cooked gently, salted, in butter, tossed often, until tender but not browned

The following to be joined to the stew (usually scattered over the surface) only at the moment of serving:

Green vegetables (peas, beans, peeled broad beans), rapidly parboiled

(with rabbits and chickens)   The liver (cut into small pieces), the heart (thinly sliced), the gizzard (fleshy parts cut free of all gristly skin and thinly sliced), sautéed, salted, together in butter for a few seconds

Croutons, cooked gently in butter, tossed often, until golden and crisp but not hard; they may be tossed at the last minute over a higher flame with a persillade—finely chopped or pounded garlic mixed with chopped parsley. For a formal presentation, the stew meats are presented on a heated platter, sauce and other garnish poured over, and the croutons are fashioned—2 or 3 to a slice—from thin slices of bread, in the form of triangles, a clove of garlic rubbed over each crisp triangle,

293

a point of each dipped first in sauce, then in chopped
parsley, and arranged, crown-like, parsleyed tips pointing out, around the edge of the platter

Chopped fines herbes (tarragon does not mix well with
herbs other than parsley, chives, and chervil, but it may
be used alone, discreetly, and is more interesting with
white meats; it also goes well with tomatoed sauces),
fresh basil flowers and leaves torn to fragments, finely
chopped fresh marjoram flowers and leaves, small
amount of finely chopped tender young savory (best
mixed with parsley)

The strips of fat pork, rolled and tossed until well coated in the
mixture of garlic, herbs, and seasoning, are each forced with one's
finger into a deep, narrow incision pierced with the grain of the
meat using a small knife; depending on the size and the structure
of each piece of meat, it may receive one, two, or three lardons. The
double purpose of seasoning interiorly, forming tiny pockets of iso-
lated flavor, and nourishing it to keep it moist is served particularly
well with long-cooking stews, although rabbit—and especially the
saddle section—also profits from this treatment. The aromatic elements may be altered to taste. The meats should be larded before
being put into a marinade.

Use, if possible, a heavy copper *plat à sauter* for the browning
process, large enough to hold all the pieces of meat at their ease, side
by side. Lacking that, use a skillet and transfer everything to a large
cocotte for the braising process.

If the garnish includes lean salt-pork lardons, begin cooking
them in the fat over a medium flame until they begin to take on
color. Add the carrots and onions and cook all together, stirring or
tossing regularly, for about ½ hour, removing the lardons and putting vegetables aside as each arrives at the correct stage of surface
crispness and color. The carrots and onions should be lightly colored,
the onions caramelized but not dark brown. Empty them into a
sieve, being certain that no fragment of onion remains in the pan (it
would burn over the high heat necessary to brown the meat, lending
an acrid taste to the sauce), and return the fat to the pan.

If the pieces of meat have been marinated, drain them (collecting the liquid for subsequent moistening), sponge each dry with a

towel or absorbent paper, and salt on all sides. Brown them over high heat in the same pan and the same fat used for the vegetables, turning the heat up or down as necessary to keep them from either stewing or burning and, when all are regularly colored on all surfaces, sprinkle over the sugar (if included), turning the meats around, permitting it to caramelize lightly, thus reinforcing the color of the sauce and effacing the flat sweetness of the sugar.

Lower the heat, sprinkle over the flour, and continue turning the pieces of meat until the flour is lightly colored. Turn the heat up and moisten, first with the marinade—if the meats were marinated—or with wine, scraping vigorously all the surfaces of the pan with a wooden spoon or spatula to dislodge and dissolve all traces of caramelized adherences. If tomato is used, add it at this point, reducing it with the wine so that it may cook apart a bit, mingling with and coating the meat—or, if no wine is used, add the tomato, stirring around well before adding the other liquids. Return the onions and carrots to the pan, add the garlic (if it has not been added with the marinade) and the cayenne, and tuck the bouquet garni into the heart of the thing. If an *eau de vie* is to be added, heat it in a small saucepan, set fire to it, and, when the flame has subsided, pour it over. Add enough stock or water to barely cover the contents of the pan, gently packed together so that they may be moistened with a minimum of liquid, bring to a boil, and adjust the heat so that, covered, the liquid's surface is maintained at the suggestion of a simmer (if you have been working with a pan—or with pans—too small to contain all the ingredients, transfer meats, vegetables, and bouquet to a large *cocotte* before sprinkling the pans first with sugar, then with flour, deglazing, and, finally, pouring the slightly thickened liquid over the meats and vegetables to cover). The stew may be cooked in a slow oven or on top of the stove—the precise adjustment of heat necessary to maintain the desired simmer is more easily achieved on top.

Skim off surface fat two or three times and, when the meat is tender—still slightly firm, remove it, piece by piece, to a plate and pour the remaining contents of the pan into a large, fine sieve placed over a saucepan. If a particularly delicate, translucid sauce is desired, press the solid remainder gently to extract all the juices and discard the vegetables and the bouquet. For a rougher sauce with more body, remove the carrots (they may be added to the meats to serve as garnish—overcooked and impregnated with flavors other than their own, they add little; their work has already been done), press the bouquet and discard it, and purée the onions and garlic into the sauce.

Return the meat to its cooking vessel, add the garnishes chosen from the first part of the list, cover, and put aside until the sauce is ready.

Bring the sauce to a boil and move the saucepan somewhat to the side of a medium flame in order to maintain a light boil at one side only of the sauce's surface. A skin will form on the undisturbed part of the surface that should be gently pulled to the edge with a tablespoon, removed, and discarded. Give it time to form—the firmer it is, the more fat and impurities will be contained in it and the easier it will be to remove. Repeat this procedure four or five times over a period of ½ hour or so. If at this point the sauce isn't sufficiently reduced (there should be only enough to generously coat the meats and garnish and it should be light-bodied but consistent—not watery), turn the flame high for a couple of minutes and reduce, stirring the while with a wooden spoon. Taste for salt.

Grind pepper to taste over the meat and garnish, pour the sauce evenly over, return to a boil over a low flame and simmer, covered, for another 15 or 20 minutes, gently shaking the pan from time to time to encourage the intermingling of flavors and the even coating of all the elements by the sauce. Remove any further evidence of fat on the surface (cast off by the lardons or the vegetables that have been cooked in butter), soaking it up with the corner of a paper towel, if in tiny globules. Scatter over the terminal garnish, freshly prepared, and serve, preferably from the cooking vessel.

DRY HEAT: ROAST AND GRILLED MEATS
(CHALEUR SÈCHE: VIANDES RÔTIES ET GRILLÉES)

An uncomplicated roast is better cooked before an open fire than in an oven, probably because it turns in a dry open air unoppressed by vapors and condensations of moisture, although, just as a fireplace that does not smoke will perfume a room deliciously with the odor of burning wood, the flames, their smoke rising with only their heat radiating outward, undoubtedly alter the flavor in a delicately different way from the heat of an oven.

But so many things influence taste . . . The eloquence of a roast slowly turning before living flames, its visible transfiguration as it contracts, swells, and, fondled by repeated basting, assumes a luxuriant brown satin glaze, has an entrancing effect on a company. If a leg of lamb spitted in a fireplace seems more succulent than its delicious counterpart roasted in an oven, so much the better—nothing, in any case, ever tastes better than it is (in the absence of euphory, things rarely taste as good as they are . . .); perhaps the ritual beauty of the thing and the excitement and suspense it engenders collaborate to rivet attentions and sharpen palates in the service of total appreciation. I remain convinced of the matter-of-fact superiority of a roast cooked in this way; beyond the fireplace, the turnspit, and something to serve as a dripping pan, no special equipment is essential—although an upright grill within the fireplace, designed to hold the burning logs, provides a more manageable source of heat—a solid face of flames—than a fire built on the hearth itself. The intensity of the heat is controlled by adjusting the distance of the spit from the source of heat.

The flavor of grilled meats depends on the nature of the wood burned: fruit woods are most satisfactory and, for rapid grills that do not need a bed of coals of great sustaining power, dried grapevine prunings, reduced in a holocaust of flame to incandescent embers in the space of a few minutes' time, will put other woods to shame. A fire fed regularly with logs for heating purposes contains an incandescent heart from which a bed of coals may be raked to the side or the front but, if a fire is built specifically for purposes of grilling, care should be taken to choose relatively small wood all of approximately the same size; the smaller wood will, otherwise, have dissipated into ash before the larger pieces are reduced to coals. A preheated heavy welded iron grill with feet 3 to 3½ inches high gives the best results. It may be placed over the coals to heat before the flames and smoke have completely disappeared, but only glowing coals should be in evidence when the meat is placed there and, for that needing a longer cooking period (poultry, lamb's shoulder . . .), the bed of coals should be deep but its intensity should be allowed to subside a bit, a film of gray ash veiling the embers' ardor. In the absence of a fireplace or a back yard in which to build a bonfire, charcoal barbecue devices are practical; when circumstances permit, a bundle of dried fruitwood branches added to the hot coals and left to blaze up and die down before grilling the meat will improve the result—commercialized charcoals often stamp foods with strange flavors.

Meats, whether oven roasted, turned in the open, grilled, broiled, or pan fried, will always cook better if at room temperature, rather than chilled, at the moment they are put to cook. A steak should be removed from refrigeration at least ½ to 1 hour earlier and a leg of lamb 2 or 3 hours earlier. Roasts should be salted some 10 minutes after being put to cook; grilled meats should be salted on the side first to be grilled at the moment they are thrown on the grill and on the other side just before turning. The searing process prevents any loss of juices that the salt might otherwise draw out.

Olive oil is the best fat for rubbing roasts and grills, both for the quality of the coloration and of the flavor. The thin sheets of fat pork (*bardes de lard*) commonly wrapped around all roasts in France are valuable only for poultry and, especially, for game birds and guinea fowl, whose breasts would otherwise be overcooked and dried out before the legs were sufficiently cooked. They should be unwrapped and frequently basted for the last 10 minutes or so of cooking. The old-fashioned method of larding a roast's surface by threading narrow strips of fat pork into and out of the flesh with a larding needle is another thing, and it is a pity that it has, for the most part, been abandoned; the lardons nourish the meat interiorly and exteriorly while permitting the surface to brown at the same time, and the decorative effect is delicious—their presence, however, should not proscribe rubbing the roast in olive oil and subsequent basting. Grilled meats should be basted but slightly each time, preferably with a brush or a bouquet of herbs, to discourage fat's falling onto the coals and blazing up.

Although I think it a mistake to scatter herbs over certain meats before grilling—good beef, for instance—any meat will be enhanced by the slight caress of smoke from a handful of herbs being tossed onto the coals shortly before removing it from the grill; the most exciting is that of rosemary.

Meats to be served rare or pink throughout, if left to relax in a warm place for a period of time relative to their size—5 minutes or so for a steak and up to ½ hour for a large leg of lamb—will be tenderer and more succulent; the heat contained within the meat will continue to penetrate to the heart and the juices will be freed, a relaxed firmness supplanting the somewhat rubbery, elastic resistance of uncooked flesh. This may not always seem practical for grilled meats (I usually place the meat on a heated plate, cover it with another heated plate or shallow bowl, and leave it for a few minutes on the edge of the grill), but it is important for a roast. For an open roast, leave it, unspitted, in the dripping pan, near the fire, covered by some preheated container; for an oven roast, remove it from the oven to arrest the cooking, turn the oven off (leaving the door open if it holds heat well), and return it to the warm oven a few minutes later.

LAMB AND MUTTON
(Agneau et Mouton)

The flesh of grass or yearling lamb (often incorrectly and confusingly called "baby lamb") is tender but its structure is that of a mature animal. It is, when of good quality, well furnished with white, dry, and rather crumbly fat and the flesh is a clear rose-tan. Older mutton has a reddish-brown flesh and the flavor is stronger, but all the methods of treating it are the same. Milk lamb, a traditional Easter dish, has a pale grayish-pink flesh, is best roasted to assume a glorious, crackly golden surface; it should always be cooked well done. It is as different from grass lamb as is veal from beef and, for those of delicate digestion, should probably be avoided. All of the following recipes are for grass or yearling lamb.

American habits of cutting lamb are a windfall to the stewmaker and a disaster for the roaster: The shanks (easily the best stew pieces for flavor, moistness, and leanness) are chopped off both the legs and the shoulders, a "leg of lamb" being often composed only of the upper half of the leg plus a section of the saddle, creating a bizarre form and a complication of bone structure at the heart of the roast that renders both decent presentation and elegant carving out of the question; the animals are usually split and often cut up in advance, thus destroying the double saddle, one of the handsomest and, when kept pink, finest of roasts . . . If you have a good butcher and order in advance, everything can be arranged. Lamb should be aged for perfect flavor and tenderness; American butchers are often more serious on this score than the French.

The spareribs are the most economical and probably the commonest stew cut. They are, for some tastes, unpleasantly fat and their structure does not permit its being removed; unless you are certain of your company, you'd best stick to the shanks. Stock will not improve a lamb stew, but a certain amount of tomato will flatter its distinctive flavor and lend warmth to the sauce. A *navarin,* the classic French lamb stew, is prepared like the stew recipe-type, moistened only with water and about ½ cup of puréed tomato (or one large, ripe, peeled, seeded, and chopped tomato) and garnished with butter-cooked little onions, carrots, and tender young turnips, tiny new potatoes being put to cook in the sauce during the last ½ hour and freshly shelled little peas during the last 10 or 15 minutes; butter-stewed artichoke hearts provide a lovely garnish, better alone than in combination with others—or precooked white beans may be drained and simmered in the stew for the last ½ hour or so. Chopping the onions finely (they may be cooked directly with the meat after it has half browned), eliminating the initial flour thickening, and increasing the quantity of tomato, the stew may be transformed into a sublime pilaf by the addition, some 45 minutes before serving, of a cup of long-grain rice that has first been cooked dry over low heat in a spoonful of butter or olive oil, stirred regularly, until the grains turn opaque or "milky." Before adding the rice, carefully skim the sauce of all fat. Stir in the rice so that no grain remains unsubmerged, and then do not touch it until it is done.

AVIGNON DAUBE
(Daube à l'Avignonnaise)
(for 6)

Were lambs' trotters marketed in the United States, they would replace the calf's foot or the pig's feet in this recipe. White beans usually accompany this *daube;* fresh egg noodles seem to me the perfect accompaniment. The white wine may be replaced by red wine. The thyme may be eliminated from the bouquet and either it alone or a mixture of dried, crumbled herbs sprinkled over the layers of meats and vegetables. The presence of dried orange peel in a bouquet is specifically Provençal and was originally that of the bitter Seville orange, or *bigarrade* (just as duck in orange was originally wild duck finished with a bit of bitter orange juice for relief: *canard à la bigarrade*). A 5- or 6-inch strip (when freshly peeled; dried, it will wither to a small curl) is about right. It is practical to keep a few dried peels ready for use in a jar; peel the orange thinly to eliminate the white inner part, string the peels up with needle and thread, and hang them so that air circulates freely around each until well dried—3 or 4 days.

The stew will be at its best if prepared the previous day, left at room temperature, uncovered, overnight, skimmed of surface fat the following day, slowly reheated, and left to simmer for another ½ hour or so.

	5 pounds lamb shanks, boned, superficial fat removed
	3 ounces fresh fatback, cut into 1- by ¼-inch strips
	Salt, pepper
	½ teaspoon finely crumbled mixed dried herbs
Marinade	1 medium onion, finely sliced
	1 medium carrot, finely sliced
	3 cloves garlic, crushed
	Thyme, bay leaf
	2 tablespoons olive oil
	1 bottle dry white wine
	1 calf's foot, large upper bone removed, split, each half cut in two crosswise (or 2 split pigs' feet)
	6 ounces fresh pork rind, cut into 1-inch squares
	10 ounces (2 thick strips) lean salt pork, cut crosswise into a dozen pieces
	Bouquet garni: Parsley (plus root, if possible), leek greens (if available), branch celery, thyme, bay leaf, strip of dried orange peel
Chopped mixture	1 pound sweet onions, finely chopped
	5 garlic cloves, finely chopped

1 pound ripe, firm tomatoes, peeled, seeded, coarsely chopped

Salt (preferably coarse)
¼ cup Cognac
Water (to cover)

Lard the pieces of meat with the strips of fatback, first tossed in the mixture of herbs and seasonings. Marinate for about 3 hours (or overnight in the refrigerator), covered, turning the pieces around in their marinade two or three times during that period.

Cover the calf's foot, the rinds, and the pieces of lean salt pork with cold water, bring to a boil, simmer for about 5 minutes, drain, and rinse.

The traditional *daubière* is a pot-bellied earthenware affair, the form of which reduces greatly the liquid's surface, minimizing evaporation and facilitating skimming. Use a 6- to 8-quart heavy utensil (earthenware, copper, enameled ironware), preferably deep of form, with a tight-fitting lid. Pour in a bit of water, arrange the foot, a handful of pork-rind squares, and some pieces of salt pork so that the bottom is completely covered. Put half of the lamb pieces on this bed, placing the bouquet garni in the middle, scatter over half of the chopped vegetable mixture and half of the remaining rinds and salt pork, pressing things firmly into place, sprinkle with salt, and repeat the procedure. Before adding any liquid, be certain that the solid elements are arranged so as to leave the fewest holes or gaps possible, a minimum of liquid being required to completely submerge them. Sprinkle with Cognac, strain over the marinade through a sieve, and add just enough water to cover. Bring slowly to the boiling point (using an asbestos pad to disperse the heat if working with a direct flame)—it should take about an hour, skim off the foam that forms on the surface, and cook, covered, at the slightest suggestion of a simmer, for about 5 hours. If to be served immediately, skim off the fat as thoroughly as possible; if left to cool, remove the fat the following day.

IRISH STEW
(for 4)

Irish stew is the common denominator of all the meat and potato *daubes* and, by virtue of its purity, it may be the best. The French have long since adopted it, and it is, apparently, closer to theirs than to the Irish heart, possibly because of its affinity to cool, young Beaujolais. A typically French refinement consists of using two different potato varieties in alternating layers, one a firm, waxy-fleshed type that will not cook apart and the other a soup variety that melts into a purée, forming the body of the sauce.

Among the closely related French provincial preparations are the Ardèchoise *bombine* (lamb stew prepared according to the recipe-type (page 291), but without flour, the sauce strained off, meat and potatoes arranged in the pot in alternate layers, the sauce poured over, baked for an hour in a gentle oven), the Alsatian *baeckaoffa* (alternate layers of mutton, pork, beef, potatoes, and onions, seasoned with garlic and herbs and moistened with local white wine—the word means "baker's oven" and that is where it is traditionally cooked for some 3 hours), and a number of variations involving the conjunction of other vegetables—carrots, turnips, coarsely shredded, parboiled cabbage . . .

1½ to 2 pounds boned lamb shanks or leftover lamb roast, cut into
   pieces or thick slices
2½ to 3 pounds potatoes, peeled and sliced thickly
1 to 1½ pounds onions, thinly sliced
Salt
1 teaspoon finely crumbled mixed dried herbs
Water (to cover)

Arrange layers of meat and vegetables in an oven casserole, beginning with one of potatoes, then one of onions, seasoning the layers as you go with a sprinkling of salt and herbs, and finishing with a thick layer of potatoes. Press the surface firmly, pour over water to cover, and cook, covered, in a 325° to 350° oven for from 2½ to 2¾ hours. Check after an hour or so and reduce the oven's heat if the contents are bubbling too rapidly.

GRATIN OF CHOPS AND VEGETABLES
(Gratin de Côtes d'Agneau aux Légumes)
(for 4)

A *gardiane*, the Provençal version of a *bombine*, is prepared in the same way, eliminating the wine and all of the vegetables except for the potatoes and the *persillade*. Starchy, soup potatoes are usually used so that, in disintegrating, they thicken the sauce and, because the dish is cooked covered in the oven, it remains a stew rather than being transformed into a gratin.

4 1-inch-thick shoulder chops, outside fat removed
Salt
3 tablespoons olive oil
½ cup dry white wine

Vegetables and seasonings (to be all mixed together in a large mixing bowl)

1 pound firm, yellow-fleshed potatoes, sliced about ¼ inch thick
6 to 8 scallions (or 1 medium sweet onion), finely sliced
Persillade (handful finely chopped parsley mixed with 2 cloves garlic pounded to paste in a mortar)
4 to 5 ounces mushrooms, finely chopped (or passed through a Mouli-juliènne)
4 tender artichokes, pared, halved, chokes removed, sliced and coated in olive oil
Salt
1 teaspoon powdered mixed herbs

Water (to cover)

Brown the chops, salted, in the olive oil, remove them to a plate and deglaze the pan with the white wine, reducing it by about half. Pack half of the vegetable mixture into the bottom of a fairly shallow oven casserole, place the chops on top, sprinkle over the wine deglazing juice, pack in the remaining vegetables, and pour over water to cover. Bring to a boil and cook, covered, at a simmer for a half hour. Uncover the casserole and bake in a 375° oven for about one hour, adding a bit of boiling water after forty minutes or so if it seems to be drying out.

SHANKS WITH GARLIC
(Souris aux Aulx)
(for 4)

2 or 3 pounds lamb shanks, outside fat removed
Salt
3 tablespoons olive oil
15 to 20 cloves garlic, unpeeled
A few tablespoons water, ½ teaspoon finely crumbled mixed dried herbs
½ cup dry white wine
Pepper

Use, if possible, a heavy copper pan of just a size to hold the shanks at their ease. It should have a tight-fitting lid. Brown the shanks, salted, lightly in the oil, toss in the garlic, and cook over very low heat, covered, turning them occasionally, for about 1½ hours, or longer to be very tender. An asbestos pad may be necessary to disperse the heat—the shanks should only very gently stew in their own juices. In heavy copper their natural juices will hold for about 1 hour—in other metals, for a much shorter time. When all liquid has disappeared and they begin to sizzle in fat, add a spoonful of water from time to time so that a film of liquid remains always in the bottom of the pan. Sprinkle with the herbs after about an hour's time.

As the meat approaches the desired tenderness, stop moistening with water so that all the liquid evaporates. When the meat begins again to sizzle in pure fat, remove it to a plate, pour off the fat, deglaze the pan with the white wine, scraping and stirring with a wooden spoon to dissolve all caramelized adherences, put the juice and garlic through a sieve to rid them of the garlic hulls, return to the pan, reduce the liquid to the staccato bubbling stage, and return the meat to the pan—there should be only enough sauce to just coat the pieces. Grind over pepper to taste.

LAMB SHOULDERS IN POT-POURRI
(Èpaules d'Agneau en Pot-Pourri)
(for 8)

The recipe may, of course, be halved; it is convenient to prepare two shoulders because of the way the tied-up melon forms fit so neatly into an oval *cocotte*, a bouquet garni wedged between them, thus solving once again the sempiternal braising problem of filling all possible space so that complete immersion may be achieved with a minimum quantity of liquid. For a single shoulder it is best to eliminate the cumbersome bouquet garni, substituting a loose bay leaf and a healthy pinch of crumbled herbs and replacing the *cocotte* with a heavy saucepan.

Boning is merely a highly simplified exercise in dissection; a superficial understanding of the structure at hand and a small, sharply pointed knife are the only prerequisites to a rapid execution (a boning knife is useful because the large handle may be firmly grasped while directing the small, pointed blade, but a sharp paring knife will serve perfectly well).

To Bone a Shoulder

Place the shoulder skin side down (cut side facing up) on the table. It contains three bones: the shoulder blade, a flat, triangular wing with a rudder-like protrusion on the under side; the marrow bone of the upper foreleg, a straight bone with knobs at either end (the dog's bone of the comic strips); the lower foreleg (shank), a straight bone that thickens and curves slightly as it moves into the knuckle.

Move the joints back and forth several times to familiarize yourself with the structure. Feel with your fingertips the shoulder blade, the better to define its form. Make a straight incision, cutting to the bone, from the point of the shoulder blade at the first joint, moving outward to the extremity of the shoulder and describing approximately the triangle's median. Fold the flesh back, to the right and to the left, from the bone, forcing with fingertips and scraping with the knife blade. When the upper surface and the borders of the shoulder blade are entirely exposed, feel your way, going slowly the

*Lamb shoulder, bones removed and rearranged in
relationship to each other; the boned shoulder tied up,
ready for cooking*

first time, with the tip and the blade of the knife, alternating with
fingertips, following the contours of the underside of the bone and
trying not to cut through the skin at the point at which the rudder
shape approaches the surface. Grasp the freed shoulder blade in one
hand and the lower part of the shoulder in the other and crack the
underside smartly against the edge of the table at the joint. The bone
will not come completely free, but will be torn out of joint so that
you may see clearly the points at which to sever tendons and cartilage
with the knife tip and where to scrape free the extremities of flesh
touching the joint.

307

Make an incision to the bone between the shoulder joint and the upper shank joint, free the flesh (the marrow bone is simple in form and the flesh offers little resistance except for the tendonous attachments at the joints) and crack the shank joint against the table edge as before; a protuberant extremity of the shank joint often breaks free at this point, but it may easily be cut free from the flesh after the marrow bone is removed. Separate the flesh from the shank bone in the same way, making a circular incision to the bone at its base, just above the hock, to free it completely. Turn the shoulder over and remove all excess fat.

2 boned lamb shoulders

Marinade	1 teaspoon finely crumbled mixed herbs (thyme, oregano, savory)
	2 tablespoons olive oil
	½ cup white wine

Persillade	1 clove garlic, pounded to a purée in mortar, mixed with:
	Small handful finely chopped parsley
	Salt, pepper

Salt
⅓ cup olive oil (in all)
Bouquet garni: leek greens, celery branch, bay leaf, thyme, oregano, parsley (plus root)
8 ounces carrots, peeled, finely sliced
8 ounces tender crisp turnips, peeled, finely sliced
1 pound onions, finely sliced
4 cloves garlic, peeled and finely sliced
1 cup dry white wine (plus the marinade)
Boiling water
1 pound eggplant, peeled, cut into ½-inch-thick wedges
3 medium-size sweet peppers (or 8 or 10 small elongated, light-green Italian peppers), seeded, sliced into strips lengthwise
1 pound firm, ripe tomatoes, peeled, seeded, and cut into pieces
1 teaspoon sugar

Handful fresh basil leaves, torn into fragments, and basil
flowers (or chopped parsley)

Marinate the shoulders for several hours or, refrigerated, overnight, turning them around several times in the marinade.

Smear the interior surfaces of the shoulders with the *persillade*
and seasonings, gather the extremities in upon themselves, forming
each shoulder firmly in your hands and turning it over on the
table, leaving only smooth skin surface in view; the form should
be that of a slightly flattened sphere. The *persillade* clings to the
surface on which it has been smeared and is, therefore, enclosed,
albeit imperfectly, within the shoulder, which has been closed up.
If another, more plentiful stuffing is used (usually a bread and *fines-
herbes*—or bread and *persillade*—I often add fresh marjoram and
egg and chopped beef marrow), the shoulder must then be tied up,
the stuffing enclosed, before turning it over. Tie up the shoulders,
using a length of about 1½ yards kitchen string for each. Feel your
way and take your time; a length of string should be first tied,
forcing slightly, around the "waist," then the form should be en-
circled in the other sense (vertically) at least four times and, if
necessary to hold it neatly and firmly in its melon form, five or six
times. Once the first vertical round is tied in place, the top-center
of the melon may be used as an apex at which point the string is
repeatedly looped and circled vertically around the melon again. It
should, in the course of its journey, be looped occasionally around
the horizontal round of string, the better to hold everything, un-
budging, in place.

Wipe the tied shoulders dry with a towel, sprinkle them with
salt, and brown them lightly on all sides in a skillet or other heavy
pan in about 3 tablespoons olive oil, over a medium flame—there
should be no smoking or burned oil. Transfer them to an oval
cocotte just large enough to hold them without forcing, the bouquet
garni fitted in between them.

Cook the carrots, turnips, and onions in the same pan, salting
lightly and adding a bit more oil if necessary, over a low flame,
stirring occasionally with a wooden spoon, for 15 or 20 minutes—
until softened but not browned. Stir in the garlic and pack the mixture gently around the shoulders and the bouquet, filling all spaces.
Deglaze the pan with the marinade, pour it and the white wine over

309

the meat and vegetables, and add enough boiling water to almost cover the shoulders. Bring to a boil and cook, covered, at a bare simmer for 1½ hours. Remove the shoulders and the bouquet and pour the vegetables into a sieve, gathering the braising liquid in a saucepan. Return the meat, the bouquet, and the vegetables to the *cocotte* as before. Reduce the liquid in the saucepan, skimming it first several times, the pan kept slightly to the side of the flame, a light boil maintained only at one section of the surface, then boiling rapidly over a high flame, stirring all the while, until slightly syrupy in consistency—it should be reduced by about two thirds.

While the meat and the first batch of vegetables have been cooking, the peppers and eggplant will have been put to cook, salted, in about 3 tablespoons olive oil, over a medium low flame, tossed regularly, until softened; add the tomatoes and the sugar and cook, tossing regularly or stirring cautiously, for about 15 minutes longer or until all of the tomatoes' water has been evaporated. Add these vegetables to the *cocotte*, pour over the reduced juices, shake the container gently to settle the contents, and cook, covered, still at a bare simmer, for another hour.

Remove the shoulders, discard the bouquet, pour the vegetables into a sieve, and, when well drained, arrange them on a large, deep heated platter. Clip the strings from the shoulders, place them on the bed of vegetables, and sprinkle the whole with basil or parsley. Skim any fat off the cooking juices and serve the liquid apart in a sauceboat. Cut the meat into wedges.

MARINATED ROAST LEG OF LAMB
(Gigot en Marinade Rôti)
(for 6 to 8)

Order the leg from your butcher ahead of time; the leg bone should be sawed off at the extremity of the shank, just above the knuckle joint, and the leg should be cut somewhat above the pelvic joint—more or less depending on the size desired—and boned as far as the joint (that is to say, the section of pelvic bone removed) but no more. Correct carving is impossible in the interfering presence of the pelvic bone, but a boned leg of lamb, whatever its other virtues,

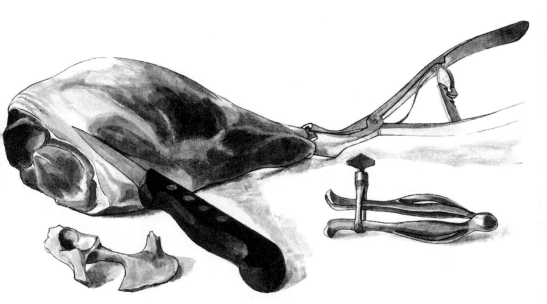

*Leg of lamb, section of pelvic bone removed; boning knife;
two different kinds of* manche à gigot *(clamp* manche
attached, screw manche *below)*

always suffers a loss of succulence that refined little forcemeats do
nothing to redeem.

Preferences in degrees of doneness may legitimately vary from
rare to pink (which means well done in France), but those who are
nervous if flesh is not cooked until gray will never understand what
a glorious thing roast lamb can be; count from 10 to 12 minutes
per pound, depending on the degree of doneness (from 45 minutes
to 1 hour and 10 minutes should encompass both extremes, size
being taken into account) and from 15 minutes to ½ hour of relaxation in a warm place (the time necessary to eat the preceding course

—the relaxation period should not be too brief, but it may be prolonged with no damage done).

If rosemary grows in abundance and if the leg of lamb is being spit roasted, shortly before unspitting it remove the dripping pan for a minute while holding a large bouquet of smoldering rosemary beneath the revolving joint . . .

1 leg of lamb, pared clean of surface fat
1 teaspoon crumbled mixed herbs (thyme, oregano, savory)
Salt, pepper
¼ cup olive oil
½ cup dry white wine

Mix the herbs and the seasonings together. Pierce the roast deeply and repeatedly on all sides with a small, sharply pointed knife, directing it on a bias toward the bone, each time forcing a small pinch of the seasoned herbs deeply into the vent with your finger. Rub all over with olive oil, pour over the wine, and turn the roast around in its marinade several times over a period of a couple of hours or so.

For an oven roast, wipe it dry with a towel (this is not necessary for an open roast), rub it again with olive oil, seasoning with salt and pepper at the same time, place it in a shallow oven dish just large enough to hold it, and start it in a 450° oven, turning it down to 375° after about 10 minutes. A spit roast is best salted and peppered only some 15 minutes after it has been turning. Begin basting, in either case, after about ½ hour, first only with the fat drippings (or with a bit of olive oil if they are too sparse), then 10 minutes or so later, as the roast begins to color, begin basting with the marinade: For an oven roast, add a spoonful to the pan from time to time, basting with the mingled juices in the bottom of the pan and adding no more marinade until the liquid in the pan has nearly disappeared; for a spit roast, all of the marinade may be added to the dripping pan, washed around that part closest to the fire occasionally to keep it deglazed, while basting regularly at the same time. The liquid will dissolve the caramelized meat juices, reducing to a syrupy consistency, and the meat, from repeated basting, will acquire a rich, glossy surface; basting and roasting should be conducted in such a way that practically no juice remains in the roasting or dripping pan when the roast is done. What little juice remains in the pan should be poured over the roast at the time of serving, so that as the meat is carved the juices that flow from within will mingle with the basting juices, a spoonful or so taken from the tilted platter to pour over each serving.

Carve at the table. If you do not have a handle especially designed to screw onto the leg bone *(manche à gigot)*, hold the bone end, wrapped in a tea towel or napkin while slicing thinly, always away from yourself, at a sharp angle almost parallel to the bone, first removing the number of slices desired from the thick, rounded fleshy section of the leg, then turning it around to slice in the same way from the thinner, more elongated muscle on the opposite side of the bone, and, finally, cutting from the bone outward near the point at which it is gripped, slicing off the shank meat; each of these sections has a different flavor and, because of the leg's construction, a different degree of doneness.

GRILLED LOIN LAMB CHOPS
("Mutton Chops" Grillés)

An unboned shoulder is also marvelous grilled, its only drawback being the impossibility of neat carving; after surface fat has been removed, it should be slashed to the bone on both sides (about ½-inch-deep slashes) several times at about 1½-inch distances to permit the heat to penetrate and cook the meat in a regular way. It is then treated in the same way as chops (herbs and oil being rubbed well into the slashes, as well); a shoulder requires about the same length of cooking time as a thick chop, but since it has only two sides on which to grill, whereas a chop has five, the former is sometimes a bit charred when finished—few people mind that and some prefer a lightly charred surface.

For those who prefer the savor of a single herb, oregano has a distinct affinity to lamb and may easily replace the thyme-savory-oregano mixture that recurs throughout this book.

The apron of a loin chop is usually rolled up and fixed into place against the filet mignon with a small skewer. I have come to prefer wrapping it fairly tightly around the entire chop for several reasons: It, unlike the filet and the filet mignon, is best well done—even rather crisp—and only in this way is its entire surface exposed

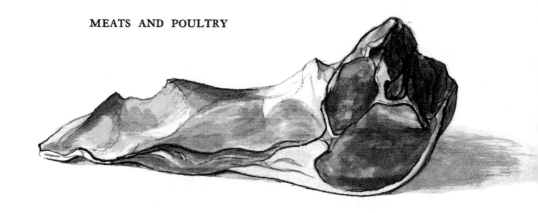

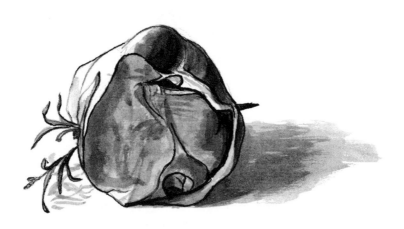

3-inch loin lamb chop unpared; pared and skewered with a rosemary branch, ready for grilling

to crisping; it protects both the filet and the filet mignon from too much exposure to direct heat so that they cook more slowly and remain, if desired, pink throughout; if the apron is rolled against the filet mignon, the protection is so thick as to keep it nearly raw, while the filet may be overcooked.

1 loin chop per person, 2½ to 3 inches thick
1 pinch mixed herbs per chop
Olive oil
Salt, pepper

Remove all fat except for the bit joining the apron (the extension of belly which is always left attached to loin chops or saddle roasts) to the filet and carefully remove all layers of membranous tissue and fat from between the thin layers of flesh composing the apron. Sprinkle lightly with herbs and rub all over with olive oil. Pull the apron gently up over the filet mignon, across the flat bone end of the chop and down against the filet as far as it will reach, fixing it in place by running a small skewer or sharpened stick through the chop, piercing the apron wrap on both sides; thus prepared, the form should be that of a solid block of approximately equal thicknesses in all senses. Grill the chops on a preheated grill over a bed of coals of moderate intensity and good depth, counting about ½ hour and turning them every 3 or 4 minutes; first sear the two exposed filet surfaces and finish cooking by turning from one part to another of the apron surface (which will be so formed as to present three additional grilling surfaces—a swelled triangular form), the longest and last amount of time being given to the apron-covered bone surface (the bone disperses the heat, which radiates around the chop and penetrates more gently to the heart—the heat should also be lessened during the last 8 or 10 minutes by spreading out the coals, moving the chops to the edge of the grill, or by raising the grill, the relaxation period being incorporated into the final part of the cooking).

LAMB VARIETY SKEWERS
(Brochettes d'Abats d'Agneau)
(for 4)

Sweet onion sections and thin slices of zucchini may supplement the vegetables, and squares of bacon or thin squares of lean, parboiled salt pork, parboiled, pared, and pressed sweetbreads, liver, or cubes of lamb filet may add to the choice of meats. Beige-colored lambs' kidneys are delicate in flavor; if dark reddish black, they tend to be strong. The lambs' kidneys may be replaced by a veal kidney, membrane removed, split lengthwise, interior fat cut out, each half sliced crosswise into ¾- to 1-inch thicknesses. Sharpened rosemary branches, a tuft of leaves left at the unsharpened end, may replace metal skewers, affording much the prettiest and most appetizing presentation. A saffron and tomato pilaf is a perfect accompaniment.

4 lambs' kidneys, surface membrane removed, each cut crosswise into 3 pieces
3 lambs' hearts, pared free of fat and the tough tubes and vessels at the entrance split, each half cut into 3 pieces
6 ounces small, firm, unopened mushroom caps, stems cut off and finely chopped
1 medium sweet onion, finely chopped
1 large sweet pepper, cut into 1- to 1½-inch squares
2 tablespoons finely chopped parsley
1 teaspoon finely crumbled mixed dried herbs
1 large clove garlic, crushed
About ⅓ cup olive oil
Salt, pepper

Combine all ingredients, except for the salt and pepper, in a large mixing bowl, mixing thoroughly but gently so that all meat and vegetable pieces are uniformly coated with oil, herbs and chopped vegetables; leave to marinate for a couple of hours if you like, turning the elements around two or three times.

Pierce the meats and vegetables alternately on four skewers, salt and pepper all sides, and grill over hot coals (or, lacking that, in the broiler) for from 12 to 15 minutes, turning the skewers every 3 or 4 minutes and brushing lightly the just-grilled surface with marinade (supplemented with more olive oil if necessary) after each turn.

SAUTÉED LAMBS' HEARTS AND LIVER À LA PROVENÇALE
(Coeurs et Foie d'Agneau en Persillade)
(for 4)

Lamb's liver is one of the most frustrating things to cook until one realizes what a very short cooking time is required; if being sautéed alone, throw in the *persillade* immediately after adding the liver strips to the hot oil and toss the lot together for no more than a minute. The sautéing pan should be heavy and large enough so the pieces of meat do not pile up on one another, causing them to bleed and stew rather than promptly searing and holding in their juices.

> ¼ cup olive oil
> 2 or 3 lambs' hearts, pared free of fat and tough vessels, split, each half cut lengthwise into 6 or 7 strips
> 6 to 8 ounces lamb's liver, sliced and cut into thin strips
> Salt, pepper

Persillade   Handful chopped parsley mixed with 1 or 2 cloves garlic, finely chopped or (for a less aggressive presence) puréed
> ½ lemon

Add the strips of lamb heart to the hot oil and sauté over a high flame for about a minute or until they are seared on all sides, lower the flame, and continue tossing for 2 or 3 minutes longer. Turn the flame high again and add the liver, seasoned, and the *persillade*. Sauté for another minute or until all of the liver strips are gray on all sides from contact with the hot oil and minuscule pearls of rose begin to appear at the surface. They are done; the hearts will have cooked for just under 5 minutes and the liver for about 1 minute. Squeeze over lemon to taste and, preferably, serve directly from the sautéing pan so as to lose no heat.

LAMBS' BRAINS
(Cervelles d'Agneau)

See "Calves' Brains," page 328, and "Pumpkin Satchels," page 233.

LAMBS' TESTICLES OR "FRIVOLITIES"
(Animelles d'Agneau; Rognons Blancs)

Of great delicacy and, in the past, much used as a garnish in combination with little *quenelles* for *vols-au-vent* and similar dishes,
testicles have, apparently, fallen from grace—at least in the cookbooks; their abundance in the market is sufficient proof that they
are still appreciated in French homes.

Whatever their ultimate preparation, they should always be
first peeled, disgorged, and parboiled (usually they are soaked for
several hours in cold water, then parboiled, before being peeled,
which serves little purpose, the impermeable skins' preventing dis-
gorgement): Only the egg-like form of flesh is retained; it is contained within a tough, loose outer skin and two inner skins, the
last of which clings tightly to the flesh. Split the skins the entire
length of the swelled surface with a sharp knife—you will have
to cut some quarter of an inch into the flesh—and carefully peel
the oval flesh form free, damaging it as little as possible. Put to
soak in a basin of cold water for about 3 hours, changing the water
two or three times. Transfer to a saucepan, cover largely with cold
water, salt, bring to a boil, simmer for 6 or 7 minutes, drain, plunge
into cold water and leave until cool. They may be kept, drained
and refrigerated, in a covered bowl or wrapped in plastic, for a day
or so before being used.

Frivolities are often braised like sweetbreads, but prolonged
cooking toughens the flesh. To best retain their tender delicacy,
cut them into ¼-inch slices and stew them simply in butter, tossing
occasionally, for 6 or 7 minutes, adding chopped *fines herbes* at the
halfway point (tarragon is very much at home in this context) and
finishing with a few drops of lemon juice. Cream may be added
or a cream and egg-yolk mixture thickened over low heat, stirring
constantly, without approaching the boil; they may be tossed in olive
oil over high heat and finished with a *persillade* and a bit of lemon
like the hearts and liver in the preceding recipe; or attractive stews
may be imagined in combination with veal kidneys, sweetbreads,
mushrooms, etc., each prepared separately to suit its demands and
combined at the last moment in the sauce of one or another. Dipped
in batter and deep fried, they are exquisite.

318

FRIVOLITY FRITTERS
(Beignets d'Animelles)
(for 4 or 5)

2 pounds lambs' testicles, prepared as above and cut into ¼-inch-thick
  slices
Marinade: the juice of ½ lemon, 1 teaspoon olive oil, salt, pepper, 1 table-
  spoon finely chopped fines herbes (including tarragon)
Fritter batter (see page 262)
Olive oil (to a depth of at least ¾ inch in the skillet or pan used for
  frying)
Handful parsley leaves
Lemon wedges (or lightly buttered tomato sauce) as accompaniment

Marinate the slices for from ½ hour to 1 hour, turning them
around a couple of times. Slip them all at once into the frying batter
and, when the oil is hot enough to sizzle when a drop of batter
touches the surface, pick them out of the batter, one by one, in a
teaspoon, making certain that each is well coated in batter before
dropping it into the hot oil. Do not try to fry too many at a time.
When golden and crisp on the underside, turn each over in the oil
with the tines of a fork and, when done, remove with a large flat
wire spoon, first to absorbent paper to drain the excess of oil, then
to a folded napkin arranged on a heated platter. Keep them covered with the napkin while frying the others. The flame may have to
be adjusted a couple of times during the frying process. When the
last fritter is removed from the oil, throw in the parsley, leaving it
only long enough to have finished sputtering—when it is quiet,
remove it, drain it a moment, and transfer it delicately to the fritters'
surface. Place lemon wedges around or pass a sauceboat of tomato
sauce apart.

VEAL *(VEAU)*

Veal sautés all follow the basic pattern outlined in the sauté recipe-type (page 291). The meat is not larded. Most are deglazed with white wine, which is almost completely reduced, lightly tomatoed, and moistened with veal stock. A veal Marengo hardly differs from the Milanese *osso-bucco* except that the sauce of the former is sieved; the bones are missing, as is the genial *gremolata* (garlic *persillade* mixed with grated lemon and orange peel) and the wonderful *risotto* accompaniment (Piedmont rice, which, by nature, is gummier than others, cooked in a suggestion of olive oil like a pilaf, onion and saffron flavored, moistened first with white wine and, as the liquid is absorbed, repeatedly remoistened with veal stock or water, stirred well after each moistening to enhance the natural gumminess, and, finally, stirred up with grated cheese and butter—a revelation in sticky sensuosity). Both, however, are deglazed with white wine and moistened uniquely with tomato—or, at the most, a bit of veal stock added as a symbolic gesture. A veal *matelotte* is moistened with about 2 parts of red wine to 1 of veal stock or water and garnished with the *Bourguignon* little onions, sautéed mushrooms, and browned salt pork lardons; calves' lungs may be prepared in exactly the same way (they should be beaten first to rid them of their air) and are delicious—the sauce, in either instance, should be cooked apart, skimmed, and reduced for a good ½ hour after the meats are done.

VEAL SHANK IN SORREL CREAM SAUCE
(Jarret de Veau à la Crème d'Oseille)
(for 4)

The delicate, classical *crème Germiny* soup and the homely *blanquette* are first cousins; this recipe is, on the one hand, essentially that of a Germiny garnished with meat and, on the other, that of a *blanquette* enhanced by the presence of sorrel. It goes without saying that it is entirely different from both in effect. Little butter-stewed onions may be added as a garnish and fresh egg noodles are the perfect accompaniment; I sometimes cook a couple of handsful of freshly shelled peas with the noodles, toss the lot in butter after being drained, and consider the ensemble pretty spectacular.

8 ounces sorrel, picked over, stems pulled off backwards, washed in a
    couple of waters, parboiled for a moment (removed from heat as soon
    as water returns to a boil), and well drained without pressing
1 tablespoon butter
3 pounds veal shank, cut across the marrow bone into slices of from 1
    inch to 1¼ inches thick (as for osso-bucco)
Bouquet garni: leek (or leek greens), parsley (including root), branch
    celery, thyme, bay leaf
1 medium (2 ounces) onion stuck with 2 cloves
Water (to cover)
Salt
Roux: 1½ tablespoons butter
        2 tablespoons flour
½ cup heavy cream
2 egg yolks
Pepper

Stew the parboiled and drained sorrel in butter over low heat, stirring regularly, until its moisture has disappeared and it is reduced to a near purée—15 minutes or so. Put it aside.

Place the slices of shank, the bouquet, and the onion stuck with cloves in a large *plat à sauter*, oven casserole, etc., just large enough to hold them neatly fitted into place in a single layer. Pour over water to barely cover, salt, bring to a boil, and cook, covered, at a bare simmer for 1½ hours or until the veal is just tender.

Remove and discard the bouquet and the onion. Remove the pieces of meat to a plate (carefully, so as not to dislodge the marrow) while pouring the liquid into another vessel and return them to their casserole, keeping covered in a warm place until the sauce is finished.

Prepare a *velouté* with the roux and the cooking liquid, pouring the latter in slowly over a low flame, stirring all the while, and, when it has returned to a boil, pull the saucepan somewhat to the side of the heat so that a light boil is maintained at one side of the liquid's surface. Cook for about ½ hour, skimming off the fatty skin that forms on the still part of the surface. The *velouté* should be only very slightly thickened; pour it over the meat, return to a simmer, and leave for another 10 minutes or so—the time necessary for the meat to become thoroughly reheated in the sauce.

Remove the stew from the heat. Pour the cream slowly into the cooled, stewed sorrel, stirring until smooth. Stir in vigorously the egg yolks and freshly ground pepper to taste. Add the mixture to the stew, stirring and taking care not to damage the pieces of meat. Return the stew to low heat and continue stirring gently until the sauce takes on a bit more body—it must not return to the boiling point, nor should it be very thick. Serve, preferably directly from the cooking receptacle.

VEAL SCALLOPS *(ESCALOPES DE VEAU)*

Veal is the most versatile of meats; its succulent juices, the flesh colored in a bit of fat, rapidly caramelize to form, when deglazed, the finest of simple meat-sauce bases; the flavor, apparently anonymous in its lack of eccentricity, is nonetheless of a sapid density and a chameleon receptivity that demand only the spark of one or a combination of other agents—wine, lemon, sorrel, mustard, herbs, aromatic vegetables—to open up a sharply defined personality. Thick chops or a small roast from a moist cut—round heel, for instance—cooked gently in a covered heavy pan, copper, earthenware or iron, in a bit of butter or olive oil with pieces of onion or whole small onions, carrot, unpeeled garlic cloves, a bouquet or a pinch of herbs, turned regularly and, once the meat and vegetables have begun to color and caramelized scrapings have formed in the bottom of the pan, moistened lightly with a white wine or one of the fortified wines, will eventually, after repeated moistenings, be enveloped in a voluptuous, syrupy glaze that is one of the glories of old-fashioned French home cooking. The process is one of repeated deglazing. The liquid must be added in small quantities at a time, never more than a film in the bottom of the pan, and it should be permitted to completely evaporate, caramelized adherences beginning to re-form in the pan before more is added. After the first couple of deglazings, it is best to substitute water or veal stock for the wine, particularly if it is one of the richly flavored fortified wines—and a close eye should be kept throughout, for a sumptuous glaze may, in a moment's time, be transformed into an acrid disaster should any element begin to burn ...

Veal birds (*paupiettes de veau,* also quaintly called *alouettes sans têtes* or "headless larks") may be glazed like the chops discussed above or they may be treated like a stew, the sauce usually being generously tomatoed. The cutlets used for their assemblage should be cut thinly from a single muscular structure so that the body of the cutlet is of a solid piece; they should be trimmed and lightly but firmly flattened (not pounded) with the flat of a large heavy knife blade or cleaver. The stuffing should be in the spirit of a *farci* (see page 185). Too often it is only ground sausage meat, which cooks into a savorless, hard, and heavy ball. A good stuffing may be prepared like the mixture of the following recipe (sweetbread loaf), substituting for the sweetbreads ½ pound or so of chopped lean veal, pork, or leftover meats and a couple of ounces of chopped fatback or beef marrow, eliminating 1 or 2 eggs, and leaning more heavily on the herbs. A heaping tablespoonful is rolled into each cutlet, its sides first neatly tucked in, and the giant cork shape is looped twice around the "waist," once around the long way and tied with kitchen string (in the south of France, housewives often secure them with thread wrapped dozens of times around, a detestable practice that may be easier than tying up a neat and simple package; to be faced with such a mess on one's plate is upsetting). The *bardes,* or sheets of fat pork often wrapped around them, nourish them very little, prevent their coloration, and render the sauce troublesomely greasy. Larding is not essential, but the meat's surface interlarded with narrow strips of fatback, using a larding needle, will give happier results than *bardes.*

Unless they be used as a wrap for veal birds, veal cutlets, being so thin, really shouldn't be cooked in contact with liquid; it is done, but they are always dry. If they are sautéed rapidly—they should be only just done—the pan will still contain enough scrapings to form the base of a simple sauce. Remove the cutlets while finishing the sauce. Formulas for sauced cutlets are endless, but they are all pretty much the same. If chopped shallots or finely sliced mushrooms find their place, they are sautéed rapidly before the pan is deglazed—usually with a fortified wine—and the liquid radically reduced (juices that drain from the cutlets are poured back into the pan). Sometimes the reduction is the sauce—or butter may be swirled into it away from the heat. Often it is finished with heavy cream, which is then boiled down to the desired consistency before the cutlets are slipped back into it to reheat (without boiling). Wine omitted, the pan may be deglazed directly with cream, a bit of lemon juice added at the last minute for relief. Dried morels may serve as a garnish and, after being soaked and cleansed, should be stewed gently apart, first in butter, then in cream, the lot being then combined with the deglazing reduction. Or any of a variety of vegetable stews may be tossed with it. Fresh parboiled little peas are an exquisite last-minute addition to a creamed sauce . . . And so forth.

The goodness of breaded veal cutlets is sealed in, the juices (that, freed by other cooking methods, may be transfigured into burnished glaze or fragrant broth) remaining virgin. They, too, should be trimmed free of any fragments of fat, skin, or nervous tissue surrounding them and slightly flattened, the muscular structure sufficiently bruised to relax and not shrink during the cooking, but they should not be pounded to paper-thin death, the fiber hopelessly crushed and unable to contain its natural moisture. An hour's marinade (in a bit of lemon juice, a few drops of olive oil, and either finely chopped *fines herbes,* including a bit of tarragon, or a pinch of finely crumbled dried herbs, including oregano) will lend relief to veal's bland savor. For sharper, but less delicate relief, the cutlets may, first salted and peppered, be lightly spread with Dijon mustard before being breaded. If marinated, they should be sponged gently dry and then salted and peppered just before breading.

A light coating of flour before the passage in egg will greatly increase the adhesive quality of the breading, but the pastiness within the casing is always vaguely unpleasant (not so if lightly floured, dipped in egg, and sautéed without being breaded—the flour then becomes an integral part of the slightly crisp, batter-like surface). I usually dredge them in freshly grated Parmesan instead of flour, but sometimes dip them directly into the egg.

The spoonful or so of water that is usually added to the egg—beaten only enough to mix yolk and white—is designed to prevent the casing's buckling while cooking.

Finely crumbled stale, but not dried out, crustless breadcrumbs give a lighter and more delicate result, but with less adhering strength than the customary finely ground dried breadcrumbs; the cutlets must be handled with greater care and, although it is essential to avoid the dispersion of loose crumbs in the cooking fat, they may never be altogether eliminated with this method.

Once the cutlets are breaded (sprinkling more crumbs over and patting them into place with your hand to ensure an even coating), transfer them to a board sprinkled with breadcrumbs and flatten each side, tapping gently with the flat of a heavy knife blade or cleaver to render the breading more compact. Finally, a crisscross pattern created by tapping each surface gently with the back of a heavy knife blade at approximately 1-inch distances will break up the surface tension, reinforcing adherent strength and creating an attractive pattern—the principle is the same as that of the regularly spaced lines that are pressed into cement sidewalks to prevent their cracking.

Deep fried in olive oil, breaded cutlets are delicious, but a normal 3- to 4-ounce cutlet divided into three or four small ones will be easier to handle. If they are cooked in a frying pan there should be a good ½-inch depth of fat (olive oil, mixed olive oil and butter, or pure butter), preheated, the heat reduced to medium-medium-low when the cutlets are put to cook. It is probably wiser to first clarify the butter if it is used alone (I rarely bother).

VEAL SWEETBREADS *(RIS DE VEAU)*

Sweetbreads are the thymus gland of a young animal; it shrivels to no more than a memory in an adult animal. It consists of two connected sections—the elongated throat sweetbread and a large full lobe called in French *la noix*. Lamb sweetbreads are treated in the same way as veal sweetbreads, but, because they are so much smaller and less presentable, they are usually treated as a *ragoût*.

Whatever the ultimate preparation, sweetbreads should first be soaked in cold water for, ideally, several hours (½ hour of soaking will not be disastrous, however), then covered generously with new cold water, brought slowly to a boil, and left to simmer for a very few minutes, drained, plunged into cold water and, when cool, freed of all fat, cartilaginous tubes, and superficial membranes (but the connective tissue holding together the sweetbread sections should be left intact). Placed between two towels, a weighted board on top, they are left for several hours—or overnight. For most purposes a weight of 4 or 5 pounds is enough, but for a particularly firm, easily manageable, and attractively presentable grilled *noix,* it is well to count up to a 10-pound weight. Dipped in melted butter, seasoned, and grilled for about 30 minutes over well-sustained but not intense wood coals, turned several times and regularly basted with melted butter—using a little brush fashioned from fresh thyme or rosemary branches, if possible—the sweetbreads' pristine beauty is best understood. Sauce is superfluous. They are most often braised (see page 68) and are, then, never better than when garnished with fresh little peas. They may be treated like a fricassée (floured, lightly colored in butter, moistened with a bit of white wine and veal stock to cover, simmered for ½ hour or so, garnished, if one likes, with precooked little onions and mushrooms, the liquid skimmed and finished, like a *blanquette,* with egg yolks or egg yolks and cream) or simply stewed gently in butter for ½ hour. However cooked, the process should be gentle and should last a minimum of 25 to 30 minutes—undercooked, sweetbreads are not pleasant.

In the following recipe, because they are trapped in suspension in a congealed pudding, the sweetbreads need not necessarily be subjected to weighting. I have tried a number of sauces with the sweetbread loaf; the one I prefer is a so-called *sauce bâtarde,* which is nothing more than flour-thickened water finished with egg yolks, lemon juice, and butter; traditionally, it accompanies poached fish (melt 1 tablespoon butter in a small saucepan, stir in 1 tablespoon flour, remove from heat, pour in slowly, stirring the while, 1 cup salted hot water, return to heat and stir until boil is reached, remove from heat, pour in an egg yolk beaten with a bit of cold water, whisking constantly, return to low heat, continue whisking until lightly thickened, but not approaching a boil, remove, add lemon juice, and whisk in about 3 ounces or approximately ⅓ cup butter, softened or cut into little pieces—it takes about as long to prepare as to read the instructions. Because the flour is not cooked, the sauce does not have a "floury taste"; it should be only lightly bound and, thanks to the whisking, frothy).

VEAL SWEETBREAD LOAF
(Pain de Ris de Veau)
(for 4)

½ pound mushrooms, finely chopped or passed through medium blade of Mouli-julienne, sautéed in 2 tablespoons butter until dry
1 medium onion, finely chopped, stewed in 1 tablespoon butter without coloring
3 ounces stale bread, crusts removed, soaked in hot water, squeezed dry
Handful finely chopped parsley
½ teaspoon finely crumbled mixed herbs (thyme, savory, oregano)
Salt, pepper, pinch cayenne
1 egg
1 pound veal sweetbreads, prepared as above, very coarsely chopped (cut into approximately ⅓- to ½-inch cubes)
Butter (for mold)

Mix together all the ingredients except the sweetbreads and butter, mashing and beating with a fork until thoroughly homogeneous. Stir in the sweetbreads delicately, to avoid crushing them.

Butter a 3-pint charlotte mold (or any mold of simple form and straight sides), press a buttered round of kitchen parchment paper into the bottom, and fill with the mixture, tapping the bottom of the mold two or three times against the tabletop to settle the contents. Poach in a *bain-marie,* the mold immersed by two thirds in hot but not boiling water in a 350° oven for about 40 minutes. Run the blade of a knife all around the sides of the mold before unmolding onto a heated serving dish. Lift the round of paper from the surface, loosening it gently and progressively with the blade of a knife if it sticks.

CALVES' BRAINS *(CERVELLES DE VEAU)*

Good fresh brains are firm-looking, the form cleanly and symmetrically defined, the surface moistly glistening in aspect; they are white with a pearl cast, only the filigree network of thread-like veins in the surface membrane showing red. These conditions are not always met—otherwise good brains are often discolored by blood clots. In any case, those whose form and whose superficial cannular structure are ill-defined, the surface dull and messy in appearance, should be rejected.

Brains should be put to soak in cold water and the vein-threaded surface membrane carefully peeled off; it often facilitates the work to dip them repeatedly in water while removing it. Usually, with healthy-looking, firm, fresh brains, it slips free with little difficulty, but, occasionally, it offers frustrating and sometimes insuperable resistance; if after further soaking, it refuses to come free, leave it ... Brains that have been badly bloodstained should be soaked again for 1 hour or so with several changes of water in order to draw from them the maximum discoloration (in professional kitchens, they are often parboiled to hasten the work of peeling, a process which, although permitting the membrane to be removed more easily, firmly stamps the flesh with a brown color and a muddy flavor that detracts greatly from their delicacy).

In the south of France and in Italy I have often eaten brains (usually those of sheep), the membrane of which had not been removed and which were put to cook raw, dredged in flour, in butter or olive oil. The crisp golden surface disguises, although imperfectly, the presence of the membranes; the flavor, without the support of court bouillon, borders on the insipid with a vaguely sweet edge— not altogether unpleasant—and the texture, even when well cooked, remains somewhat mushy. Neither is that disagreeable, but no hint is contained there of the wonderful creamy body, at once firm and melting—something of the same texture as that of foie gras cooked pinkly—that takes form through a preliminary passage in court bouillon. And the imprecise taste of faded things is transformed into subtlety and nuance by an aromatic vinegar court bouillon. Perhaps because I do not want anything else to imperfectly resemble the savor that I associate with brains—the fragrance of the court bouillon alone contains that single association for me—I reserve vinegar court bouillon for that limited use, preferring white wine in most other instances. Whatever their destiny, poach calves' brains for about 25 minutes (lambs' brains 18 to 20 minutes) in a court bouillon, slipping them gently into the simmering liquid and keeping it at a near simmer, saucepan covered, without permitting the boil to be reached. The court bouillon may first be strained to remove herbs and vegetables (there are, however, certain kitchen pleasures that are not shared at table—the beauty of a pair of brains floating among carrot and onion slices and straggles of herbs is among them. It is the only reason, also, for slicing the onion into rings rather than halving it and slicing it much more rapidly).

VINEGAR COURT BOUILLON
(Court Bouillon au Vinaigre)

3 pints boiling water
Salt
1 medium onion (3 to 4 ounces), finely sliced
2 small carrots (3 to 4 ounces), finely sliced
Bay leaf, branches of thyme (or 1 teaspoon crumbled), bouquet parsley
   (plus root if possible)
¼ cup good wine vinegar
10 to 12 whole peppercorns

Add all the ingredients, except the vinegar and the peppercorns, to the boiling water and simmer, covered, for about 15 minutes. Add the vinegar and the peppercorns and continue cooking at a simmer for another 15 minutes or so . . .

Served directly from the court bouillon, drained a moment on a towel, sliced onto a heated serving platter with bubbling brown butter poured over is the simplest and the purest way to appreciate brains. Chopped parsley may be added; capers are often added; the

329

butter is often black instead of brown (I don't understand the taste for burned butter—it is, furthermore, indigestible).

Sliced thickly (or simply split, allowing a lobe per person— lambs' brains left whole), lightly floured, and cooked in butter; dipped in batter and deep fried in olive oil, alone or in combination with vegetables (see page 165); "scrambled" (stirred gently with a wooden spoon so as to damage them as little as possible) with eggs kept creamy (see page 97), butter-crisp croutons scattered at the moment of serving: These and various gratins (*béchamel, mornay, duxelles* . . .) are all perfect methods of preparing them. See also pumpkin satchels (page 233) for a gratin of brains and creamed squash or pumpkin. The flavor is attenuated and the voluptuous texture destroyed in all recipes that call for puréeing brains.

GRATIN OF CALVES' BRAINS WITH SORREL
(Gratin de Cervelles de Veau à l'Oseille)
(for 4)

10 ounces young sorrel, picked over, well washed, parboiled for a few
    seconds, drained without pressure
About ¼ cup butter (in all)
1 cup heavy cream
Salt, pepper
Breadcrumbs
2 calves' brains, prepared as above

Stew the parboiled sorrel in about 2 tablespoons butter over a low flame for some 20 minutes, stirring from time to time. Add half the cream, reduce over a higher flame, stirring, until lightly thickened, stir in the remaining cream and season to taste.

Arrange the brains, sliced, in a buttered gratin dish, spoon over the sauce, sprinkle the surface with breadcrumbs, and garnish the entire surface with paper-thin sheets of butter shaved from a cold block of butter with a sharp knife. Bake in a 425° oven until the gratin has formed—about 20 minutes.

330

VEAL KIDNEYS
(Rognons de Veau)

Only veal kidneys have a special finesse. There are, as far as I know (Ali Bab's stuffed and braised fantasy apart), only three ways to prepare them. Whole, a thin layer of their fat is left surrounding them and they are cooked in a covered casserole either over low heat or in a medium oven, turned regularly, for from 40 to 45 minutes. To be grilled or sautéed, their fat and the thin protective membrane should be first removed; they are then split lengthwise and the fat pared out of the heart. Rub the halves in olive oil for grilling, season and grill first on the cut side for a couple of minutes, turn them, and, as soon as tiny pearls of blood appear at the surface, remove them.

A simple, classic recipe for sautéed veal kidneys is given in *The French Menu Cookbook*. For a rapid, sauceless sauté, try them *à la Provençale,* the split halves sliced crosswise more thinly (about ¼ inch thicknesses) than for a regular sauté, tossed rapidly, seasoned, in a heavy pan over high heat in butter, olive oil, or a combination. After a minute's tossing add a handful of mixed finely chopped parsley and garlic (or mix the parsley with garlic pounded to a purée for a more delicate flavor), toss for another minute, sprinkle over lemon juice, and serve . . . Croutons are a welcome garnish.

CALF'S LIVER *(FOIE DE VEAU)*

On the French market, one finds *foie de veau* and another mysterious and darker-colored liver baptized *foie de génisse* (literally "heifer's liver"). The butchers carry no other products claiming to derive from the heifer. In parts of the United States, similarly obfuscatory methods are deployed to confuse the public, calf's liver and so-called veal liver being differently colored and differently priced.

Sublime calf's liver is pale beige with a pink cast. Livers of a

331

well-sustained rose hue may, nonetheless, be very good. The tightly clinging sheer surface membrane must be carefully peeled off; it shrinks in contact with heat, warping or otherwise deforming the liver.

Calf's liver is nearly always sliced and pan fried in butter, thin slices being cooked rapidly (and usually imperfectly) over high heat, thicker slices more slowly over lower heat. It must always be pink throughout, the heart of the flesh having just turned firm, its juices in released suspension within the tender structure (those accustomed to eating liver overcooked find even calf's liver "strong"; the strong taste, in company with an ugly, dull, dry texture, appears only—and then with progressive intensity—as grayness begins to pervade the moist pink realm). A few drops of lemon juice may be welcome to some people; bacon, fried onions, or fortified wine deglazing juices can only obscure its perfect finesse.

Thick slices (¾ to 1 inch) rubbed with olive oil and cooked on a well-heated grill over coals of no more than moderate intensity deserve all of one's favorite superlatives. The time is probably about 4 minutes to a side—but, once turned, watch them; press the surface with your finger to test firmness, and the moment the first tiny rose and translucent pearl of liquid begins to ooze up through the grilled surface remove them to a heated platter. It is impossible to grill thin slices correctly and useless to attempt to cook liver, thick or thin, in a broiler.

Recipes for braised whole livers are common enough, though not commonly executed. A true braising process necessitates a more or less prolonged cooking whose raison d'être is to permit a slow and progressive interpenetration and intermingling of the braising liquids and the natural juices of the material being treated. The quality of melting tenderness that one hopes to achieve is dependent on the combined dissolution of the meat's (or vegetable's) primitive structure, and this perfect fusion of sapid essences. Any meat, on the other hand, whose qualities depend on the flesh's remaining rare or pink, requires a precisely opposed treatment: there can be no question of a liquid's being absorbed from outside (except by marination before the seared seal is put). The meat's structural composition, while relaxed by a gentle penetration of heat, must, above all, not be broken down.

If my definitions are acceptable, then it must follow that the notion of braising a calf's liver is nonsense. And so it is. By which I do not mean to suggest that the thing cannot be good—if the liver has been correctly "braised," the cook will have taken every possible precaution to *prevent* its braising while, at the same time, respecting all of the time-consuming formal complications integral to a true braising process: The liver will have been marinated (a great pity, but, if one prefers to deform its flavor, a roast, too, can be marinated), its entire surface will have been larded with a hundred tiny lardons, and it will have been seared; aromatic braising bases *(mirepoix* or *duxelles)* will have been prepared in advance as well as veal stock or *demi-glace,* destined to share with the marinade and a fortified wine the moistening honors; truffles and cèpes or morels may find their place; and, of course, but half submerged in liquid, it must be basted. The trick is to arrest the cooking before the seared surface is so damaged, its resistance weakened by contact with external liquids, as to permit the commencement of a braising process. The liver, if its surface has not been too damaged, will be pink and will have retained its own juices, untainted by outside savors, and the sauce, if it is good, will owe its success to the quality of its initial ingredients, having drawn, ideally, nothing from the liver—it may as well have been prepared apart.

All of which leads us to roast liver: It requires absolutely no preparation (its delicacy and beauty would be masked by a sauce) and its flesh looks and tastes exactly as "braised" liver *should* taste; it is one of the most exquisite things I know. Mushrooms, in one form or another (mushroom pudding, purée of mushrooms, *cèpes sautés à la Bordelaise,* creamed morels . . .), accompany it perfectly, as does a choice of vegetable purées.

ROAST CALF'S LIVER
(Foie de Veau Rôti)
(for 4)

1 whole calf's liver (or a 2-pound section of veal liver), surface membrane
  removed
Olive oil
Salt

Choose a heavy, low-sided container just large enough to hold the roast with a bit of space around—a small skillet or an enameled ironware gratin dish, for instance. Rub the liver liberally with olive oil, sprinkle it with salt, and put it into a 450° oven: Its specific treatment will depend on the quality of the oven; it should be seared at high heat, continue cooking at low heat, and relax at a temperature that permits it to remain hot, the heat contained within it continuing gently to penetrate to the heart of the roast. With my oven, which is extremely hermetic, holding heat for long periods of time, I start it out at from 450° to 475°, turning the oven off immediately and the roast is ready some 30 to 35 minutes later, the oven having gradually descended to about 200°. With friends' ovens I have usually found the best method to be: (1) 8 to 10 minutes at about 450°; (2) another 10 minutes or so with the thermostat reduced to 275° to 300°; (3) 10 to 15 minutes with the oven turned off. It must, above all, not be left for too long a time at a searing temperature. Five minutes more than the time prescribed in a warm oven during the relaxing period will not harm it.

Transfer it to a heated platter and carve it at table, using a very sharp knife and slicing it as thinly as possible—no more than ¼-inch-thick slices, serving onto heated plates. A turn of the pepper grinder . . .

BEEF *(BOEUF)*

Beef stews (prepared like the sauté recipe-type) in a number of regions assume the name of *estouffade* or one of a number of dialectical variations on that word. Most *estouffades* are simplifications of the genial *boeuf Bourguignon,* the traditional garnish of lean lardons, little onions, and mushrooms being eliminated or altered, the red wine, in some instances, being replaced by combinations of white wine, tomato bouillon, water . . . Often the sauce is not passed and purified but merely skimmed of surface fat before serving.

Black or green olives creep into a number of Provençal beef stews, dried orange peel may join the herb bouquet, and, in the curiously named *grillade des mariniers* (the mariniers—or sailors—in question are the Rhône river boatmen), bizarre overtones of anchovy and capers—probably more pleasing to the Provençal palate than to others—lace the sauce, whose liquid constituents are vinegar and water.

Oxtail (in America, it is usually more richly endowed with fat than in France and it is as well to pare off the excess), cut into sections, lends itself admirably to a *Bourguignon* or an *estouffade* treatment. Its structure does not permit of interlarding, but moist succulence is ensured by a particularly gelatinous constitution. It demands a bit more cooking time than other stew cuts (something over 3 hours, precise timing depending on the age of the animal). It is also a splendid *pot-au-feu* element and, left over, is delicious stewed gently for ½ hour or more in a tomato sauce and accompanied by a pilaf or fresh noodles—or simply coated with melted butter and breadcrumbs and gently grilled, butter-basted, until golden and heated through, accompanied by mustard.

Leftover *pot-au-feu* meats should not be cooled in their bouillon —they will turn flabby and tasteless. Boneless (or, in the case of spareribs, subsequently boned) leftover *pot-au-feu* cuts are transformed into *mirotons,* the meats sliced very thinly (an easy task when cold and firm), warmed, and gently simmered in a sauce made of onions and the *pot-au-feu* bouillon, lightly tomatoed. Onions in quantity—to taste—are finely sliced, gently stewed in butter until melting soft but not colored, sprinkled lightly with flour, and, after a moment's cooking and stirring, moistened with a tablespoonful each of vinegar and tomato purée to each approximate cup of bouillon; a pinch of powdered herbs may be added; then the sauce is simmered for a good ½ hour. A *miroton* is perhaps better transformed into a gratin (alternate layers of the boiling sauce and cold meat slices, beginning and ending with sauce, liberally sprinkled with fresh breadcrumbs lightly colored in butter, are cooked ½ hour or so in a 350° oven). The gratin can be simple or include vegetables (finely sliced, sautéed zucchini or peeled, sliced, fried, and drained eggplant, in alternate layers with beef and sauce or arranged as a border around the edges of the gratin dish) or may be arranged within a border of noodles or mashed potatoes (if the potatoes, too, are left over, best doctor them up a bit by the addition of an egg, a suspicion of grated nutmeg, or a handful of *duxelles* ...).

335

Beyond the suggestions in the preface to this chapter, there is little to be said about grilled or roast beef. It is my conviction that, if one dislikes the idea of rare meat, there is no point in eating these cuts and that, if the meat is aged and of fine quality, no sauce will enhance its natural, clean, robust flavor. The filet is the tenderest but the least flavorful of grilling and roasting cuts. In the service of extravagance and out of mingled curiosity and suspicion, profiting from the number of mouths to feed, my students and I recently prepared in class Lucien Tendret's celebrated but rarely executed filet of beef: The whole filet is split, incompletely, lengthwise, opened out, whole truffles forced into some twenty slits and a handful of peeled pistachios into tiny intermingling slits; the opened filet is folded closed into its original form, tied up, the surface larded with a larding needle, put to marinate overnight with herbs, white wine, and a bit of olive oil, and roasted—7 minutes per pound—the next day, accompanied by a buttered juice composed of reduced deglazing marinade, a bit of lemon juice, chopped parsley, truffle peelings pounded to a purée . . . The perfumes were heady and exciting and the thing could hardly be said to have been bad, but a simple truffle stew or a simple roast beef would have, one or the other, made a great deal more esculent sense.

BEEF AND ONIONS IN BEER
(Carbonnade du Nord)
(for 4 to 6)

1 pound sweet onions, halved, thinly sliced
About ⅓ cup olive oil (or lard, for authenticity)
Salt
2 pounds lean beef (shoulder or round) cut into ¼-inch-thick slices, edges slashed
2 teaspoons brown sugar
3 tablespoons flour
2 cups beer
1 cup stock or pot-au-feu bouillon
2 bay leaves

2 teaspoons finely crumbled mixed dried herbs (thyme, oregano, savory, marjoram . . .)
Pepper

Cook the onions in something over half the oil in a skillet over a low flame, stirring or tossing regularly, until softened and lightly caramelized—turn the flame up slightly, if necessary, toward the end in order to color them. Empty them into a sieve over a mixing bowl or over the oven casserole that will serve for cooking the dish, being certain that no fragment of onion remains in the skillet.

Pour the drained fat back into the skillet, add a bit more oil, if necessary, and, over a fairly high flame, brown the slices of steak, first salted. This will have to be done in two or three shifts; remove those that are done to the strainer with the onions and pour back into the skillet, from time to time, the fat and juices that drain from the onions and seared meat. When all the steaks have been browned, turn the flame low, add the sugar, stir around, then add the flour and cook, stirring, for a few moments and deglaze with the beer, adding it slowly and stirring the while, scraping well to loosen all caramelized adherences. Stir in the stock, bring to a boil, and remove from the heat. Taste for salt.

Arrange the slices of meat in alternate layers with the onions (three layers of meat slices and two of onions), a bay leaf and a sprinkling of herbs on each layer of onions. Pour over the liquid— the contents should be well immersed; add a bit more beer or some water or stock, if necessary. Bring to a boil on top of the stove and cook, tightly covered, in a 300° to 325° oven for about 3 hours, testing for tenderness after some 2½ hours. Carefully lift all fat from the surface, first with a tablespoon, then with absorbent paper, before serving. Season with pepper at table and accompany with steamed potatoes or fresh egg noodles. Customarily, beer is drunk with it—I prefer a cool, light-bodied, young red wine.

HOT COUNTRY TERRINE
(Terrine Paysanne)
(for 4)

8 to 10 ounces lean salt pork (unsmoked bacon), rind removed, sliced
(by machine) to ⅛-inch thicknesses (twice that of packaged bacon)
1½ pounds lean beef (shoulder or round) cut into ¼-inch-thick slices,
edges slashed
Olive oil
Red wine or water (for deglazing)
1 teaspoon finely crumbled mixed herbs: 1 bay leaf ground to powder,
pinch ground allspice, salt, mixed together
About 3 tablespoons Cognac
About ⅓ cup red wine
About ⅓ cup stock or pot-au-feu bouillon (the amount necessary to just
immerse the meats)
Flour for dough

Cover the slices of salt pork with cold water, bring to a boil,
drain, and rinse. Brown the steaks (in two or three shifts, transferring them to a plate when finished), drain off the fat from the pan,
and deglaze with a bit of red wine or water.

Choose a terrine (earthenware or enameled ironware) of a size,
as nearly as possible, corresponding to that of the steaks. Arrange
alternate layers of steak and salt pork slices, beginning with a steak
and finishing with slices of salt pork, sprinkling the surface of each
steak with the seasoned herb mixture. Pour over any juices that may
have drained from the steaks, the deglazing liquid, the Cognac, and,
finally, the wine and the stock, first a bit of one, then a bit of the
other, in order to finish with approximately equal parts of each when
the meats, well packed into place, are just submerged.

Prepare a flour-and-water dough containing a bit of oil (which,
as the paste cooks, will prevent it from hardening to the point of
being nearly unbreakable—one risks breaking fragile earthenware
when breaking the seal of the paste, otherwise). Roll it out into a
long ribbon on a floured board and fit it into the ridge designed to
receive the lid before pressing the lid into place. Put the terrine into

a 450° oven and, after about 15 minutes, turn the oven down to about 275° to 300°. Count 3 hours. Break the seal and carefully lift off all the surface fat before serving.

BRAISED, STUFFED OXTAIL
(Queue de Boeuf Farcie Braisée)
(for 4)

The preparation is relatively long, requiring a couple of hours' preliminary work and, in all, some 6 hours' attention on the following day, the last 2 of which should be more or less undivided. The result is attractive but unprepossessing in appearance; the flavors are sumptuous, well worth the time spent. Served cold, it is an altogether different experience—and at least as good. If a section is left over, choose a small oval terrine just large enough to contain it without forcing; if to be unmolded, line the bottom with the remaining braised vegetables and braising liquid, placing the section of tail on this bed; if to be sliced and served directly from the terrine, place the meat first in the bottom, pouring vegetables and juices atop, then pour over to cover the remaining reduced stock—doctored with a bit of sherry if desired—and refrigerate for a day.

It is of the greatest importance that the stock be undersalted, for it will be subjected to not only a reduction by half, doubling its salt content, but also a subsequent and continuing reduction during the final braising process. See page 103 for its preparation: It can cook longer than a veal stock; maximum flavor will have been drawn from the ingredients after about 4 hours' cooking time, but the bones will continue to release their gelatin for several hours longer. I usually put it to cook as soon as the tail is boned, simmering it for 3, 4, or 5 hours, leave it to cool overnight, degrease it, add more water if necessary, and simmer it for several hours longer before straining it.

The truffle may be eliminated from the stuffing (a breath of its soul will be sacrificed); mushrooms or *duxelles* may be added, but should not be thought of as a substitute, for they bear no relation, one to the other. If the truffle is retained, best prepare the stuffing the previous day, refrigerating it overnight, so that its perfume may permeate the mixture.

339

The size and shape of the cooking vessels should both correspond to those of the stuffed tail, that used for poaching the wrapped and tied tail representing about twice the volume of the oval *cocotte* used for the final braising; the flesh shrinks radically during the first cooking process, and when braised (further shrinking is imperceptible) it should be contained in a receptacle permitting partial immersion by a minimum of reduced stock.

To Bone an Oxtail

In guise of instruction, the cookbooks say, "Bone an oxtail without piercing the flesh." The practitioner who is able to bone an oxtail without ever piercing the flesh is a rare bird; I know none. The flesh is tough and sinuous and the cartilaginous extremities of the vertebral joints are not tender and easily sliced through as in smaller and younger animals. Even using a small, razor-sharp, and sharply pointed paring knife (a boning knife is too large to work with precision), it is practically impossible to avoid the knife's slipping from time to time. Furthermore, as one progresses down the tail, the spinal protuberances themselves often tend to pierce the flesh's surface, sheathed only by a taut, tough and sheer membrane. The lesson to be drawn from this is not to worry; do the best you can, but do not imagine that a few slits here and there are a disaster.

Only the first six joints are boned, the terminal third of the tail (8 or 10 inches) being cut off and joined to the bones for preparing the stock. The vertebral extremities touch the surface of the flesh on the top and on the underside the entire length of the tail; the sides, at the upper half, are fleshy and pose no problem. The tail should be boned from the underside, slit open, following a median line described by the points at which the bones touch the flesh's surface. It is useless to attempt to describe the complex form of the bones to be removed (there are five major protrusions to each vertebra whose contours should be closely followed); the first and largest at the fleshy base of the tail is easily removed and can be studied, the better to know what to expect from the succeeding and progressively smaller units. The cartilaginous attachment at each joint is easily sliced through and each bone should be removed as it is freed from the flesh. Work mostly with the tip of the knife, scraping and keeping the blade tip always in contact with the bone—go carefully when approaching the flesh surface and, as soon as bone gives way to carti-

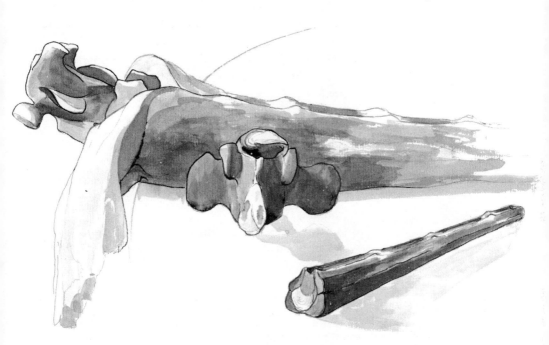

An oxtail, first bone removed, second bone exposed

lage, slice through, leaving the cartilage embedded in the flesh. The boned tail, its tip cut off, should describe an elongated triangle some 10 to 12 inches wide at the fleshy base and 18 to 20 inches in length.

	1 boned oxtail
Marinade	Finely crumbled mixed dried herbs (thyme, oregano, savory) 1 tablespoon olive oil 1 cup dry white wine

Stuffing

6 ounces chopped beef marrow (pried out of the bone with a knife, not poached)

8 ounces lean chopped beef

2 cloves garlic, peeled and puréed

3 ounces fresh or stale (but not dry) breadcrumbs (without crusts)

½ teaspoon finely crumbled (or freshly powdered) mixed dried herbs

Handful finely chopped parsley

1 large truffle, coarsely chopped (or finely chopped truffle peel)

Salt, pepper, pinch ground allspice

2 tablespoons Cognac

1 egg

2½ to 3 quarts stock (prepared from the bones, the emptied marrow bone, and any available lean beef trimmings)

6 to 8 ounces each sweet onions and carrots, peeled and chopped or cubed into a coarse brunoise (½- to ⅓-inch squares)

Sprinkle the meat lightly on both sides with herbs and put to marinate, turned well and folded in the oil and the wine, in a covered crock, refrigerated, overnight.

The firmness of the stuffing is important and is ensured by the marrow's being well chilled. If it has not been prepared in advance and chilled, be certain that both meat and marrow are chilled and thoroughly combine all the ingredients, using a fork rather than your hands, whose warmth would soften the mixture.

Remove the tail from its marinade and spread it out, boned side facing up, on a square of cloth (that will be used for wrapping it up before being tied—I use old sheets, torn into squares). Mound the stuffing evenly along the center of the upper two thirds of the tail, fold the lower third in a flap up and over the surface of the stuffing, draw the edges of the tail together at the point where the flap has been folded, running the trussing needle and a 2½-foot length of string through, tie the far end of the string in a knot and sew up the length of the tail and the opening at the wide base, spiral-wise, pierc-

342

ing the edges at approximately 1-inch intervals. Clip the string, leaving several inches hanging free. The stuffing will be loosely contained in the sewn-up tail; despite the important loss of fat from the marrow, the stuffing will swell somewhat, whereas the flesh of the tail shrinks. Don't worry if a bit of stuffing is visible through inadvertent slits. Wrap gently but firmly, the cloth pulled tight, gathering together and twisting the cloth at one end of the package and tying it tightly. Loop the string 3 or 4 times around the length as if tying up a roast, tie the other end of the cloth, gathered and twisted, and clip off any excess. Place the package in its pot, pour over the marinade, and enough warm but not boiling stock to cover well (if you have not quite enough stock, add water). Bring to the boiling point and adjust the heat so that the liquid will just simmer, counting 2½ hours from the time that a continued simmer has been reached. Carefully lift off all the fat from the surface two or three times during the last hour of poaching (there will be a good cupful).

Remove the wrapped tail to a platter (or, better, to a small pastry grill placed on a platter), clip the strings, unwrap it, permitting the cloth to drain, and leave the meat to drain while reducing the stock and sweating the vegetables. The liquid drained from the wrapping cloth and the piece of meat will be very fatty; it can be poured into a bowl, chilled, the fat removed in a piece, and added to the leftover stock later.

Skim the stock, a light boil maintained at one half of the surface, pulling the skin that forms to the other side with a tablespoon and removing it, repeatedly, over a period of about ½ hour. Lift loose floating fat from the surface with absorbent paper. When no more traces of fat are visible and a skin no longer readily forms on the surface, turn the flame high and reduce at a rolling boil to about half of its original volume.

Scatter the *brunoise* of onions and carrots in the bottom of the *cocotte* that will serve for braising the tail (no fat, no liquid, no seasoning) and put, covered, into a 350° oven for about ½ hour, checking from time to time—they should sweat and become semitender without coloring. Remove the lid and leave them for another 5 or 10 minutes or until they just begin to stick to the bottom, a suggestion of golden edges appearing here and there.

Place the drained tail, sewn side down, on the bed of vegetables, ladle over enough hot reduced stock to immerse the meat by from

343

one half to two thirds (if the *cocotte* is just large enough to contain it at ease, only something over half of the remaining stock will be necessary), and braise at a bare simmer for an additional 2 or 2¼ hours, basting every 10 or 15 minutes, the first hour covered over a low heat, and the second hour uncovered in a 325° to 350° oven. Use a tiny ladle for basting and, during the period in the oven, take care to scoop up vegetables with the braising liquid, scattering them over the surface so that they, as well as the surface of the meat, will acquire a rich, caramelized glaze.

Remove carefully, with spatulas, to a heated serving platter, clip the string at the knot, pulling gently from the other end while holding the meat in place, to remove it. Serve the remaining vegetables and braising liquid apart in a preheated sauceboat.

TRIPES

Because tripe is sold precooked, the mythical *tripes à la mode de Caën* and a host of other folklorique and *daube*-like recipes are either impossible or impractical to prepare. Others of the *daube* family may be simplified and given only a couple of additional hours of gentle cooking with the happiest of results. *Tripes à la Niçoise,* for instance: a bed of *mirepoix,* a parboiled split calf's foot, large bones removed, tripe cut into narrow 2- or 3-inch strips, salt and a generous sprinkling of herbs, a glass of white wine, peeled and seeded, chopped tomatoes or canned ones, crushed or chopped garlic, sometimes a very light flour thickening; the dish is brought to a boil and barely simmered, tightly covered, for a couple of hours. Prepared in this way, tripe is often gratinéed, as in Florence—spread in a shallow oven dish, sprinkled with Parmesan, and put for 15 minutes in a hot oven.

Most recipes that call for precooked tripe, because that which is commercialized is prepared without any aromatic support, will be improved by an hour's simmering in a richly flavored (onions, carrots, and lots of herbs) court bouillon: Hot, *à la vinaigrette;* "sauced" with stewed sorrel in soft scrambled eggs; sautéed *à la Lyonnaise* (sliced onions cooked apart, tossed with thin strips of sautéed tripe,

344

the pan washed up with a bit of vinegar). Or, as with the Lyonnais *tablier de sapeur,* several hours in a marinade may sufficiently re-vivify the somewhat emasculated product (I have more than once known friends, incomprehensibly trepidant at the thought of tripe, to be seduced by this preparation): 3-inch squares of tripe marinated for several hours in a mixture of lemon juice, mustard, white wine, a few drops of olive oil, salt, pepper, chopped *fines herbes*—the mari-nade should be plentiful enough to only coat the pieces, which should be well turned around in it from time to time; the tripe then dipped in beaten egg and fresh breadcrumbs, left to set, basted with melted butter, and grilled with repeated bastings for 6 or 7 minutes on each side. Serve with *sauce tartare.*

TRIPE AND POTATO TERRINE
(Pot-au-Four)

For well over a year, two Ardèchois friends had spoken to me repeat-edly of two preparations remembered sentimentally from childhood —vulgar, rustic, robust, savory dishes: the *bombine* and the *pot-au-four.* But neither friend had practical experience in the kitchen and their memories of these dishes were mainly those of a general expe-rience, memories of specific details being vague and often contradic-tory. Furthermore, the gastronomic chroniclers had, in their repeated dragnetting of the provinces for obscure, traditional family recipes, somehow missed these two, and no recipes were to be found in any of the cookbooks known to my friends or to myself. They were insistent that I should re-create these recipes for them and, finally, managed to gather together five other friends and contemporaries originally from the Ardèche; in the course of an hour's discussion and occasionally violent disagreement, I was able, finally, to define both dishes in a general sort of way. The *bombine* is a mutton and potato dish (see page 303). Some, in discussing the *pot-au-four,* re-membered the presence of olives, others of finding always a collec-tion of *osselets* in the bottom of the earthenware cooking utensil (*osselets* are the small digital bones from calves' or pigs' feet, well known to French children, who play tiddly-winks type games with them), no one remembered onions but everyone was certain that garlic was present, several remembered "a lot of bay leaves," and so forth.

With the first tryout, there were several serious faults: The potatoes were sliced much too thinly; there were far too few in relation to the quantity of tripe; the *osselets* were too large (I had used a calf's foot instead of a pig's foot); the juice was too "rich" (I had moistened the dish with a veal stock) . . . I later met the mother of one of my friends—an old lady who had learned to prepare these dishes from her mother but who, having fallen victim to the deep-freeze and other facilities, had prepared neither for some quarter of a century. Her memory, however, confirmed my final recipe with the exception that the olives should be green instead of black (I do not like green olives in cooking; if readers care to try them, they should first be parboiled for 5 or 10 minutes before being added to the preparation).

The black olives should be either of a sort prepared in herb-flavored brine or a very simple natural preparation in which the flavor is clean and almost "sweet." Strong-flavored olives, like the Greek ones, should not be considered—better eliminate the olives altogether.

> 1 pig's foot, large bone removed, split, covered with cold water, parboiled for 10 minutes, drained, and rinsed
>
> 1½ pounds beef tripe, cut into approximately 2-inch squares
>
> 8 ounces pitted black olives, parboiled for a minute and drained

Aromatic Mixture
> 2 teaspoons crumbled thyme (or mixed dried herbs)
> 1 mounded tablespoon finely chopped garlic
> 1 handful finely chopped parsley

> 3 or 4 bay leaves
> Salt
> 2½ pounds potatoes (preferably of a firm-fleshed variety that does not disintegrate while cooking), cut to approximately ¼-inch slices
> Water (plus any leftover meat roasting juices)
> Flour for dough

Use a 4- to 5-quart oven casserole (earthenware or enameled ironware). Place in it the halves of pig's foot plus enough pieces of tripe to line the bottom, sprinkle with the olives, the herb and garlic mixture, and a bay leaf, salt lightly, add a layer of potatoes, one of tripe, more seasoning and aromatic mixture, etc., finishing with a layer of potatoes. Press the surface to pack the contents slightly, pour in water to cover, bring gently to the boiling point on top of the stove, fashion a ribbon of dough from flour, water, and a bit of oil, rolled with your hands on a floured board, and seal the lid to the edges of the casserole. Count about 4 hours in a slow (275°) oven.

PORK *(PORC)*

There is an edge—somewhat flat, slightly sweetish, fatty, and insidious—to fresh unsalted or uncured pork that palls on many a palate. The most successful remedy is to play something else a bit sweet against it, often supplemented by a sharp or acid element. The American spoonful of cold tinned applesauce as an accompaniment to roast pork may not be very exciting but, more imaginatively used (sliced and sautéed in butter; cored and peeled cross-sectional slices prepared as fritters with unsweetened batter), apples are among the more useful accompaniments to fresh pork (to blood sausage also).

Sage is the herb most often used and, if it is fresh, it does its work well; dried, it tends to lend a musty flavor. Inch-thick pork chops, fat trimmed, seasoned, rubbed in olive oil, 2 or 3 fresh sage leaves pressed to each side, grilled over wood coals for about 8 minutes on each side, are very good indeed and perfectly accompanied by apple fritters. Sage is a powerful herb, but the quantity used in this instance will not be aggressive, for the leaves only caress the chops with their perfume and are not, themselves, eaten—often some disappear into the bed of coals.

In stews, pork is treated as other meats; in the south often as a *civet,* prepared in red wine, heightened by marc (instead of Cognac), the herb mixture strengthened with a bit of sage, the sauce finished with a mixture of blood and finely chopped or pulverized liver; in

347

the north, it is prepared as a *carbonnade* with beer (like the beef recipe, page 336); in the Touraine, soaked and pitted prunes may be added to a red or white wine stew. Count on 1½ to 2 hours cooking from the time of moistening.

PORK CHOPS AND APPLES IN MUSTARD SAUCE
(Côtes de Porc aux Pommes à la Moutarde)
(for 4)

2 pounds apples, quartered, cored, peeled, sliced thinly
1 tablespoon butter
4 pork loin chops about ¾ inch thick, pared of excess fat
Salt
¼ cup dry white wine
1 cup heavy cream
About ⅓ cup Dijon mustard (to taste)
Pepper

Spread the apples in a lightly buttered gratin dish (large enough to hold the chops placed side by side without forcing) and bake in a 400° oven for 15 minutes.

Meanwhile, cook the salted chops in a bit of butter over medium heat until nicely colored on each side—7 or 8 minutes per side. Arrange the chops on the apples' surface, deglaze the pan with the white wine, reducing it by half, and dribble it over the surface.

Mix the cream and the mustard, adding the latter progressively and tasting. Salt lightly, pepper to taste, and pour the mixture over the chops and apples, shaking the dish gently to be certain the cream penetrates the bed of apples. Bake 15 minutes longer at the same temperature.

FENNEL MARINATED ROAST PORK
(Porc Rôti au Fenouil)
(for 4)

The hint of anise in wild fennel, usually reserved for fish preparations, is a perfect foil to the dullness of fresh pork, bringing a vibrant
delicacy to its flavor. Wild fennel is much more richly perfumed than
the bulb fennel found in the market, but if the former is unavailable,
the feathery leaves of bulb fennel may be substituted—the pastis will
reinforce their somewhat attenuated accent. The subtlety of mingled
flavors is more pronounced when the pork is eaten cold the following
day.

Potatoes and large sweet onions, both baked in their skins, the
skins of the latter removed before serving, a chunk of butter placed
on each, are a good accompaniment . . . Or little new potatoes cooked
gently in butter, sautéed, with a handful of unpeeled garlic cloves.

2 pounds single loin roast, boned (ask your butcher to bone it if you
   prefer, but not to tie it up), pared of all but a thin sheet of surface fat
Large handful of chopped tender leaves and branches of fresh fennel
1 tablespoon (or 2 if cultivated fennel is used) pastis (Ricard or Pernod
   51)
1 cup dry white wine
Salt, pepper

Pierce the meat, with the grain, with a sharply pointed, narrow-
bladed knife, the length of the roast, 3 or 4 times through the filet,
once through the filet mignon (the muscle corresponding to the filet
in beef) and two or three times through the apron, forcing generous
pinches of chopped fennel into these slits in sufficient quantity so
that, when the roast is carved, the cross-section will present a pattern
of green spots. Place the meat in a large mixing bowl, sprinkle over
the remaining fennel, add the pastis, and ⅔ cup of the wine; marinate, unrefrigerated, a plate covering the bowl, for 4 or 5 hours, turning the meat around in the marinade two or three times during this
period.

Lift the meat out, leave it to drain for a few minutes in a sieve

349

placed over the marinade, sponge it dry with absorbent paper, salt and pepper the interior lightly, and roll it up into its original form, the apron wrapped around the outside as far as it will go. Tie it up, sprinkle the outside with salt, and roast it, using a small skillet or heavy gratin dish as a roasting pan, for about 1 hour and 10 minutes in all, beginning it at 450° and turning the oven down to 350° after some 10 or 15 minutes. After ½ hour begin to baste regularly with its fat and about 20 minutes before removing it from the oven, drain the fat from the roasting pan, pour in the marinade, and continue basting regularly. The end of the cooking time should correspond to the moment, more or less, that the liquid of the marinade is completely evaporated, the bottom of the pan containing only caramelized adherences and additional fat drawn from the roast, the roast itself handsomely glazed from repeated basting. Transfer the roast to a heated serving platter, removing the strings, discard the fat from the pan, and, over a high flame, deglaze with the remaining white wine, reducing it by about two thirds. Pour the juice over the roast and, when carving, serve a spoonful of the mingled deglazing liquid and the juices that escape from within the meat over each slice.

EARS, RINDS, AND TAILS
(Oreilles, Couennes, et Queues)
(for 4)

Some 10 years ago, after a long and arduous day of tasting in the vineyards of Beaujolais country, having returned to Lyons late in the evening, a hungry handful of our group left the others to their beds and unearthed a bistro called La Queue de Cochon. I have never returned, self-inflicted duty having led me, on subsequent trips, to new experiences among the array of celebrated restaurants in the star-studded Lyonnaise region. But neither have I ever so enjoyed a meal in that region—if it could be called a meal—as I did the huge platter of boiled ears, rinds, and tails that was served us in an atmosphere of a kind that is already anachronistic in a fast-changing world; the bar was small—an old-fashioned carved wooden affair—and three colorful ladies stood, each with a glass of Beaujolais in hand, awaiting, perhaps not too hopefully, the evening's client; the dining room, too, was small, the floor scattered with sawdust, the lighting rather dull with only the brass rails gleaming and, at the marble-topped tables, all the clients were eating ears, tails, and rolled-up rinds and drinking the house Beaujolais. The Beaujolais was six months old, light and cool—a green and ravishing explosion of fruit. I no longer remember how many bottles passed that evening . . .

Any pork destined to be boiled will be better if salted down with a sprinkling of herbs for a couple of days first.

Served ungarnished as a first course or, as a main course, accompanied by boiled potatoes (which may be scrubbed and thrown, unpeeled, into the pot with the meats a ½ hour before removing them from the heat), a *ravigote* (vinaigrette to which has been added finely chopped onion, chopped *fines-herbes,* and capers) or a *gribiche* sauce will be appreciated (or each guest may fabricate a sauce to taste from a table laden with dishes of chopped onion, peeled hard-boiled eggs, capers, *fines-herbes,* gherkins, mustard, horseradish, vinegar, and olive oil). *Gribiche* (3 hard-boiled egg yolks still tepid, salt, pepper, 1 teaspoon mustard, 1 cup olive oil, 1 tablespoon vinegar) is supposed to mount like a mayonnaise but rarely does and is none the worse for it—some people add a raw egg yolk to the cooked yolks to ensure its mounting; sour gherkins, capers, *fines-herbes,* and the egg whites, all chopped, are stirred into the emulsion. Accompanied by lentils, cooked apart, imperfectly drained and tossed with butter and chopped parsley, sauce is impertinent. Snout may be added to the ears, rinds, and tails.

4 pigs' tails
2 pigs' ears
4 strips of rind (about 2½ by 8 or 9 inches each)
Coarse salt and mixed dried herbs for salting down
8 to 10 ounces peeled carrots
Large bouquet garni: thyme, bay leaf, branch celery, parsley plus parsley
    root, if possible, leek greens, branch of lovage (if available)
1 large onion stuck with 2 cloves
Salt (if necessary)

351

Pack the meats into a terrine or large mixing bowl, the layers generously sprinkled with coarse salt and lightly but evenly sprinkled with dried herbs and leave, covered, in a cool place, or, lacking that, refrigerated, for a couple of days. Discard the liquid, rinse the meats, cover well with cold water, bring to a boil, and simmer for about 10 minutes (or until the rind is supple enough to be rolled and tied). Drain and rinse.

Roll the strips of rind up tightly and tie a string around each. Cover the meats again with a large amount of cold water, bring to a boil, add the carrots, the bouquet, and the onion stuck with cloves, skim, and regulate the heat to keep the liquid, the pot covered, at a bare simmer. After 1 hour's time taste the cooking liquid for salt. Count about 2¼ to 2½ hours, testing for tenderness. When serving, split the ears in two—or cut them into narrow strips (there is little to them but cartilage—therein lies their deliciously crunchy, but sufficiently tender, goodness).

RABBIT *(LAPIN)*

One thing has not changed in France: Everywhere in the country and wherever in the villages a few yards of space can be found, there are rabbit hutches, rabbits being famously reproductive and inexpensive to raise. One often sees people wandering along the roadsides, in the fields, or on the hillsides with great burlap bags collecting weeds and herbs, clipping tender shoots from the branches of trees and shrubs, to supplement the rabbits' regular diet of kitchen debris, soups made of stale bread crusts, and whatnot.

The French affection for rabbit is general (the roadside inn whose menu includes *gibelotte* is certain to be the choice of all passing truckdrivers); if, in the past, it was considered in bourgeois households to be "common"—which means only that it was eschewed for Sunday or occasional meals, being sacrificed, instead, for weekday stews—it has now come into its own, the Sunday chicken having lost all claim to its antique titles of nobility (the Sunday leg of lamb now costing the eyes of one's head and the Sunday *pot-au-*

feu demanding more time than today's housewife willingly devotes to the kitchen). For rabbits, like the hysterical guinea fowl, although now commercially raised, stubbornly reject the mass-production treatment applied to chickens, and their flesh still retains some of the qualities of once-living creatures. Many in the cities, are in despair before the pasty-fleshed and tasteless scourge of chickens on the market; rabbits have gained greatly in popularity.

Opinions differ as to whether the flesh of domesticated rabbit is "insipid" or "delicate"—the same foolish quarrel that is often dedicated to veal. There is no doubt but that, for many preparations—and in particular those involving rich and robustly flavored sauces like *civets* or *poivrades*—a few hours in a marinade is an improvement. This is not true of wild rabbit, whose flesh has a much more pronounced and personal flavor, less gamy but otherwise not unlike that of hare; a marinade only masks its finesse, lending it too strong a flavor rather than a welcome support, as in the instance of the domestic cousin. But for that difference, recipes for the two are interchangeable. Wild rabbit should be young (tender ears, easily torn); there is no problem with commercialized domestic rabbit, it being always killed young—at about 3 months.

Because wild rabbit is shot, it bleeds internally, the flesh being infused with some of the blood, lending it part of its quality (this is true of all game), the remainder gathering in the rib cage, imprisoned there by a thin membrane separating it completely from the abdominal area. If a blood-thickened sauce is planned, this should be carefully emptied into a bowl and beaten with a tablespoon of vinegar to prevent its clotting (hutch rabbits are bled from the jugular vein before being skinned, the vinegar beaten in immediately).

There are a number of standard methods of killing rabbits; since I have no first-hand experience, I quote from a serious and sensible book on rabbit raising and care:

> The classic method of killing a rabbit is to deal an abrupt blow to the nape of the neck, either with the side of the hand or with a round stick, so as to rupture the spinal column. When the blow is well delivered in the right place, death is instantaneous, but an internal hemorrhage occurs at the point at which the blow was dealt.

353

The stretching method, also destined to break apart the vertebrae at the base of the skull, seems preferable because it does not provoke a blood clot.

One holds the rabbit by the hind feet in the left hand, the head seized in the right hand, the thumb firmly pressed against the spinal column at the base of the skull; with an abrupt movement, one pulls, stretching the rabbit while forcing the head completely backward, the thumb serving as fulcrum point; the rupture of the vertebrae at the base of the skull provokes instant death.

Most professional killers sacrifice rabbits in this way and their dexterity is really extraordinary, many being able to kill, skin and gut fifty rabbits per hour.

To skin a rabbit, cut off the forepaws at the first joint, hang it, tied firmly with a cord between paw and heel, from one hind leg, cut a circular incision through the skin just above (or just below, since the rabbit is hanging) the heel or first joint, taking care neither to sever any tendons nor to cut into the flesh (pinch the skin between thumb and forefinger to keep it distant from the flesh while cutting it); slit the skin on the inside surface of the leg in a straight line from the circular incision to the base of the tail and peel the skin free, leaving it to hang loosely. Switch the cord to the other hind leg, leaving the exposed leg hanging free, and repeat the process. Cut through the base of the tail with a small sharp knife, leaving the tail attached to the skin and, pulling gently, peel the skin back, glove-like, turning it inside out. The knife will be needed again to sever the ears from the base of the skull (they, too, remain attached to the skin) and to help loosen the skin from the skull, slicing it free, finally, at the mouth. Slit the belly from the anus to the apex of the rib cage, discarding all the insides except for the liver, heart, and lungs.

To cut up a rabbit for a sauté, use a large, heavy, sharp knife, cutting with pressure rather than chopping with a cleaver, which leaves splintered bones in its wake. Cut off the head and split it in two symmetrically (it will add flavor, and many people enjoy nibbling at the cheeks and the brains); slice the forelegs free (they are not jointed to the body, but only attached muscularly); detach the liver and cut across the body, separating the rib cage from the saddle;

354

cut the rib cage crosswise in two and the saddle into three sections; split the section of backbone connecting the hind legs to separate them.

Rabbit may be sautéed without liquid additives, garnished or lent the same savory supports applied to chicken sautés (see "Chicken," pages 371–372), counting the same cooking time as for chicken. Colored first in fat, smothered in braised cabbage, its deglazing juices dribbled over, and left to braise gently for about 45 minutes, it is a comforting winter dish; or replace the cabbage by half-braised fennel.

Rabbit is most often prepared as a stew along the lines of the sauté recipe-type, page 291. (I have indicated there 30 to 40 minutes' cooking time from the moment of moistening, but that is largely a question of taste. With about 30 minutes, the flesh will be slightly firm, but moist; those who prefer it to be "falling off the bone" should count closer to an hour.)

A *civet* (larded interiorly, red wine marinade, a bit of Cognac added to the moistening elements, sauce sieved, skimmed, and reduced, *Bourguignon* garnish of lardons, mushrooms, and little onions) is finished by stirring in a mixture of the liver, the lungs (these puréed through a vegetable mill or a sieve), and the sieved blood, the sauce returned to the boiling point and simmered very gently for but a few minutes (if you do not have the rabbit's blood, it may be replaced by ¼ cup of pig's blood purchased from a pork specialty butcher—or, if the notion of a blood-thickened sauce is distressing, the stew will be perfectly good without it). Rather than dressing the stew classically with garlic-rubbed crouton triangles neatly disposed around the border of the platter, leave it in its cooking vessel without loss of heat and scatter the surface with little golden butter-crisp croutons, tossed at the last minute over a higher flame with a handful of chopped parsley mixed either with finely chopped garlic or with puréed raw garlic.

The Provençal *lapereau en poivrade* is a sort of amalgam of recipes applied traditionally to hare *(à la royale, poivrade, civet).* It is also (but need not necessarily be) blood-thickened; white wine replaces the red of a *civet,* a large handful of unpeeled garlic cloves are added while the rabbit is being sautéed, the mushrooms and onions are eliminated from the garnish, and 5 minutes before the sieved sauce (being certain that all the onion and garlic have been puréed into the sauce), simmered, skimmed, and reduced, is removed from

355

the heat, a scant teaspoonful of coarsely broken-up peppercorns is thrown in. The sauce is then resieved over the rabbit pieces to eliminate the solid pepper.

Gibelotte is another of those magic words whose mere utterance causes saliva to run in a French mouth. My dictionary places its origin in the old French *gibelet* ("a dish of birds"). Both words, in any case, are obviously derived from *gibier* ("game"), and *gibelotte* may, at one time, have been an indiscriminate label attached to all soups or stews made of small feathered and furred game. Today it means only rabbit and white wine stew. It is thought of as vulgar, popular, unrefined (in this context, all considered to be positive virtues): *un plat canaille*. And, as if duty-bound to respect the dish's connate vulgarity, most cooks determinedly prepare it in the sloppiest possible manner, some cookbooks, moreover, specifying that it should be boiled rather than simmered: Rabbit, cut-up onions, lardons are all fried up together; flour, thyme, bay, mushrooms, white wine, and water are thrown in; and the lot is boiled until done . . . The elements are all there and it is not bad—how could it be? But the rabbit is dry and stringy, the mushrooms are black, and the sauce is greasy, something less than digestible. Boiled potatoes accompany it. The Provençal version is perfumed with mountain savory and dubbed *chasseur*.

With a modicum of respect and very little effort a *gibelotte* can be transformed into a savory and attractive dish with no compromise imposed on its humble pretensions: The pieces of rabbit need neither be larded nor marinated and, assuming the cooking to have been conducted at a gentle simmer, the sauce carefully degreased, it is not absolutely necessary to strain the sauce. But one should not forget that, before its straining, its skimming, and its proper reduction, it is nothing but an inconsistent soup full of half disintegrated debris, full of promise but not yet a sauce. Garnishing elements may be eliminated; but, if they are included, at least the little onions and the mushrooms should be prepared apart and, having conceded this much to refinement, the sauce may as well be strained and purified, its sapid and textural unification offsetting the individual textures and flavors of the garnish; if the sauce is a confusion of taste and texture, added garnish will only reinforce the confusion.

Any of the garnishes suggested in the recipe-type go well with rabbit; little butter-stewed onions, alone or in combination with others, are always welcome, as are crisp croutons (in the absence of potato garnish).

Steamed potatoes, rice pilaf, or fresh egg noodles are the usual accompaniments; in most instances, I prefer the latter. For a change, a finely sieved and generously buttered lentil purée is a good thing.

A basic *gibelotte* sauce may be finished in a number of ways. Two particularly exciting transformations consist of (1) slowly stirring in a mixture of (parboiled and drained) butter-stewed sorrel and heavy cream (about ½ pound fresh sorrel or ¼ cup sorrel purée to ¾ to 1 cup cream—more or less of each to taste) and returning to the boiling point; fresh egg noodle accompaniment; (2) stirring in a mixture of about ¼ cup (more or less to taste) Dijon mustard and ¾ cup heavy cream; garnish of scraped, rinsed, and dried little new potatoes, sautéed gently in butter until tender and pale gold and drained on absorbent paper before being eased into the sauce and simmered for a minute, served sprinkled with *fines herbes;* no accompaniment.

A rabbit fricassée is a *gibelotte* finished like a *blanquette,* bound with egg yolks (or egg yolks and cream). A mushroom purée may also attractively finish the sauce (½ pound raw mushrooms passed through a mechanical device, sautéed, seasoned, in butter, a bit of lemon juice for bleach, until all liquid has vanished), creamed or not —or egg-yolk-bound, if one likes . . . Artichoke hearts, first stewed in butter, are a pretty garnish with a mushroom sauce.

SAFFRON RABBIT STEW WITH CUCUMBERS
(Lapin Sauté à la Toucassaine)
(for 4)

1 rabbit, cut up for sautéing
Salt
3 tablespoons olive oil
1 large onion (about 4 ounces), coarsely chopped
5 or 6 cloves garlic, unpeeled
½ teaspoon sugar
1 mounded tablespoon flour

357

⅛ to ¼ teaspoon powdered saffron (to taste)
Small pinch cayenne
1½ cups dry white wine
Water

Garnish   1 large, firm ripe tomato (5 to 6 ounces), peeled, seeded, coarsely chopped (or equivalent of seeded and drained preserved tomatoes)
1 pound firm fresh cucumbers (small with undeveloped seeds, if possible)
The rabbit's liver
¼ cup butter
Salt, pepper
1 handful fresh basil leaves (and buds and flowers, if in flower)

Use a large, heavy *plat à sauter*. Lacking that, begin in a large skillet, transferring everything to a casserole at the time of moistening.

Salt the pieces of rabbit and color them in the hot olive oil, adjusting the flame to medium after a couple of minutes. Add the onion and the garlic cloves immediately after turning the rabbit pieces over, shifting rabbit and onions regularly to prevent the latter from browning. When the rabbit pieces are sufficiently colored, sprinkle with sugar, turn the pieces over, and a minute later sprinkle over the flour, lowering, at the same time, the flame. Displace all the contents of the pan, turning the rabbit pieces over two or three times during a period of about 5 minutes—the flour should be lightly colored. Sprinkle over the saffron and cayenne and continue turning things gently around and over until all the elements are saffron-stained. Turn the flame high and pour in the white wine, scraping the bottom of the pan at all points and repeatedly with a wooden spoon until all adherent material has been dissolved into the sauce. Add enough water to the boiling sauce to just cover the contents of the pan, return to a boil, and cook, covered, over a very low heat, at a bare simmer, until the rabbit is tender, but still slightly firm—about ½ hour for a young rabbit.

Remove the pieces of meat to a platter and strain the sauce

through a sieve, working the debris vigorously with a wooden pestle to purée the onions and garlic—only the garlic hulls should remain in the sieve. Scrape the purée from the underside of the sieve and stir it into the sauce. Return the rabbit pieces to their cooking vessel, add the tomatoes and the cucumbers (see below), distributing them regularly and shaking the pan to settle the contents. Grind over pepper to taste and leave, covered, in a warm place while finishing the sauce.

Skim off any fat that has risen to the surface of the sauce. Bring it to a boil, pull the saucepan a bit to the side of the flame, adjusting the heat so that a light boil is maintained at one side of the surface. Skim (skin) each time a skin forms on the still surface area, gently gathering it to the edge with the tip of a tablespoon, lifting it free and discarding it. After 15 or 20 minutes, the sauce should be fat free; if it still seems light-bodied (it should be relatively so) or over-abundant, reduce over a high flame, stirring all the while with a wooden spoon, to the desired consistency.

Pour the sauce over the rabbit and garnish, shake the pan gently, bring to a simmer, and leave, covered, over very low heat for about 10 minutes—long enough for the pieces of rabbit to be thoroughly re-heated and for the flavors to intermingle. Sprinkle with the sautéed liver (see below) and the basil, the leaves torn into tiny pieces rather than chopped with a knife (if tiny-leafed variety, leave the leaves whole). Cover and leave, off the heat, for another 5 minutes, permitting the basil to expand. Accompany with a rice pilaf.

Garnish Preparations

Stew the tomatoes, salted and peppered, in 1 tablespoon butter over low heat, tossing them occasionally, for about 10 minutes. If the liquid is still abundant, turn up the flame and reduce rapidly, shaking the pan all the while.

Peel and rinse the cucumbers. If they are small, the seeds still unformed, they may be cut crosswise into ½-inch lengths. Larger cucumbers should be split either into halves or quarters, depending on their size, seeds removed and cut into ½-inch to 1-inch lengths, depending on thickness (the dictates of the nineteenth century still oblige the professional cook to pare them in the form of large olives —the waste of time and cucumber involved makes no sense in the home kitchen unless one's guests are addicted to mechanical decoration). Plunge them into heavily salted water and simmer for no more than a minute—they should not be cooked, only ever so slightly softened—drain and put them to stew gently in 2 tablespoons butter, tossing from time to time, for 6 or 7 minutes—they should be tender, but absolutely intact.

Cut the liver into small pieces or thin strips and toss, seasoned, in hot butter for a few seconds—long enough to turn the pieces gray; they should remain pink inside.

RABBIT PAPILLOTES
(Lapin en Papillotes)
(for 4)

The recipe indicates only the rear of the rabbit; there is practically no flesh on the rib section and the forelegs, and although they are as nicely flavored as any part of the rabbit and are the least likely to dry out during cooking, they are too skimpy to serve, at least first. If more than one rabbit is being prepared, these pieces can be put aside with the heads for a stew. Otherwise, split the rib cage, marinate it and the forelegs with the rest, and put all four pieces into a single large *papillote* to serve as seconds. (The liver cannot be used in this preparation; rabbit livers are extraordinarily large, one being a sufficient portion for a person. Cooked gently, seasoned, in butter on each side until firm but still pink, it is surpassed in delicacy only by calf's liver.)

The aluminum foil is not as attractive as parchment paper, but the preparation is extremely rapid and the result otherwise as good. Care should be taken that no sharp edges or fragments of splintered bones are bared, perhaps piercing the aluminum foil and thus letting either steam or juices escape during cooking. The rabbit pieces may each be wrapped in a slice of bacon and, there too, if the bacon is fixed with a toothpick or other sharp stick, it must be so placed as to not touch the foil casing.

The saddle of the rabbit, cut across into two equal sections and the two hind legs

Snail butter (1 large clove garlic pounded to a paste, 2 heaping table-

spoons finely chopped parsley, large pinch finely ground mixed dried
herbs, salt, pepper, 3 tablespoons butter, all mashed together until
thoroughly mixed)
Finely crumbled mixed dried herbs (thyme, oregano, savory, marjoram—
your choice)
¼ cup olive oil
Salt, pepper

Pierce each piece of meat deeply, a number of times, using a
small and sharply pointed knife and following the grain of the meat
(straight through from one cut side to the other for the saddle sections; pierce at a sharp bias, almost parallel to the bone, but directed
toward it, for the legs), forcing a healthy quantity of snail butter
into each vent as you go. Sprinkle the pieces lightly but evenly with
dried herbs, turn them around in a bowl with the olive oil, and leave
to marinate for several hours (if time permits—not essential).

Enclose each, salted and peppered at the last minute and well
coated with oil, in a large (12- to 14-inch) square of aluminum foil,
placed flat on a table, the sides drawn up, pinched together and
folded twice upon themselves (or more when necessary to avoid
bizarre forms), firmly pinched for air-tightness, the pinched border
forming a crest the length of the vaguely omelet shape. Place them,
not touching, on a flat pastry sheet and bake in a hot oven (450°) for
from 35 to 40 minutes. Slit open at table. A potato or a vegetable
gratin provides a good accompaniment.

STUFFED, ROAST SADDLE AND HINDQUARTERS OF
RABBIT
(Râble de Lapin Farci au Four)
(for 4 to 6)

A whole unboned stuffed roast rabbit may be a thing of beauty, but
it is impossible to carve; the stuffing is crushed and scattered and the
flesh shredded as one attempts to sever sections of the backbone and
the large quantity of stuffing engulfed by the rib cage can only be
reached with a spoon once the initial carnage is finished. A boned
stuffed saddle is cut into neat slices without further ado.

Preparing a rabbit; spinal column separated from back but still attached

To Bone a Saddle

Cut the rabbit in two at the vertebral joint between the second and third rib, the two terminal ribs adhering to the saddle section (scrape the meat free from the remainder of the ribcage and from the forelegs and put it aside with the liver and the heart for the stuffing; the bones will be joined to the neck, the head, and those from the saddle to prepare a stock).

A small, sharply pointed paring knife is easier to work with than a boning knife: Lay the saddle out flat, back to the table, legs farthest away from you (best work seated and relaxedly). Remove the ribs from the inside surface of the thin apron of flesh, pinching the flesh downward, away from the rib on each side, slipping the point of the knife through the flesh just beneath the rib and slitting it free; break it loose from its point of attachment to the spinal column.

The median described by the spinal column inside the carcass serving as a starting point, loosen the flesh progressively the entire length of the backbone, working mostly with the tip of the knife, following carefully the undulating cross-like contours of the vertebrae. Don't attack the filets until the filets mignons have been folded outward, remaining attached to the filets but exposing the wing-like protrusions to each side of the vertebrae. Loosen the flesh between the wings of joining vertebrae with the knife tip. Now free the filets almost to the back, leaving the summit of the spinal column attached the whole length.

The final detachment of the length of spinal column is the only delicate part of the operation, for each vertebra is terminated by a cartilaginous attachment reaching to the outside surface of the flesh; to avoid piercing the flesh at any point, one must snip through each vertebral extremity, leaving its cartilaginous tip embedded in the flesh, the tip of the knife then describing an inverted U to free the flesh between joining vertebrae. It may be easier to break off sections of two or three vertebrae as they are freed from the back, and one may, without inconvenience to carving, leave the final joint at the base of the tail.

To Lard the Saddle

Turn the saddle over, legs spread out, back facing up. Cut the fatback into long strips about ⅛ inch square (it is easier to cut if well chilled). A larding needle with a hinged crochet at the larger, hollow end (rather than the classic splayed blades) will prevent the lardons from slipping free of the needle while larding. The needle should pierce the flesh with the grain (in the sense of the length of the saddle and of the legs rather than running crosswise), shallowly, surfacing again at about ¾ inch, pulling the lardon in its train so as to leave a ¾-inch section embedded in the flesh; each lardon is then trimmed, leaving about ¼ inch visible at each end (1¼- to 1½-inch lengths, in all, but it is only practical to work with much longer lengths, trimming after they are in place). Lard in rows of alternat-

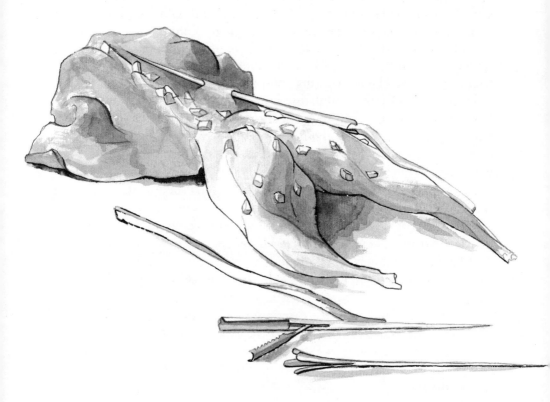

Preparing a rabbit; seen from the back, in the process of being larded—two different kinds of larding needles illustrated

ing alignments (the flesh of the second row being pierced on a line with and at the halfway point between the points at which the lardons of the first row have surfaced).

A pound of green chard leaves without ribs, parboiled, squeezed dry, and chopped, will render the stuffing even more *bonne femme* in spirit and more rustic in flavor.

It is possible to leave the rabbit whole (removing the eyes for aesthetic reasons), but the spinal column, from the rib cage to the base of the tail, must, in any case, be removed; in this case, there being nothing from which to prepare a stock, the breadcrumbs are soaked either in water or in the strained marinade and squeezed dry (the marinade saved for basting).

Parboiled little peas scattered over the rabbit at the moment of serving affords a pretty picture and a delicious accompaniment—or parboiled, drained, and butter-stewed, creamed sorrel will marry wonderfully.

> The larded saddle and hindquarters of a rabbit, saddle boned
> (About 4 ounces pork fatback for larding)

Marinade
> 1 medium onion, finely sliced
> 2 or 3 cloves garlic, crushed
> Large pinch crumbled mixed dried herbs (or branches of thyme)
> 2 bay leaves
> 1 tablespoon olive oil
> 1 cup dry white wine

Stuffing
> Stock (bones, split head and neck of rabbit, 1 quart water, sliced carrot, cut-up onion, herbs, very little salt, skimmed, simmered, covered, for 2½ to 3 hours, strained)
> 1 large clove garlic
> 3 ounces stale bread, crusts removed, crumbled
> 2 tablespoons Cognac
> Duxelles: 2 tablespoons butter
> 1 medium onion, finely chopped
> 6 ounces mushrooms, finely chopped or passed through Mouli-juliènne
> Salt, pepper
> Handful finely chopped parsley
> Juice of ½ lemon
> Suspicion freshly grated nutmeg (optional)
> 1 teaspoon finely crumbled (or freshly powdered) mixed dried herbs
> The liver and heart of the rabbit, finely chopped
> 6 ounces lean loin of pork (or veal), chopped

365

3 ounces fresh pork fat, chopped (or beef marrow or
   softened butter)
Salt, pepper
2 eggs

Thin sheet of fresh pork fat (optional—may be replaced
   by buttered parchment paper)
Olive oil (to rub the roast)
Salt, pepper
1 cup heavy cream

Marinate the boned and larded section of rabbit for several
hours, turning it around and over in the marinade two or three times
(or, covered and refrigerated, marinate overnight). Just before preparing the stuffing, remove it from the marinade, sponge the outside
surface dry with a towel, and leave it, back down, on the towel, waiting to be stuffed. Strain the marinade.

Reduce the strained stock, over a high flame, in a small saucepan,
to a syrupy consistency—there should be only about ⅓ cup remaining. Pound the clove of garlic to a paste in a mortar, add the breadcrumbs, the Cognac, and the reduced stock, mashing and mixing
with a fork to an even consistency.

Duxelles: Stew the onion gently in butter until softened but not
colored, add the mushrooms, seasoned with salt and pepper, turning
the flame high, and toss until all liquid has been evaporated and the
mixture is dry enough to begin sticking slightly to the pan, stir in the
parsley, then a moment later add the lemon juice and nutmeg and
remove from the heat.

Mix together the *duxelles* and all the other stuffing ingredients
in a large mixing bowl, using your hands, squishing, swirling, and
beating until completely homogeneous.

Begin sewing the rabbit up before stuffing it, allowing a single
long (about a yard) length of string, passing the trussing needle first
through the flesh joined by the legs at the base of the tail and tying
the end of string, then sew, in a spiraling manner, holding the
borders of the aprons together and piercing them ¼ to ½ inch from
the edge at about 1-inch intervals, closing about one third of the
belly. Spoon stuffing into and at the entrance to the sewn-up area, lift

366

*Preparing a rabbit; stuffed and sewn, legs tied together,
trussing needle still threaded*

the rabbit, legs hanging down, and shake it gently to settle the stuffing into place, replace it on its back, and spoon the remainder of the stuffing, mounded, into place; because the flesh shrinks during cooking and the stuffing swells, the stuffing should not be tightly packed. But, with an overabundance of stuffing, one may place a rectangle of sheet pork fat *(barde)* over the molded surface of stuffing and continue sewing without drawing the borders of the belly aprons completely together, the string thus forming a zigzag pattern across the *barde*'s surface. Cut a round of *barde* (or buttered kitchen paper) to hold the stuffing in place at the open end of the saddle, tucking the

367

edges in between the wall of flesh and the stuffing, and, when the whole length of belly has been sewn, continue, crossing the string several times from border to border, forming a large hatchwork to hold the protective *barde* or paper in place.

Use a shallow oval gratin dish just large enough to hold the roast easily. Place it, larded back up, in the dish, cross the bone ends of the hind legs and tie a string around them to hold them in place, dribble olive oil over the roast, patting with your hand to evenly distribute it, salt and pepper the surface, and roast for about 1½ hours, beginning at 450°, turning the oven down to 350° 10 minutes later, and, after about 20 minutes, beginning to baste with the fat from the roasting dish. As the tips of the lardons and the surface of the roast begin to take on a bit of color (after, say, 30 to 40 minutes— one must feel one's way), start basting with the marinade, 3 or 4 tablespoons at a time, continuing to baste regularly and, when the liquid is almost completely evaporated, adding more marinade until (after a theoretical 1 hour and 10 minutes' of total roasting) the marinade is all gone. Continue basting, watching carefully, until no liquid remains, the juices in the pan having separated into caramelized adherences and loose fat (it happens in a moment's time); remove and discard the fat from the pan and begin basting with the cream, 3 or 4 tablespoonsful at a time, never letting the pan run dry. After another 20 minutes or so the cream should be used up, the rabbit thickly coated with a voluptuous clotted and mottled glaze. Transfer to a large, preheated serving platter (to facilitate carving), remove strings, clipping the knot and pulling gently from the other end of the string, holding the roast in place the while. If a paper seal was used to replace the *barde,* remove it. Spoon over what remains of the reduction of basting liquid, taking care not to obscure the attractive pattern of browned lardon tips.

RABBIT SAUSAGES
(Boudins de Lapin)
(18 to 20 boudins)

In old cookbooks, *andouillette, boudin,* and *saucisse* are more or less interchangeable terms, the first two identifying practically any bound and precooked mixture that takes the form of a sausage, is usually but not necessarily stuffed into a sausage casing, and is reheated by grilling (an *andouille* is a large *andouillette* and shares with *cornichon* the additional and derogatory meaning of "dolt"); *Le Cuisinier Méridional* (1855), for instance, gives one recipe for *andouillettes* whose stuffing is a truffled mixture of lambs' sweetbreads, chopped roast chicken, chicken livers, and the roof of beef mouth, bound with a stiff *velouté* and eggs and another of pounded, cooked white meats, cow's udder, and *panade* with beaten egg whites added.

Today *andouillette* means chitterling sausage and *boudin* most often means *boudin noir,* or blood sausage (*boudin blanc* is casing stuffed with a pounded raw white meat—chicken or pork—and *panade quenelle* forcemeat and poached).

Prepare these sausages in advance (they may be kept refrigerated for several days—or they may be deep frozen) and, before being served, bring them to room temperature, rub them with olive oil, and grill over hot wood coals (or broil) until golden and slightly crisp—about 10 minutes, turning every 2 or 3 minutes. A generously buttered, fine-textured lentil purée accompanies them perfectly—as does a potato purée.

Chopping the different meats separately by hand, to varying degrees of finesse, is a valuable refinement, but, pressed for time, you may put everything together through a meat grinder with satisfactory results.

If you cannot get blood, eliminate it rather than discarding the recipe; if you cannot find sausage casing, fashion the *boudins* by hand, rolling them in flour, place them in a large, buttered *plat à sauter* or skillet, pour in boiling water (against the side of the pan so as not to disturb the *quenelles*) to cover generously and poach at the suggestion of a simmer, covered, for 10 minutes; remove to a pastry grill to drain and cool and wrap individually in plastic or aluminum foil for storing. Dip in egg and roll in breadcrumbs, cooking until crisp and golden in half butter and half olive oil (or baste with butter and grill).

Panade: 1 cup milk
      3 ounces stale bread, crusts removed, crumbled
8 ounces finely chopped lean pork tenderloin
1 rabbit, all flesh removed (about 1 pound) from bones and chopped, less finely than the pork, lungs, heart, and liver are chopped

6 ounces fresh pork fatback, chopped or cut into tiny cubes

6 ounces sweet onions, finely chopped, gently stewed in 2 tablespoons butter until soft and yellowed but not browned

The rabbit's blood (beaten with a tablespoon of vinegar and strained) or ⅓ cup pork blood (from pork specialty butcher)

2 ounces shelled, unroasted pistachios, put for a minute or so in boiling water, drained, rubbed vigorously in a towel to remove skins, coarsely chopped

5 eggs

1 teaspoon powdered mixed dried herbs

1 teaspoon (if available) finely chopped flowers and leaves of fresh marjoram

Salt, pepper, cayenne, allspice

About 4 yards of sausage casing (pork specialty butcher)

Boil the milk and the bread together, stirring and, finally, beating with a wooden spoon until the *panade* is stiff and homogeneous. Add to the chopped meats, mixing loosely.

Add the blood to the stewed onions and cook over very gentle heat for about 5 minutes, stirring. Stir into the bread and meat mixture—enough to attenuate the heat, then add all the other ingredients, mixing and squishing well with hands. Taste for seasoning (not very pleasant in this condition—spit out).

Soak the intestinal membrane in tepid water acidulated with vinegar until soft and supple. Lacking professional material, it is easier to cut the casing into 2-foot lengths. Use a large plastic funnel to stuff them, gently stretching one end up and around the funnel tube to receive the stuffing and leaving the other end untied until the entire length of casing is stuffed (to avoid trapping air inside). Force the stuffing through the funnel with your fingers and into place in the casing, squeezing or forcing with your hands, and molding each 2-foot length into 4 very loosely packed sausages, no air bubbles remaining inside. Tie the ends with string and twist, tying at intervals to form the sausages.

Slip them into a large pot of hot but not boiling water, bring barely to the boiling point, and poach at the suggestion of a simmer for 10 minutes. Drain, drop them into a basin of cold water until cooled, and then drain on absorbent paper, gently sponging them dry before wrapping to store.

CHICKEN *(POULET)*

When dealing with chickens, a sauté is not a stew, for a true stew, it is claimed, never contacts a liquid during the cooking process (why only chicken should be distinguished with correct denominations is a mystery). There are hundreds of formulas for chicken sautés (they may be applied, as well, to rabbit, milk lamb, or baby goat), but they are all the same: The cut-up chicken is colored in butter, olive oil, or a combination of the two, covered, and cooked gently for another 15 or 20 minutes (a garnish, usually precooked, is added at some point during the last 15 minutes), and a rapid sauce is prepared by deglazing, usually with white wine, occasionally with red wine, sherry, or another fortified wine or, very rarely, with a blazing brandy (in Normandy the pan is deglazed with flaming applejack and the reduction finished with cream); the sauce is finished, often only by swirling butter into the deglazing reduction, sometimes with cream, tomato, prepared sauces, etc., boiled down to the desired consistency, butter whisked in away from the heat. Normally, the chicken pieces are dressed on a platter with their garnish and the sauce is poured over at the moment of serving. The most practical method of operating in a home kitchen—and one that eliminates the loss of precious heat—consists of coloring the chicken in a large skillet or *plat à sauter*, transferring the pieces to an oven casserole to finish cooking (the garnish being added at this time or a few minutes later), deglazing the original cooking receptacle, draining off the juices from the casserole into the deglazing liquid, and pouring the finished sauce back over the chicken and its garnish, which will then be served directly from the casserole.

Chicken breasts, to remain moist, can support but a short cooking period; color them after the other pieces, adding them to the casserole only 8 to 10 minutes before finishing the sauce (or remove them from the casserole early if they have been started at the same time as the other pieces, keeping them in a warm place and returning them at the last minute), or forget about them, preparing your sautés with legs only . . .

371

If the sauce is to be creamed, it is just as well to have a bit of fairly thick *velouté* on hand to lend it body.

Vegetables, alone or in combination, constitute the most rational garnish (certain fantasies involve grapes, bananas, melon, apples . . . with results not destined to please all palates; and crayfish is a persistent accompaniment to many *grand-cuisine* chicken preparations) —butter-stewed artichoke hearts; asparagus tips; glazed carrots (usually in combination with other vegetables); little new potatoes sautéed gently in butter until lightly colored (often in combination with lean lardons and little onions); thinly sliced, rapidly sautéed little zucchini; parboiled little peas (added at the last minute—or, if very tender, added raw when the chicken is transferred to the casserole); rapidly parboiled and butter-stewed cucumbers; drained *ratatouille* (its liquid reduced with the deglazing liquid); sautéed mushrooms, cultivated or wild (chicken smothered in *chanterelles sautées à la Provençale*—see pages 207 and 208, the liquid that has first been drawn from them reduced to a syrup and added to a white wine deglazing reduction—is a wonderful thing); and, of course, truffles (deglaze with Cognac for black truffles; if you should come by one of the white Piedmont truffles flown fresh from Italy during the months of October and November, shave it paper-thin over the chicken only a minute before serving, simple white-wine deglazing mounted with butter). Tarragon often perfumes a chicken sauté; cook a bouquet of fresh tarragon with it and discard the bouquet before saucing the chicken and sprinkling with *fines herbes*—I sometimes dribble over a very short white wine reduction and simply drop globs of stiff heavy cream on the surface, leaving it to half melt and mingle with the juice during the service. Liquid cream is best incorporated into the sauce and either radically reduced or given binding support by a *velouté*.

A chicken sauté garnished with a vegetable stew (little onions, artichoke hearts, broad beans or peas, lettuce *chiffonade*—see page 168) prepared apart and added to the chicken 10 minutes before finishing the sauce, its juices reduced with those of the chicken and the deglazing liquid and buttered away from the heat, cannot fail to excite admiration.

Chicken stews, all prepared like the sauté recipe-type, take a host of names: *coq-au-vin* or *estouffade à la Saint-Emilionnaise* (red wine moistening, *Bourguignon* garnish); *poulet au sang* or *coq en barbouille* (the same thing finished with blood—see discussion of *civet* under Rabbit, page 355); *coq à la flamande* (with beer); *coq-au-Riesling* (self-explanatory); fricassées (all with white wine and, like a *blanquette*, finished with egg yolks, usually combined with cream—*géline à la Tourangelle* is, theoretically, a fricassée prepared with an old hen . . .). Gizzards, the lobes of flesh carefully sliced free of the gristly skin, can be transfigured into a dozen different and glorous *ragoûts,* choosing the possibilities from and respecting the methods of the recipe-type—they are done in ½ hour's time but will not suffer from 2 hours' cooking. Breasts are best reserved for other preparations.

A preparation resembling that of American fried chicken—with the difference that the chicken pieces were first marinated—was current French fare until a century or so ago. Old books recommend fairly rough marinades (wine, spices, and herbs in great variety, vinegar, onions, garlic, orange and lemon zests, olive oil); bitter (or Seville) orange was squeezed over at the moment of serving, or the marinade was reduced and used as a sauce, or both. The rare recipes in books from this century simplify the marinade to *fines herbes*, lemon juice, and olive oil. After a couple of hours in either marinade, the chicken pieces are sponged dry and either dredged in flour or dipped in batter and fried. I have found the archaic marinade to be better with chicken legs and prefer the simpler modern version with breasts. The total eclipse of *marinade de poulet* is even less comprehensible in view of the excruciating poverty of integral flavor in the commercially raised chicken of today and of its crying need for outside support. A marinated whole chicken, split down the back, opened, flattened, legs fixed through slits in the abdominal skin (preparation identical to that of the split, stuffed chicken except for loosening and stuffing the skin), grilled over a well-sustained but not violently hot bed of coals (about 40 minutes in all, turning several times and basting, but counting a good two thirds of the cooking time, beginning and finishing, with the split-open surface face to the coals), is delicious, and young guinea fowl or pheasant prepared like this and kept slightly underdone is a revelation. A potato *paillasson* is the perfect accompaniment.

SAUTÉED CHICKEN AND FENNEL
(Poulet Sauté Eygalières)
(for 4)

4 pounds bulb fennel, tougher outer stalks removed (saved for soups
or other preparation), "strings" pulled from surface of exposed stalks
(like stringing celery), bulbs split, parboiled 5 or 6 minutes, drained
Salt
⅓ cup olive oil
2 heads garlic, cloves separated, superficial chaff removed, unpeeled
Pepper
1 chicken, cut up (or 4 or 5 legs, thighs and drumsticks separated or not,
as preferred)
½ cup dry white wine
Liver, heart, and fleshy lobes of gizzard, cut into small pieces and tossed
rapidly, seasoned, in a few drops of olive oil over a high flame
Chopped parsley mixed with finely chopped feathery fennel leaves

Cook parboiled fennel halves and garlic cloves, salted, in preheated olive oil (large *plat à sauter* or skillet) over medium heat
for about ½ hour, turning the contents carefully from time to
time, until lightly colored. Transfer, neatly arranged, to a large
gratin dish, draining the cooking oil back into the pan, grind pepper
over the fennel, and keep hot in the oven while sautéing the chicken.

Sauté the chicken, first seasoned, in the same oil until nicely
colored on all sides, arrange the pieces on the bed of fennel and
garlic, deglaze the skillet with the white wine, scraping sides and
bottom with a wooden spoon and reducing by about half, dribble
over surface of the chicken, press a sheet of aluminum foil over the
surface (which prevents drying out from direct contact with heat
while permitting the braising juices to evaporate and reduce).
Count 35 to 40 minutes in a medium (375°) oven. Remove the
aluminum foil, scatter over the freshly tossed giblets and the chopped
herbs, and serve.

STUFFED, BRAISED CHICKEN LEGS WITH FENNEL
(Cuisses de Poularde Farcies, Braisées au Fenouil)
(for 4)

Substitute any stuffing you like if the truffle peels are not easily come by—one of those suggested for the split, stuffed, and baked chicken or simply a fabrication of breadcrumbs, egg, herbs, dried or fresh, precooked onion or raw garlic purée . . . Stuffed legs may, of course, be treated like any of the stews as long as the elements in the stuffing marry with those in the sauce.

A mixture similar to the truffle stuffing was recently fabricated in one of my classes to stuff raviolis (the fat pork was replaced by a chunk of white cheese and an egg yolk was added). They were, justifiably, a great hit, served with bubbling brown butter poured over, no cheese.

If the truffle stuffing is retained, it is best to bone and stuff the legs the preceding day to permit the truffle aroma to penetrate the chicken's flesh.

To Bone the Legs

Cut off the knobs from the drumstick bones, severing the tendons. Using a small, sharply pointed knife, slit the flesh on the skinless surface the length of the thigh bone, forcing the bone free mostly with fingertips, knife tip aiding to sever the tendon attachments at each extremity and to separate it from the drumstick bone. Free the flesh from the upper end of the drumstick bone in the same way and gently pull the bone, holding the leg in the other hand, thumb and curled forefinger pressed against the bone to prevent the flesh's being torn loose as the bone slips out.

Stuffing	½ small garlic clove
	Salt, pepper
	1 pinch each crumbled dried thyme and oregano
	3 ounces truffle pieces and peelings
	1 mounded tablespoon grated or finely chopped fresh pork fatback

375

Handful (1 ounce) finely crumbled stale but not dry
bread, crusts removed

1 tablespoon Cognac

Stock (1 or 2 tablespoons to moisten)

4 boned chicken legs

2 pounds bulb fennel, prepared and parboiled as in
preceding recipe

⅓ cup (3 ounces; 6 tablespoons) butter (in all)

Salt, pepper

Veal or chicken stock (2 to 3 cups—to cover)

Pound the garlic to a paste with the seasonings and the herbs,
add the truffle debris, and pound until reduced to a granular purée.
Add the fatback and the breadcrumbs, sprinkle with Cognac, and
mash with a fork (or work with your hands), adding enough stock
to bring it to a malleable consistency.

Stuff the legs (without packing—the flesh shrinks and the
stuffing swells). Each leg will use something less than a foot of
string, but the work is easier if a much longer length is threaded to
the trussing needle. Sew the borders of the skin together, starting
at the top of the leg, run the needle through the drumstick tip, and
tie the two ends of string together, pulling gently to form a neat
package of the stuffed leg.

Cook the fennel, seasoned, in half the butter over medium
heat, tossing or turning it from time to time, for about ½ hour.
Remove to a plate and color the seasoned stuffed legs in the same
fat. Return the fennel, if the receptacle is earthenware or heavy
copper (if a skillet is used for coloring, transfer everything to a
casserole, deglazing the skillet with some of the stock and pouring it
over), arranging neatly to permit maximum covering with minimum
liquid, pour over stock to cover, and cook, covered, at a bare simmer,
for about 50 minutes, degreasing the surface two or three times and,
after ½ hour, gently turning the legs over.

Remove legs and fennel, draining well, clip the strings and
remove them from the legs, pour the cooking juices into a small
saucepan, and return fennel and legs to their casserole, placing the
legs on the bed of fennel. Keep covered in a warm place while reducing the braising juices.

376

Lift as much fat as possible from the surface of the liquid, skim (skin) for 10 minutes or so, a light boil maintained at one side of the pan, and when no more fat is visible, reduce by half over a high flame. Whisk in the remaining butter (softened or cut into small pieces) away from the heat and pour over the meat and fennel.

BRAISED CHICKEN LEGS WITH LEMON
(Poulet au Citron)
(for 4)

The lemon and garlic alliance is borrowed from French Catalan cooking. Were the dish prepared in that country, Banyuls, a fortified wine vinified in much the same way as Port, would replace the white wine in this recipe.

Serve a plain, uncondimented pilaf or parboiled and steamed rice as an accompaniment.

20 to 25 large, firm, crisp garlic cloves, peeled without crushing, parboiled for 5 minutes, and drained
2½ cups veal or chicken stock
4 chicken legs
Salt, pepper
3 tablespoons butter
1 lemon, peeled (all white inner peel removed), thinly sliced, seeds removed
2 tablespoons flour
½ cup dry white wine

Poach the parboiled garlic cloves for about 40 minutes in the stock, covered, kept at a slight simmer.

Color the seasoned chicken legs in butter over medium heat (20 to 25 minutes) and transfer them to an oven casserole. Strain the stock to remove the garlic cloves, taking care not to damage them. Scatter the garlic over the chicken pieces, distribute the lemon slices, and put the casserole aside, covered, until the sauce is prepared.

Remove any excess fat from the pan in which the chicken was browned (leaving just enough to absorb the flour), add the flour and cook, stirring, over low heat for a few moments. Deglaze with the white wine over high heat, stirring and scraping with a wooden spoon, add the stock, and pour into a small saucepan; this is important, the small surface permitting a more rapid and complete skimming and degreasing of the sauce while preventing, at the same time, an exaggerated reduction. Skim (skin) for about 15 minutes, removing any traces of loose fat from the surface with absorbent paper. Pour the sauce over the chicken and its garnish and cook, covered, in a 375° to 400° oven for 40 to 45 minutes. The lemon will have almost completely disappeared into the sauce; the garlic cloves should be absolutely intact with a consistency of melting purée; the sauce must be tasted to be believed.

GARLIC CHICKEN
(Poulet "aux 40 Gousses d'Ail")
(for 4)

The garlic, squeezed from its hull and spread onto grilled crisp slices of rough country bread as one eats the chicken, will be appreciated by all who do not share the mental antigarlic quirk; if the bread can be grilled over hot coals, the light smoky flavor will be found to marry particularly well with the garlic purée.

For variety's sake, turn, quarter, and choke 3 or 4 tender young artichokes, coating them immediately in the recipe's olive oil before mixing all the ingredients together.

1 chicken, cut up as for a sauté (or 4 legs, thighs and drumsticks, separated)
4 heads (6 ounces) firm garlic, broken into cloves, cleared of loose hulls, but unpeeled
⅔ cup olive oil
Salt, pepper
1 teaspoon finely crumbled mixed dried herbs (thyme, oregano, savory)
1 large bouquet garni: large branch celery, parsley and root (if available), bay leaf, leek greens, small branch lovage (if available)
Flour for dough

Put everything except the bouquet into an earthenware casserole, turning around and over repeatedly with your hands to be

378

certain of regularly dispersed seasoning and liberal and even coating of oil. Force the bouquet into the center, packing the chicken around and filling all interstices with garlic cloves. Prepare a dough of flour, water, and a dribble of oil, roll it into a long cylindrical band on a floured board, moisten the ridge of the casserole, press the roll of paste into place, and press the lid on top. Cook in a 350° oven for 1 hour and 45 minutes and break the seal of paste at the table.

CHICKEN GRATIN
(Poulet au Gratin)
(for 4)

The recipe is given for a whole chicken. It is best prepared with pieces all of a kind. Wings lend themselves perfectly. If prepared with breasts, they should be only just colored in the sautéing process, the flesh not quite firm from cooking.

The acidity of the white wine and the lemon causes the cheese custard to curdle during the cooking, creating a texture that, personally, I find pleasant but which may not please everyone. Try it . . .

> 1 frying chicken, cut up
> Salt
> 2 tablespoons butter
> Large handful finely crumbled stale but not dry bread, crusts removed, crumbled
> ⅓ cup white wine

Cheese Custard ¾ cup heavy cream
> 3 egg yolks
> Salt, pepper
> 3 ounces freshly grated Gruyère
> Juice of ½ lemon and deglazing liquid

Salt the chicken pieces and cook them in the butter over a medium heat until nearly done and lightly colored on all sides— about 20 minutes, adding the breasts only after the first 10 minutes. Transfer them to a gratin dish of a size to just hold them, arranged side by side. Cook the crumbs in the chicken's cooking butter until slightly crisp and only slightly colored—still blond, stirring. Put them aside (don't worry if a few remain in the pan) and deglaze the pan with the white wine, reducing it by about half.

Whisk together the cream, egg yolks, seasonings, and cheese, then incorporate the lemon and the deglazing liquid. Spoon or pour the mixture evenly over the chicken pieces, sprinkle the surface with the breadcrumbs, and bake at 400° for 20 to 25 minutes or until the surface is nicely colored and the custard is firm.

PROVENÇAL CHICKEN PILAF
(Poulet Sauté au Riz à la Provençale)
(for 4)

Sautés, stews, trussed whole chickens, and chicken pilafs, all doctored to suit the Mediterranean palate with olive oil, tomato, cayenne, garlic, peppers, onions, olives . . . are abandoned to a confusion of names that shift aimlessly among ingredients and garnishes from one reference book to another, *poulet à la Nimoise, à la Niçoise,* or *à la Basquaise* in one becoming *à la Vauclusienne, à l'Arlésienne,* or *à la Marseillaise* in the other—none all that different from *à la Portugaise* or *à l'Espagnole.*

If prepared in a sauce, rather than as an element in a pilaf, deglaze with white wine after the vegetables have been sautéed, and add tomatoes at that time, preparing a pilaf, plain or saffroned, apart as accompaniment.

Butter-stewed artichoke hearts may be added at the same time as the olives; slices of eggplant fried in olive oil and drained and/or coin-thin slices of zucchini sautéed rapidly in olive oil provide a delicious terminal garnish. For a guestless meal, prepare it with wings alone—or leftover backs and necks.

1 cut-up chicken (or 4 legs)
Salt
3 tablespoons olive oil
1 medium onion, chopped

1 large sweet red or green pepper, emptied of seeds and cut into narrow strips
3 cloves garlic, finely chopped
1 cup long-grain rice (preferably non-treated), rinsed and well drained
1 teaspoon crumbled oregano flowers
About ⅛ teaspoon saffron (to taste)
1 pinch whole saffron flowers (for effect)
Small pinch cayenne
Handful pitted rinsed black olives (not strongly flavored—the Niçoises are the best, but do not bother to pit them)
1½ cups boiling water (or chicken stock)
3 large ripe tomatoes, peeled, seeded, and cut up (or, out of season, preserved tomatoes)
1 tablespoon butter
Pepper
½ teaspoon sugar
Fresh basil (if unavailable, substitute chopped parsley)

Use a large heavy copper *plat à sauter* or a wide earthenware *poëlon*. Brown the chicken pieces, salted, in the olive oil, remove them to a plate, and replace them by the onion and pepper, cooking over low flame and stirring regularly until soft and lightly colored. Sprinkle with salt (if moistening with chicken stock, take its saltiness into consideration), add the chopped garlic and the rice, stirring regularly with a wooden spoon until the rice turns milky-opaque in aspect, sprinkle over the oregano, the two saffrons, and the cayenne, stirring until the rice is saffron-stained, scatter over the olives, pour in the boiling liquid, and put back the chicken pieces, adding any juices that may have drained from them. Cover and cook over very low heat, a bare murmur at the liquid's surface, for 15 minutes.

Gently stew the tomatoes, seasoned, sugar added, in the butter, stirring or tossing occasionally. Add them to the pilaf, strewing them regularly over the surface with their juices, without disturbing the rice, and leave again, tightly covered, over low heat, for another 15 minutes. Remove from heat, sprinkle surface with torn-up basil leaves and flowers, cover, and let stand another 5 minutes or so before serving.

381

SPLIT, STUFFED, BAKED CHICKEN
(Poulet Fendu Farci au Four)
(for 4)

This recipe has excited a great deal of enthusiasm in my classes. It seems to be possessed of a multitude of virtues, the ease of its preparation and the beauty of its presentation being not among the least; the breasts, moreover, being both protected from the direct onslaught of heat and nourished by the melting fats of the stuffing, remain moist and are delicately perfumed; the skin, basted from within as well as from without, crispens evenly to a rich golden brown, a miracle of beauty and flavor; it is elastic and, unlike stuffed flesh, will not shrink in contact with the heat, splitting beneath the pressure of a swelling forcemeat. I have often packed as much as a 2-inch thickness of stuffing between most parts of the flesh and the skin with perfect results.

Carving presents no problem, and it would be a pity not to carve it at table. A fairly large, stiff-bladed boning knife, which is, nonetheless, a good bit smaller than the usual carving knife, is the easiest to work with; split the bird in two (the breast bone, wishbone, and collar bone, having been broken and partially separated when the bird was flattened out, offer little resistance); delicately cut through the skin and the stuffing with the knife tip, in an arc described by the leg joint and the contour of the thigh, from the split edge to the outside extremity of the thigh; slip the knife beneath the thigh, loosening it, and far down, at the point of its contact with the backbone, cut through the fragment of vertebra—the breast and the leg will slip apart.

The stuffings I find most interesting are a *cheese and fresh sage* ravioli filling (3 ounces ricotta or other fresh white cheese mashed with 4 tablespoons softened butter, an egg beaten in, seasoning, several finely chopped fresh young sage leaves, chopped parsley, and, finally, a large handful of freshly grated Parmesan and a small handful of breadcrumbs), *spinach* (same recipe as the filling for stuffed *crêpes*—see page 229), *zucchini* (recipe following), and *mushroom* (like the preceding recipes, the vegetable being replaced by 8 or 10 ounces of mushrooms, finely chopped or passed through the medium

382

blade of a Mouli-juliènne and sautéed in butter over high heat until dry, a bit of lemon added). A handful of rapidly parboiled little peas or skinned tender broad beans is an attractive addition to the mushroom stuffing, or it can be treated to more fanciful variations: A quantity of unpeeled garlic cloves gently stewed with eggplant in olive oil until both are purée-tender, the two sieved together and incorporated into the cheese and mushroom mixture is quite spectacular; shredded prosciutto may be added, as may be dried morels, soaked and butter-stewed; retaining the sautéed juliènned mushroom base, the cheeses may be eliminated, the mushrooms mixed only with breadcrumbs and softened butter—*fines herbes* will help— or soft crumbs soaked in heavy cream; mushrooms, crumbs, and snail butter mashed together, and so forth . . . An egg binds but is not absolutely necessary. If the vegetable preparations are added still hot or warm to the butter and cheese mixtures, the whole becomes soupy and difficult to manage; cool them or chill them first.

The stuffing may often be sufficient garnish in itself; a potato *paillasson* (see page 217) is a perfect supplementary garnish.

To Prepare the Chicken for Stuffing

Note: The following directions are for chickens as they are usually dressed, throat and abdomen ripped open, for the American market; in France, chickens are bled from the beak and the intestines are unraveled through the anus before being marketed, the skin being punctured at no point. If you have the good luck to find an unemptied chicken (Kosher butchers sell them), singe it, cut off the head, the oil duct above the tail, and the feet at a halfway point, leaving about 1½ inches beyond the drumstick heel (the extra length makes it much easier to secure the leg ends in the abdominal slits); slit the neck skin along the *back*, detach it from the neck without tearing it, cut off the neck and split the chicken down the back before emptying it; the abdominal skin thus remains intact, as does the neck skin, which serves as a flap that folds over the throat opening and is tucked beneath the stuffed chicken, sealing it.

Split the chicken the entire length of the back, beginning at the tail, using heavy poultry shears, and cutting it, as nearly as possible, through the center of the backbone. Open it out on a chopping board, skin side up, the joints joining drumstick and thigh forced inward, facing. With the flat side of a mallet or cleaver—or with the heel of your hand—flatten it out with a firm (even violent) whack, fracturing breastbone, ribcage structure, collarbone, and wishbone (don't try to remove any of the broken ribs from beneath —they are attached to thin sheets of flesh that help contain the stuffing).

Only at the summit of the breastbone, at the extremities of the drumsticks, and, to each side, the length of the spinal column is the skin securely attached to the flesh by tendons; it should remain so at these points. Elsewhere only fragile and easily ruptured membranes keep skin and flesh together. Take care not to tear the skin (intact, it is supple and resistant to tearing but, once a section is torn, the flaw transforms itself easily into a gaping wound): Work, first with fingertips and, as the skin is progressively loosened, with your entire hand, reaching in through the throat cavity and separating the skin, first from one breast, then from the thigh, and, finally, from the drumstick. Before you have the drumstick in your hand, your fist and wrist will be nearly lost to view (proof of the skin's supple resistance); repeat with the other breast and leg. If the butcher's original damage was serious, now is the time to patch things up with a needle and some kitchen string. Cut off the wing tips at the second joint, leaving shoulder section attached—or fold them under.

	1 split chicken, skin loosened
Marinade	1 teaspoon crumbled mixed dried herbs (thyme, oregano, savory)
	3 tablespoons olive oil
Stuffing	3 ounces fresh white cheese (ricotta or cream cheese— or cheese may be replaced by 2 ounces soft breadcrumbs, soaked and mashed with ⅓ cup heavy cream)
	⅓ cup butter (in all: 2 tablespoons for sautéing zucchini; 1 tablespoon for stewing onion; the remainder for stuffing)
	Salt, pepper
	Large pinch finely chopped fresh marjoram leaves and flowers (if unavailable, substitute fines herbes)

Chicken split and stuffed beneath the skin, ready for roasting

1 egg
1 medium onion, finely chopped, stewed gently in butter
    for 15 minutes without coloring, cooled
1 pound small, firm zucchini, juliènned, salted, squeezed,
    sautéed, and cooled (see page 243 for method)
Large handful freshly grated Parmesan

Sprinkle the chicken on both sides (but not beneath the skin) with herbs, pat and rub generously with olive oil, and leave to marinate for an hour or two.

385

Mash the white cheese and butter together with seasonings and fresh herbs, using a fork; add the egg, mashing; then, stirring briskly, put in the onion and the zucchini, and, finally, the Parmesan, adding enough to bring the stuffing to a firm, stiff consistency.

Stuff the chicken, taking a handful of stuffing at a time and forcing it into place, pushing with the fingers of one hand beneath the skin while molding and forcing with the other from the outside. Coat drumsticks and thighs well first before worrying about the breasts. When all of the stuffing is in place, fold the neck-skin flap (if there is any) over the throat orifice and tuck it beneath the bird. With a small sharply pointed knife, pierce the web of skin and thin flesh between the inside of the thigh and the tip of the breast, making a slit just large enough to receive the drumstick tip. Force the drumstick gently up and push its tip through the slit to the underside. Place the bird in its roasting pan (a large skillet or a round, shallow earthenware baking dish are ideal receptacles) and mold the surface with your hands to force the skin and stuffing into a plump version of the natural form. Salt and pepper and roast, starting at 450° and turning the oven down to about 375° some 10 minutes later. Start basting regularly after ½ hour. Count 50 minutes to 1 hour, depending on the size of the chicken, and if, after about 40 minutes, it seems to be coloring too rapidly, turn the oven down further, placing a sheet of aluminum foil loosely over the bird.

Transfer to a round, heated serving platter; don't attempt to serve the juices—they are too fat and the dish needs no sauce (chill scrapings and juices, discard the fat, and use for flavoring a dish of leftovers).

GRILLED CHICKEN BREAST ROLLS
(Filets de Volaille en Crottes d'Âne)
(for 4)

4 chicken breasts, boned and skin removed

Handful chopped fines herbes (parsley, chervil, chives, tarragon—whichever available)

1 heaping tablespoon finely chopped shallots (preferably gray shallots—if neither gray nor red are available, substitute onion and a couple of crushed cloves of garlic, the latter to be discarded after the marination)

½ teaspoon finely crumbled oregano flowers
3 or 4 ounces finely chopped mushrooms
The juice of ½ lemon (1 tablespoon)
3 tablespoons olive oil
Coarsely ground pepper (or peppercorns crushed in a mortar)
Salt

Make certain that no fragment of bone remains attached to the breast. Open them out, separating the filet from the filet mignon to form an approximate heart shape, flatten with the side of a cleaver or a large knife, and spread them out on a platter covered with all the ingredients except salt. Turn them around and over several times during a 1- or 2-hour period. Salt each filet lightly, coat well with the chopped vegetables from the marinade, roll it up carefully, and fix with 3 or 4 toothpicks. Salt the outside lightly and grill on a preheated grill for from 10 to 12 minutes, turning them every 2 or 3 minutes and basting regularly the colored surfaces, adding more olive oil to the marinade if necessary.

CHICKEN BREASTS AND ZUCCHINI WITH MARJORAM
(Blancs de Volaille Sautés aux Courgettes à la Marjolaine)
(for 2 or 3)

1 pound zucchini, thinly sliced
Salt, pepper
2 tablespoons butter
1 teaspoon finely chopped fresh flowers and leaves of marjoram (substitute ½ teaspoon finely crumbled dry, if necessary—or switch to fresh tarragon)
The breasts of 1 large chicken, skin, bones, and fat removed, filets and filets mignons separated and cut into strips ½ inch thick by 2 inches in length
½ cup heavy cream

Use, preferably, a heavy copper *sautoir* or *plat à sauter*. Toss the zucchini, seasoned, in 1 tablespoon butter over a high flame for about 6 minutes—until barely tender and hardly colored. Toss in the marjoram and put aside. In the same pan, with the other tablespoon of butter, over a high flame, toss the seasoned breast strips for no more than 3 minutes. They may stick at first; gently displace with a wooden spoon. As soon as they become firm and rubbery, return the zucchini to the pan, toss the two well together, add the cream, swirl, and toss. It is ready when the cream reaches a boil. Accompany by a pilaf.

CHICKEN LIVER CUSTARD
(Flan de Foies de Volaille)
(for 4)

Restaurant owners in the Lyonnaise and Bressoise regions faithfully serve a crayfish sauce with this custard. It is a marriage dictated by tradition (and by Lucien Tendret) rather than by harmony. A creamed tomato sauce, a *sauce suprême*, or a rapid *sauce bâtarde* (see page 326) will all serve perfectly. A chicken liver custard is an exquisite thing, but it does not take well to garnish and belongs to the realm of first courses. Cold, it is another kind of splendor and needs no sauce.

A custard (liver or not) that is subjected to an excess of heat, be it ever so slight, will break; the body (which, when correctly cooked, is set in a moist and trembling, tender suspension) shrinks within itself, shot with holes bound in a honeycomb of vaguely rubbery structure, its precious liquid cast off in the unmolding. It is difficult, under the circumstances, to give precise oven temperatures; the important thing is that the water of the *bain-marie* must never approach a boil. Keep an eye on it and, if there is the slightest suggestion of a simmer, turn the thermostat down further, leaving the oven door open for a minute to reduce the heat.

Considering the relatively small proportion of livers (they make up less than one third of the bulk of the mixture), the result has an astonishingly pure-liver effect; the quantity may be reduced for a more custardy effect and a more attenuated liver flavor.

6 to 8 ounces chicken livers (all traces of green stain removed)
2 ounces beef marrow (pried out of bone, not poached)
1 clove garlic, puréed
1¾ cups milk

2 eggs
3 egg yolks
Salt, pepper
Butter (for mold)

The liver, the marrow, and the crushed garlic may be reduced together to a purée in a blender or with a mortar and pestle. In any case, the resultant purée must be stirred together with all the other ingredients, the lot passed through a fine sieve and whisked until smooth. Pour into a generously buttered 3-pint charlotte mold, into the bottom of which has been pressed a round of buttered parchment paper (fold a square of paper in quarters and continue folding, over and over, from the central point to the center of the triangular base until only a wide-based needle remains; measure it out from the approximate center of the overturned mold, clip off the excess, open it out, and butter it). Cook in a *bain-marie* (the mold placed on a small grill or folded towel within a larger container that is filled with warm but not hot water to the level of the custard surface—about two thirds of the mold's height) in a 300° to 325° oven for about 1 hour and 15 minutes, or until the center is firm to the touch, the edges having just begun to shrink from the sides. Leave to relax for 5 or 6 minutes before unmolding; when unmolded, delicately peel off the round of paper, and, if you like, coat lightly with the chosen sauce, serving the rest in a sauceboat apart.

PRESERVED GOOSE *(CONFIT D'OIE)*

Foie gras, itself, remains, even in the regions of its production, a luxury product, gracing the tables only on very special occasions. It enjoys, there, a quality of reverence shared, perhaps, only by the truffle. (I once listened in amazement to a Périgord farmwife describing—in what was intended to be a vehement denial that the raising of geese destined to produce foie gras involves cruelty to animals—the tenderness and gentleness with which the birds are treated and, with mounting enthusiasm and in the most extraordinarily sensuous

389

language, the suspense and the excitement experienced as the moment arrives to delicately slit the abdomen, to lovingly—ever so gently—pry it open, exposing finally the huge, glorious, and tender blond treasure, fragile object of so many months' solicitous care and of present adoration. One sensed vividly the goose's plenary participation, actively sharing in the orgasmic beauty of the sublime moment for which her life had been lived.)

Duck foies gras are rarely tinned commercially and a large proportion of them remain to embellish the home tables, but the prized fattened goose livers are mostly sold, fresh or sterilized, far from home. Their by-products, however—rendered goose fat and preserved goose—remain to stamp a distinctly different personality on the cooking throughout the southwestern part of France. Perhaps the best way to understand, analytically, the flavor that goose fat can impart to a preparation is to sauté raw potatoes, cut to any form, in it—and its power to refine a texture is perfectly demonstrated in a *garbure*. Omelets are prepared in goose fat, macaroni is flavored with it, soup vegetables are removed from the soup, fried in goose fat, and returned to the pot (unless you prefer to spread it on toast while eating foie gras, the fat from a tin of foie gras should be scrupulously saved for some small preparation that will appreciate it)—in short, goose fat permeates this food no less than does butter the food of Normandy or olive oil the food of Provence. The indigens' claim that it is the only altogether digestible cooked fat should be taken with a grain of salt.

Only a goose especially fattened for the production of foie gras will be fat enough to be preserved in its own fat without a compensating addition of lard. In a country where not only is this practice abhorred, but where the deep freeze has replaced most other methods of preservation, to preserve a goose may seem like a quaint anomaly. Necessity, today, plays no role, but the necessity of the past through which a unique flavor was created may tempt us to imitate its methods to recapture a glimpse of a world apart—there is no other way to an empathic comprehension of the soul of cooking throughout the entire lower lefthand corner of the map of France.

Confit d'oie is often served simply reheated, lightly browned in a bit of its fat, and garnished with potatoes or cèpes sautéed in goose fat, or sometimes with sorrel purée stewed in goose fat . . . Those who have not grown up on preserved goose will best appreciate it reheated in an undersalted liquid preparation (warmed for ½ hour in a pot of lentils or beans and added to any of a variety of thick vegetable soups); this produces an interchange normalizing both elements.

The neck (skin) is, traditionally, stuffed and preserved also, rewarmed in a pot of lentils or braised cabbage, sliced to serve—or served cold, sliced thinly like a sausage, as an hors d'oeuvre. If your goose passes through normal commercial channels, the neck will be in no condition for stuffing; order it from a Kosher butcher or ask a farmer to behead it close to the neck, keeping the neck skin intact. Remove it at the time of cutting up the goose, first cutting off the wings at the shoulder joints and separating the neck skin from the rest by cutting, front and back, between the holes left by the removed wings. Peel the skin backwards from the body toward the head end and off the neck, turning it right side out again. Sew up the small end, stuff it with the finely chopped liver, fleshy lobes of gizzard, heart, and lungs of the goose, a thick, boned, chopped pork chop, herbs, spices, and seasonings to taste, sew the large end closed, even out the stuffing in its enclosure with your hands, and refrigerate until the salted goose is ready to be cooked. Chopped truffle peelings are often added. Peeled chopped pistachios or a few green peppercorns may be added . . .

An approximately 8-pound goose (or 5½ to 6 pounds cleaned and cut up)
Herbs (bay leaf, thyme, oregano, savory)
About ½ cup (4 ounces) coarse (or Kosher) salt
The goose's fat
1 pound lard (more or less depending on the quantity of fat contained in the goose)
About ⅔ cup water

If you have a bird with feet still attached, remove them, blister the skin of the feet regularly over a flame, and remove it with the help of a towel or paper toweling. Cut the bird up, breast split in two, legs left whole, neck detached from back, back cut into 3 or 4 flat-shaped pieces; wings and feet.

Sprinkle salt and herbs into the bottom of a large stoneware jar, an earthenware *marmite*, or a porcelain or enameled ironware receptacle, taller than it is wide, pack in layers of the goose pieces, sprinkling each layer with salt and herbs. Leave, covered, in the coolest part of the house for 2 days and 2 nights.

Wipe the pieces dry with a clean towel (paper toweling will turn soggy, fragments will tear loose and cling to the flesh), discarding liquid and herbs in the jar.

Put the goose fat, lard, and water into a large skillet or *plat à sauter*, heat over medium low flame, and when the lard is melted but before the goose fat is entirely melted, arrange the cut-up goose in the pan so that, as nearly as possible, all pieces are submerged. Cook, covered, lowering the flame if necessary to keep the fat only lightly bubbling. The neck, feet, and wings may be removed after about 50 minutes to 1 hour (the stuffed goose neck, which requires about 45 minutes, replacing them). The larger pieces require from 1½ hours to 1¾ hours.

The stuffed neck, which will be eaten in the days to come, can be cooled, wrapped in plastic, and refrigerated. Arrange the other pieces in a stoneware jar or other non-metallic container (not glass, which would break in contact with the hot fat), closely, leaving a minimum of air space, and pour over the hot fat, completely covering them. Leave to cool and refrigerate, tightly covered (heavy aluminum foil held in place with a rubber band, for instance). To remove pieces of *confit* without damaging them, it is usually necessary to heat the jar in a *bain-marie* until the fat is melted, making certain each time that all remaining pieces are submerged before permitting the fat to congeal again.

DESSERTS

MANY people are happy to finish a meal with cheese, especially if a red wine other than that served with the principal course has been chosen to accompany the cheese platter. For others, a glass or two of a fine Sauternes, unaccompanied, is welcome and sufficient food and drink at the end of a meal. Fresh fruit is a good dessert. In season, fresh strawberries, peaches, or figs (the latter peeled, a cross cut into the upper part of each, pinched open like a baked potato and well chilled), coated with a raspberry purée (fresh or deep-frozen raspberries passed either through a nylon drum sieve with a pastry cook's *corne* or plastic disc or through a stainless steel sieve with a wooden pestle and sweetened to taste) are a perfect dessert; peeled fresh almonds may be scattered on top or whipped cream diluted with raspberry purée served on the side. (The acidity may, to some extent, interfere with the perfect analytical appreciation of an accompanying Sauternes). Or one's glass of red wine filled with fresh strawberries or sliced peaches, sugar-sprinkled, will terminate a meal in beauty.

France produces many dessert wines other than Sauternes; many tend to be flat and flabby in effect—cloying but otherwise destitute of character (this may be true also of generic Sauternes, whose

393

labels indicate no more specific origin). None has the depth or the intricate structure of a Sauternes at its best—the nervous, sensuous, pulsating body whose background of delicately etched bitterness lends relief to and is masked by a complexity of fresh and sun-dried fruit associations and whose sweetness is vibrant. These astounding wines are so consistently pitted against quarrelsome desserts that it is not surprising to see the Sauternais wine growers arising indignantly in a body to condemn their being served at the end of a meal, dictating instead that they assume the role of apéritif or that of companion to foie gras, avocados, fish in sauce, or Roquefort cheese. Celebrated menus of the past are cited to prove that the time-honored placement of a Sauternes is at the head of a menu—and it is true that a Château d'Yquem very often opened the gamut of wines (Champagne inevitably closed it, which, although "brut" was not then fashionable, is compelling enough proof that the taste of our ancestors was not invincible).

Not only is it difficult to ally a Sauternes successfully to a first course, but it is also practically impossible to follow it with a wine, red or white, that will not suffer from its juxtaposition to the penetrating intensity of the Sauternes—nor, for my part, can there be any question of drinking a Sauternes throughout a meal. Few, moreover, would deny that a brut Champagne or other dry white wine is a truer apéritif or appetite sharpener. It seems to me wiser to search out those desserts that best accompany the wines of Sauternes rather than to risk unbalancing a menu by their displacement.

The cellars of our gastronomic temples all harbor great Sauternes from rich vintages—noblesse oblige—but their menus rarely list a single dessert of a discretion designed to flatter or to lend relief to their qualities. Sauternes are best served well iced—colder even than most white wines—and certain hot or tepid desserts will afford an exciting contrast (ices and ice creams will annihilate any wine, as will excessive sweetness; the proximity of chocolate is a disaster; desserts soaked or blazed in distilled alcohols will paralyze the palate). The dessert should be less sweet than the wine itself. The richer the wine, the greater is one's choice of dessert possibilities. The best recent vintages are 1962, 1967, and 1970; the greatest "living" Sauternes are probably still the fantastic 1921s, but it is possible that the '67s will develop into near peers. A wine like the admirable Château Filhot, which, although lacking none of the depth and vitality of its more classical neighbors, tends to be somewhat less sweet and lighter of body, may be more difficult to place on a dessert: Hot or tepid apple desserts are among the most perfect of Sauternes companions (baked apples; fritters; sliced apples sautéed in butter, rolled, unsweetened, into *crêpes*, arranged in a buttered gratin dish, sprinkled with sugar—heavy cream may first be spooned over— and heated in a hot oven until the sugar is lightly caramelized; half-baked pastry shell lined with butter-stewed sliced apples, a sugared quiche mixture of beaten eggs and heavy cream poured over, baked until swelled and set; or a discreetly sweetened American butter-crust apple pie . . .). Eating pears (slightly underripe, halved, peeled, and cored, simmered for a couple of hours in red wine with sugar, a pinch of cinnamon, and a strip of orange peel, served tepid or cold), fresh figs (peeled, sprinkled with sugar, a film of water in the bottom of the pan, baked for 20 minutes in a hot oven), dried figs (simmered in wine, with or without thyme), peaches (peeled and poached in a red wine and sugar syrup, the poaching liquid radically reduced to serve as a sauce), or the *raisiné,* a variety of seasonal fruits stewed in the unfermented must drawn from the newly filled wine vats, which is made in all wine-growing areas at the time of the grape harvest (you can approximate it by boiling up ripe, black-skinned grapes, straining them through a sieve, reducing somewhat with sugar to taste, and simmering sliced apples and pears, whole figs, cubes of pumpkin—quince is often added—or whatever fruits are available, in the juice, stirring regularly to prevent sticking) also serve well. Nutty and, in particular, almond-flavored (but not *pralinés*) desserts marry well with Sauternes, as do any of the starchy puddings—bread; rice; noodle or vermicelli; tapioca; semolina . . .

With the exception of the melon ice, all of the following recipes will welcome an accompanying Sauternes.

ALMOND AND PISTACHIO LOAF
(Pain des Houris)
(for 4)

Served directly from the oven, this is a soufflé. Tepid, much of the body is lost, but the savors may more easily be appreciated. Cold, it is moist and compact, heavy but delicious.

Candied peels: 1 tablespoon each slivered strips of orange and lemon
  peel, parboiled for a few seconds and drained
⅓ cup water
1 tablespoon sugar

4 ounces shelled almonds, parboiled for a couple of minutes, rubbed
  between towels, and skinned
2 ounces shelled pistachios, treated as above
½ cup sugar (plus sugar for sprinkling on the surface)
¼ cup white wine
3 eggs, separated
Small pinch salt
1 tablespoon butter

Combine the juliènned, parboiled orange and lemon peels with
the sugar and water, bring to a boil, and simmer until the liquid is
almost entirely reduced, the peels coated with a thick syrup, but remove from the flame before the sugar begins to caramelize.

Pound the almonds and pistachios together in a mortar until
well crushed into a coarse purée, add the peels and a bit of sugar,
and continue pounding, adding sugar from time to time, until the
mixture becomes too stiff to work easily. Continue pounding, alternating additions of white wine and sugar until both are used up.
Add the egg yolks and work vigorously, pounding and stirring with
the pestle.

Beat the egg whites with the pinch of salt until they stand
firmly in peaks, fold a healthy spoonful into the mixture in the
mortar, then turn the contents of the mortar into the bowl containing the remaining egg whites, and fold the two gently together.

Pour into a buttered gratin dish and bake at 375°, the dish
immersed by half in a larger pan containing hot water, for about
25 minutes, or until the center of the pudding is firm to the touch.

APPLE AND BREAD PUDDING
(Pudding Crème aux Pommes)
(for 4)

For this and any of the following apple recipes, russet or Canadian apples will be the best choice. They are hard to find; use whatever varieties are available, leaning on the abundant Golden Delicious only as a last resort. Serve tepid, accompanied or not by a *sabayon* sauce (½ cup sugar, 3 egg yolks, ⅔ cup white wine, and a bit of grated lemon peel whisked in a small heavy saucepan in a *bain-marie* of nearly boiling water over low flame until thick—the water should not boil).

1 pound apples, quartered, cored, peeled, sliced
Large handful (about 2 ounces) stale breadcrumbs, without crusts
About ½ cup butter
Pinch powdered cinnamon
1 cup milk
2 eggs
⅓ cup sugar
Small pinch salt

Cook the apples in about 3 tablespoons butter, tossing from time to time, until tender and translucid—20 to 30 minutes. Cook the breadcrumbs in the remaining butter (eventually adding more if necessary) over very low heat, stirring regularly, until they are uniformly golden and crisp.

Spread the crumbs in the bottom of a lightly buttered gratin dish, arrange the apples on the bed of crumbs, sprinkle lightly with cinnamon, whisk together the milk, eggs, sugar, and salt, and pour the liquid slowly over the apples so as not to displace them. Bake at 325° for about ½ hour.

GRATED APPLE LOAF
(Pain de Pommes Rapées)
(for 4)

I am beholden to my sister-in-law, Judith Olney, for this recipe. Serve it hot or warm—not cold—accompanied or not by fresh heavy cream.

1 pound apples, quartered, cored, peeled, coarsely grated or passed through medium or fine blade of Mouli-juliènne
About ⅓ cup sugar (in all)
Pinch powdered cinnamon
4 ounces finely crumbled stale but not dried bread, without crusts
¾ cup butter

Mix the apples with ¼ cup sugar and the cinnamon. Mash the breadcrumbs, 2 or 3 tablespoons sugar, and ½ cup softened butter together with a fork. Melt the remaining ¼ cup butter in a small heavy frying pan and pack the breadcrumb mixture against the bottom and sides with a fork to form an even shell. Fill with the apple mixture, packing with the fork, and cook over a low flame, covered, for about 15 minutes or until the edges of the bread-crumb casing begin to show brown. Finish, uncovered, in the oven (375°) for another 15 minutes. If the contents of the pan do not slide freely with gentle shaking, loosen the bottom with a spatula before unmolding.

BAKED APPLE CURDS
(Brouillade aux Pommes)
(for 4)

Serve hot, tepid, or cold, with or without heavy cream.

1 pound apples, peeled, quartered, cored, sliced
¼ cup sugar (plus 2 tablespoons for sprinkling later)
3 eggs
Small pinch salt

Sprinkle the sliced apples with the sugar, tossing well, and leave, covered, overnight. Beat the eggs and the salt lightly, as for an omelet, and gently stir in the apples. Heat the butter in a heavy frying pan until bubbling, pour in the mixture, and, a few seconds later, transfer to a medium (350°) oven. Stir every 10 or 15 minutes, turning the mixture over in spoonfuls, chopping it with the side of the spoon, and smoothing the surface with the back of the spoon. Count 1 hour in all and, after 45 minutes, sprinkle with 2 table-spoons sugar, turn the oven higher, and if, after 15 minutes, the surface is not sufficiently caramelized, pass for a few seconds be-neath a hot broiler.

APPLE TART
(Tarte aux Pommes)
(for 4)

A *pâte sablée* or crumbly pastry, cookie-like, is the usual base also for jam tarts, a thin layer of jam replacing the apples in this recipe and a latticework of pastry strips pressed on top for decorative purposes. Any fairly thick puréed jam or fruit "butter" may replace the apri-cot jam as a glaze in this recipe—I usually use one made of wild plums.

Sablée pastry 1 cup flour
       3 tablespoons sugar
       ¼ cup softened butter
       Tiny pinch salt
       1 egg

       1 pound apples
       Sugar (to sprinkle surface of tart)
       Puréed apricot jam

Combine the pastry ingredients in a mixing bowl, stirring and mashing with a fork until fairly consistent, then work with finger-tips until everything is absorbed in a coherent mass. Transfer to a floured pastry marble or board and knead for a couple of minutes, pushing small sections of the mass against the floured surface and away from yourself with the heel of your hand; gather it together in a ball and begin again—it will, at this point, be soft and sticky; wrap it in plastic or waxed paper and refrigerate for at least a couple of hours.

If using a cookie sheet, butter it lightly. If your oven is fitted with a solid metal plaque, use it, removing it from the oven before heating and lining it with parchment paper or aluminum foil, the surface lightly buttered.

Roll out the dough as rapidly as possible, being certain that it is always lightly coated with flour—it sticks easily. Turn it over two or three times while rolling—the given proportions should form a circular sheet approximately 14 inches in diameter. Fold it and transfer it to the buttered plaque; then spread it out. It is extremely fragile; if it should tear, don't worry—patch it up. Roll the edges up to form a border, pressing all around with the tines of a fork.

Halve the apples, core them and peel them (don't do it ahead of time—they will turn brown). Slice each half crosswise into ⅛- to ¼-inch thicknesses and arrange the slices, starting just inside the border of the pastry, in concentric circles, slices overlapping and circles overlapping. Sprinkle the surface with sugar and bake in a 350° oven for about 1 hour, checking progress regularly after 45 minutes. Paint the surface of the apple slices with the puréed jam, using a pastry brush—or simply dribble it around with a teaspoon, smearing it regularly over the surface of each apple slice with the back of the spoon. Slip the tart onto a large flat, round platter; serve hot, tepid, or cold.

BREAD PUDDING
(Pudding au Pain)
(for 4)

3 ounces stale but not dry bread without crusts
1 cup milk
⅓ cup sugar
1 tablespoon Kirsch

Handful pistachios parboiled for a minute, rubbed in a towel to remove
skins, chopped
4 egg yolks
2 egg whites
1 tablespoon butter

Put the breadcrumbs to soak with the milk in a mixing bowl,
add the sugar, Kirsch, pistachios, and egg yolks, combining thoroughly, beat the egg whites until they stand in peaks, fold them in
gently, pour into a liberally buttered gratin dish and bake at 400°
to 450° for from 25 to 30 minutes or until swelled, browned, and
firm in the center. Serve directly from the oven. A *sabayon* sauce
(page 397) is probably the best accompaniment; apricot sauce or
crème Anglaise are also possibilities.

COFFEE CUSTARD
(Crème au Café)
(for 4)

These proportions will fill four small individual ramekins—small
portions, but it is a rich essence. It is good accompanied by heavy
cream. Serve at the same time simple butter cookies, *tuiles,* palm fans
(puff pastry sprinkled with sugar, rolled up from opposite edges to
meet, sliced crosswise, and baked), *pets de nonnes*, etc.

1 cup freshly ground coffee
1½ cups milk
Caramel: 2 tablespoons sugar; water
⅓ cup sugar
Tiny pinch salt
3 egg yolks

Stir together the coffee and 1 cup of milk in a saucepan over
medium flame until a full boil is reached, remove from the heat,
and leave to infuse until tepid. Strain through a sieve lined with a
cloth, pressing and twisting the cloth to extract as much milk as
possible.

401

Boil the 2 tablespoons sugar with 1 tablespoon water in a tiny saucepan, watching carefully—after the slurry boiling stage is passed, the sugar begins, first imperceptibly and then very rapidly to color. Remove from the heat the moment the right, rich, but not dark caramel color appears, pour in 2 or 3 tablespoons water and dissolve the caramel, stirring and returning to the heat for a few moments, if necessary.

Combine all the ingredients, whisk thoroughly, and cook in a *bain-marie* on top of the stove, the water kept just below the boiling point—or, if you are using a heavy copper saucepan, the custard may be cooked directly over a tiny flame. Stir constantly with a wooden spoon and remove from the heat as soon as the mixture is the consistency of a heavy sauce, coating the spoon easily—it must not approach the boiling point. Pour into ramekins or into a single deep serving dish and chill.

FIGS WITH THYME
(Figues au Thym)
(for 4 to 6)

1 pound dried figs
2 cups red wine
2 or 3 small branches of thyme (or ½ teaspoon crumbled dried thyme tied in a bit of muslin)
3 tablespoons honey

Combine all ingredients in a saucepan and cook at a simmer, covered, for about 1 hour, turning the figs over from time to time in their liquid if not completely covered. Remove the figs to a serving dish, discard the thyme, and reduce the cooking liquid over a high flame by about one third—or to the consistency of a light syrup—and pour over the figs. Good either tepid or chilled. Serve a dry cookie-like thing on the side.

MELON AND CHAMPAGNE ICE
(Granité de Melon au Champagne)
(4 to 6)

Buy more melons than you need and taste them before using them—flavorless melons will make a flavorless sherbet. If they are of a size that half shells will contain the right quantity for individual servings, cut them in two—if larger, lift off a lid as for a jack-o'-lantern to empty them, serving from the shells into sherbet glasses. In Europe, tiny melons no more than 2½ to 3 inches in diameter are perfect for individual servings; I have never seen such small versions of the American cantaloupe or muskmelon. If you have large enough deep-freezing facilities, deep freeze the shells, otherwise chill them thoroughly.

⅔ cup sugar
½ cup water
Cantaloupe melons to provide 2 cups purée
2 tablespoons lemon juice
1 cup iced Champagne
¼ cup Cognac

Boil the sugar and water together and leave to thoroughly cool before mixing it with the melon purée (sieved), lemon juice, and Champagne. Freeze in ice-cube trays, loosening the mixture from the sides and stirring from time to time, as it freezes. Best start it several hours ahead of time. Just before serving, turn it into an iced bowl, working it a bit with a fork if too firm—it should be just slightly mushy. Rinse out the frozen or chilled melon shells with the Cognac, pour it into the ice, mix, and then fill the shells with the ice.

ORANGE BAVARIAN RICE
(Riz à la Maltaise)
(for 4)

Blood oranges are usually used for this dessert and the characteristic color is a rich, cold red. California oranges lack the color, but are perfect for flavor.

Gelatin   1 calf's foot, large bone removed, split

5 cups water

¾ cup sugar

Pinch powdered cinnamon

Juice of 1 orange and 1 lemon plus several thin strips of peel

1 egg white

⅓ cup white wine

1½ cups milk

¼ cup sugar

Small pinch salt

Strip orange peel

1 tablespoon butter

½ cup long-grain rice, parboiled for about 8 minutes, drained, rinsed, and drained well again

1 egg yolk

1 cup orange juice

1 cup of the above gelatin

1 cup heavy cream

Almond oil (or a tasteless vegetable oil)

2 tablespoons each thinly peeled orange and lemon peel, cut into tiny thread-like julienne, blanched for a few seconds and drained

2 tablespoons sugar

⅓ cup water

Prepare the jelly the previous day (if time does not permit, use commercial gelatin in the recipe, following instructions on the package for quantity, dissolving it in ½ cup water and augmenting the quantity of orange juice in the recipe by ½ cup).

Soak the foot in cold water for several hours. Cover generously with cold water, bring to a boil, simmer for 8 or 10 minutes, drain, rinse well, and return to a clean saucepan, cover with 5 cups water, return to a boil, skim, and cook, covered, at a bare simmer for about 7 hours. Strain the liquid through a sieve, refrigerate overnight, and cleanse the surface of all traces of fat, wiping it finally with a cloth dipped in hot water and wrung out.

Heat enough to melt and add the sugar, cinnamon, orange and

lemon peels, and the juices. Beat the egg white and the white wine together in a large mixing bowl, pour in slowly the other mixture, whisking all the while, pour back into the saucepan, bring to a boil, still whisking, and leave at a simmer, whisking from time to time, for about 15 minutes. Strain through a tightly woven cloth (dish towel, section of sheet . . .) lining a sieve.

Combine the milk, sugar, salt, orange peel, and butter in a saucepan, bring to a boil, remove from the heat, and leave to steep until tepid. Discard the orange peel, add the parboiled rice, return to a boil, and leave, covered, over very low heat (or in a slow oven), without disturbing it, for ½ hour. The milk should be completely absorbed; should any remain, strain it off and discard it. Stir in the egg yolk and leave the rice until nearly cool. Stir in the orange juice and the cup of gelatin.

Whip the cream until semifirm but not stiff (the dessert will be dry and cottony if the cream is whipped stiffly), fold it and the rice mixture thoroughly together, and pour into a lightly oiled mold. Tap the bottom smartly against the tabletop a couple of times to settle the contents and refrigerate for 5 or 6 hours—or overnight.

Cook the blanched julienne of orange and lemon peel in the sugar and water at a gentle simmer until a nearly complete reduction, the julienne being coated with a thick syrup.

Unmold the bavarian rice just before serving and decorate the surface with the candied julienne.

PEAR UPSIDE-DOWN TART
(Tarte aux Poires Renversée)
(for 6)

The receptacle chosen to serve as a pie dish should be of a heavy material and able to support the heat of a direct flame. It should be deeper than the ordinary American pie dish in order to contain a sufficient quantity of wine during the first part of the cooking process. A frying pan is perfect if your oven is large enough to take the handle; the lid to a large *pommes Anna* mold, a *tarte tatin* mold, or a round, enameled ironware gratin dish will serve equally well. The proportions given here are for an approximate 10-inch mold.

The dessert may be served hot, tepid, or cold but should, in any case, be unmolded only just before serving to prevent the pastry's being soaked in the cooking juices.

7 firm, slightly underripe eating pears, split in half, cored, and peeled
½ cup sugar
½ teaspoon powdered cinnamon
About 2½ cups red wine
Short pastry (pâte brisée): see page 247

Arrange pear halves in the pan, cored surface facing up, the wide end of each pressed against the side of the pan, the elongated tips pointing in toward the center of the pan so that the ungarnished areas form a fairly symmetrical star shape. Split the remaining pear halves and fill the empty spaces, slender tips pointing out, wide ends meeting in the center so that, when unmolded, the body of pears will form a neat geometric pattern.

Sprinkle over the sugar and the cinnamon, pour over red wine to cover, bring to a boil, and cook, covered, at a simmer, for from 1 hour to 1 hour and 10 minutes or until the pears are tender, lending no resistance to the tip of a sharp knife, but still firmly intact. Drain all the liquid into a saucepan, holding a lid firmly against the pears' surface so as not to displace them. Reduce the cooking liquid over a high flame, stirring from time to time, until only about ½ cup remains, the boil having arrived at the cottony, puffy, slurry stage, the liquid a consistent syrup. Dribble the syrup regularly over the pears' surface.

Roll out a round of pastry; prick it 4 or 5 times with a knife tip; it may be cut to the exact inside dimensions of the pan or rolled out slightly larger, the edges rolled up and crimped either with the floured side of your thumb or with fork tines and laid gently upside down over the pears. Bake in a 375° to 400° oven for about 40 minutes or until the pastry is golden and crisp. Unmold with care—if a frying pan has been used, the handle will prevent its being unmolded onto the center of the platter; place the platter upside down over the pan, its edge pressed to the handle's point of attachment, turn everything over at once and ease the tart into the middle of the platter. The pears often spread slightly in the unmolding—push them gently into place, pressing all around the outside with the back of a tablespoon or a spatula.

FRIED PUFF BALLS
(Pets de Nonne)
(about 40 fritters)

In pre-nineteenth-century cookbooks, these little fritters are called *pets de putain*. I have been unable to pinpoint the moment—certainly early—during the nineteenth century at which, with a somewhat irreverent insouciance, they were distinguished by the more respectable title of *pets de nonne*, the largest of the lot being attributed, traditionally, to the Mother Superior.

The mixture is an ordinary *pâte à choux*, the same that, baked in various forms, is transformed into *éclairs, profiterolles, gâteau St.-Honoré*, etc. One of its more attractive forms is that of the Burgundian *gougère* (3 ounces Gruyère cut into tiny cubes replacing the sugar and grated peel of this recipe; dabs arranged in a circle with a spoon or pastry bag, the crown sprinkled with more Gruyère cubes, and the batter baked at 400° for about 40 minutes, pierced regularly with a knife tip after ½ hour to permit the interior to dry out).

Both the drying of the paste over the fire and the incorporation of the eggs is tiring arm work. If, after the mixture begins to achieve a certain consistency, the handle of the wooden spoon, standing vertically, is grasped in one's fist, forearm held horizontally in relation to the spoon handle, the movement coming from one's shoulder as one stirs firmly, rhythmically in a circle, the forearm will suffer less from fatigue.

1 cup water
⅓ cup butter
½ tablespoon sugar
Pinch salt
1 teaspoon (loosely filled) grated lemon rind
1 cup (instant-blending type) flour
4 eggs
Olive oil (or other vegetable oil) for frying

407

Combine the water, butter, sugar, salt, and lemon rind in a saucepan, bring slowly to a boil, and, as soon as the butter is completely melted, remove from the heat. Add the flour all at once, stirring, first carefully, then, as the mixture pulls itself together, vigorously. Return to the heat and continue to stir, roughly and rhythmically, for 3 or 4 minutes or until the mass clings persistently together, leaving the bottom and sides of the saucepan clean, and its surface assumes a sweaty, shiny aspect. Remove from the heat and, forming each time a well in the center, add the eggs, one at a time, stirring each time until the mixture begins to unify and then beating vigorously.

A skillet or a large omelet pan, filled two thirds full with oil, is deep enough for frying. If using a deep fryer, don't use the basket; a large, round, flat, wire skimming spoon (*araignée*) is the most practical for removing the fritters from the fat; lacking that, use a slotted skimming spoon. The oil should sizzle when a bit of batter is dropped in, but it should not be too hot—the fritters need to cook long enough so that exterior coloration coincides with their interior drying out. Don't overcrowd the pan—fritters swell to about four times the size of the raw dab of dough. Drop in teaspoonsful, dipping the spoon into the hot fat each time before spooning up the dough. Roll them over in the oil with a nudge of the teaspoon tip to encourage even coloring. Drain on absorbent paper and sprinkle with sugar or with confectioners' sugar.

THE THIRTEEN PROVENÇAL CHRISTMAS DESSERTS
(LES TREIZE DESSERTS DU GROS SOUPER)

The Parisian Christmas Eve *réveillon* differs little in spirit from the New Year's *réveillon*. It is a public and mundane celebration that, for those who respect the tradition of the midnight mass, does not begin until afterward. Restaurants are booked far in advance, and oysters, Champagne, foie gras, truffles, roast turkey, and *bûche de Noël* usually mingle among the elements of the menu (the *bûche*, most often a construction of *Génoise* and variously flavored butter creams, is characterized by a log-like form and excessive sweetness; its principal virtue lies in the fidelity with which creams, chocolate curls, and meringues simulate wood grains, bark, and mushrooms).

The ritual, pre-midnight mass, Christmas Eve supper in Provence is strictly a family affair. A certain flexibility of detail exists within its nonetheless rigid form: Garlic soup (*aïgo bouido*) may or may not preface the meal, followed by or replaced by either *petits-gris* (a variety similar to but smaller than the huge Burgundy snails that are tinned and exported—they are first starved for a few days, bathed in salt and vinegar, well washed, and cooked for 2 or 3 hours in a heavily fennel-flavored white wine court bouillon) and *aïoli* or crisp celery hearts and *anchoiade* (a thick vinaigrette whose body derives from pounded garlic and anchovy filets); salt cod and its alternative *raito* or *capilotade* sauces, although traditional, are sometimes dethroned by other fish and other sauces (an octopus *daube,* for instance, which takes the quaint appellation of *tripes de mer,* or "sea tripe"); gratins of spinach and hard-boiled eggs, creamed chard ribs, or salsify are common follow-ups, but any winter vegetable preparation may supplant or supplement them. Each element seems to have been deliberately chosen for its humble and homely character, and the intention becomes flagrantly evident when one examines the lavish-sounding thirteen desserts: They are chosen from among seasonal fresh fruits (oranges, tangerines, pears, apples, bananas), sun-dried fruits (figs, raisins, dates), nuts (almonds, hazelnuts, walnuts), candied chestnuts, candied almonds, candied fruits, almond and honey nougatines, sometimes a local pastry (spinach tart, for instance—parboiled, squeezed, and finely chopped spinach, sautéed with olive oil or butter, liberally sugared, flavored with grated lemon peel, and baked in a Provençal olive-oil crust, a butter short crust, or a *pâte sablée* with a pastry latticework atop), and the immutable *pompe à l'huile* with its accompanying homemade sweet wine (*vin cuit*), so useful for dunking (*pompes* garnish all Provençal tables on Christmas Eve and have apparently done so for many centuries). The meal is an homage to the fruits of nature—a Provençal Thanksgiving.

PROVENÇAL CHRISTMAS CAKES
(Pompe à l'Huile, Pompe de Noël, Gibassier, Fouace)
(about 12, each 4 inches in diameter)

Home baking is not one of the French vices; baking, it is felt, is what bakers and pastry cooks are made for. The Provençaux carry that attitude to an extreme—and they think of pastry, moreover, as being for children; the adults eat it, for the most part, only on religious holidays, tradition having assigned a different pastry to each. Few housewives have ever prepared *pompes* in their kitchens, and published recipes tend to be largely folklorique galimatias. For all practical purposes of description, they are flat cakes made of sweetened bread dough that has been enriched by the addition of olive oil; it is probable that the addition of egg to the dough is a fairly recent amelioration and it is certain that a larger proportion of sugar than that recommended in the following recipe often goes into their confection (orange blossom water, which stamps many Provençal pastries with a vague, sickly memory of stale and faded perfume, usually is added to a *pompe* dough, as well). The *pompes* sold in the village bakeries tend to be hard, tough, greasy, and heavily anise-flavored.

When shorn of ritual and symbolic glory—and when homemade—they are pleasant tea biscuits or a perfect accompaniment to stewed fruits, fresh fruits macerated in wine or ices; I find them innocent to the point of being innocuous (although I enjoy dunking them in my morning coffee), but friends and neighbors never fail to wax enthusiastic when offered them.

The Niçoise *fougassette* is made in the same way—about ⅛ teaspoon saffron is usually stirred into the flour before preparing the dough and sometimes fragments of candied fruits are pressed into the surface of the little breads at the same time that their surfaces are slit with the razor blade.

Pompes are sometimes called *fouaces,* but the term or one of its variations *(fougasse, fougace),* depending on the region, is more widely used outside of Provence to describe a similar *galette*—country cousin and undoubted ancestor of the elegant *brioche,* whose only difference is in the substitution of softened butter for olive oil in the dough; like *fougassettes, fouaces* are often saffron-flavored.

Pompes are traditionally cut into large rounds of from 6 to 7 inches in diameter; a 4-inch diameter seems to me to produce a more attractive article of a more practical size.

The French equivalent of American "instant-blending" flour has been used for testing proportions—a bit more in terms of volume may be required of other flours.

½ ounce compressed yeast (or 1 tablespoon dried yeast)
1 tablespoon sugar
½ cup tepid water
About 3 cups instant-blending flour (just under 1 pound)
Salt
½ cup brown sugar
2 teaspoons grated lemon peel
1 egg
¼ cup olive oil

Add the tepid water to the yeast and sugar (first mashing the yeast and sugar together with a fork if the yeast is compressed) and leave in a warm place to ferment for 15 minutes or so.

Put the flour in a mixing bowl, make a well in the center, add all the other ingredients, including the yeast-water mixture, stir with a fork, working from the center gradually outward, until thoroughly mixed, then transfer to a floured board and knead well, eventually picking up the mass and heaving it back against the board repeatedly in between kneadings. When the dough is elastic and no longer sticky, form it into a ball, return it to the mixing bowl, and leave, covered with a towel, in a warm place for a couple of hours or until the volume has nearly doubled. Turn it out onto the floured board, punch it down, and knead lightly (not too much or it will not want to be rolled out), then flatten as much as possible with the palm of your hand, turning repeatedly to keep both surfaces floured, and roll out to a thickness of from ¼ to ⅓ inch. Use a large, opened tin can or an overturned bowl to cut out rounds, transferring them to a flat baking sheet (or foil-lined oven plaque). Gather the scraps into a ball and roll them out again—or simply flatten them into another *pompe* with your hand. Slit the surface of each with a razor blade, forming a crisscross design—two slits each way if the *pompe* measures about 4 inches in diameter. Leave, covered with a towel, in a warm place to rise for another hour or so; they will rise but slightly (by about one third). Bake at about 400° for 20 minutes or until a rich deep brown and crusty. Slip onto a pastry grill to cool.

TWELFTH-NIGHT PASTRY
(Gâteau des Rois)
(for 6 to 10)

The ritual of the thing—and the accompanying wine—may be more amusing than the pastry itself. The *gâteau des Rois* in the Parisian region—and, generally, in northern France—is a simple *galette* of puff pastry, the surface crisscrossed with a knife tip and painted with egg before being baked; sometimes it is a confection, less fanciful in form but resembling in composition a *Pithiviers,* of sweet, buttered, and lightly egg-bound almond paste, spread between plate-sized rounds of puff paste. Throughout the southern half of France, it is a ring of leavened pastry, brioche-like, whose composition varies greatly from one region to another and from one baker to another: The dough may be less richly endowed with butter and eggs; a heavy, sweet syrup in which grated orange and lemon peel have been cooked is often added as well as a liqueur of some sort (or some orange blossom water); a variety of candied fruits, citrus dominating, may join or replace the cherries. A *gâteau des Rois* contains either a dried bean or a small porcelain or plastic trinket (known, in any case, as *la fève,* or broad bean) and the person whose portion of pastry contains it is crowned king or queen for the evening.

A celebration of the Epiphany (although scholars suggest that its origins may be pagan), its sacred significance has long been tenuous; the devout during the seventeenth century abominated the tradition of the *gâteau des Rois* because of the excessive debauchery to which it led. Prosper-Montagné cites a tract from the period whose tone suggests that the author may have been a temperance leader:

Large groups gather (on the Twelfth-Night) to elect a king; he chooses his cabinet members and then the celebration begins, continuing for days with the festivities multi-plying until all purses are empty and the creditors arrive.

The sons hasten to imitate the example; they elect their king also and organize elaborate banquets either with stolen money or at their parents' expense, the better to school themselves in the ways both of luxury and of larceny.

Nowadays the game is an innocent excuse for friends to gather together and drink a couple of bottles of Champagne; it is apparently still great fun, for hardly is everyone recovered from celebrating the advent of the New Year than people begin gathering to *tirer les Rois* and it goes on throughout the month of January, the person crowned being designated as the next to receive; quite distinguished company is apt to turn loud and bawdy in the joyous atmosphere. (If you want to play the game, you will need, in addition to the ingredients listed, a gilt, cardboard crown . . .)

It is as well not to attempt the following preparation during the hot summer months. Use, if possible, a marble slab for kneading and forming the pastry and a flexible, plastic pastry cook's *corne* for scraping. I have used "instant-blending" flour in this recipe (not because I prefer it for this kind of recipe, but because it more nearly resembles its American equivalent than ordinary pastry flour); it weighs about ⅔ ounce more per cup than regular flour—if weighing instead of measuring, count 12 ounces flour, in all.

Leavened dough	1 cake compressed yeast (or 1 package dried yeast)
	1 tablespoon sugar
	½ cup tepid water
	1¼ cups flour (plus ¼ cup for kneading)
Batter	1 cup flour
	4 eggs (room temperature)
	¼ cup butter (room temperature, cut into small pieces)
	Salt
	1 cup butter (room temperature)
	1 dried white bean
	4 ounces candied (glazed) cherries
	1 egg yolk beaten with a bit of water
	About 3 tablespoons sugar

413

Add tepid water to the yeast and sugar (first mashing them together if using compressed yeast), leave in a warm place for about 15 minutes to ferment, and stir the flour in, progressively, until the dough is only just stiff enough to handle—a bit less firm than ordinary bread dough. Scrape out onto a lightly floured marble and knead for about 10 minutes, pushing sections of the dough repeatedly away from yourself with the heel of your hand. Scrape your hand clean, form the dough into a ball, lightly floured so that it will not stick to your hand, and heave it, repeatedly and mercilessly, against the marble. Form it again into a ball, lightly floured, return it to the mixing bowl, and leave, covered with a tea towel, in a warm place for about 1 hour or until doubled in volume.

Stir the eggs and the ¼ cup butter into the salted flour and beat, either with an electric mixer or with a wooden spoon, for a long time —until the batter is elastic, the surface glistening and slippery in aspect.

Combine the dough and the batter in the largest of the mixing bowls, mix loosely at first, until the dough no longer resists, and then stir in a wide circle with a wooden spoon, held vertically, grasped firmly in your fist, forearm held at a right angle to the spoon handle, the motion directed from the shoulder, until completely unified. Add the cup of butter, either pinched into small fragments or squeezed repeatedly through your fingers (approximately 1-ounce chunks at a time) to soften it and disperse it to the point of being readily absorbable. Mix, as before, but only until the butter is completely absorbed.

Scrape the dough down from the sides of the mixing bowl, cover with a plate, and leave at room temperature—68° to 70°—for about 5 hours, away from drafts (the bowl may be placed in the middle of a bed, the corners and edges of a heavy blanket lifted loosely up and over it). Scrape the dough loose from the sides and beat it until reduced to its original, unleavened volume. Leave, covered, long enough to begin rising again—½ hour or so—and refrigerate overnight.

The following day, turn the chilled dough out onto a lightly floured marble, scraping it free from the bottom of the bowl, flip it over to flour all surfaces, flatten slightly, press the bean and all but a dozen of the cherries into the surface, and roll the mass in such a way as to enclose the garnish, forming it rapidly, partly by rolling and partly by molding with your hands, into a sausage something over 2 feet long, the ends slightly tapered. Shape in a circle, twisting the ends lightly around each other to simulate a simple knot, and transfer, lifting the ring rapidly with both hands, to a thinly buttered pastry plaque placed beside the marble. Re-form it neatly, embed the remaining cherries in the surface, and leave in a slightly warm corner of the kitchen, covered with a tea towel, for about 2 hours or until approximately doubled in volume. Paint all exposed surfaces with the beaten egg-yolk mixture, sprinkle lightly with sugar, and bake for 40 minutes, starting in a 450° oven that is then turned down to 400°. Turn it around after 25 minutes or so if not coloring evenly (or, if coloring too rapidly, lay a sheet of aluminum foil lightly over the surface—it should, however, be a rich, deep, burnished golden brown when cooked). Slip onto a pastry grill to cool—or partly cool (it is best eaten freshly baked and, preferably, warm).

CANDLEMAS CRÊPES AND COOKIES
(CRÊPES ET NAVETTES DE LA CHANDÊLEUR)

Except in Marseilles, where all the bakeries prepare the little boat-shaped sugar cookies called *navettes* for the second day of February, all over France *crêpes* are prepared to celebrate Candlemas. No particular subsequent treatment is requisite—they may simply be eaten as they come from the pan, lightly buttered and sprinkled with sugar or spread with jam or jelly and rolled up . . .

CRÊPES WITH FIGS AND CHARTREUSE
(Crêpes aux Figues à la Chartreuse)
(for 4 to 6)

Wonderful desserts can be made with *crêpes;* their greatest pitfalls derive, no doubt, from their versatility—not in itself a fault, but a quality that teases many a cook into overstepping the boundaries of sense and taste. One should never lose sight of the fragile and delicate, thin, tender thing that is the *crêpe* itself. How, transformed into a dribbling, spongy sop for a complicated cocktail of alcohols, can the little *crêpe* be good?

A good preparation is that of *crêpes* lightly spread with a sugar and butter *pommade* into which has been incorporated either a fruit juice or purée and a small amount of a liqueur or brandy whose flavor is particularly compatible with that of the chosen fruit (pineapple-Kirsch, banana-rum, hazelnut-Cognac, and tangerine-Curaçao are classic examples; the chosen liqueur or brandy replaces the Cognac in the preparation of the *crêpes* also). The *crêpes* are folded in four and reheated (arranged slightly overlapping in a buttered gratin dish, brushed with butter, sprinkled lightly with sugar and a few drops of the same liqueur as that of the *pommade,* and put for a few minutes in a very hot oven). *Crêpes Suzette* (although more incendiary crimes have been committed in Suzette's name than in any other) are a case in point (tangerine juice is used, in part, for moistening the *crêpe* batter, Curaçao replaces the Cognac, and the *pommade* is flavored with tangerine juice and Curaçao). The following recipe is in a similar spirit; the herbal aura is quite unusual, thyme lending support to the famous secret formula, and, to me, it is particularly attractive in a dessert; a fine Sauternes, well chilled, marries excitingly with it.

Apart from the color, green Chartreuse varies from yellow Chartreuse in that it is less sweet and it contains a higher concentration of herbal infusion and a higher degree of alcohol; for all those reasons, I prefer it to the yellow. Whether green or yellow, the aged product labeled "VEP" is much more interesting.

1 recipe crêpes (see page 260), made with milk and butter, substituting 2 tablespoons Chartreuse for the Cognac
1 recipe "Figs with Thyme," page 402, doubling the quantity of honey (or substituting for the honey ⅓ cup sugar)
About ¼ cup Chartreuse
2 or 3 tablespoons sugar
About 2 tablespoons butter

The fig-cooking juices should be reduced to a fairly thick syrup; stir in 2 or 3 tablespoons of Chartreuse—enough to bring it back to a light, syrupy consistency.

Cut the figs in two, removing the tips of the stem ends if they are tough. Roll two or three fig halves into each *crêpe,* first dribbling over a few drops of Chartreuse, and arrange the *crêpes,* flap side down, side by side in a buttered gratin dish. Spoon over the syrup—there should be no more than enough to just coat the *crêpes.* Sprinkle lightly with sugar, place a thin strip of butter on each *crêpe,* and heat in a 500° oven for about 10 minutes. Serve on heated plates.

MARSEILLES CANDLEMAS COOKIES
(Navettes de la Chandeleur)
(12 cookies)

½ cup sugar
2 tablespoons butter
Small pinch salt
1 egg
1 cup flour

Cream the sugar, salt, and butter together with the back of a wooden spoon until of a regular, crumbly consistency, beat in the egg, and gradually stir in the flour. Knead slightly on a lightly floured board or marble until consistent. Roll walnut-size lumps on board or between the palms of your hands into tapered sausage shapes, place on a lightly buttered flat baking sheet, and slit the length of each sausage shape to about ¼ or ⅓ its depth with the tip of a sharp knife. Leave, covered with a towel, in a warm place for 1 or 2 hours and bake at 350° for about 25 minutes or slightly less, depending on the oven.

Index